# A Dictionary of Nafsan, South Efate, Vanuatu

## OCEANIC LINGUISTICS SPECIAL PUBLICATIONS

*Numbers 1 through 28 may be accessed online through JSTOR.*

1. English in Hawaii: An Annotated Bibliography. Stanley M. Tsuzaki and John E. Reinecke. 1966.
2. An Ivatan Syntax. Lawrence Andrew Reid. 1966.
3. Manobo-English Dictionary. Richard E. Elkins. 1968.
4. Nguna Texts. Albert J. Schütz. 1969.
5. Nguna Grammar. Albert J. Schütz. 1969.
6. A Grammar of Kaliai-Kove. David R. Counts. 1969.
7. Chrau Grammar. David D. Thomas. 1971.
8. Philippine Minor Languages: Word Lists and Phonologies. Edited by Lawrence A. Reid. 1971.
9. Japanese Pidgin English in Hawaii: A Bilingual Description. Susumu Nagara. 1972.
10. Kapampangan Syntax. Leatrice T. Mirikitani. 1972.
11. Isneg-English Vocabulary. Morice Vanoverbergh. 1972.
12. Outline of Sre Structure. Timothy M. Manley. 1972.
13. Austroasiatic Studies, Parts I and II. Edited by Philip N. Jenner, Laurence C. Thompson, and Stanley Starosta. 1976.
14. A Bibliography of Pidgin and Creole Languages. Compiled by John E. Reinecke, Stanley M. Tsuzaki, David DeCamp, Ian F. Hancock, and Richard E. Wood. 1975.
15. A Handbook of Comparative Tai. Fang Kuei Li. 1977.
16. Syntactic Derivation of Tagalog Verbs. Videa P. De Guzman. 1978.
17. The Genetic Relationship of the Ainu Language. James Patrie. 1982.
18. A Grammar of Manam. Frantisek Lichtenberk. 1983.
19. The History of the Fijian Languages. Paul A. Geraghty. 1983.
20. For Gordon H. Fairbanks. Edited by Veneeta Z. Acson and Richard L. Leed. 1985.
21. The Causatives of Malagasy. Charles Randriamasimanana. 1986.
22. Echo of a Culture: A Grammar of Rennell and Bellona. Samuel H. Elbert. 1988.
23. A Guide to Austroasiatic Speakers and Their Languages. Robert Parkin. 1991.
24. Tonality in Austronesian Languages. Edited by Jerold A. Edmondson and Kenneth J. Gregerson. 1993.
25. Tinrin Grammar. Midori Osumi. 1995.
26. Toward a Reference Grammar of Tok Pisin: An Experiment in Corpus Linguistics. John W. M. Verhaar. 1995.
27. An Erromangan (Sye) Grammar. Terry Crowley. 1998.
28. From Ancient Cham to Modern Dialects: Two Thousand Years of Language Contact and Change. Graham Thurgood. 1999.
29. Grammatical Analysis: Morphology, Syntax, and Semantics: Studies in Honor of Stanley Starosta. Edited by Videa P. De Guzman and Byron W. Bender. 2000.
30. Nhanda: An Aboriginal Language of Western Australia. Juliette Blevins. 2001.
31. Bislama Reference Grammar. Terry Crowley. 2004.
32. Otto Dempwolff's *Grammar of the Jabêm Language in New Guinea*. Translated and edited by Joel Bradshaw and Francisc Czobor. 2005.
33. A Grammar of South Efate: An Oceanic Language of Vanuatu. Nicholas Thieberger. 2006.
34. William J. Gedney's Comparative Tai Source Book. Thomas John Hudak. 2008
35. Kokota Grammar. Bill Palmer. 2009.
36. A Dictionary of Mah Meri as Spoken at Bukit Bangkong. Nicole Kruspe. 2010.
37. William J. Gedney's Concise Saek-English, English-Saek Lexicon. Thomas John Hudak. 2011.
38. Sivisa Titan: Sketch Grammar, Texts, Vocabulary Based on Material Collected by P. Josef Meier and Po Minis. Claire Bowern. 2010.
39. A Grammar of Mavea: An Oceanic Language of Vanuatu. Valérie Guérin. 2011.
40. A Study of Saisiyat Morphology. Elizabeth Zeitoun, Tai-hwa Chu, and Lalo a tahesh kaybaybaw. 2015.
41. A Dictionary of Nafsan, South Efate, Vanuatu: M̃p̃et Nafsan ni Erakor. Nicholas Thieberger with Members of the Erakor Community. 2021.

Publications may be ordered electronically from www.uhpress.hawaii.edu or by mail from University of Hawai'i Press, 2840 Kolowalu Street, Honolulu, Hawai'i 96822, USA.

Oceanic Linguistics Special Publication No. 41

# A Dictionary of Nafsan, South Efate, Vanuatu

## M̃p̃et Nafsan ni Erakor

*Nicholas Thieberger*
*with Members of the Erakor Community*

University of Hawai‘i Press
*Honolulu*

Printed in the United States of America

26 25 24 23 22 21 6 5 4 3 2 1

**Library of Congress Cataloging-in-Publication Data**

Names: Thieberger, Nick, author.
Title: A dictionary of Nafsan, South Efate, Vanuatu = M̃p̃et Nafsan ni Erakor / Nicholas Thieberger with members of the Erakor community
Other titles: M̃p̃et Nafsan ni Erakor | Oceanic linguistics special publication ; no. 41.
Description: Honolulu : University of Hawai‘i Press, 2021. | Series: Oceanic linguistics special publications ; 41 | Includes bibliographical references.
Identifiers: LCCN 2020054659 | ISBN 9780824890148 (hardcover) | ISBN 9780824890544 (paperback) | ISBN 9780824890513 (adobe pdf) | ISBN 9780824890537 (epub) | ISBN 9780824890520 (kindle edition)
Subjects: LCSH: Nafsan language—Dictionaries—English. | English language—Dictionaries—Nafsan.
Classification: LCC PL6261.Z5 T45 2021 | DDC 499/.5—dc23
LC record available at https://lccn.loc.gov/2020054659

Printer-ready files provided by the author.

University of Hawai‘i Press books are printed on acid-free paper and meet the guidelines for permanence and durability of the Council on Library Resources.

# Contents

# Acknowledgments

I would like to thank the following Nafsan speakers for their help with this work: Silas Alban; Endis Kalsarap; Kalsakar Wayane; Manuel Waiane Kalopong; Jack Kallon; and Joel Kalpram. Thanks also to: Rosey Billington, whose work on the phonetics and phonology of Nafsan has been very helpful in finalising the dictionary; John Lynch for comments; Margaret Bowman for copy-editing; Megan Ellis for design and layout; Chandra Jayasuriya for producing the maps. Ross Clark and Murray Garde kindly acted as reviewers of the final manuscript. Jack Kallon proofread the near-final version and made valuable corrections.

Thanks also to Sean and Lisa Bracken, Kalsarap Namaf, Ralph Regenvanu, and William Wayane for support during initial fieldwork. Jean Claude Rivierre kindly provided the wordlist he produced in 1965 with Maxime Carlot. In addition to those already named, in 2015–2018 the following helped with checking the dictionary at workshops in Erakor: Kalonuk Albert; Elisa Alphonse; Johnny Alphonse; Alice Andrew; Linuk Apisai; Fanny Atuary; Maturine Carlot-Tary; Lionel Emil; Touran Emile; Kaar Albert Erikan; Maureen Isabelle George-Nikahi; Tookoune George; Ernest Joseph; Gino Joseph; Jackob Joseph; Joel Joseph; Michael Joseph; Elder Louis Peras Josephe; Silas Kalfabun; Kalkot Kalfapun; Malau Kalkot; Timteo Kalmet; Abet Kalokis; Asael Wayane Kalopong; PS Arron Kalopong; Samsen Kalopong; Tarimar Kalopong; Norman Kalotiti; Carol Kalpram; Kaltapu Kaltack; Remy Kaltack; Rosemary Taun Kaltack; Toufau Kaltack; Nicole Kaltak; Timothy Kaltak; Gray Kaltapau; Rita Kaltapau; Glenda Lalier; Marik Maal; Leimau Malas; Kaltang Martin; Yokopet Ngui; Lina Kaloros Smitson; Leitang Sope; Malini Sope; and Marie Zacharie.

The group 'Dictionary ni Nafsan' on Facebook has also been very responsive in answering questions about meanings of words.

This dictionary was initially stored in Toolbox software (https://software.sil.org/toolbox/) and then transferred to Fieldworks Language Explorer (https://software.sil.org/fieldworks), both products of the Summer Institute of Linguistics whom I thank for making this software freely available.

This work was done while I was employed at the University of Melbourne and was assisted by Australian Research Council grants QEII DP0984419, Future Fellowship FT140100214, and the ARC Centre of Excellence for the Dynamics of Language CE140100041.

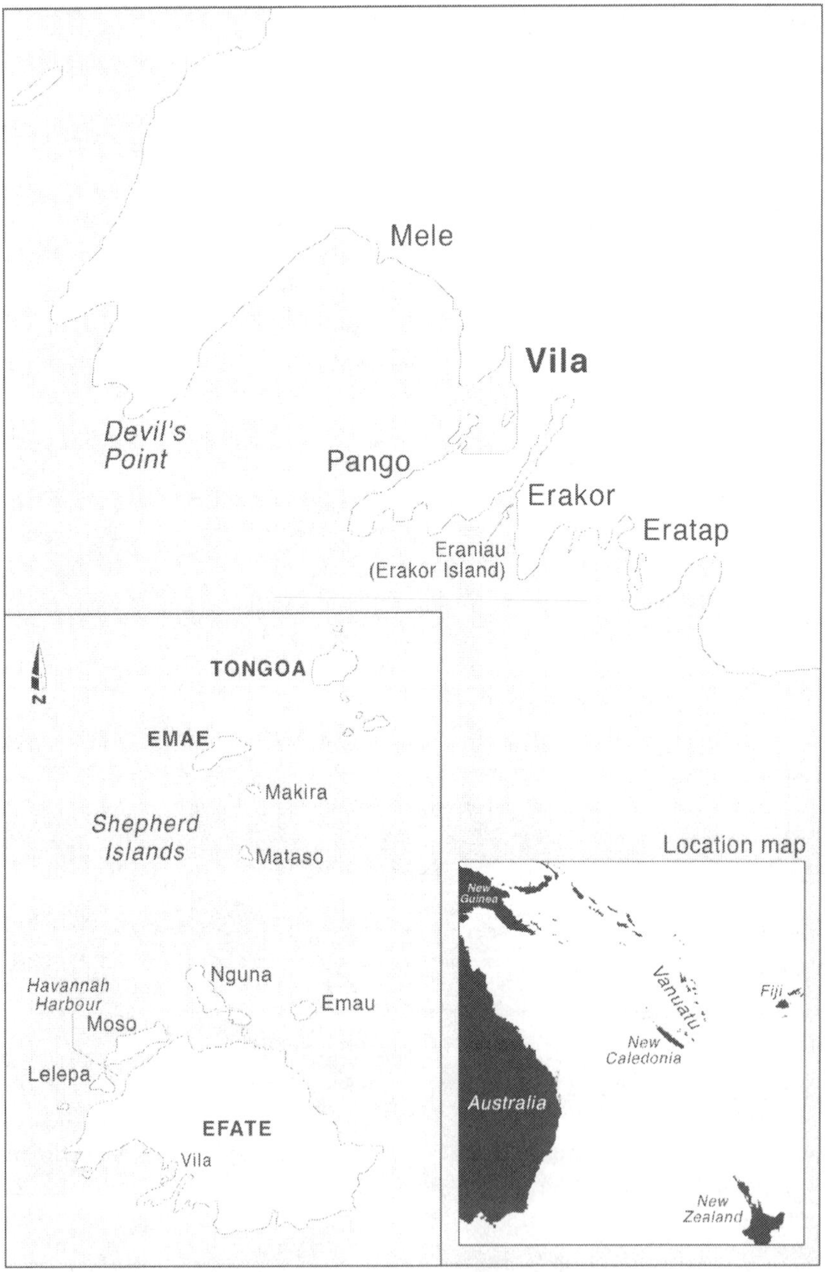


**Map 1: Map of Efate. Location of Efate and the villages of Pango, Erakor, and Eratap, where Nafsan is spoken. (Map produced by Chandra Jayasuria)**

# Introduction

Nafsan[1] (also known as South Efate) is spoken by some 6,000 people in the villages of Eratap, Erakor, and Pango in Efate, Vanuatu. I began work on the dictionary when writing a grammar (Thieberger 2006) and collection of stories in the language produced as *Natrauswen nig Efat* (Thieberger 2011). Later, in a series of workshops in Erakor from 2015 to 2018, many other people from Erakor contributed to editing and adding to the dictionary. In each of these years in week-long workshops Nafsan speakers discussed drafts of the dictionary page by page. They considered spellings and suggested new words and new senses of existing words. They also determined ways of presenting Nafsan that are more suited to community use of the work than the linguistic presentation I had used in my grammar, as will be discussed below.

We set up a Facebook group that extended these workshops into an online community that allowed us to keep working on the dictionary, me in Melbourne with questions that were quickly answered online by people in Erakor.

There are slight differences between the Nafsan spoken in Pango, Eratap, and Erakor and this dictionary is based on the way people in Erakor speak Nafsan.

Identification of plants and animals has been conducted over time with a number of individuals to check names as best as possible. However, it may be that a name, for example for a shellfish, is given for a specific shell when in fact the name may refer more generally to shells of the same type or appearance. Plants whose English or botanical names have not been identified have been included with a description.

**Photo 1: Some of the participants in the 2017 dictionary workshop, at Arron Kalopong's church hall. (Author's photo)**

**Photo 2: Some of the participants in the 2018 dictionary workshop, at Lameri in Erakor village. (Author's photo)**

There is more work to be done to make this a more comprehensive dictionary and any comments or corrections are welcome.

A list of all material prepared in Nafsan as a result of my research can be found online from this site: http://www.nthieberger.net/sefate.html. This includes retyped historical materials, Christian translations, and stories recorded and transcribed since the mid-1990s. An Android app of this dictionary, including audio of many of the words, is available here: https://rebrand.ly/nafsandictapp.

South Efate has fifteen consonant phonemes and ten vowel phonemes, as can be seen in Table 1. Voicing is not phonemic. In a common convention in the writing systems of Pacific languages, the letter *g* represents a velar nasal, like the sound of *ng* in English, and is also alphabetised as a *g* and not as a separate cluster *ng*. The letters *nr* represent a single sound, a prenasalised alveolar trill, that is ordered in the dictionary as two letters, again to avoid confusion. The letters *m̃* and *p̃* represent co-articulated stops which are produced by combining *g* and *m*, or *k* and *p*. These two letters are not given separate sections in the dictionary and are alphabetised along with *m* and *p* respectively. Similarly, double vowels are alphabetised as two letters and not as a single segment, and do not have separate sections in the dictionary. Nafsan speakers decided that it was less confusing to sort these letters in this way and to use the English alphabetical order.

**Table 1. Examples of Nafsan Sounds**

| Spelling | International Phonetic Alphabet | Example Word |
|---|---|---|
| a | a | n**a**m̃nam̃ 'grass' |
| aa | a: | w**aa**k 'pig' |
| e | e | tokap**e** 'green-winged ground dove' |
| ee | e: | nam̃l**ee**natu 'footprint' |
| i | i | **i**nrok 'after, behind' |
| ii | i: | t**ii**k 'no, nothing' |
| o | o | nal**o**f 'track' |
| oo | o: | ft**oo**k 'niece or nephew' |
| u | u | **u**ti 'skink sp.' |
| uu | u: | **uu**r 'prawn' |
| f | f | **f**ket 'sour' |
| g | ŋ | nala**g**la**g** 'scale (of a fish)' |
| k | k | na**k**te 'my' |
| l | l | **l**ak 'marry' |
| m | m | **m**isleo 'tune' |
| m̃ | ŋ͡m | **m̃**aat 'snake' |
| n | n | **n**ametrau 'family' |
| nr | nᵈr | **nr**p̃ei 'bark (of a dog)' |
| p | p | **p**are 'to be blind' |
| p̃ | k͡p | **p̃**as 'pick (a flower)' |
| r | r | **r**owat 'sago palm' |
| s | s | **s**aof 'visit' |
| t | t | **t**afra 'whale' |
| w | w | **w**ailu 'yam sp.' |
| y | j | **Y**esu 'Jesus' |

## Interesting Words in Nafsan

For English speakers looking at this dictionary there are some words that are unusual in the meanings they encode. Each culture and language pays attention to particular things relevant to its cultural tradition and Nafsan is no exception. There are, for example, many named types of yams, taro, breadfruit, bananas, and coconuts, and many trees and plants are named and Nafsan speakers know their uses. There are many terms around cooking with an earth oven (*uum*), and two named constellations of stars represent the oven and the tongs (*nkem*) used to move food and stones in the oven.

Giving and exchange are an important part of South Efate life, so there are words for these with slightly different meanings to English. For example, *sautog* is a gift given, like rent, with no expectation of a return gift, whereas *tigpiel* is an exchange, also used for the gift given by a bride at a wedding. The ordinary word for 'give' is *tu*, but giving an important gift uses the verb *ptu.*

Many more canoe parts are named in Nafsan than we typically know words for in English, unless we have technical knowledge – words like 'washstrake' (*kortas*), or 'cross-member' (*nakiat*), or 'the peg that attaches the outrigger to the cross-member' (*laak*).

There are names for spirits of various kinds, like *sputan*, *ntwam*, *m̃pau*, *lilip̃,* *maarik*, *mtulep*, *naferkaal*, *napum̃*, or *natopu*, and the people who can help dealing with them, the *munwei*, *teleekot*, and *kulru.*

## Earlier Wordlists of Nafsan

Despite translating a number of works into Nafsan, the earliest missionaries did not leave any wordlists or dictionaries of the language. While there was some variation in the spellings used in the earliest translations, the most commonly used system of that time has continued to be used and is often still considered the authoritative form of spelling for the language. The only major difference between that earlier system and the one presented in this dictionary is the current recognition of vowel length (by writing double vowels) and the use of a tilde over the *m* and *p* to show the sound is a co-articulated stop (*m̃* and *p̃*). The tilde seems to have been introduced sometime in the late twentieth century, it is present in Kalsarap's personal writing from the 1980s and 1990s and in the book *Tesa! Mal natrausuen*, published in 1983, but not in writing from the 1950s and earlier.

Shirley McRae, a missionary teacher at the Iririki District School (IDS) school in the 1950s, wrote a list of fewer than a hundred words that she kindly gave me (McRae, Shirley. n.d.).

Arthur Capell produced a wordlist of various Efate languages sometime in the 1950s.[2]

Jean-Claude Rivierre, working with Maxime Carlot Korman in the 1960s, produced a wordlist of Nafsan.[3] I used that list in prompting speakers, but it contains some items that were not known by speakers today and so they are not included in the published dictionary.

## Old Words

All languages change over time, and there are some Nafsan words that are not used today but can still be found in the old stories and translations created since the 1860s or in the hymn book *Natus Nalag*. Anyone interested in these words can look at the collection of texts listed below. These old words are included in this dictionary if they were remembered by at least one speaker today, and they are marked as being an old word not generally known today.

## Place-Names

There are many Nafsan place-names that apply to areas as small as a person's yard (*elol*), through to large geographic features (islands, coastal points, reefs, hills). These names feature in stories, for example, about how the land was formed (e.g., the story of Katapel in Thieberger 2011:51, 76, 82, or M̃aatleplep, ibid.: 66). For the purposes of mapping names, places were located either by going there

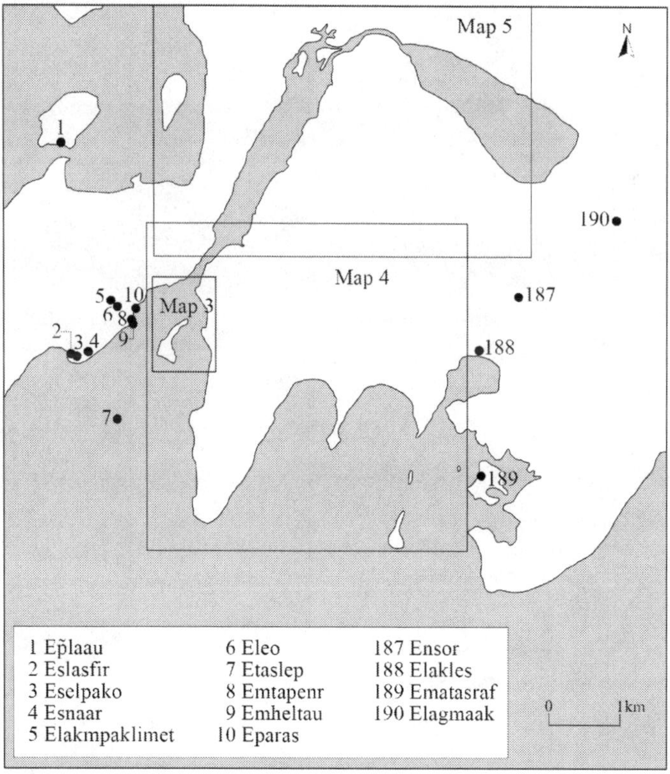


**Map 2: Some place-names of South Efate. (Map produced by Chandra Jayasuria)**

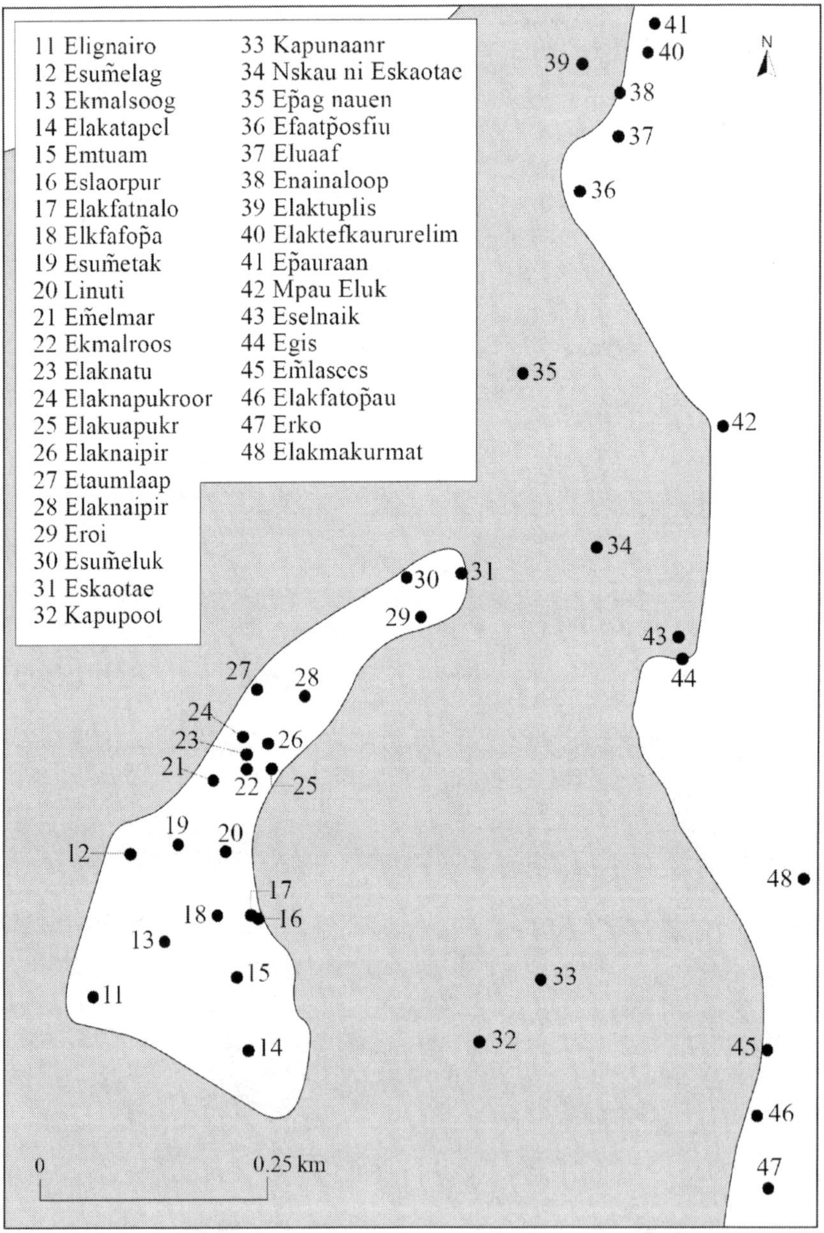


**Map 3: Some place-names of South Efate. (Map produced by Chandra Jayasuria)**

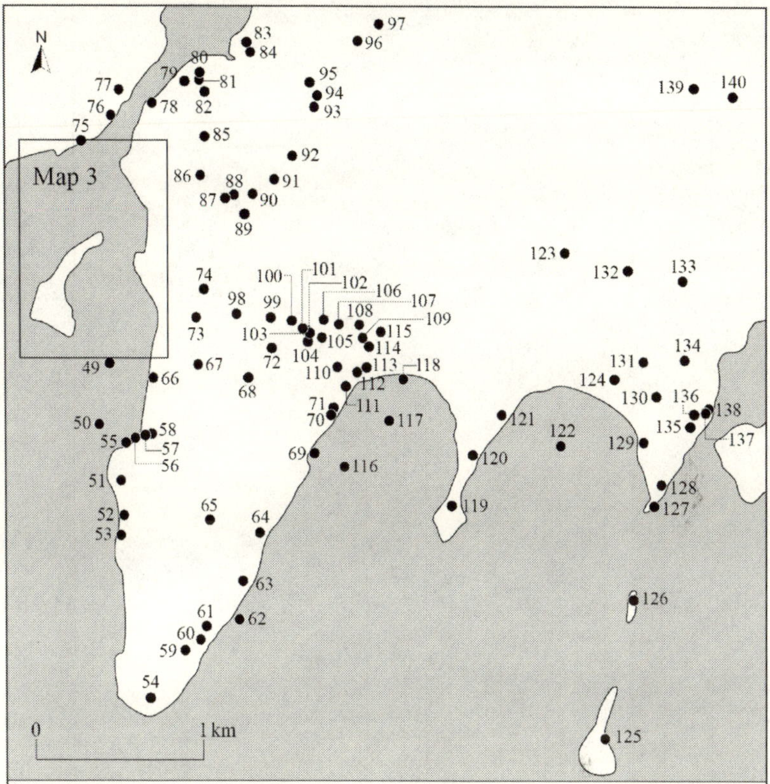


49 Eranm̃at
50 Elakfaatkor
51 Ep̃auraan
52 Ekamlat
53 Em̃aas
54 Nagis
55 Ekofemat
56 Nariaar
57 Emat
58 Elukewar
59 Elakmtulepkafuur
60 Elkau
61 Elakfatkor
62 Eslaorelkau
63 Ejipt
64 Elakligkari
65 Em̃elae
66 Epakm̃aal
67 Elakmpakrau
68 Etanoru
69 Emetatog
70 Etaumlap
71 Elauesuur
72 Eslaatmat
73 Napup̃ur
74 Eroi
75 Elaknraopet
76 Emetp̃er
77 Emetaikes
78 Elaknareo
79 Elaknraupet
80 Elakfaatp̃aum̃osu
81 Ekiip
82 Erkari
83 Elukewaar
84 Elwaaf
85 Emetator
86 Eraam
87 Emterik
88 Emetnamkanr
89 Elaksaofenu
90 Eniu
91 Elaknkasp̃o
92 Elaknakoumal
93 Erota
94 Eptam
95 Etil
96 Em̃urmlao
97 Ekasuup̃
98 Etkonmat
99 Elakmpaktaarp̃etu
100 Erp̃aak
101 Emlas
102 Elaknalo
103 Elakntalierik
104 Elakmemer
105 Ekofpei
106 Ereare
107 Ep̃alig
108 Elakntamlaanr
109 Enailom
110 Etraau
111 Ep̃ulei
112 Elukm̃orun
113 Ep̃kaul
114 Etraau
115 Ensor
116 Pasis ni Emetatog
117 Etmaat
118 Nskau ni wor
119 Em̃ut
120 Efookto
121 Elauesuur
122 Ekasiik
123 Elkaap̃
124 Elaknasu
125 Ekapum̃lep
126 Ekapum̃rik
127 Etmaat
128 Eter
129 Emtap̃lel
130 Ep̃uus
131 Ekofnaniu
132 Em̃ormaanr
133 Esfiriao
134 Em̃elfaat
135 Eaar
136 Elaknawen
137 Eslaorep̃us
138 Efman
139 Etaumlaap
140 Epakrar

**Map 4: Some place-names of South Efate. (Map produced by Chandra Jayasuria)**

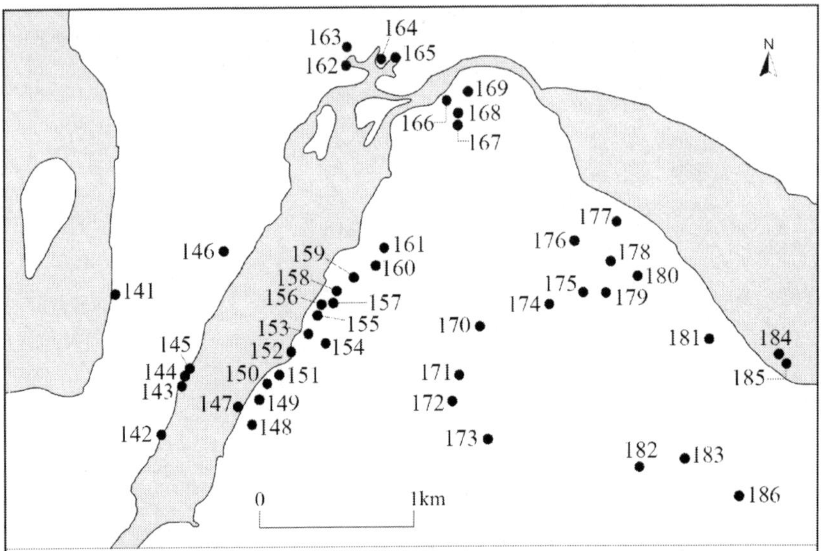


141 Elakuraupet
142 Em̃aas
143 Elakmlet
144 Elakratkas
145 Efatkepil
146 Elaknamook
147 Nskau ni Kaloros
148 Elakmparomwaal
149 Ekasufaat
150 Em̃lenap̃erik
151 Esunaot
152 Ep̃uul
153 Eselnaptam
154 Esum̃laanr
155 Etaartaar
156 Emetaip̃ur
157 Em̃lenap̃erik
158 Elaknaap̃
159 Em̃orwerik
160 Elaknkasmul
161 Emetaarwarof
162 Elaknapktay
163 Eroog
164 Etasrik
165 Elakmpkawenr
166 Enslaar
167 Enam
168 Emaas
169 Ekoftau
170 Etanamoos
171 Ematas
172 Efatfot
173 Elakntali
174 Elakntaamal
175 Emeltafra
176 Ep̃aal
177 Elakligkau
178 Emtenm̃ap
179 Em̃elp̃au
180 Emetraar
181 Emetnayam
182 Esfiriau
183 Em̃laliu
184 Emten
185 Elaukai
186 Ep̃lak

**Map 5: Some place-names of South Efate. (Map produced by Chandra Jayasuria)**

with a Global Positioning System device, or by plotting on a google earth map with speakers. There are some 190 names that appear in the maps below. There are undoubtedly many more place-names than appear on these maps, but these were the ones recorded over a number of workshops and in conversations over the course of several years.

## Texts in Nafsan

The first publication in this language appears to be *Nadus iskei nig Fat* (1864), a seven-page booklet of biblical material, printed in Aneityum and translated by local teachers on Efate, followed by other work translated by the Rev. Donald Morrison (at Erakor, 1864–1867), then Rev. James Cosh (1867–1872), and then the Rev. Dr James Mackenzie (1872–1912). The earlier work appears to be in Nafsan, more particularly the Erakor/Pango dialect of Nafsan, but the later material produced by Mackenzie and Macdonald is a mixture of pan-Efate/Shepherds dialects. There are also a few written texts from the twentieth century. I have found copies of as many of these early sources as I can and have digitised images and converted these sources to a searchable text format (see the list at the end of this introduction). The only secular book produced by speakers of Nafsan is *Tesa! Mal natrausuen* (Wai et 1983) which contains thirteen stories in a monolingual volume.

In addition, I recorded more than 100 texts with people in Erakor village from the mid-1990s and transcribed them. Copies of all of these texts and recordings can be found in the PARADISEC collections NT1 (http://catalog.paradisec.org.au/collections/NT1) and NT3 (http://catalog.paradisec.org.au/collections/NT3). These texts provide many of the example sentences in this dictionary and a book of these texts was produced in 2011 (Thieberger 2011). Note that the spelling of some words used in these texts has changed over time and with the input of speakers at dictionary workshops.

## Early Translations from Efate

This is a list of work written in Nafsan, going back to the earliest sources. I have scanned and converted a number of these to text and have put copies into the PARADISEC archive. An identifier in the PARADISEC NT3 collection is given for items that are available online in that collection (https://catalog.paradisec.org.au/collections/NT3).

Anon. 1864. *Nadus iskei nig Fat.* Aneityum: Mission Press. NT3-NadusIskei.
Anon. 1864. *Nalag Nig Efat*. Aneityum: Mission Press.
Anon. 1866. *Nafsanwi nig Iesu Krist nag Mark i mtir i.* Trans. D. Morrison. Sydney: Sheriff and Downing. NT3-MarkNafsan

Anon. 1868. *Nalag nig Efat.* Trans. D. Morrison. Sydney: Mason, Firt, nigar asler (Mason, Firth and Co). NT3-NalagNigFat.

Anon. 1871. *Nafsana wi nig Iesu Krist nag Yoan ki mtir i* [translator James Cosh]. Printed for the British and Foreign Bible Society at the 'Daily Southern Cross Office'. Auckland, New Zealand. NT3-Ioane.

Anon. 1874. *Kenesis natus a bei nag Moses ki mtir i.* Trans. Cosh, J. Sydney: British and Foreign Bible Society. NT3-kenesis.

Anon. 1875? *Nafisan nafousien.* Sydney: F.Cunninghame and Co. NT3-NafisanNafousien.

Anon. 1877. *Tusi Fe.* Sydney: F.Cunninghame and Co.

Anon. 1880. *Nawisien Nig Nagmer Apostol.* Sydney: F.Cunninghame and Co. NT3-Apostols.

Anon. 1885. *The Gospel according to John, Tus Nanrognrogona Uia ni Iesu Kristo nag Ioane i mitiria.* Trans. Mackenzie, J. Macdonald, D.D. Sydney: F.Cunninghame and Co.

Anon. 1892. *Tusi nalag Efate Niu Ebrites.* Sydney: F.Cunninghame and Co.

Anon. 1911. *Efatese primer, catechism and hymn book.* Havannah Harbour, Efate, New Hebrides. Melbourne: Arbuckle, Waddell & Fawckner, Printers, 20-22 McKillop Street. NT3-catechism.

Anon. 1918. *Tusi Nalag, Efate, Niu Ebretes.* Sydney: Epworth Printing and Publishing House.

Anon. 1919. *Natus bei ni nafisan ni Efate.* Sydney: Epworth Press. NT3-NatusBei.

Anon. 1919. *Tusi tab fao (New Testament).* Trans. Mackenzie, J. Macdonald, D.D. Melbourne: British and Foreign Bible Society.

Anon. 1923. *Nafakoron ni aliat. Erakor Efate, New Hebrides.* Nouméa: Imprimerie A.-L. Laubreaux. NT3-nafakoron.

Anon. 1923. *Scripture History.* Sydney: Epworth Printing and Publishing House. NT3-scripturehistory.

Anon. 1979. *Natus nalag.* NT3-NatusNalag.

MacDonald, Daniel. 1875. *Tus Narogorogoanauia Ki Iesu Kristo, Anigita Nawota Go Nagmolien, Luka Eka Mitiria, Nimetnafisan 13, 14, Go 15; Naligana Nalotuena Ru Tolu Ru Nea.* 1875. Printed at the Glasgow Foundry Boys Society's Press for Havannah Harbour, Efate.

MacDonald, Daniel. 1883. *The Gospel according to Luke Translated into the Language of Efate, New Hebrides.* Melbourne: M. L. Hutchinson.

## Notes

1 Nafsan has the ISO-639-3 code erk, and the Glottolog code sout2856
2 Images of this work can be found here: http://catalog.paradisec.org.au/collections/AC2/items/VEFAT21
3 A text version of this wordlist is here: http://catalog.paradisec.org.au/collections/NT3/items/rivierrewordlist

## References

McRae, Shirley. n.d. *Phrase book: English-native dictionary New Hebrides Presbyterian Mission.* [physical copy in the National Library of Australia. Digitial copy: https://catalog.paradisec.org.au/collections/NT3/items/phrasebook]

Thieberger, Nick. 2006. *A Grammar of South Efate: An Oceanic Language of Vanuatu*. Oceanic Linguistics Special Publication, No. 33. Honolulu: University of Hawai'i Press.

Thieberger, Nick. 2011. *Natrauswen nig Efat, Stories from South Efate.* http://repository.unimelb.edu.au/10187/9734

Thieberger, Nick & Chris Ballard. 2008. Daniel Macdonald and the 'compromise literary dialect' in Efate, central Vanuatu. *Oceanic Linguistics,* Volume 47:2: 365–382.

Wai, Kalop̃ong, Kalsal Kaltapau, Kaltafer Kaltak, Harry Kallon, Maxime Carlot, Harris Takau, & Alfred Carlot, 1983. *Tesa! Mal natrausuen*. Port Vila: USP Centre.

# Using the Dictionary

The dictionary is presented in two sections. The first lists words of Nafsan in alphabetical order with definitions in English. The second section, the finderlist, lists English terms and their Nafsan equivalents. For some topics, like trees, birds, or insects, lists of words are included under those headings, in addition to occurring in the alphabetical list. Bislama words in the finderlist are in italics.

Each dictionary entry has information set out as can be seen in the example entry for *mtir* below.

**Main word (other form of the word)** [*part of speech*] [definition] [example sentence] [example translation] [cross reference]

**mtir (mtri)** *verb*$_a$ **1)** to write. *Tiawi ni teetwei gar ru supnekin mtir; tiawi ru kano mtir.* The old people from long ago didn't know how to write, they couldn't write. **2)** to paint. *cf:* namtirwen.

If there is more than one meaning, then each is given a numbered sense as in the example above where sense (1) is *to write* and sense (2) is *to paint.*

When a noun can take a possessive ending (like a body part, for example) then the word given in the dictionary is the bare word or stem, with the third person form given in brackets following. For example, the word for name is *nagi*, and 'his/her/its name' is *nagien*, so the way it appears in the dictionary is *nagi* (*nagien*). The word for 'arm' is *nar*, but to say 'her or his arm' you would say *narun*. In the dictionary this is presented with the word that means 'arm' first, followed by the word that means 'his or her arm', for example, *nar* (*narun*). If the 3rd person singular is the same as the stem, then the third plural is given in brackets to show what is added because it is not always predictable, for example *namlun* 'skin' has the plural form *namlur* 'their skin' given in brackets.

Many locations are made by putting the 'location prefix' *e-* before a noun, for example, *etalm̃aat* 'at the garden', *esum̃* 'at the house', and you have to take off the *e-* to find the word (*talm̃aat*, *sum̃*) in this dictionary.

Nouns can be formed by putting *na-* before a verb and *-wen*, or *-ien*, after it, so for example, *nrom* 'to love' has a noun form *nanromien,* that means 'gift'.

While all verbs can be made into nouns in this way, many do not appear as nouns in the collection of texts and so they are not included as headwords in this dictionary. The most common verbs made into nouns are included as words in the dictionary.

In discussion with Nafsan speakers we have decided not to include homonym numbers (a subscript number after a word) in this dictionary.

Some pronouns are written with '=' following, for example, *p̃a=*, and this shows that they are attached to the following word (they are called pronoun prefixes in the dictionary). Note that these pronouns are written separately from the following verb in example sentences in this dictionary, following preferences expressed by Nafsan speakers at dictionary workshops. In the grammar of Nafsan I conclude that these are proclitics and so in other work I have written them as attached to the following verbal information. They are not used in the same way as free pronouns and so they are distinguished in the dictionary by using '='.

Some verbs start with a *p* that can change to an *f* for the irrealis form (e.g., *pestaf*/*festaf*); that is, when the action it describes has not happened or is being used in a command. It is the *p* initial form that is listed in the dictionary, with the *f* form following in brackets, for example, *preg* (*freg*). Entries for these words listed under *f* in the dictionary do not give a definition but refer back to the *p* initial form.

For some pairs of verbs it is not clear if they are a single word or two words, for example *preg pta* or *pregpta* 'make good', *mro sa* or *mrosa* 'think badly'. Some people want these written as one word and some want them written as two. If the combination of two verbs are used very often together then they are written here as a single word, we could say that they have become words themselves (they are lexicalized).

Some verbs are given with their third singular object form in brackets following the headword; this is due to the unpredictable nature of the vowel that is introduced to allow the object marker to appear. Sometimes, if the third person singular and the stem are identical, then either no form is provided, or the third plural form is given in brackets following the headword.

There are different kinds of verbs in Nafsan, depending on whether they can take an object as a suffix (ambitransitive, $verb_a$), or if they are intransitive ($verb_i$), or transitive ($verb_t$). Some verbs typically only appear as the second of two verbs and are marked as $verb_2$. For some verbs it is not yet clear what class they belong to and their part of speech is given as *verb*.

Scientific names are, in general, given by identifying a plant or animal from a reference book, not by having voucher specimens identified by the herbarium or similar authority. Where it is unclear if the animal or plant is exactly what the scientific name applies to, a question mark is included here.

It is hoped that further work on biological identification will be aided by this approximate identification.

An online version of an earlier version of this dictionary which includes audio of words being spoken can be found here: http://paradisec.org.au/SELexicon /index.htm.

This dictionary is part of a larger database of words and texts in Nafsan that can be found here in FLEx format: http://doi.org/10.4225/72/56FA0C5A7C98F. This includes archaic words and Bislama terms that were not included in the present dictionary.

All recordings are also archived in the Pacific and Regional Archive for Digital Sources in Endangered Cultures (PARADISEC.org.au). For more information about the grammar of Nafsan, see Thieberger 2006.

# Abbreviations and Glossary

| | |
|---|---|
| **adjective** | a word that modifies nouns, for example, *pram* 'tall' |
| **adverb** | a word that modifies verbs or sentences, for example, *em̃ae* 'far away' |
| **auxiliary** | one of a small set of verbs that occurs before the main verb |
| **cf.** | compare, look at another word that is similar |
| **cm** | centimetres |
| **COMP** | complementizer, used for *na* when it starts a new clause |
| **conjunction** | a word that joins words or sentences, like *go* 'and', *ko* 'or' |
| **demonstrative** | a word that points to something, words like 'that', 'this' |
| **determiner** | used for the word 'the' |
| **directional** | directional particle, follows a location to indicate direction (*mai* 'from', *pa* 'to', or *to* 'at') |
| **e.g.** | for example |
| **idiom** | idiomatic usage, a way of using the word that is usually not predictable from its definition |
| **interjection** | words that are used as sentences themselves, like *nta* 'okay', *ale* 'alright' |
| **interrogative** | question words like *fei* 'who', *ngas* 'when', *nafte* 'what' |
| **IPA** | International Phonetic Alphabet |
| **noun**$_{i}$ | inalienably possessed noun, also known as a directly possessed noun, for example: *naar* 'hand', *naarun* 'his/her hand'; *napot* 'belly button', *naptom* 'your belly button' |
| **particle** | a small group of words that don't fit into other parts of speech, like *pe* 'intensifier', used between two of the same word to intensify the meaning, like *maon pe maon* 'to sweat and sweat' |
| **prefix** | gets attached to the word that follows, like *te* 'the' in *tewarik* 'the few' |
| **preposition** | a word that tells you about the location of a noun, for example, *maloput* 'in the middle', *skot* 'with' |
| **preverbal** | words that are not verbs that go before the verb |

| | |
|---|---|
| **pronoun prefix** | the small words that go in front of a verb phrase to tell who is doing the action, like *ka* 'I', *ku* 'you' |
| **pronoun suffix** | the small words or single letters that go after a verb to tell who is receiving the action, like *-r* 'them', *-k* 'you' |
| **sp.** | species |
| **spp.** | species (plural) |
| **verb$_2$** | second verb in a compound verb (for example, *sok* is verb$_2$ in *mrosok* 'think a great deal' based on *mro* 'think') |
| **verb$_a$** | ambitransitive verb that can have the object marked as a suffix (for example, *kam* 'to step on', *kamti* 'to step on it') |
| **verb$_d$** | ditransitive verb, a verb that takes two objects, like *tu* 'give' (give something to someone) |
| **verb$_i$** | intransitive verb, like *trok* 'agree' |
| **verb$_t$** | transitive verb, like *kop* 'chase' |

# Nafsan to English Dictionary

# A AA

**a=** *pronoun prefix* I (1st person singular realis subject). *A muur ka fa me a mtak nlaken naflak neu pato ke fo watgi, i tap leeg mau.* I wanted to go but I was afraid because my *naflak* who were there would hit him, it was not right.

**aaf** *noun* fish spp., anthias (small groupers, perchlets, basslets, soapfishes). (*Serranidae*). *cf:* aaf ni nariuriu, patru.

**aaf ni nariuriu** *noun* fish sp., cigar wrasse. (*Cheilio inermis*). *cf:* aaf, patru.

**aal** *noun* shellfish sp., type of Turbo. (*Turbo chrysostomus* or *Turbo petholatus*).

**aal** *noun* sun. *I to pi mal kotfaan aal ki to na ke mtar.* It was afternoon, the sun was about to go down.

**aas** *noun* day after tomorrow. *cf:* naas.

**aas** *noun* coconut crab. (*Birgus latro*).

**afam** *noun* fish sp., humphead wrasse, Napoleonfish. Can get to be very large (a metre) and it sleeps vertically. (*Cheilinus undulatus*). *cf:* patru.

**afoka** *noun* avocado (English word used for foreign fruit). (*Persea americana*).

**afsak** *noun* turtle (general term). (*Idiom: 'He is really a turtle.' He is tricking us, he is a liar.*)

**ag** *pronoun* you (2nd person singular subject or object). *Go raiten i tli na, "I tiik, ag ku kano pan nlaken ag ku sees."* And its mother said, "No, you can't because you are little." *Kineu a kano taulu ag.* I can't marry you.

**akam** *pronoun* you (2nd person plural subject or object). *Go teesa nanwei i na, "Kineu a tae skot akam."* And the boy said, "I can come with you."

**akit** *pronoun* we (1st person plural inclusive subject or object). *Akit tu pitlak naik laap me naik i skei i pi map̃er naik sees me i tap muurin nag ke lek ko ke ur naor mram kai ures mau.* We have many fish, but this fish, the *map̃er*, is a small one and it doesn't like to see light or be in a bright place.

**alak** *noun* honeyeater, incl. silver-eared honeyeater, Vanuatu mountain honeyeater (type of bird). (*Lichmera incana*).

**ale** *interjection* okay; and then. *Ale teesa sees nen i to kai.* Okay, this small child cried. *A to weswes hotel ale i pitlak masta i skei, natam̃ool i skei i mai tli na i muur teweswes sanpe.* I was working at a hotel and then someone, a boss, came and said he wanted (me to) work somewhere else.

**aliat** *noun* day. *Or i kano siwer aliat me i tae siwer p̃og go natam̃ool nega ru muurin nag ke to negar traus nafte kin i pan leka natokon nig Ambae ko Santo.* Yes, he can't travel in the day, but he knows to travel at night and his people wanted him to tell them what he'd seen in the village at Ambae or Santo. *cf:* naliati.

**aliat faitaumlap** *noun* Thursday (learning day). *cf:* faitau.

**aliat fnau** *noun* Wednesday (court day). *cf:* fnau.

**aliat kaaru** *noun* Tuesday (second day). *cf:* kaaru.

**aliat motu** *noun* midday (the big middle day). *cf:* motu.

**aliat pei** *noun* Monday (first day). *cf:* pei.

**aliat p̃oot** *noun* Friday (day for dividing and sharing things out). *cf:* p̃oot.

**aliat tap** *noun* Sunday (holy day). *cf:* tap.

**aliat toknak** *noun* Saturday (a day to prepare). *cf:* toknak.

**almtar** *noun* sunset. (*Idiom: 'The sun is going down.' Old age is approaching, end of one's life is getting close.*)

**altuk** *noun* **1)** island cabbage. *Me ser nrak nen kin ru freg kapu ru pus altuk.* But every time they made laplap they put in island cabbage. **2)** cabbage.

**alu (aluen)** *noun$_i$* uncle (father's brother). *cf:* awo, **apaap**.

**am̃kano (am̃kanor)** *noun$_i$* heart.

**anisakel** *noun* plant sp., bougainvillea.

**anrar** *noun* fish sp., cardinalfish. (*Apogonidae*). *cf:* p̃op̃or.

**apaap** *noun* father, father's brother (address term, used by those in *naflak* other than *kram* and *namkanr*). *Go nanronrogon nen kin a nrogo na tete apaap ru sat teesa me ru pag ki nkas.* And I heard that some men ('fathers') got some kids to climb trees. *cf:* gka, taata, tem.

**apu** *noun* grandfather. Note: added to the last syllable of some names, e.g., *apu + Kalorip = apurip. Asaraf, go komam u nrogo kin apu me ati nigmam ru to nigmam trausi na i pi natam̃ool nen i pram, i pram kotkot.* Asaraf, we have heard our grandfather and grandmother tell us that he was tall, really tall.

**apu motu** *noun* great-grandfather.

**apu sees** *noun* grandson with the same name as his grandfather. *cf:* apu.

**ara** *noun* yam sp., red inside, sweet.

**arkao** *noun* shellfish sp., trochus.

**arleeg** *adjective* skilful. *Malnen ku nep maan ku mpalua go ru soso ki arleeg.* When you throw a stone at a bird and you hit it, they say you are skilful.

**arm̃afaf** *noun* box crab. (*Calappidae*).

**armatu** *adjective* right-handed. *cf:* arworksu, maur.

**armaur** *verb* left-handed.

**arsa** *adjective* clumsy, not skilful.

**arum** *verb$_i$* skin nearly ripe. mrapil.

**arworksu** *adjective* ambidextrous, someone who can use both hands. *cf:* armatu, maur.

**asel (aslen)** *noun$_i$* friend; *aslak nmatu* 'girlfriend'. *Too go taap̃es ra tm̃er pi asel kir.* The chicken and the swamphen were friends.

**aslel** *noun* fish sp., striped mackerel. (*Rastrelliger kanagurta*).

**aslot** *noun* worm.

**ataat** *noun* albino. *Ataat nen nalun i taar ko naskon i taar ko i miel.* An albino has white hair and his skin is white or red.

**ataf** *noun* helper, chief's assistant.

**ati** *noun* grandmother. *Go nasum̃tap nen, i wel ki mal ni ati me apu mana, komam u skul wes.* And that church, in the time of grandmother and grandfather, we went to school there. *cf:* ati sees.

**ati motu** *noun* great-grandmother.

**ati sees** *noun* granddaughter with the same name as her grandmother. *cf:* ati.

**atlag** *noun* **1)** moon. **2)** month. There are two women in the moon, *Leiriki* (small one) and *Leilepa* (big one). *Ligal* is an old name for the moon. A red moon means there will be a cyclone. *A weswes atlag i tol, me a leka iwi, me a mer ler mai to esum̃ to.* I worked for three months, and I found it good, but I came back and stayed at home.

**atlag foum** *noun* **1)** new month, next month (also *atlag nen tu* 'next month'). **2)** new moon.

**atlag fsofus** *noun* moon, new moon.

**atlag kaaru** *noun* month after next month.

**atlag malik** *noun* no moon.

**atlag mrem** *noun* moonlight, shining light.

**atlag pei** *noun* first month, e.g., last month, the month just past (also *atlag nen pa* 'last month').

**atlak** *noun* owner. *Atlak sa, ko natopu ni san i tkali, ga ru faafat wes.* The owner here, or the *natopu* from here, touched him, they believe in him.

**atmat** *conjunction* and, used to join numbers only, so, for example, *ralim atmat itol* 'thirteen' (ten and three).

**atol** *noun* egg. *Akam ko fo to lekor atol, me kineu ka fo mer ler pak naur ni Efat.* You will look after the eggs, and I will return to Efate.

**atol kanr** *noun* rice (lit: black ant egg). (*Oryza sativa*).

**aure** *adjective* skilled, be skilled at singing. Someone who is *aure* can lead a choir.

**awe** *interjection* exclamation, used to show surprise.

**awo** *noun* uncle, your mother's brother, the term you call your uncle (address term). *cf:* alu, **apap**.

## E EE

**e** *particle prefix suffix* location, this is usually prefixed to the location noun or place-name, but can also appear following a location noun or place-name. For example, sum̃ 'house', esum̃ 'at the house'. *Me nanwei ga ke fo pak e talm̃aat, i slat nafnag i paunamru ke mai psi esum̃.* The man would go to the garden, get food, carry it and put it in the house. *Gar ra nru mat peen Epakrar e.* They both died at Epakrar.

**efare** *noun* **1)** meeting area, place usually cleared of vegetation for large meetings. **2)** men's house.

**ekate** *noun* the side of a canoe that is away from the outrigger (left-hand side).

**ektem** *preposition* outside (as in outside a house). *Go i nrik wou ki na, "Ko to, ko fo to me ka fak ektem."* And he said to us, "You stay, you will stay and I'll go outside."

**elag** *preposition* **1)** above. **2)** high, up. *Maan i nrir ur elag.* The bird flies above.

**elagsau** *noun* heaven.

**elau** *noun* sea. *Go selwan elau i mu go raru i m̃el, go u tu tm̃alu raki Tangoa, Santo.* When the sea was high, and the boat floated, we left for Tangoa, Santo. *cf:* namoos, ntas.

**elkao** *noun* coral fence, stone wall, once used as a protective wall for the village.

**elol** *noun* yard. *cf:* em̃lel.

**eluk** *noun cf:* luk.

**em̃ae** *adverb* **1)** away. *Selwan ka fak em̃ae p̃a ta mai pak esum̃ neu mau.* When I go away don't you come to my house. **2)** far, distant. *P̃a nrus kin ke fak em̃ae.* Move it so it is far away.

**emat** *noun* cemetery, graveyard.

**emat (ematen)** *noun$_i$* grave. *If wel kuf lek tete nkas i ftom emat nigneu.* If you see a tree growing from my grave. *Go emater gar ra tefra to, tkal mees.* And their graves lined up there, up until today.

**em̃au** *noun* clearing, a cleared piece of ground. *cf:* limuti.

**emeromen (emermen)** *noun* **1)** earth. **2)** world. *Ru po tp̃a ki nafsan nen ru pak ser naor emermen.* They would send information to every country in the world.

**em̃lel** *noun* yard. *cf:* elol.

**em̃rom** *preposition* inside. *Go i sa kin ka fo psir em̃rom ni kaset gakit.* And it is bad if I tell a lie on our cassette.

**en** **1)** *verb$_i$* lay, stay doing something. *Naik seserik ru en fam.* The small fish stayed and ate. *Maarik i pen Ermage i en pan pan pan.* The spirit (Maarik) was at Erromango, it stayed and stayed. **2)** *auxiliary* used to mark an ongoing activity. *Ntwam i na i to kai mrokin na, "Kai pe en mrokin pan kai pe tok nrus mroput."* The devil stopped and thought, "I thought about this and I am a little worried." **3)** *auxiliary* inside, be inside. *cf:* entaak, entan.

**enflos** *verb$_i$* sleep badly, toss and turn in sleep. *Teesa i entan sa, i enflos.* The child is laying uncomfortably, it is sleeping badly.

**enkot** *verb* lay and break something by laying on it.

**ensok (ensoki)** *verb$_a$* lay on, brood (of a fowl). *Too i to ensok atol.* The chicken is laying on the egg. *Ku ensok narun.* You sleep on his arm.

**entaak** *verb$_i$* sleep on the side. *cf:* en, entan.

**entaf** *verb* to be the main one of, to be the head of, to encompass. *Ru tok lek maan i nru ra tok pan paakor kir. Go i tap pi negar ru skei mau, me tete natkon nag ru entaf kir. Maan nen kaaru i taar, go kaaru i got.* Two birds would appear to them. And it wasn't just at their villages, but at a number of villages, of which theirs was the main one. This bird was white and the other one was black.

**entan** *verb*$_i$ lie, lay down. *cf:* en, entaak.

**ep̃ag** *noun* bedroom. *cf:* etkuum.

**ep̃ag** *noun* south.

**ep̃au** *noun* north.

**ep̃rom** *noun* special place, a private special place.

**erfale** *noun* cave. *U to pan me u ta lek erfale ni Litrapog mau.* We went but we didn't see Litrapong's cave.

**esan** *noun* here. *Komam ko fo matur esan, ematool pulp̃og, ko fo sel naot negar pak elau Lefenpis.* We will sleep here, tomorrow morning we will take their chief to the beach at Lefenpis.

**esem** *noun* outrigger side of a canoe (usually the right-hand side). *Maloput raru go nsem̃ i pi esem.* (The area) between the canoe and the outrigger is called '*esem*'. *cf:* nsem.

**etak** *noun* **1)** toilet. *Ka fak etak.* I will go to the toilet. **2)** place for throwing rubbish.

**etan** *preposition* below, underneath, down. *I pag ki nkafik pak elag, me Ririal i to etan.* He climbed up the nakavika and Ririal stayed down below. *cf:* paketan.

**etan mpam (etan mpamun)** *noun*$_i$ scapula, shoulder blade.

**etan ntaf** *noun* downhill.

**etik** *preposition* edge, on the side of a hole or a cave. *cf:* natik, nrau.

**etkuum** *noun* lounge room. *cf:* ep̃ag.

**etog** *noun* foreign place. *Or maarik nen i lek loto, raru stimer i lek raru nlae tete natir i tol go stimer sernale nig nam̃er nig etog i lek silua.* Yes, this man saw cars, a steamboat, a sailing boat with three masts and a steamer, he'd seen all these foreigner's things.

**euut** *noun* beach, shore. *Selwan ku kano los ku pato euut m̃as to.* When you can't swim, you stay on the beach.

## F

**fa** See: pa

**faafat** *verb*$_i$ believe, trust. *A faafat i tilm̃ori.* I believe he speaks the truth.

**faag** *verb*$_i$ riddle, tell riddles. *cf:* nfaag.

**faai** *noun* fish sp., stingray (general term).

**faai** See: paai

**faai kuul** *noun* fish sp., bluespotted ribbontail ray. (*Taeniura lymma*).

**faai mantu** *noun* ray sp., with black skin that can be scraped off. Identified as both manta ray (but see *roktaar*) and devil ray.

**faai p̃og** *noun* fish sp., spotted eagle ray. (*Aetobatus narinari*).

**faai pumat** *noun* fish sp., bluespotted stingray. (*Dasyatis kuhlii*).
**faai suar** *noun* fish sp., eagle ray.
**faakot** See: paakot
**faan** See: paan
**faar** *verb$_i$* smooth pandanus leaves to make them ready for weaving. *Ku mrokin nen p̃a freg m̃iit, go p̃a fo pei pak nlak naki, ale p̃a fo faar.* You want to make a mat, so you first go to a pandanus tree, then you smooth the pandanus leaves.
**faar** *noun* light, also used to mean eyes (maybe from French *phare* 'lighthouse'). *P̃a pnot faar gaag.* Close your eyes. *cf:* namet.
**faareki** See: paareki
**faat** *noun* stone. *Faat sees i tp̃ofu raru p̃ur.* A small stone can wreck a big canoe.
**faat** *noun* vatu, money. *Ale i pan sor tete sernale hotel, nen ke sel faat sees.* Then he goes and sells something at the hotel, to get a little money.
**faat ni uum** *noun* top stones of an oven. *Nafet faat ni uum ru miel malen ru ftin.* The top stones are red when they are heated.
**faatfag** *noun* stone, top stones used to cover a *kapu* in the earth oven.
**faatfar** *noun* **1)** rock that is under the sea most of the time, but is exposed in low tides and sticks out of the water. **2)** coral formation or 'bommie', a rock that is used to make lime by baking it on a fire. *Ku pan slati elau, p̃a mai, p̃a traf nam̃or, ku pu nkap kerkrai, nkap nmarteu (nator). Ku sat faatfar ku psi pakelag nkas nmarteu nen i tu, ku tp̃ili. I sor faatfar panpan i frafer. I frafer, ru tae to malsees. Us i wo, ale i slatlu natoon ni nkas. Ale faatfar m̃as, natoon knen i taar i tu. Ku pan pai, ale ku pai. Ale ku pan preg nasum̃ ki, tikon ki nasum̃ ki, taos simen.* You get it from the sea, you come and dig a hole, you put in strong dry wood. You take the *faatfar,* you put it on top of the wood, you burn it. It burns the *faatfar* until it cracks up. It cracks up, then you wait a little while. The rain washes the rock pieces from the wood. The ashes from the *faatfar* are white. You pack it up. Then you can make a house from it, the walls of the house, like cement.
**faatftak** *noun* bottom stones of an oven.
**faatmaama** *noun* sharpening stone. *cf:* maama, pkal.
**faatmpasok** *noun* stone used to hold a mat down.
**faatsal** *noun* stone that floats, pumice. *cf:* naf.
**faftae** *interjection* thank you, this is the Polynesian term that is widely used by Nafsan speakers. *cf:* **psawi**.
**fag** *verb* be scabby, to be covered in sores. *Me nmatu nen i trau fag.* But this woman was covered in sores. *cf:* nfag.
**fag** *verb$_i$* smoulder (of a fire that is glowing or smoking but no flame is visible). If the flame is visible then it is said to *sor*.

**failuk** See: pailuk

**faitau** *verb*$_i$ learn, study. *Nasum̃ nen ru to, teesa ru to faitau wes, ru maui saprek, tarp̃ek.* The houses, where children would go to study, they were all broken. *cf:* plaksok, tafnau, tefaitau.

**fakfak** *noun* shellfish sp., cone (no poison). (*Conidae*).

**fakis (faksi)** *verb*$_a$ decorate.

**faksaar** *noun* protection, something that protects you.

**faksaarsa** *noun* poison.

**falus** See: palus

**fam** See: pam

**famnrog** See: pamnrog

**fam̃or** See: pam̃or

**fan** See: pan

**fanei** *verb*$_i$ **1)** dissolve (as of sugar in water or smoke in the sky). **2)** fade.

**fanfan** *verb*$_i$ wash the face.

**fanikoro** *noun* tree sp., has fruit that looks like vanilla pods, with pretty flowers, and can be used for firewood.

**faresor** *noun* tree sp., used for timber posts, firewood, burns well.

**farfar** *noun* wagtail (bird) with a black breast.

**farfar** *verb*$_i$ **1)** shake, as in a leaf shaking or other small movements. **2)** move about quickly.

**farfarsa** *verb* **1)** mess things up, be messy. **2)** to shake a rattle announcing the presence of a group of people (or *waal*). **3)** wobble, as in the wobbling fat from an animal (an old word).

**faria** *adjective* poor.

**fas** See: pas

**fati** *noun* boil that comes up on fingers. *cf:* nmak, nmanuk, p̃onfer.

**fatkau** *adjective* **1)** hooked, anything shaped like a hook. **2)** *noun* piece of hooked wood used to pull grass or wood that you will cut. *cf:* tkau.

**fatkau** *noun* barb of a spear. *Ku tae preg fatkau timen gaag.* You can put a barb on your arrow.

**fatlas** See: patlas

**fatma** *noun* grater for making laplap with root crops and bananas. *cf:* naures, skeitrai.

**fato** See: pato

**fau** See: pau

**faus** See: paus

**fe** *verb*$_a$ read. *I sup̃ne ki nam̃er taar. I tae na namuurien ga m̃as. Ru malik ru sup̃ne kin fe natus.* He didn't know white people. He only knew his own way. They were in the dark, they didn't know how to read a book. *cf:* fef.

**feek** *noun* cockroach.

**fees** See: pees

**fef** *verb*$_i$ read, reading a letter or a book. *Neu a to muur ka fef ser nrak.* I want to read all the time. *cf:* fe.

**fei 1)** *pronoun* who. *Talm̃aat ni fei?* Whose garden? *Fei mana?* Who (all)? *U tap tae fei kin ke fo mos mam pak ist Hog Haba mau.* We didn't know who would take us to east Hog Harbour. *Fei kin ke fo pamir?* Who will eat them? *cf:* nafeifeien.

**fei** See: pei

**fekfek** *verb*$_i$ **1)** show off. **2)** show something you are proud of. *cf:* pesp̃ur, polmatmat.

**ferfer** *verb*$_i$ mark rhythm. *Ag ku ferfer ukelele gaag.* You keep rhythm on your ukelele.

**fesfes** *verb*$_i$ cheep (of birds).

**fesrae** See: pesrae

**festaf** See: pestaf

**fetkasu** *verb*$_i$ jealous, be jealous.

**fgan** *noun* bait, used for fishing or hunting.

**fi** See: pi

**fiar** *verb*$_i$ be unafraid of. *Me kineu a fiar kin, kat natrauswen ga i nrak laap i to neu traus.* But I wasn't scared of it because he had told me his story many times.

**fiet** *verb* fierce, to be a good fighter. *cf:* ple.

**fiif** *verb*$_i$ **1)** to be twisted, to be rolled up, to be curly (e.g., of hair). Followed by *ki* it can mean 'to tie up'. *Nap̃kas i fiif.* The grain (meat) of the wood is twisted. *Ag p̃a fiif ki string, kineu ka fo palus.* You roll up the line, I'll paddle the canoe. *Tuk fiif ki naniu su po slatir pelpel pak esum̃.* Let us tie up the coconuts, then take them home quickly. **2)** spin. *Ku nrog np̃aum i fiif a? Ku na p̃a tarup̃ nlaken nanrur i teflan.* You feel your head spinning, eh? You almost fall over because of the earthquake. *cf:* lfek.

**fiikot (fiiktofi)** *verb*$_a$ **1)** tie a cloth or rope onto oneself, e.g., a towel wrapped around the throat. **2)** fasten a mat around your body, a sign of high rank. *cf:* nanrepnrep, nap̃lai, nasieg, nrepnrep, pisp̃lolo.

**fiisok** *verb* wrap a cloth around something, wind a cloth around yourself.

**fiit** *verb*$_i$ run. *P̃a fiit p̃elp̃el.* You run fast. *P̃a fiit!* Go quickly! *cf:* pelpel.

**fios** See: pios

**fis (fsei)** *verb*$_a$ whip, with a rope. *Me masta nen i sa, tete nrak i fsei ki stokwip.* But a bad master, sometimes he would whip him with a stockwhip. *cf:* fisktof, sm̃anr.

**fisfis** *verb*$_i$ masturbate, whip yourself.

**fisktof** *verb* whip. *Me tewan i fisktofi, boy i kano pregsa ki. Me naskon ke fo miel nlaken stokwip i kerkrai.* But some he would whip, and the boy couldn't do anything about it. But his skin would be red, because the stockwhip was strong. *cf:* fis.

**fitkaskei** See: pitkaskei

**fitlak** See: piatlak

**fkaar** *verb*$_i$ joke, give cheek. *cf:* pesfkaar.

**fket** *adjective* sour, to be spicy (like chilli), food which 'bites' you. It can also describe the feeling of a hornet's sting. *Ntal, nawi, chili, ru nomser fket.* Taro, yam, chilli, they are all spicy.

**fket** *adjective* biter, describing a characteristic of a person or animal that bites. *cf:* kat.

**fkofuk** *adjective* swelling of the skin, could be from allergy or insect bite.

**fkop** *verb$_i$* chase, follow fish. *P̃a fan fkop ntas.* You chase fish at sea. *cf:* kop, kpas.

**fla** *preverbal* conditional particle. *Tete gar ru fla tap tkal fifti mau. Gar ru nrfal m̃as.* Some may not have reached fifty. There were only a few of them.

**flak** See: plak

**flefil** *noun* shellfish sp., pearl oyster. (*Pinctada margaritifera*). *cf:* toor.

**flor** See: plor

**flos** See: plos

**fnagot** *noun* shellfish sp., Turbo shell (small one).

**fnau (fnaus)** *verb$_a$* preach, judge, teach. *Natam̃ool nen kin i su i pi natam̃ool fnau nen i po patlasir.* The man who came down to meet them was a preacher. *cf:* aliat fnau, tafnau.

**fneslu** *noun* shellfish sp., moon shell, shell is white, flesh is white, black operculum. It lives in the sand. (*Naticidae*).

**fo** See: po

**foik** *noun* fish sp., batfish. *cf:* talmat.

**fokfkaal** *verb$_i$* comfort. *Ku pes fokfkaal kin.* You comfort him.

**fol** See: pol

**folfol** *verb$_i$* behave. *Folfol wel nmatu.* Behave like a woman. *cf:* pol.

**folfol sa** *verb$_i$* **1)** bad behaviour. **2)** copulate.

**folfolm̃ak** *verb$_i$* **1)** rub. *I folfolm̃ak ki namten.* He rubs his eyes. **2)** shake out, like a tablecloth, or clothes being washed, or shaking hands to dry them. *Ku folfolm̃ak ki nkal.* You wash the clothes.

**foum** *adjective* new. *Malen kin i pa raru foum i pak nai tefla.* When he pushed the new canoe he went to the sea just like that. *cf:* met.

**fraa** *verb$_a$* **1)** beg. **2)** ask. *Ku fraa naat nen ke weluok.* Ask that man to help you.

**frafer** *verb$_i$* scatter, go away from. *U preg nalotwen i nom kin me ko fo frafer pak klas fserser.* We finished praying then we scattered to our different classes.

**frak** *verb$_i$* to be late. *Ku frak nafnag.* You are late with the food.

**frap̃o** *noun* beetle (general term).

**freg** *verb$_i$* carry a basket on your head, or hanging from a rope around your forehead (only of women). *I freg ki napor.* She carries a basket. *cf:* p̃aunamru.

**freg** See: preg

**fregfu** See: pregfu

**fregnrog** See: pregnrog

**fregwel** See: pregwel

**fro** *verb* look after, keep safe for someone, typically of food or belongings.

**frofur** *noun* rash, swelling and itchiness on the skin, heat rash.

**frulsei** *verb$_i$* wash a baby after birth (an old word, not used today).

**fsar** *verb* grab, wrestle.

**fser** *noun* fish sp., vermiculate rabbitfish or forktail rabbitfish. (*Siganidae*).

**fser** *adjective* 'own', the one associated with a particular person. When it follows a word it means that it belongs to the person. *Nasum̃ fser.* One's own house.

**fserser** *verb*$_i$ different, to be. *Ke piatlak kaai, go ke fo piatlak wiit, go ke fo piatlak naik, go ke fo piatlak tefserser i laap nen i to slati elau, ntas.* There were shellfish, and octopus, and fish, and many other different things that she would get from the sea.

**fsofus** *adjective* young, to be. *Akit tefsofus ni malfane, taos kineu, kineu plak nafet teesa nanwei fsofus ni taos Erakor mees.* We young people of today, like me, me and all the young men in Erakor today.

**fsok** *verb* sex, to have sex. *cf:* ftik, tik.

**fsup̃** *verb* sting (as in a wasp sting or a stingray's tail sticking into you).

**fsup̃** *verb*$_i$ pointed, to be pointed, pitch, summit, pointed; something sticking up. *Nasu i fsup̃ pak elag.* The roof is pitched high. *Nawi nen i ftom kai fsup̃ pak elag.* This yam grew and pointed upwards. *cf:* nafsup̃.

**fti** *noun* fish spp., scorpionfishes. (*Scorpaenidae*).

**ftik** *verb*$_i$ sex, to have sex with. Use *ftik* instead of *tik or tki* to avoid embarrassment (slang). *cf:* fsok, tik.

**ftil** *verb*$_i$ gossip. *A ftil skot ag.* I gossip with you.

**ftin** *verb*$_i$ **1)** hot, to be. (*Idiom: 'His hand is hot.' He has money.*) **2)** angry, be angry. *I preg np̃au ftin pak naot.* They made the chief angry (lit: they made the chief's head hot). *cf:* maet.

**ftir** *noun* fish sp., stonefish, small one (smallscale scorpionfish). (*Scorpaenidae*). *cf:* p̃iit.

**ftiti** *verb* crowded. *Teesa ru mai matur skot apap go iak ru ftiti nawol i skei.* Children come and sleep with their father and mother and are crowded into one bed.

**ftok** *noun* cane (*nasul*) when straightened and ready to make arrows (*timen*). *cf:* naus.

**ftom** *verb*$_i$ grow, a plant just starting to grow; *nawi ftom* 'germinated yam'. *I po to ftom.* It is growing.

**ftook** *noun* niece or nephew.

**ftu** See: ptu

**ftup̃** *verb*$_i$ fight, hit someone in a fight. *Tete ru ftup̃, wel ki ru min ru ftup̃ wel ki pregi ru preg problem laap.* Some fight, they drink and they fight, causing many problems. *cf:* nafkal, tup̃.

**fuelig** *noun* basket, an open woven set of two panels made of coconut leaves, used to carry large items or to carry rubbish. *cf:* likat, napor, nroog, tasaal.

**fuelig araskei** *noun* coconut leaf split and leaves woven together to make a mat that is used for the wall or roof of a house.

**fuet** See: puet

**fuet** *adjective* marked, to be, e.g., the way that skin is marked after it is hit by something.

**fuetsok** See: puetsok

**fufuel** *verb*$_i$ disappear. *Pulp̃og san ntas i ures nasum̃ ru nomser fufuel.* In the morning here, the sea came in and all the houses disappeared.

**fuk** See: puk

**fuknra** *noun* fish sp., twinspot snapper, red snapper, mangrove jack. It is quite likely to have *mam* ciguetera poison. (*Lutjanidae*).

**fulful** *verb* twirl, spin from one's hands. *cf:* **pul**.

**fum̃** *verb$_i$* bud. *Namlas nen i fum̃.* The bush is flowering. *cf:* nafum̃.

**fumasei** *noun* fish sp., picasso fish, strong skin, or brush-sided filefish.

**fumatol** *noun* fish sp.

**fum̃os** *noun* fish sp., strong skin, dark coloured (orange-lined triggerfish?).

**funfnaal** *verb$_i$* make a mess.

**funfnoi** *verb$_i$* **1)** blurring. **2)** disappearing from view. *cf:* krakfunfnoi, surfunfnoi.

**funfunmet** *noun* flickering light.

**funrei** *noun* ant sp., white ant, termite. *cf:* ofet.

**funrei** *noun* wriggler, mosquito larva.

**fup̃eel** *noun* fish sp., sand bass. (*Centropomidae*).

**furaru** *noun* banana sp. *cf:* nanrmem.

**furfur** *noun* bundle of *nmarteu* coconuts.

**fuserek** See: puserek

**fusuer** *verb$_i$* growl, a noise made to show you are grumpy. *Apap i maet ki iak go i to fusuer.* Dad was angry with mum and he was growling.

**fusurtol** *noun* competition.

**fuu** *noun* fish spp., triggerfishes, but see also *p̃arp̃or*. (*Idiom: Fuu p̃aru aliat skei 'Become the fat fish of the day.' Fatten oneself up with money, which gets all spent by that person in only one day.*) (*Balistidae*). *cf:* p̃arp̃or.

**fuu** *verb$_i$, adverb* **1)** quick, go quickly. *A siwer fuu, a fuu reki talm̃aat.* I walk quickly, I go quickly to the garden. **2)** blow hard (of the wind). *Nlag i fuu.* The wind blows hard.

## G

**ga** *pronoun* **1)** he/him, she/her, it (3rd person singular subject or object). *Me katom i tae na ga i kano kraf pelpel, taos menaal, menaal i tae sef pelpel.* But the hermit crab knew that it couldn't crawl quickly like the barracuda, the barracuda could go quickly. **2)** his/hers. *Me i nrik kori sees ga nen kin na, "Tak fak san pe."* And he said to his dog, "Let's go back there." **3)** for his/her benefit. *Ale gavman i tua ntan. I ga sevei ki.* Then the government gave him ground. It surveyed it for him. *cf:* nega.

**gaaf** *noun* **1)** metre, one metre, length of one arm. **2)** material, piece of material, also a scarf.

**gaag** *pronoun* **1)** yours (2nd person plural possessive). *Ku pan sai ki raru gaag i to slaor.* You push your canoe into the passage. **2)** for your benefit (2nd person plural benefactive). *Me i pitlak natam̃ool nen kin ke fo mer gaag preg naul nkas nen ke tuok p̃a mingi, go p̃a fo mer m̃ool.* But there are people who will then give you leaf medicine to drink, and you will become healthy again. *cf:* negaag.

**gakit** *pronoun* **1)** our (1st person plural inclusive possessive). *Go i pi Kaptin Jemis Kuk. Malnen i mai i paam̃or naurur gakit i pi New Hebrides.* And it was Captain James Cook. When he found our islands, these became the New Hebrides. **2)** for our benefit (1st person plural inclusive benefactive). *A muurin na ka gakit traus natrauswen sees iskei.* I would like to tell us all a little story. *cf:* negakit.

**gamus (negamus)** *pronoun* **1)** you (2nd person plural object), typically *mus* is used rather than *gamus*. *I pi tenag a na ka nrik mus ki nen ko tae.* That is what I can tell you, so that you will know. **2)** for you (2nd person plural benefactive). *Kafo gamus tao atol ke to rak to san tok.* I will leave two eggs for you here. **3)** yours (2nd person plural possessive). *Apu natopu gakit, i muur teesa nmatu gamus.* Our ancestor spirit wanted your daughter.

**gar** *adjective* dry, to be. *Malen elau i mat kerkrai, mat toop, go nskau i gar userek.* Then the sea was really low and the reef was completely dry.

**gar** *pronoun* **1)** they, them (3rd person plural subject or object). *Gar ru pitlak na ntan nen naot nig Efil i tuer kin Emlap̃o, san kin Kawenu i tkos.* They had land that the chief of Ifira gave them at Emlap̃o, where Kawenu (college) is. **2)** theirs (3rd person plural possessive). *Ru po kop namuurien gar i toop.* They would follow their own minds too much. **3)** for them (3rd person plural benefactive). *Ra po gar pregpta ki suker pan i nom ra sol tete pret.* We (two) will prepare sugar for them, we'll get some bread. *cf:* negar.

**gawa** *interjection* that's it, that's the way. Expression often used to conclude a part of a story or to confirm what has just been said. *Nanre ni French ru ta muur independens na ke mai pelpel mau nlaken ru muur na ru mer ptu ki ntau i lim, me nanre ni Inglis gar ru tuer ki, go gawa, ru panpan ru preg naflewen.* On the French side they didn't want independence to come quickly, they wanted to give it in another five years, but on the English side, they gave it, and, that was it, they had an argument. *cf:* gawan.

**gawan (gawanki, gawankia)** *interjection* like that, an expression used to refer to a previous discussion. *Nser ni taap̃es, tene, i pi teni taap̃es. Me tene i pi teni too. Gawan ki.* The swamphen's comb, it belongs to the swamphen.

But this is the rooster's comb. That's it. *cf:* gawa.

**gien** *verb* act as. *Maarik Samuel ga i gien ki nafinaotan tu Apu Kalmet kin i tok pes nam̃leen.* Maarik Samuel was acting chief, but Apu Kalmet took the right to act in his place. *cf:* surosur.

**gka** *noun* father (address term used by members of *naflak namkanr*). *cf:* apap, taata, tem.

**gkar** *noun* tree sp., devil nettle. Note: stinging nettle tree. (*Dendrocnide latifolia*). *cf:* nkraful.

**gkar (nkar)** *noun* handle of a pot.

**gki** *interjection* expression used for 'come and take this', 'here it is', 'look at this'.

**gkis** *interjection* exclamation, used to draw attention or to start a conversation.

**gkof (gkofus)** *verb*$_a$ roast fish on the stones separate from laplap. *cf:* tanum̃.

**go** *conjunction* and. *Selwan kin ku tai, i pitlak nsem go i pitlak nakiat.* When you cut, there is the outrigger and there is the cross-member (of the canoe).

**go** *demonstrative* **1)** used after a noun to form a question, e.g., *ga go?* 'who is that?' **2)** that one just mentioned. *Ale i pei kin kin teflan go i trau mur me i na, "O a trau semsem lek namrun go."* So he showed her and she laughed and said, "Oh I am glad to see this."

**gog 1)** *verb* be ready to jump. Like an animal ready to defend itself or to jump away. **2)** *noun* goalkeeper in football.

**golgol** *adjective* to be toothless (of baby or old person). *Teesa nen i pi golgol i to pam kumol nen ru krakfufua.* A toothless baby only eats kumala that they have mashed.

**gor** *verb*$_i$ snore, also used for the noise a pig makes. *cf:* ur.

**gos** *verb*$_i$ get a flu, cold, sickness. *Kineu a gos.* I have a cold.

**got** *adjective* black, to be. *Namtir nen i got.* That colour is black. *Nam̃er got me nam̃er taar. Navy, army nametrau nam̃er fserser.* Black men and white men. Navy and army, all different men.

## I Ii

**i=** *pronoun prefix* he, she, it (3rd person singular realis subject). *Me i pitlak namrun i skei i to nam̃oru.* And there is this thing that stays out in the deep sea.

**iak** *noun* **1)** mother, mother's sister, father's sister, and women in that generation to the speaker (address term). *Iak neu i mat me apap neu m̃as i m̃ool to.* My mother is dead but my father is still alive. **2)** aunt. *cf:* rait.

**ifmertiik (kefmertiik)** *idiom* otherwise.

**ilfot** *number* nine. *cf:* kilfot.

**inrok** *adverb* after, behind, later, also used to talk about the next event in a story. *Ag p̃a fei me kineu ka fo inrok.* You go first and I will come behind. *Me inrok nen, malen kin tu sat independent, go ru po sapot ki independent.* But after that, when we got independence, they supported independence.

**inror** *noun* pig too old to have piglets.

**inruenru** *adjective* each. *Nrakpei i welkia i pitlak adminstresen ni Britis go Franis ru pitlak ospital inruenru, go tete sernale inruenru.* Back then, there was the British administration and the French and they each had hospitals and each had everything. *cf:* limlim, patpat, toltol.

**ipi** *number* how many?, used following a time measure, like *ntau ipi* 'how many years?'. *A tap tae ntau ipi i to Eum̃ mau.* I don't know how many years he was at Teouma.

**iuui** *interjection* exclamation, called out when embarrassed, for example.

## K

**-k** *pronoun suffix* **1)** my (1st person singular direct possessive) when suffixed to inalienable body part. *P̃a leka af sik naaruk p̃a tao nawes.* You'll see I raise my hand, you put down your paddle. **2)** you (2nd person singular object) as object marker on a transitive verb. *Ku muurin paus ki naik ke fo tuok ki.* If you ask for fish, he will give it to you.

**ka=** *pronoun prefix* I (1st person singular irrealis subject). *Ka nrikir ki nafsan ni tiawi i skei.* I'll tell you a story from the old people.

**kaaf** *noun* crab.

**kaafat** *adjective* fourth. *Kineu a pi teesa kaafat gar.* I am their fourth child. *cf:* paat.

**kaai** *noun* **1)** shellfish sp., cockle. (*Arcidae*). **2)** vagina (slang).

**kaaifar** *noun* shellfish sp.

**kaaiflu** *noun* shellfish sp.

**kaaikuk** *noun* shellfish sp.

**kaainmet** *noun* shellfish sp.

**kaaitlak** *noun* shellfish sp.

**kaaiuwi** *noun* shellfish sp.

**kaak (kaak naniu)** *noun* coconut mat, mesh formed by the coconut palm, used for straining liquids.

**kaakas** $verb_i$ sweet, to be.

**kaal** *noun* digging stick. *Komam u pregnrogo ki kaal p̃afp̃of me u kano nri mpak.* We tried with a big digging stick but we couldn't dig the banyan.

**kaanr** *noun* **1)** black ant. **2)** fire ant.

**kaap̃** *noun* ghost crab. (*Ocypode cerathopthalma*).

**kaaru** *adjective* **1)** other. *Teni natkon kaaru i maet.* The one from the other village got angry. **2)** next, second. *Aliat fnau kaaru.* Next Wednesday. *P̃a mer pan slat tekaaru mai.* You go and get another person. *cf:* nru, p̃tae.

**kaat** *verb* taste by taking a small bite. *cf:* kat.

**kaatol** *adjective* third. *Naimat kaatol ga i to Ep̃uf ru soso ki M̃autol.* The third lake was at Ep̃uf and they called it M̃autol. *cf:* tol.

**kafeer** *noun* crab, brown sea crab, about 12 cm across, not eaten.

**kafkaf** *verb$_i$* search by moving things around.

**kaflag (kaflagi)** *verb$_a$* lift up something that is covering something else, like lifting up a tablecloth to see what is under it.

**kafrali** *noun* crab, big brown crab.

**kaftaal** *verb* search for something by moving something else out of the way, as in to separate the bush looking for something.

**kaftan** *noun* crab, a sea crab that is not eaten. It is white, and buries itself in the sand.

**kai** *verb$_i$* to cry. *I kai panpan go tep̃afp̃of ru na ru to ru mai paus ki na, "I ku kin ku to kai?"* He cried until the adults asked him, "Why are you crying?" *cf:* kait.

**kai=** *pronoun prefix* **1)** then **2)** echo subject, takes the place of a subject pronoun when the subject is already known. *Ra slat sernale ni talm̃aat kai pa.* They (two) carried everything from the garden and they went.

**kai=** *pronoun prefix* I (1st person singular perfect subject). *Go kai ler mai lek tmak go raitok.* And I went back and saw my father and my mother.

**kaiaraskei** *noun* shellfish sp., abalone (general term).

**kaifar** *noun* kneecap.

**kaimes** *verb$_i$* create, invent. *cf:* preg.

**kainintas** *noun* barnacle.

**kaip̃aar** *noun* shellfish sp., Venus clams (general term). (*Veneridae*).

**kaisur** *noun* shellfish sp., ornate mactra. (*Mactra ornata*).

**kait** *verb$_t$* cry for, to cry for something or someone. *Me teesa nmatu nen nmatu nen i to kait na, nafarun. I kaiten panpan.* But this girl cried for her wings. She cried and cried for them. *cf:* kai.

**kaitao** *noun* fish spp., jacks and trevallys. (*Carangidae*).

**kaiwi** *noun* shellfish sp., virgate tellin. (*Tellina virgate*).

**kal** *verb$_i$* dress, be dressed, to dress oneself. *I kal su.* She is dressed. *Me komam malpei u kano kal ki nkal ni nanwei.* But back then we couldn't dress in men's clothes. *cf:* nkal.

**kala** *interjection* exclamation, like 'wow!'. *Kala i mten!* Wow, it is heavy!

**kalafiai** *noun* fish sp., a big parrotfish.

**kalap̃og** *noun* fish sp., bumphead parrotfish. (*Bolbometopon muricatum*). *cf:* nuo.

**kalapus** *noun* gaol (from Bislama).

**kalim** *adjective* fifth. *cf:* lim.

**kalnrog (kalnrogo)** *verb$_a$* try clothes. *Nkal nen i sees, p̃a pei kalnrogo.* This shirt is small, try it first.

**kalo** *noun* male name marker (an old-fashioned word). This cannot be used as a pronoun. *Kalo ku wan* *go i pa?* Who is that (man) going there? *cf:* li.

**kalo** *interjection* hesitation, used when thinking about the word you want to use. *Ga i to natik Ertap, nagis ni Emtaftin, nagien nana, kalo fei kia?* He stayed at the end of Eratap, at Emtaftin point, his name was, um, who was it?

**kalsaar** *noun* stick, for husking coconut.

**kalsiu** *noun* small women's spear, made of various hardwood, e.g., black palm, hardened in fire, or other wood such as *nagi* or *tap̃ir*.

**kaltag** *noun* dragonfly.

**kalum̃** *noun* spider.

**kalus** *noun* shellfish sp., cockle (general term). (*Cardiidae*).

**kaluspam** *noun* shellfish sp., Spengler's mactra. (*Scissodesma spengleri*).

**kam (kamti)** *verb$_a$* step on, walk on something. *A tap lek m̃aat nen mau, a siwer pan trau kamti.* I didn't notice the snake, I walked along and just stepped on it.

**kamkor** *verb$_a$* to block a road with people.

**kamkot (kamktofi)** *verb$_a$* stand on and break into pieces. *P̃a kamkot nkas nen ki pe mtet.* Stand on this tree and break it into pieces, it is rotten. *cf:* kamp̃or.

**kamnrog (kamnrogo)** *verb$_a$* feel with the foot. *P̃a fei kamnrog nakirles nen i mkal ko i tiik.* Feel this coral with your foot and see if it is sharp or not.

**kamp̃or (kamp̃rai)** *verb$_a$* stand on and break. *I pato elag go i kamp̃rai kapa ne, smen ne malnen i tarp̃ek mai i matmat.* He went up and he broke the cement roof and fell through and died. *cf:* kamkot.

**kamsok (kamsoki)** *verb$_a$* brake, stop quickly.

**kamti** *verb$_a$* take stones from the fire with tongs. *Faat nen ki pe ftin tlasi, p̃a kamti ke fak etik.* This stone is hot enough, take it out and put it to the side.

**kanin** *adjective* rippled, sea is slightly rippled so you can't see into it.

**kano 1)** *auxiliary* cannot, to be unable, used before the verb, e.g., *kano siwer* 'can't walk'. Also used as the verb. *Nat nen i kano pes.* That man can't talk. *Ru kano totan skot apap me iak reki natrauswen.* They can't sit with their father and mother for stories. **2)** *verb$_i$* cannot, to be unable. *Go nmatu i kano taos mees.* And the woman couldn't do like (one can do) today.

**kano** *noun* man; *kano ni nafkarwen* 'joker'. *Me, kano i skei ga i kus to, i kus to leker.* But this man hid, he hid and he looked at them. *cf:* nam̃er, nanwei.

**kano lak** *noun* bridegroom.

**kanotaar** *noun* breadfruit sp., type of breadfruit that you can cook quickly. *cf:* naptam.

**kanrsip** *noun* tube of bamboo (for carrying water).

**kaori** *noun* tree sp. (*Agathis macrophylla*).

**kapil** *noun* scar, a healed cut on skin.

**kapkaap** *noun* swiftlet (type of bird).

**kapu** *noun* laplap, pudding made of grated vegetable (e.g., manioc, yam, taro, banana) mixed with coconut milk and baked underground on hot stones. *Me mees nmatu ke muur ke furi ke freg kapu, ga ke fan tm̃en slat nafnag.* But today it is the woman who prepares food, makes laplap, who gets food.

**kapuenrar** *noun* fish sp., flounder. (*Bothidae*).

**kapuer** *noun* old person, someone with white hair.

**kar** *verb*$_i$ itch, scratch (like a chicken scratching), fiddle.

**kar (karo)** *verb*$_a$ scratch. *P̃a neu kar ntakuk.* You scratch my back.

**karkor** *noun* jellyfish.

**karo** *adjective* grey, to be.

**karo** *verb*$_i$ topless, have no shirt on.

**karo** *verb* gather together items in your hands, like everything on a table clutched to your body.

**karo usrek** *verb*$_i$ naked. *syn:* puu.

**kasfaas** *noun* cicada.

**kat** *preposition* because of, due to. *I fla pan pnak, wat natam̃ool kat mane ga.* He might steal or hit a man for his money.

**kat (kati)** *verb*$_a$ bite. *Kori i kat naat.* The dog bit the man. *cf:* fket, kaat.

**kat naniu** *verb*$_a$ husk a coconut with one's teeth. *Kalsar ke fla tiik go p̃a trau kat naniu m̃as.* If there is no wooden stake (to husk coconuts) then just use your teeth.

**kat p̃orp̃ros npatin** *verb* grind one's teeth.

**kat soksok npatin** *verb* **1)** close one's mouth, refuse to drink. **2)** grind one's teeth, also a sign of anger.

**katmanuksa** *noun* insect that bites and hurts a great deal. It is bigger than a cricket, and has wings. It lives in the bush and comes out at night.

**katnaam** *noun* mosquito.

**katnraap** *noun* soursop; custard apple is *katnraap ni nam̃er taar* 'whitemen's soursop'.

**katnrog** *verb*$_a$ taste.

**katom** *noun* hermit crab, land hermit crab. (*Coenobitidae*). *cf:* katp̃aar.

**katp̃aar** *noun* hermit crab that lives in the sea. The one that lives on the shore is *katom*. (*Diogenidae*). *cf:* katom.

**katp̃o** *verb* selfish, greedy, to be. *Kano nen i tae katp̃o toop, i to preg naik laap me i to mal ptu kir tu natam̃ool.* This man is so greedy that he catches many fish but doesn't share them with people.

**katsok** *verb*$_i$ hold between one's teeth. *Go lisaan i katp̃on tefla, i trau katsok nanwen sa.* And the clam was greedy for it (the snake) and it just held the snake's neck in its teeth.

**kau** *verb*$_i$ row a boat with oars.

**kau** *interjection* exclamation (people say it came from Mare in New Caledonia).

**ke=** *pronoun prefix* he, she, it (3rd person singular irrealis subject). *Ser nrak natam̃ool i muurin nag ke fak namoos.* Every time, the person wanted to go to the sea.

**kefi** *adjective* how much?, how many? *Ku muur magko kefi?* You want how many mangoes?

**kel** *verb*$_i$ hold onto something, touching but not grabbing it. *Malnen ra kel ntakun, go Kaltog i kel ntak Selwin teflan go rakai ler mai pak esum̃, Erakor.* Then they held his back, Kaltong held Selwin's back like this and they came back to the house at Erakor. *cf:* kelsok, tkal.

**kel sman** *verb*$_i$ drive (hold steering wheel) (any vehicle). *cf:* pu sman.

**kelsok** *verb*$_i$ cling. *Go komam Sam, ra pan pueti me i kelsok namet nega go nasum̃ i pi m̃eltig nag ke tarp̃ek.* And Sam and I went to grab him, but he clung on to the door of the house, which was about to fall down. *cf:* kel.

**kerkerai 1)** *verb*$_i$*, auxiliary* strong, to be. **2)** *adjective, adverb* brave. *I piatlak natam̃ool kerkerai nig nafkal i nru nag ru sosor ki m̃aau.* There were two strong warriors called *m̃aau.* **3)** *adjective* hard. *cf.* **nakerkeraian**

**kfakor** *verb* cover a *koof* 'shed', usually a temporary shelter in the garden.

**kfet** *adjective* dry taste, like an unripe banana. Astringent.

**ki** *preposition* to, with, of. *Go nrak i laap ru to paakor ki natam̃ool.* And often it would appear to people.

**ki=** *pronoun prefix* he, she, it (3rd person singular perfect subject). *I na i mai go ki pam nana nm̃arteu ne, i lek nm̃arteu ne trau pami.* He wanted to go and eat this coconut, he saw this coconut and ate it.

**kia** *demonstrative* here, this one, used as a way of talking about something that has just been mentioned, and also as part of idiomatic expressions *gawankia, welkia,* both meaning something like 'thus'. *Ga kia!* That one now! *A me kineu a na ka fo pam akam kia me akam ra sef.* Ah, I wanted to eat you, but you ran away. *cf:* kis, welkin.

**kig** *noun* fish sp., unidentified fish.

**kii** *verb*$_i$ ring (of ears). *Ku los toop ntas go ntalgem ru kii.* You swim a lot in the sea so your ears ring.

**kil (kli)** *verb*$_a$ dig the ground (with a tool), also dig to harvest food. Note that different terms are used for harvesting different crops. *cf:* kis, pupuet, traf.

**kilfot** *adjective* ninth. *cf:* ilfot.

**kilkil** *noun* seagull (type of bird), a white bird with brown spots. Its meat is tough but it is eaten.

**kin** *particle* **1)** that, which (complementiser) when following a verb. *Ale mal naseeswen neu a mroperkati kin nanrur p̃ur nen kin i mai.* Okay, when I was young I remember that a big earthquake happened. **2)** that, which (relativiser) when following a noun. *Go ga kin i pi taklep neu.* And he was my older brother (he was firstborn). **3)** that, used to start a new sentence, but referring back to earlier information.

*Ko katom i tae na menal i mat go katom i win. Kin i win na, nareswen, ale katom i preg nafsan.* And the hermit crab knew that the barracuda had died and the hermit crab had won (the race). He won the race, so the hermit crab told a story.

**kin (kinti)** *verb$_a$* pinch. *Ku kinti.* You pinch it. *Ku kin naat.* You pinch someone.

**kineu** *pronoun* I, me (1st person singular subject or object). *Natrauswen tilm̃ori nen kineu a to trausi.* (This is) a true story I am telling.

**kinlep** *noun* thumb.

**kinliu** *noun* **1)** finger, middle finger. **2)** toe, middle toe.

**kinm̃aat** *noun* **1)** finger, index finger. **2)** toe, big toe.

**kinrik** *noun* **1)** little finger. **2)** toe, little toe.

**kintapul** *noun* **1)** ring finger (the finger that's used for wiping yourself after going to the toilet). **2)** second toe.

**kipwi** *noun* Indian myna (type of bird). (*Acridotheres tristis*).

**kirkis (kirksi)** *verb$_a$* tickle. *Teesa i muur selwan ku kirkisi.* The child laughs when you tickle her.

**kis** *preposition* now, here, at this place. *Kis a to san to.* Now that I am in here. *Ga kis!* That's him now! *cf:* kia.

**kis (ksi)** *verb$_a$* **1)** press, push down; *kis ntafatun* 'stand with hands on hips'. **2)** turn on (lamp). (*Idiom: Kisfu np̃au kaanr. 'Poke the ant's head.' Deliberately remain silent after doing something, so as to pretend that you hadn't done it.*)

**kis (ksi)** *verb$_a$* harvest kumala. Note that different terms are used for harvesting different crops. *cf:* kil, pupuet, traf.

**kispu** *verb* harvest a new garden for the first time.

**kispuen** *noun* middle of a mat, where the two parts join.

**kispun** *verb* **1)** abort; *kispun teesa* 'abort a child'. **2)** squeeze to death.

**kistup̃ (kistup̃a)** *verb$_a$* poke, tickle quickly.

**kit** *pronoun* **1)** we (1st person plural inclusive subject). **2)** our (1st person plural inclusive direct possessive). *Nlaken akit nrakit ga i skei m̃as.* Because our blood is just one blood. **3)** us (1st person plural inclusive object). *I mai i pregsa ki kit.* He comes and hurts us.

**kitsa** *verb$_i$* envy, to be envious; to covet. *Selwan nat i preg namrun wi tete nat ru kitsa kin.* When someone does something good, some people envy them. *cf:* ktekit.

**klaru** *adjective* seventh. *cf:* laru.

**klat** *noun* germinated coconut.

**klates** *adjective* sixth. *cf:* lates.

**klatol** *adjective* eighth. *cf:* latol.

**klet** *noun* shellfish spp., conches (general term); *klet nraan* 'shell with "fingers"'. (*Strombidae*).

**klet** *noun* sow, female pig. *cf:* pwok, waak.

**klop** *noun* knot in bamboo or cane. The piece of cane between the knots is called *malmal*.

**knen** *adjective* of it, its own. *Nlaken nawesien knen i ta wi mau.* Because its work was not good. *Natrauswen kaaru, i mer pitlak nalag knen.* The next story has its own song.

**knopun** *noun* fish spp., filefishes, puffers (but see *pakosgal*), balloonfish. (*Monacanthidae, Tetaodontidae*).

**ko** *conjunction* or, also used to form questions. *Ru fla psi ntas ko ru fla psi sa.* They may have put it in the sea or they may have put it here. *I wi ko?* Are you good, or?

**ko=** *pronoun prefix* **1)** we (1st person plural exclusive irrealis subject). *Tiawi ru preg nafsan go ru fla tili na ko fan gar preg talm̃aat, ko fo pa.* The old people might tell us to go to make their garden and we have to go. **2)** you (2nd person plural irrealis subject). *Go akam ko fo nomser pak namrun nen kin ke fo mai akam ko fo nomser pakes.* And you will all go to this thing that is coming (in the future), you will all go to it.

**kof** *verb* be possessed by a devil who makes you unable to move (typically at night).

**kof** *verb* hang down (of cloth hanging, or of a flying fox [*mantu*] hanging). *Selwan ru siwer pan nalur i kof kor namter me selwan ru pul ki nap̃aur go nalur ki mer ler pak nap̃aur pan.* When they (the white women) walked, their hair hung over their eyes, but when they shook their heads, their hair moved back.

**koi=** *pronoun prefix* **1)** you (plural perfect subject) **2)** we (1st exclusive perfect subject). *Me malen u mai go koi pe nomser tu, nawesien i tiik.* But then we came and we all stayed, there was no work.

**koiaf** *noun* guava. (*Psidium guajava*).

**kol** *verb$_i$* shout. *A muur na ka nrik mus ki na tuk fo kol.* I want to ask you to shout.

**kom (komi)** *verb$_a$* suck.

**komam** *pronoun* we, us (1st person plural exclusive subject or object). *Or ga i taos malpei nmatu komam u mtak ki taos nkal ni nanwei.* In the olden days, women, we couldn't wear men's clothes. *cf:* mam.

**kon** *verb$_i$* to be stuck. *I kon faat.* It is stuck to a stone.

**konafnako** *noun* fish sp. goatfish (general term). (*Mullidae*). *cf:* susmraknaniu, suus.

**konr** *noun* shellfish sp. (*Strombus*).

**konrkai** *noun* pig, female pig which has no piglets.

**koo** *verb* kiss.

**koof** *noun* hut, shelter in the garden, temporary shelter made for special occasions.

**kookon** *adjective* bitter, to be.

**kool** *adjective* crippled, to be. *I pi kool.* He is crippled.

**kool** *noun* sea urchin, black one.

**koom** *noun* fish sp., grouper. *cf:* p̃aup̃al, p̃autop.

**koor** *noun* fence, fishtrap. *cf:* laak, tokor.

**kop** *verb*$_t$ **1)** chase. *I kop napel.* He chases sardines. **2)** follow. *I to kop namuurien ga.* He follows his own thinking. *cf:* fkop, kpas.

**kopnan** *noun* plant sp., used as ringworm medicine. It is also planted to stop a disease in a garden that kills plants. (*Plectranthus scutellarioides*).

**kor (koren)** *noun*$_i$ sister, also mother's or father's sibling's daughter. *I pan patu sari, me koren nra nen ra preg nafnag i to.* He went walking around, but his two sisters got the food ready. *Go a pitlak p̃aluk i pat go korek i skei.* And I have four brothers and one sister.

**kor (kro)** *verb*$_a$ block a blow, parry, also used as the second part of many verbs, e.g., *nriikor, tiikor, kfakor, tunkor. Ku kor ki narum selwan naat i na ke nrpagik.* You block with your arm when someone wants to hit you. *Ru puet kor main wes, main ru sal ur puetkor main nen raru ru kano sil.* They pulled the mines there, mines were drifting around, they pulled the mines so that boats can't come in.

**korflefil** *noun* flower, periwinkle flower.

**kori** *noun* dog.

**kortas** *noun* washstrake, wooden rail built onto the upper rim of a canoe to strengthen the side and to keep out water.

**kos** *adjective* used to intensify the meaning of a noun, e.g., *namlas kos* 'dense forest', *ntwam kos* 'strong (smelly) devil'.

**koser** *noun* fish sp., crescent-banded grunter. Terapon jarbua.

**kot** *verb*$_i$ *to* cut laplap.

**kotfaan** *noun* **1)** afternoon. **2)** evening. *I pi kotfaan selwan aal i to na ke mtar.* Evening is when the sun starts to go down.

**kotfak** *noun* **1)** half, a small amount of something. *Ko fo paakot tete namuurien nigmam ke nom me kotfak mane ko fo sati ler mai.* We would buy what we wanted, but we would have change to take back because the price was very low. **2)** leftover food. *cf:* naknafnag, nakon.

**kotfeel** *noun* flying fox, red flying fox and white flying fox. *cf:* mantu.

**kotieu** *noun* piece of laplap.

**kotkoot** *adverb* really, emphasises a verb or adjective, e.g., *pramkotkoot* 'very long', *malpei kotkoot* 'long ago', *teetwei kotkoot* 'very long ago'. *Gar nen kin me malpei kotkoot misnari i preg nfaptaiswen.* Long long ago, they, the missionaries, did the baptisms.

**kpas (kpasi)** *verb*$_a$ chase. *Ki nrik mtulep kin nag, "Ag p̃a tok me kineu ka mer pak talm̃aat pan, ka fan leel waak p̃ur na kia i kpas kit."* He told his wife, "You stay, but I will go back to the garden, to look for the big pig that chased after us." *cf:* kop, fkop.

**kraf** *verb* crawl (of crabs and animals). *Me katom i tae na ga i kano kraf pelpel, taos menaal,*

*menaal i tae spit.* But the hermit crab knew that it couldn't crawl quickly, like the barracuda; the barracuda could go quickly.

**krak** *verb$_i$* crawl (of babies and people).

**krakfai** *verb* sore, the feeling of pain that you have when you hit a wound or sore on your body.

**krakfufu (krakfufua)** *verb$_a$* crush something into small bits, cut in pieces.

**krakfunfnoi** *verb$_i$* erase, rub out (more than *surfunfnoi*). *cf:* funfnoi, surfunfnoi.

**krakpel** *verb$_i$* do something by accident.

**krakpes** *verb$_i$* make noise. *Go teesa ru fla to preg nakrakpeswen p̃og mana.* And if young people make noise at night, for example.

**krakp̃og** *verb* conquer, defeat.

**krakp̃orp̃or** *verb* break something like wood or bones, making a noise.

**krakpun (krakpni)** *verb$_a$* **1)** kill. *A krakpun natam̃ool i skei.* I killed a man. *Naat nen i tm̃en krakpni.* That man killed himself. **2)** turn off, switch off a light. *cf:* wat.

**kraksmanr (kraksmanri)** *verb$_a$* drop something accidentally.

**kraksok** *verb$_i$* **1)** catch, as in catch a disease. *Me ru kraksok na disentri.* And they caught dysentery. **2)** understand, catch on. *A pan go a po kraksok franis.* I went and I learned French.

**kraktof (kraktofi)** *verb$_a$* **1)** break (a branch). **2)** chop into pieces.

**kram** *noun* axe (originally made of clam, *kram*). *Tuk p̃rai nkas ki kram.* We split firewood with an axe. *cf:* lisaan.

**kram** *noun* shellfish spp., clams and miters, shellfish – general term for several types of shellfish including giant clams. Types include *kram nap̃rai, kram p̃og, kramp̃o, kramp̃el.* (*Tridacnidae, Mitridae*).

**kram** *noun* sugarcane, variety of sugarcane.

**kramkon** *noun* giant clam.

**kramp̃el** *noun* adze with a flat blade, used to shape the outside of a canoe, with the finishing work done with *limur*. *cf:* limur, took.

**kramp̃el** *noun* clam that lives in the sand. Also the name of a clan or naflak.

**kramp̃og** *noun* sugarcane sp., a dark red colour, nearly black. Each section is short, but thick. Also the name of a clan or *naflak.*

**kramteu** *noun* sugarcane sp.

**kramtig** *noun* shellfish that leaves tracks on beach sand.

**krapei** *verb* fish sp.

**krip** *noun* whip, made of *naplel,* for example; used to control animals.

**krokur** *verb$_i$* startled, to be; to be surprised. *Naat i krokur selwan ku kol kin.* The man is surprised when you shout out to him.

**krum** *verb$_i$* cross one's arms.

**krusperi** *noun* wild berry. (*Passiflora foetida*).

**kruuk** **1)** *verb$_i$* collect, gather, pick up off the ground. **2)** *verb$_2$* gather, used as the second part of a verb, *srakruuk* 'people coming together', *paakruuk* 'coming together as a group', *taakruuk* 'carry everything in your arms'.

**ksaar** *noun* garden that is left half cleaned and has gone back to being bush again. *cf:* namlaskos, m̃p̃akus, namlas.

**ksakes** *adjective* green, to be; now also used for blue. *Ksakes blu, ksakes grin.* Blue, green. *cf:* mlakes.

**ktekit** *verb$_i$* against, to be against. *A ktekit kik.* I'm against you. *cf:* kitsa, putkau.

**ku** *verb* why, for what reason? Mostly used in the expression *i ku* or *nlaken i ku* 'why'. *Ku ftup̃ nlaken i ku?* Why are you fighting? *P̃a ku?* What are you doing? *Tete ka fo tae tli na, ru ku, rui pe ta mro ki natopu mau a?* Some, I will tell you, they questioned, they didn't believe in the spirit (*natopu*) at all. *cf:* nafte.

**ku=** *pronoun prefix* you (2nd person singular realis subject). *I ku kin ku to kai?* Why are you crying?

**kue** *verb* do something. *Ku kue kin?* What are you doing?

**kuf** *verb* fight, physical fight (slang).

**kufa** *noun* shellfish sp., 5 to 8 cm long.

**kui=** *pronoun prefix* you (2nd person singular perfect subject). *Me ag kui pe fam ko i tiik?* Have you eaten or not?

**kuk** *verb$_i$* to shrink, to get smaller.

**kulmam** *noun* person who can see supernatural beings, like ghosts, but doesn't have to be a *kulru* or *munwei*. *cf:* kulru, munwei.

**kulmer** *noun* light-skin, e.g., person with both European and Ni-Vanuatu parents.

**kulru** *noun* clever, in a psychic sense, a healer. *Or, natam̃ool nen i pi kulru welkia tenamrun ke fo mai me ga ke fo pei nrik nam̃er laap ki.* Yes, this is a clever man and if something is going to happen in the future he will tell everyone about it first. *syn:* teleekot. *cf:* kulmam, munwei.

**kulsa** *noun* skin sickness, black spots.

**kumol** *noun* kumala, sweet potato. (*Ipomoea batatas*).

**kursm̃anr** *verb$_i$* slip, as in a person slipping when walking. *cf:* soksm̃anr.

**kus** *verb$_i$* hide. *I maet go ki sef pan kus namlas, i pan kus namlas, go ki to ur namlas.* He got angry and he ran away to hide in the bush, he hid in the bush, and he wandered in the bush. *cf:* uus.

**kuskor (kuskro)** *verb$_a$* hide while approaching (as in prey), hide and watch. *Me selwan i mai p̃ulmatlen i mai, kuskor mtulep Katapel.* When he came in the morning, he came and hid from Katapel. *cf:* p̃oo.

**kusu** *noun* **1)** rat. **2)** mouse.

**kut (kuti)** *verb$_a$* squeeze, press in one hand, hold firmly.

**kut (kutun)** *noun$_i$* louse. (*Pediculidae*).

**kut p̃orp̃rai** *verb$_a$* crush in one's hand. *P̃a kut p̃orp̃rai pur atol me p̃a npa kin ke fa.* Crush that eggshell and throw it away.

**kuuf** *noun* arrow for killing birds. It has a flat or round end so that it stuns the bird and knocks it to the ground. (*Idiom: This word is used as a term of abuse for a man, implying he is not a sharp arrow.*).

**kuul (kuulti)** *verb*$_a$ cover (as in a blanket); wrap (as in a present). Note that *kul* is also 'skin'.

*cf:* nakul.

**kuulkor (kuulkro)** *verb*$_a$ cover, as in covering laplap.

**kuulkul** *verb*$_i$ cover.

**kuut** *noun* seed of breadfruit.

# L

**laag** *noun* fly (as in the insect).

**laak** *noun* fence for a pig. *cf:* koor, tp̃er.

**laak** *noun* peg used to hold the outrigger (*nsem*) to the cross-member (*nakiat*) on a canoe.

**laap** *adjective* many, more. *Nlagwat i mai, go i piatlak nasum̃ laap kin ru sa, ru tarp̃ek.* The cyclone came, and there were many houses that were damaged, they fell over.

**laas** *noun* cup; *laas naniu* 'coconut shell', *laas p̃ur* 'basin'. (*Idiom: You've gone over the limit, something bad happened because of what you did. One day it will end badly. The glass is too full.*)

**lag (laga)** *verb*$_a$ sing. *I pan kam ntas go i po lag, i preg nalag.* He went to the sea and he sang, he sang a song.

**laga** *verb* repeat what someone has said. *I to laga tenen kin natam̃ool ki pe tli.* He repeated what the man said.

**lagi** *adjective* **1)** fancy. **2)** proud.

**laglag** *verb*$_a$ scale, to take the scales off a fish.

**laglaga** *verb*$_i$ cast a spell. *I laglaga kik.* He casts a spell on you.

**lagsu** *noun* wind, east wind (lit: downwind). *cf:* tokelau.

**lai** *verb*$_a$ spit out. *A lek nap̃re ki ntwam i skei i to lai nuasog.* I dreamed of a devil that spits smoke. (*Idiom: 'Spit it out.' Say what you mean.*)

**lailaipako** *noun* fish sp., fiveband flagtail.

**lainmar** *verb* breathe out quickly.

**lak** *verb*$_i$ marry, to; to be wed. *Telaap ni mees ga, teesa nmatu me teesa nanwei telaap ru tm̃er skotir to me ru ta lak mau.* Many these days, many girls and boys, stay together but they aren't married. *cf:* nlakwen, taulu.

**lakle** *noun* sores, thick large sores (not boils).

**lakle** *noun* owner of a building who lives in the building.

**lakor** *auxiliary* maybe, might be. *I lakor pi i paat ko i lim.* There might be four or five. *Ke fo lakor mai.* Maybe he'll come. *A lakor pes sa.* I might have said the wrong thing.

**laktau** *noun* vine sp., a white vine near the sea. Drinking an infusion of this plant cools you when you are overheated.

**lalu** *verb$_i$* absent (of an octopus, when you look at the octopus's hole in the rock and it has gone). You can take a stone from the hole back to your house and then the next day when you go back the octopus will be there in that place.

**lao** *verb$_a$* **1)** plant, as in planting something that has a trunk that stands up. If it is a root crop, then the word to describe planting is *tan*. *A lao nua nkas.* I plant fruit trees. **2)** spear, as in *lao naik* 'spear a fish'. **3)** stand, to stand something up, establish. *Tete naat ru tok pregnrogo ruk lao ki political empire.* Some people tried to establish a political empire. **4)** gouge, as in gouging out the inside of a canoe. **5)** land, as in a bird landing on something. *cf:* tan, laoutu.

**lao** *noun* fish sp., sandperch. (*Pinguipedidae*).

**lao** *verb* drip. *cf:* laolao.

**laokinasusu** *noun* fish sp., nebulous wrasse. (*Halichoeres nebulosus*). *cf:* patru.

**laokor (laokro)** *verb$_a$* obstruct with something that stands vertically. *Loto i sef toklos wou go a laokro ki nmalnkas i skei.* The truck was coming towards me so I put out a log to block it. *cf:* sogkor, tikor.

**laokot (laoktof)** *verb$_a$* break; *laokot nanuen* 'break one's neck'.

**laolao** *verb* fall (of water over a waterfall). *cf:* lao.

**laop̃or (laop̃ro)** *verb$_a$* break. *I kursm̃anr kai laop̃or narun.* He slipped and broke his arm.

**laorpek** *noun* fish sp., small white fish which lives in the mangroves and seaweed.

**laosok (laosoki)** *verb$_a$* **1)** pound. *Me malnen rukoi pe laosok silua ru tur pek.* When they finished pounding it, they sewed up the bag. **2)** plant something.

**laotu** *verb* stand up. *Trawot nen i tu me esan i laotu wes tu ru soso ki Elunak.* Trawot is there, and the place where he is standing is called Elunak. *cf:* lao.

**laru** *number* seven. *Nrak pei natkon ni Erakor Efat ru pi natkon i laru.* At that time, the village of Erakor, Efate, was seven villages. *cf:* klaru.

**lat (lati)** *verb$_a$* cut (e.g., using scissors) hair, clothes, paper.

**latana** *noun* lantana, you can use the leaf on cuts.

**lates** *number* six. *Tiawi ra nru nen ra piatlak teesa i lates.* These two had six children. *cf:* kelates.

**latkor** *verb* cover the walls of a *koof* 'hut' with coconut leaves.

**latlat** *verb$_i$* froth (as of water boiling, or froth on a stream, or lather with soap).

**latol** *number* eight. *cf:* klatol.

**lau** *verb$_i$* dance. *cf:* nlauwen.

**laufal** *noun* pineapple.

**laulau** *noun* food on the table at a feast.

**lee** *verb$_i$* look, see. *Malen tmen i tm̃en nrea, i lee pak euut.* Then his father turned around, he looked to shore. *cf:* nalelewen.

**lee sulsul** *verb$_i$* squint, like when the sun is too bright. *cf:* p̃il.

**leefra (leefra wes)** *verb$_a$* to check.

**leeg** *verb$_i$* **1)** be straight. **2)** be correct. *Sernale rui pe nomser leeg.* Everything is alright. *cf:* matu, metmatu.

**leekot** *verb* foresee, have a premonition, usually made by a *munwei* (a magic man).

**leel** *noun* bracelet, rolled pandanus leaves. *cf:* tarim.

**leel (leeles)** *verb$_a$* look for. *Ag ku to leel naul nkas reki nalkes?* Are you looking for leaves for medicine?

**leepilieli** *verb* look at something that does not belong to you. *cf:* polpilieli.

**lees** *noun* tree sp., pawpaw. (*Carica papaya*).

**leeser** *verb$_i$* look around, trying to find something. *Me malen oof i tu leel naik i tu leeser. Oof sees i tu leeser panpan i ta lek makou mau.* When the heron looked for fish, it was looking around. The little heron was looking around and around but it didn't see the lobster.

**leet** *noun* epilepsy.

**lei (leir)** *verb$_a$* pick fruit.

**lek** *verb$_t$* look at, see something. *Selwan u pan kai lek nra.* When we came, we saw blood.

**lekor** *verb$_i$* watch over, beware, care for. *p̃a lekor m̃aat ke fo katik.* Watch out or that snake will bite you. *p̃a lekor nanrogtesan!* Watch out for the accident!

**lel** *noun* turtle shell.

**lelep** *noun* black stone, used for cooking in a ground oven.

**lelkau** *verb* avoid something by walking around it. *cf:* lelu.

**lelu (lelua)** *verb$_a$* avoid. *Ku lelua kai pa.* You avoid it and go. *cf:* lelkau, talel.

**lemis (lemsi)** *verb$_a$* **1)** look at. *Go i pi sup̃ wi nen kin komam me ko lemsi go ko tae.* It is a good fashion that we can look at and know (that we should follow). **2)** visit. *Aliat tap nen pan a pan lemis raitok nasum̃ namsaki.* Last Sunday I went to visit my mother in hospital.

**lep** *adjective* big. *cf:* p̃ur.

**leperkat (leperkati)** *verb$_a$* **1)** copy. *Gawan ki kai pe tli, ru to leperkat toop. Go naftekin ru leka na i sa ru pregi. Me ru na i wi.* As I said, that's because they copy too much. And the bad things that they see, they do it. But they say it is good. **2)** watch over. **3)** look after (as in a child), or watch over a cooking pot. *Me p̃a fo to mai leperkat emat nigneu.* And you will come to look after my grave. **4)** look out, beware, be careful, check if someone is there. *P̃a leperkati ka fo watgik.* Look out, I am going to hit you.

**ler** *verb$_i$*, **1)** return, repeat. *Ler ki nafsan* answer. *A tok lerekir nen ruk fo mer ler ki nafsan.* I'm waiting for them to answer. *Nalag nen i wi, ku tae ler wes?* That's a good song, can you repeat it?

**2)** *auxiliary* return; *Ler pakor* reappear; *Ler paakot* repay.

**lereki** *verb*$_i$ **1)** look forward to something. *A to lerekik p̃a fo mai.* I am looking forward to you coming. **2)** depend on someone doing something, depend on something happening.

**lesap̃** *verb*$_t$ don't recognise something when you have been away for a while. *Ku lesap̃ nat.* You don't recognise the man.

**leskes** *noun* tree sp., type of tree with small seeds. Trunk can be smashed and used to poison fish. Dry seeds can be used to burn like kerosene. Fruit looks like *katnraap* 'soursop'. There are green and red versions.

**lesmp̃au (lesmp̃aun)** *noun*$_i$ skull.

**lesok** *adjective* important, useful.

**letae (letaer)** *verb*$_a$ **1)** realise. *Malfanen a letae nra i ta pi wak mau me i pi nra natam̃ool.* Now I can see that this is not pig's blood but human blood. **2)** recognise. *Telaap ru letae go teflan kin ru weswes ki tp̃er, go tete, tete ru piatlak, na tete sup̃ nen kin gar me ru mer tae pregi nen kin ru nrus ki ntan. Ru to puet ntan sees, a?* Many recognised how to make a fence, and some had a certain way so that they could move the land (boundary). They took a little land, eh? **3)** identify. *cf:* mrotae, nrogtae.

**leusus (leususi)** *verb*$_a$ investigate, follow along looking closely into something.

**lewi** *verb*$_i$ admire, like. *Nam̃er nen ru pa raru mai. Go tete ru mai lewi ki naur.* Those men came paddling their canoes. And some came and liked the look of the island. *A lewi ki nasum̃ gaag.* I like your house.

**lfalof** **1)** *verb*$_i$ walk in the bush. *Ko mai tuk fan lfalof.* Come let us go and walk in the bush. **2)** *verb* leave tracks as you walk that others can follow. *cf:* nalof.

**lfek (lefek)** *verb*$_i$ **1)** around, to go around. *P̃a fa me p̃a fo mer lfek mai.* You go but you will have to turn around. *Ku lfek ki Efat.* You go around Efate. *Taos, teetwei gar ru to preg tp̃er i lfekor natkon.* As in the old days they built a fence around the villages. **2)** spin, as in *np̃au ki lfek* 'my head is spinning'. *cf:* fiif.

**lgaru** *verb*$_i$ double or cross weave of a mat. *cf:* lgaskei.

**lgaskei** *verb* single weave of a mat. *cf:* lgaru.

**li (lei)** *noun* female name marker (an old-fashioned word). This cannot be used as a pronoun. *limtak* 'scared woman', *kalmtak* 'scared man', *limuur* 'woman who wants things', *kalmuur* 'man who wants things'. *Li ku wan go i pa?* Who is that (woman) going there? *cf:* kalo.

**liaki** *verb*$_i$ **1)** heap up something, like rubbish pushed away from a path. **2)** together, be together, be in one place; set something aside, keep something out of sight.

**lig (ligi)** *verb*$_a$ pour out.

**ligligp̃au** *verb*$_i$ shake one's head, to refuse.

**liit** *noun* wasp which stings.

**liit ni ntan** *noun* insect like a hornet or big wasp.

**likat** *noun* basket made from coconut leaf and used to carry garden produce. *cf:* fuelig, napor, nroog, tasaal.

**liksaal** *verb*$_i$ hang, as in a bat or flying fox hanging, or a person hanging by their hands.

**lilip̃** *noun* spirit, a female spirit said to have large breasts (*lisepsep* in Bislama).

**lim** *number* five. *A muur ke lim.* I want five. *Me naliati i lim i nom go i po los go i po fam.* And after five days were over she would wash and she would eat. *cf:* kalim.

**limen** *verb* poke out one's tongue.

**limlim** *verb*$_i$ share out five ways. *cf:* inruenru, patpat, toltol.

**limnai (limnair)** *verb*$_a$ lick.

**limur** *noun* adze with a curved blade. *cf:* kramp̃el, took.

**limuti** *noun* cleared piece of land, for example, to play sport on. *cf:* em̃au.

**lipeep** *noun* butterfly.

**lisaan** *noun* **1)** shellfish sp., clam, giant clam, hippopus clam. (*Hippopus hippopus*). **2)** vagina (slang). *cf:* kram.

**litas** *noun* box jellyfish which can hurt you with its *tai* 'sting'. (*Chironex fleckeri*).

**litot** *noun* bêche-de-mer, sea cucumber (general term). *Litot i laap esan i pi nalap̃o go nawen.* There are lots of bêche-de-mer where there is soft mud or sand. (*Holothuriidae*). *cf:* nap̃laepako, taag.

**liu** *verb*$_i$ piled, to be heaped up. *Naniu ru m̃el mai kai liu tu etan tu.* The coconuts fell and piled up here.

**lkaukot** *verb* jump over, go across something.

**lkolik** *verb* **1)** hang gifts (like cloths or mats). **2)** hang yams on a rack or a frame. *Ku lkolik ki nawi.* You hang the yam on the rack. *cf:* nalkolik.

**lm̃es** *noun* top stone of a ground oven.

**lof (lofi)** *verb*$_a$ rub, also used for buttering bread.

**loflof** *verb*$_i$ rub and rub, rub yourself.

**lom** *adjective* wet, to be. (*Idiom: 'His feet are still wet.' An insult, meaning he is a newcomer, still wet.*)

**lom (lomi)** *verb*$_a$ take a photo. *cf:* lomlom.

**lomlom** *verb*$_i$ take a photo (intr). *cf:* lom.

**loof** *noun* breadfruit sp., type of breadfruit that cooks quickly. There are two types, *taar* 'white' and *m̃nam̃on* 'yellow'. *cf:* naptam.

**loof** *noun* sword, made of wood, used in fighting.

**loop** *noun* bamboo. *Nam̃er got ru tok preg nasum̃ ki loop.* Black men make their house from bamboo. (*Bambusa*). *cf:* nam̃lalop.

**loor** *noun* coconut cream, made by squeezing coconut flesh. *cf:* loorktal.

**loorktal** *noun* thick coconut cream, made by cooking *loor* until it thickens. *cf:* loor.

**loot** *noun* sores on the foot, athlete's foot, tinea.

**los** *verb$_i$* bathe, wash oneself; swim. *Selwan ku m̃ilo ku los.* When you are dirty you take a bath. *Ku preg teesa i los.* You bathe the child. *Tiawi ru po los mai pak naor nen kin i gar.* The old people swam and came to a place that was dry. *cf:* waaf.

**lot** *verb$_i$* **1)** pray. **2)** worship. *cf:* nalotwen, tp̃otur.

**lp̃eslilip** *noun* staghorn, a plant that lives on branches of a tree.

**ltia** *verb$_i$* weave the end of a mat. *Ku pau m̃iit na ku pak nametp̃agon ale ku ltia ki.* You weave the mat to the end, then you *ltia ki* 'weave the ending'. *cf:* ti.

**lu** *verb$_i$* vomit. *Kai pe lue ki nmalok.* I vomited the kava. *A lu tuer.* I vomit on them.

**-lu** *suffix* fully, completely. Added after a verb to indicate the action is complete, as in *satlu* 'take all of', *puetlu* 'pull out all of', *weslu* 'carry all of'. *Ale katom i po to euut po mai pamlu namten.* So the hermit crab would be in the sea and would eat all of his eyes.

**luk** *noun* well, water source. *Malnen mtulep Katapel i mai i termau pak eluk sees ga nen, malnen kin i pa ke fo mailum nre faat nen i tkos.* When Katapel came, she went to her small well and slowly turned the stone that was there.

**lukor (lukro)** *verb$_a$* draw curtain.

**lukot** *verb* **1)** train a vine to grow a certain way. **2)** tie up an animal.

**lul** *verb$_i$* **1)** roll things up, like mats or clothes. **2)** roll fibre to make string (coconut, hibiscus, etc.). *cf:* tal.

**lul** *verb$_i$* pierce, poke into, as, for example, in a dart hitting something. *Me ke fo lul ki naknin ru fak nmal nanr pa.* But he would come and stick his fingers in the middle of the bananas and then go.

**lum̃nre (lum̃nrea)** *verb$_a$* turn inside-out.

**lup̃ (lp̃a)** *verb$_a$* pour. *Ku lup̃ ti.* You pour tea. *Tu lup̃ nakir nen tu pan pai elau.* We pour out the coral that we filled (our bags with) at the beach.

**lupir (lupri)** *verb$_a$* unroll (e.g., fishing line).

**luuk** *noun* the cavity in a canoe, the dugout part of the canoe.

## M M̃

**-m** *pronoun suffix* **1)** your (2nd person singular direct possessive) when suffixed to inalienable body parts. *Ku nrog np̃aum i fiif.* You feel your head spinning. **2)** me (1st person singular object) when suffixed to reflexive. **3)** us, exclusive (1st person plural exclusive object) when suffixed to reflexive. *Ag ku pitlak ntaewen, ag p̃a fo tm̃om mtiri.* You have the knowledge, you will write it for us.

**maa (maan)** *verb$_a$* **1)** grate using *fatma,* e.g., grate vegetable onto leaves to make laplap. **2)** sharpen. *Ku maa masmes.* You sharpen a knife. *cf:* trai, maama.

**maaf** *verb$_i$* **1)** open (as of a flower). **2)** start, something beginning (as of a war). **3)** burst (as of a boil). **4)** hatch (as of an egg). *Mama itrau pam̃or atol i skei me i pi atol mlau, i na i to me ra sati mai pak esum̃. Ale rakai to pan pan trau maaf ale i pi teesa sees i skei.* The mother found this egg, it was a swamphen's egg, and they took it home. Then they kept it and it just hatched and it was a small child. *cf:* tafafu.

**maafmaaf** *noun* crumbs of hard food. *cf:* map̃apun.

**maag** *verb$_i$* open, be open (e.g., of a door, or a clam shell, or one's mouth). *Me welkia MCA ga i maag ki nam̃er p̃rakot, nanwei p̃rakot, ru mai pan na ru pak MCA ale malen ru pa, go ku mer tae pak talpuk gaag pa.* But the MCA is open to anyone, they can come to the MCA and when they go there, you can go to your own group. *Selwan skul i maag, go komam kin u pi tepei nen u sil skul.* When the school opened, we were the first to go to the school.

**maag** *verb$_i$* stare, look at (e.g., a performance); admire (and see *maag* 'to be open'). *A to maag wes nlaken i trau p̃onp̃tae.* I admire it because it is so different.

**maagko** *noun* mango (from English).

**maak** *verb* don't know. *A maakmaak to.* I'm there not knowing anything. *cf:* sup̃neki.

**m̃aak** *verb$_i$* peek, take a quick look at something.

**maal** *noun* hawk, swamp harrier. (*Idiom: 'The hawk steps down on land.' Old age arrives, a person becomes old and can no longer do things or go about places as they did at first.*)

**m̃aal** *adjective* smooth (as of a coconut, the outside cleaned well). *I pan kai tak naniu nen i m̃aal.* He husked the coconut until it was clean.

**m̃aal** *verb* throw small things, like stones, money, bits of wood.

**maalep** *verb$_i$* observe five days after death. *cf:* up̃lim.

**m̃aalm̃aal** **1)** *noun* clearing, a cleared area of land. **2)** *noun* clean place. **3)** *adjective* clear. *cf:* p̃au m̃aalm̃aal.

**maama** *verb* sharpen something, like a knife. *cf:* faatmaama, pkal, maa.

**maama** *verb* mash food for a baby. *Ki to ni teesa maama ki nafnag.* He is mashing food for the child.

**maan** *noun* bird (general term). *I piatlak maan ni ntas, maan ni namlas, maan ni esum̃.* There are saltwater birds, bush birds and house birds.

**maan** *number* uncountable, too many, very many.

**maan nap̃lo** *noun* Mackinlay's cuckoo-dove (type of bird). (*Macropygia mackinlayi*).

**maan ni nmalfa** *noun* aeroplane. *cf:* raru ni nmalfa.

**maar** *noun* fish sp., fusilier (common mojarra).

**m̃aarak** *adjective* **1)** courageous. **2)** eager, active.

**maarik** *noun* **1)** husband. *Ku tae nrik maarik gaag ki na ke mai. A muur ka traus skoti.* You tell your husband to come. I want to talk to him. **2)** mister, term of respect. *Naliat i laap maarik naot i to preg nsaiseiwen.* On many days the chief called meetings. **3)** spirit, respectful way of referring to a male spirit. *cf:* mtulep, natopu.

**maariktakun** *noun* brother-in-law (the one you show your back to).

**maas** *verb*$_i$ cooked, to be. *Nafnag ki pe maas.* The food is cooked.

**maasp̃ok** *verb*$_i$ undercooked, not fully cooked.

**maat** *verb*$_i$ to be low tide. *Panpanpan me, elau ki pe mat pak kotfaan.* Until the tide was out in the afternoon *cf:* nmaat.

**m̃aat** *noun* snake.

**m̃aau** *noun* giant, strong man, warrior. *M̃aau ru laap, ru to preg nafkal toklos m̃aau ni Ertap, me Ep̃ag, me Em̃el.* Many warriors, they had battles with the warriors from Eratap, from Pango, from Mele.

**maet** *verb*$_i$ angry, to get angry with. *A maet ki naat selwan i to tilusus kineu.* I get cross with a man when he talks about me. *cf:* ftin

**maf** *verb*$_i$ mature, grow older.

**m̃afei** *verb* grab something firmly, squeezing and lifting, like grabbing hold of hair when you are in a fight, or grabbing hold of leaves of a plant.

**mafmaf** *verb*$_i$ broken, be broken, be smashed into pieces.

**mai 1)** *verb*$_i$ come, move towards. *Ru to sol nalotwen ke mai pak naur Erakor.* They brought Christianity to Erakor island. *Mai!* Come in! **2)** *auxiliary* become. *Hebrida nen to, mees i mer mai pi Sentapoen.* That Hebrida, today it has become Centrepoint. **3)** hither, used as a directional particle to mean coming towards a location. *Fotres ni Franis navy i skei i po nigmam mos nafnag mai.* A (flying) fortress from the French navy brought food for us. *Selwan mis i mai to naur Erakor, go gar ru pato, tete ru pato Ep̃uf mai.* When the missionaries came to stay at Erakor island, some of them were there, and some came from Bufa. *cf:* pa.

**maikel** *noun* seahorse. (*Hippocampus*).

**mailum** *adjective* **1)** slow; *mailum fkar* 'giggle'. *Ka fo siwer ka fo mailum nrook pan totan.* I will walk, I will slowly bend and sit down. **2)** soft. *Ag ku sat kaal nen i pi altuk i mailumlum go ku po na p̃a nri mpak ki.* You took a digging stick that is made out of a cabbage tree, it is soft, and you are about to dig a banyan tree with it. **3)** weak; *mailum tkali* 'dab' (touch gently). **4)** easy. *cf:* tal.

**m̃ak** *noun* erection (of penis).

**m̃akm̃ak** *verb* peek, spy on.

**makol** *noun* sugarcane sp. *cf:* nafakton, nap̃rai, naus, traares, tumel.

**makos** *noun* sandalwood. (*Santalum austrocaledonicum*).

**makot** *verb*$_i$ broken. *Natuen i makot.* His leg is broken.

**makou** *noun* lobster, clawed crustacean. *Malen i kam leeg ki nfal ni makou go makou i puetsok natwen, i katsok natwen.* When he stepped right into the lobster's hole, the lobster grabbed his foot, it bit his foot. *cf:* pepep, unr, uur.

**mal 1)** *noun* time; *mal ni teetwei* 'ancient'. *P̃a mai mal p̃rakot m̃as.* You come any time. *Tete mal ke fo mai.* Some time that will come (i.e., the future). **2)** *verb* hour; *mal i nru* 'two o'clock'.

**mal 1)** *verb*$_i$ refuse, not want to. *Or selwan nalotwen ke mai toop, tiawi ru to preg talm̃aat, ko ru to preg nalotwen m̃as. Ru mal ki nafkal.* When Christianity took over, the old people made gardens or they just prayed. They refused to fight. **2)** *auxiliary* not want. *Tete nes ru mal slasol, ru na kineu kin ka to.* They didn't want just any nurse, they wanted me to come.

**mal** *noun* **1)** weather. *Mees mal i sa.* Today the weather is bad. **2)** season; *mal tortor* 'hot time, summer', *mal namlanri* 'cold time, winter'.

**mal sees** *noun* awhile. *P̃a pepei to raki kineu mal sees.* Wait here awhile with me.

**malep** *noun* widow, widower.

**m̃aler** *adjective* calm (of the sea).

**malfane** *adverb* now, the time at which the event takes place. In a story set in the past, *malfane* refers to that time rather than the time when the story is told. *Go pailet, pailet i to Emlap̃o i mai i p̃elgat ket, sil mai pak em̃rom ale malfane u kwarantin.* And the pilot – he was at Malapoa – came and opened the gate, we went inside (the harbour), then we had to be in quarantine.

**malier** *verb*$_i$ be ashamed. *Ku malier nafte ku pregi i sa.* You are ashamed of the bad thing you did.

**malig** *verb*$_i$ spilled, to be spilled. *A preg nai i malig.* I spilled the water.

**malik** *noun* **1)** dark, night. *Kai pak nasum̃ malik ntau i skei go atlag i tol.* And (he) went to gaol ('dark house') for a year and three months. *Ki us nalfen panpanpan ki pe tok malik, nmalko sa ki pe tok mai.* He followed its tracks until it was dark, deep darkness was coming in. **2)** darkness, time before Christianity. *A muurin nag ka gamus traus tete natrauswen nig tiawi negakit nig teetwei selwan Efat i malik.* I want to tell you a story of our old people from long ago when Efate was in darkness. *cf:* mram, nmalko.

**m̃alit** *verb*$_i$ bang, explode. *Ku kraksmanr namrun i mel mai tik ntan i m̃alit.* You dropped something and it exploded on the ground.

**malkolik** *noun* cloudy, overcast.

**malmal** *noun* section, part, e.g., between knots of bamboo or cane.

*Ntas i slakot naur sees i pi malmal i pat.* The sea split the small island into four sections.

**m̃alm̃al** *noun* grass skirt.

**malnen** *adverb* as, at the time when, then. *Malnen ru muur kapu go ru to gar preg kapu.* When they want laplap, they would get them laplap. *cf:* selwan.

**malof** *verb* leaning over, like a tree leaning over.

**maloput** *preposition* middle. *U preg camp maloput Efat, u puet telefon waia pak Forari.* We camped in the middle of Efate; we took the telephone wire to Forari.

**m̃alosak** *verb$_i$* look up.

**malpa** *noun* clearing, space between things.

**malp̃al** *noun* coward.

**malpei** *adverb* before, a long time ago. *Malpei nmalok i tiik, mal ni apap nigmam mana, nmalok ru ta ius ki nmalok teflan mau.* Before, in our parents' time, there wasn't kava, they didn't use kava like they do today.

**malp̃erik** *noun* goshawk (type of bird), which flies very quickly. (*Accipiter fasciatusaustrale*). *cf:* malpwas, sokfal.

**malpwas** *noun* brahminy kite (type of bird) with a white breast. (*Haliastur indus*). *cf:* malp̃erik, sokfal.

**maltali** *noun* club, type of club or hitting stick (an old word not used today).

**m̃altelit** *verb* to crack, as in the noise made by a tree before it falls, or a firecracker exploding. *Nkap ni kapu i to m̃altelit.* The laplap fire is making a cracking noise.

**maltotae** *verb$_a$* **1)** avoid. **2)** ignore. *A maltotae namsaki gaag.* I don't want to know about your sickness.

**mam** *pronoun* **1)** we, us (1st person plural). **2)** ours (1st person plural possessive) (inclusive and exclusive). *Go natam̃ool inru ra to plaksok mam.* And two people would teach us. *cf:* komam, mom, nigmam.

**mam** *verb$_i$* ripe, to be. *Nuankas ru mam.* The fruit are ripe. *cf:* mamis, mamp̃ok, mamtop.

**mam** *verb$_i$* poisoned, to be poisoned by, for example, ciguetera. Drink an infusion of *naul nakur* to stop the ciguetera. Bleed a large fish to reduce the chance of it causing *mam*. *I pam naik me i mam wes.* He ate the fish and then he was poisoned by it. *Naat i mam naik, i kraksok namamwen ni naik.* The man was poisoned by the fish, he got fish poisoning from the fish. *cf:* namamwen.

**mamis** *adjective* nearly ripe, to be (of fruit, but not of coconuts). *cf:* mam, mamp̃ok, mamtop.

**mamp̃ok** *adjective* half ripe, to be (of fruit, but not of coconuts). *cf:* mam, mamis, mamtop.

**mamtop** *adjective* over-ripe, to be (of fruit, but not of coconuts). *cf:* mam, mamis, mamp̃ok.

**mana** *adjective* **1)** group, follows a word to define an expected group: *apap mana, iak mana* 'a group of fathers, a group of mothers', *ati mana* 'grandmothers'. **2)** approximately, used after a time, e.g., to say 'roughly at that time'; *tri klok mana* 'around three o'clock'. **3)** and so on, like that. *Me mees nen teesa ru to preg nalag mana.* But today the kids make songs and so on. *Fei mana p̃a traem tli.* Who all (is it), you try and tell it?

**m̃aniek** *verb* be busy, fiddle around purposefully.

**manim̃aat** *noun* bird, white sea bird, maybe seagull or albatross.

**manin** *verb* feel dizzy from being up high, or the feeling you get being on a swing; vertigo.

**maniot** *noun* manioc, cassava. The leaves are not generally eaten. (*Manihot esculenta*).

**mankerkrai** *noun* hawk, eagle (strong one) (type of bird).

**mankotik** *adjective* wounded, to be.

**manmon** *noun* roll of banana or manioc, e.g., in island cabbage (*simboro* in Bislama) cooked in coconut milk in a pot, unlike *nsem̃mantu,* which is cooked in an oven. *cf:* nsem̃mantu.

**manmun** *noun* prisoner, someone who is punished for a certain period of time but still has their rights as landowners, unlike *nafit*. *cf:* nafit.

**m̃anopnop** *adjective* round, to be perfect, as of stones for the oven, a fat child, or an orange without marks on it.

**manreu** *verb$_i$* thirsty, be thirsty. *Ku manreu ka fo tuok nai p̃a min.* You are thirsty, I will give you water to drink.

**mantap̃arp̃ar** *number* million.

**mantas** *noun* brown booby (type of bird). (*Sula leucogaster plotus*).

**mantilsei** *noun* **Pacific swallow**. (*Hirundo tahitica*).

**mantu** *noun* flying fox. *Ore mantu nen i to Erontp̃au teetwei ga i to pan, i to pak Ermag.* The flying fox that was at Rentapau long ago has gone, it went to Erromango. *cf:* kotfeel.

**maomao** *verb$_i$* **1)** be tame, not wild. *Ra mer kano ple. Me rak maomao. Ra pi teskei mau.* They can't argue anymore. And they are tame. They are one now. **2)** mediate, resolve differences between people in a dispute.

**maon** *verb$_i$* sweat, to. *cf:* nmaono.

**m̃aor** *noun* fish sp., slipmouth. (*Leiognathidae*).

**maos** *verb$_i$* tired, to be. *Komam u weswes u maos u muurin na ko to wi, ko fo pei maos.* We worked and we got tired; if we want to stay well, we would first have to get tired.

**map̃apun** *noun* bits of broken things, like ceramics or wood. *cf:* maafmaaf.

**map̃el** *verb$_i$* bend in half, e.g., bend your knees. *Nmatu nen malen i matur i tm̃en map̃el.* That woman bends her knees to her chest when she sleeps.

**map̃er** *noun* fish sp., small, has black and white markings. Good to eat but not everyone likes it, not good for asthmatics. Swims with *weel.*

**map̃eriat** *noun* fish sp., angelfishes. (*Pomacanthidae*). *cf:* taligme, tiftif.

**map̃or** *verb$_i$* broken. *Raru gaag i map̃or p̃a fo sm̃oli go p̃a fo pa.* Your canoe is broken, you can caulk it and then you can go. *cf:* p̃or.

**map̃rap̃or** *verb$_i$* broken.

**mapul** *noun* Pacific imperial pigeon. (*Ducula pacifica*).

**mapul ni ntaf** *noun* Baker's imperial pigeon. (*Ducula bakeri*).

**mar** *verb$_i$* **1)** breathe. *Natam̃ool nmaron i pram.* The man is panting (long breath). **2)** smell. *Ku mar ki nafnag ale p̃a fo pami.* You smell the food, then you eat it. *cf:* nmarom̃iit.

**mar** *verb* lucky. *I mar kin i pitlak bas foum i skei.* He is lucky that he got a new bus.

**marikwi** *noun* fish sp., Indo-Pacific bonefish. (*Albula glossodonta*).

**marmar** *verb$_i$* rest. *Nasnal dei ni Vanuatu i skei, ga, ru to marmarwes.* On Vanuatu's national day they will have a rest. *I pi ntau mau malen a marmar, go a risaen.* It was a whole year that I was resting, and then I resigned.

**mas (masi)** *verb$_a$* **1)** saw, e.g., cut wood. *P̃a fo mas nkas, nap̃raat ke skei me p̃a fas kin Elakmamiel.* You would cut some wood, a piece of hibiscus, and put it at Elakmamiel. **2)** circumcise. **3)** clean, peel, e.g., yam. *cf:* tef.

**mas** *verb$_i$* sweep. *cf:* sertao.

**m̃as** *adverb* only, just. *Ag m̃as.* Yourself, just you. *A pitlak nam̃olien wi me kai pe kano siwer pak etalm̃at, kai pe to esum̃ m̃as to.* I have had a good life, but I haven't been able to walk to the garden, I have just had to stay at home.

**m̃asei** *noun* star.

**m̃asei lep ni kotfaan** *noun* evening star.

**m̃asei lep ni pulp̃og** *noun* morning star.

**m̃asel (m̃asle)** *verb$_a$* take out the rib of a leaf.

**m̃asenrsenr** *adjective* slippery, to be.

**m̃aser** *verb$_i$* hiccup.

**masktof** *verb* cut with a knife.

**m̃asm̃as** *verb* empty, be nothing. *Raru i m̃asm̃as to i tiik ki namrun wes.* The canoe is empty, it has nothing inside it.

**masmes** *noun* knife.

**m̃asok** *adjective* mature, adult, full grown (of a person).

**masoksok** *adjective* firm, to be firm, solid (as in a well-built house).

**masol** *verb* turn, go in a new direction. *P̃a masol matu!* Turn right!

**masp̃rai** *verb$_a$* cut in half, e.g., peeled banana which one cooks.

**m̃asrot** *verb$_i$* fall apart, be destroyed; *ntan i m̃asrot* 'landslip'. *Sum̃ i m̃asrot.* The house was destroyed. *cf:* p̃asrot.

**mat** *verb$_i$* die, be dead; *nmaten* 'the dead body', *mat karkar* 'really dead', *matpel* 'half dead'. *Go i pregi panpan Efat negakit nen* *natam̃ool ru mat panpan natam̃ool rui tiik.* And it came to be that our Efate, people died, until there were no people. *cf:* naatmat, nmaten, pun.

**mateu** *noun* fish sp., boxfishes, trunkfishes and puffers. (*Ostraciidae, Tetraodontidae*).

**matit** *adjective* **1)** smooth, to be. **2)** flat, to be.

**matmaal** *verb*$_i$ **1)** faint. **2)** be unconscious.

**m̃atoktok** *noun* strong, brave man.

**matol** *adjective* thick, to be, as in a thick pile of things, but also as in a thick soup, or kava that has not been strained properly.

**matool** *noun* **1)** tomorrow, the next day. *Me ke fo mer kuk p̃og reki matool.* And she would cook again at night for the next day. **2)** the future. *I pi if wel kin nafet teesa ni matool, tenen i to matool, i fla mai plak nametmatuan p̃tae.* It may be that the children of tomorrow, the ones of tomorrow, they may have a different knowledge.

**matu** *adjective* **1)** right side. *Go namrun nen i m̃alit go aian i skei i pregkot natuen a tap tae natuen maur ko matu mau, me natwen i makot.* This thing exploded and the iron hit his leg, I don't know if it was his left leg or his right leg, but his leg was broken. **2)** correct, real. *Go ga kin ru to rikod kin ru to map to me i tiik ga nagi matu ga ru soso ki Tipuet.* And he recorded it and they mapped it, but its real name is Tipuet. *cf:* leeg, metmatu, nmatu.

**matu** *adjective* ready to eat (of food). *P̃a kil nawi ki pe matu.* Dig out the yam, it is ready.

**matuktuk** *verb*$_i$ wither, wilt, as a cabbage leaf does once it has been picked.

**matuktukurik** *noun* insect, black beetle-like insect with orange on the top of its back which eats the whitewood of canoes (an old word, not known by many today).

**matur** *verb*$_i$ sleep. *Ser p̃og natam̃ool ru nomser matur.* Every night everyone sleeps. *Namtek i matur selwan a pilo pram.* My eyes go to sleep when I've been awake for a long time.

**maturkor (maturkro)** *verb*$_a$ care for, watch over.

**mau** *particle* not, used as the second part of a negation, following the verb phrase. *Me i tap metpaakor nafsan nig apap nega mau.* But he didn't forget his father's story.

**mau (maui) 1)** *adjective* all. *Ru mau to ru sef.* Everyone was escaping. **2)** *adjective* whole. *Nua i mau.* The fruit is whole (unbroken).

**m̃au naliati** *noun* day, whole day.

**maumaau** *noun* the very end, used to emphasise the noun it follows, as in *mp̃agon maumaau* 'at its very end'.

**m̃aunaliati** *verb* accomplish the day's work. *A semsem nen kai pe m̃aunaliati ni mees.* I'm happy that I finished today's work.

**maur** *adjective* left side, left-handed. *cf:* armatu, arworksu.

**maurkat** *noun* left-handed person.

**maurkat** *noun* mangrove, a tall type of mangrove, used for house posts and for the crossbeam of a canoe that holds the outrigger. Also used for spears.

**maus** *adjective* half dry, to be (as of wood).

**me** *conjunction* **1)** but. *Me ki mro kin ki i warik me, namrun nen i pi tenamrun p̃ur a?* She thought there were only a few, but this thing (spirit) was something big, eh? **2)** after. **3)** and. *Nam̃er ni Sak Pei, me Pot Lori, me ru to oof polet mai pak hospitel.* People from Shark Bay and Port Lory would come in to hospital with bullet wounds.

**me** *verb$_i$* flood.

**me** *verb$_t$* urinate, piss. This is a transitive form of the intransitive verb *mem,* one of the small set of couplets in which a distinction between an intransitive and transitive stem can be made. *A me nkas. A meir.* I piss on the trees. I piss on them. *cf:* mem, name.

**meel** *noun* **1)** shade. **2)** shadow.

**m̃eem̃** *noun* fruit of a *napuk* 'helicopter tree' that twirls down to the ground. *cf:* napuk.

**meer** *noun* moth sp., a brown moth. *cf:* tagralim.

**mees** *adverb* today; *meesp̃og* 'tonight'.

**meet** *verb$_i$* prefer one thing over another one. *Me gar ra muur rak neu meet.* They (two) wanted to give preference to me.

**m̃el** *verb$_i$* float. *SS Morinda, go selwan elau i mu go raru i m̃el, go u tu tm̃alu raki Tangoa, Santo.* When the high tide came in, SS Morinda slipped off and we left for Tangoa, Santo.

**m̃el** *verb$_i$* escape, slip out of one's hands, fall off.

**m̃elm̃el** *adjective* loose, to be (as in a tooth).

**m̃eltig** *preposition* close, next to; *em̃eltig ki 10 klok* 'nearly 10 o'clock'. *Me telaap ru ta muurin ru fi m̃eltig ki tiawi mau.* But many people don't want to be close to the old people.

**mem** *verb$_i$* piss. *Selwan a min nai toop, a muur ka mem.* When I drink too much water I need to piss. *cf:* me.

**memelim** *noun* shellfish sp., Mauritian conch, also general term for cones. (*Strombus decorus decorus, Conidae*).

**menaal** *noun* fish sp., barracudas, also *menaalmiel*. (*Sphyraenidae*).

**mer** *auxiliary* **1)** again, in turn, then; *mer ler psi* 'return something', *mer ler lak* 'remarry', *mer ler mag* 're-open'. *Komam ra mer tuer tete nanromien sees.* Then we two gave them a small present. **2)** would have, used in expressions where an expected outcome does not happen. *Af mer pa me a fla lakor wel Jimmy Steven ko af lakor mat Solomon.* If I had gone, I would be like Jimmy Stevens (who went to the Solomons and came back alive), or I would be dead in the Solomons.

**mer** *verb*$_i$ numb, cramped, to be.

**meramok** *noun* fish sp., which lives in anenomes, and moves in and out of them.

**mermer** *verb*$_i$ **1)** rule, as of a chief ruling a village. **2)** look after a group of people, like the Bible says that God looks after people. **3)** brood, a chicken covering its eggs. *cf:* mrag.

**mes** *verb*$_i$ play, as in play a game, or play music. *Kineu a mes skot teesa.* I play with the child. *cf:* nameswen.

**met** *adjective* **1)** raw, to be. **2)** unripe. *Nua nkas i ta met.* The fruit is still unripe.

**met** *adjective* new, brand new. *cf:* foum.

**metmaat** *noun* conjunctivitus, eyes are red with pus (lit: dead eyes).

**metm̃akur** *verb*$_i$ covet, wanting something that belongs to someone else.

**metmatu** *verb*$_i$ wise, to be. *I metmatu ki sernale ni namlas.* He knows about everything to do with the bush. *cf:* leeg, matu, nametmatuan, ntaewen, tae.

**metmatur** *noun* sensitive grass. (*Mimosa pudica*).

**metmatur** *adjective* sleepy. *A weswes nanom p̃og a pi metmatur.* I worked yesterday and I am sleepy.

**metmer** *verb*$_i$ get cramp (an old word, not used much today).

**metp̃ag** *noun* verdict, judgement or sentence of a court. Also a doctor's verdict about your health.

**metp̃akor (metp̃akro)** *verb*$_a$ forget. *Me welkia namroan nigmam teesa, i sees, u sat tete me tete u metp̃akro.* Our thinking, we young people, it is slight, we get some things, but some things we forget.

**m̃etu** *verb*$_i$ sneeze.

**mgal** *noun* shell, large mother of pearl shell, like *flefil.*

**mgal** *verb* disclose something that was unknown before. *Ku maet ki nat, ra ple panpan malne ku mgalgua naftekin ki pe pregi.* You are angry with a man, so you argue until you disclose to him what he did.

**miel** *adjective* red.

**m̃iit** *noun* mat, woven from pandanus and used for practical purposes (sitting and sleeping on) and also for exchange in ceremonies.

**mil** *adjective* wild. *Waak mil, too mil.* Wild pig, wild fowl.

**m̃ilo** *adjective* dirty, to be; *nam̃ilo* 'dirt'.

**mimi** *noun* breast. *Raiten i tua mimi i sus wes.* The child's mother breastfeeds her child. *cf:* nais.

**min (mingi)** *verb*$_a$ drink. *Me i pitlak natam̃ool nen kin ke fo mer gaag preg naul nkas nen ke tuok p̃a mingi, go p̃af mer m̃ool.* But there are people who will then give you leaf medicine to drink, and you will become healthy again.

**minrog (minrogo)** *verb*$_a$ taste a drink, try by tasting. *cf:* pamnrog.

**mir** *verb*$_i$ dye hair. *cf:* tuai.

**misleo** *noun* tune, sound, noise. *cf:* smokle.

**mismai** *noun* bush, 'wild peanut'. You drink a tea made from its leaves to treat skin problems. The plant's name ('missionary come') seems to be because the plant was brought by the missionary Miss Macrae. *cf:* nalepleptau.

**m̃it** *adjective* short, to be. *A mer pei taakotkot loop ru to m̃it.* First I'll cut bamboo into short pieces.

**mkaal** *noun* ant. *Mkaal miel i to preg nasum̃ nap̃lau ntan.* Red ants make their house in the garden. *Mkaal taar seserik ru to krakpun nkas.* Small white ants eat tree trunks. *cf:* tup̃roor.

**mkal** *adjective* sharp. *Masmes i mkal.* The knife is sharp. *cf:* pkal.

**mkalkal** *verb$_i$* itch, be itchy. *cf:* namkalkal.

**mla** *verb$_i$* rotten, to be; of food, to smell it is bad. *Nafnag nen ku psi i to ektem ke fo mla.* Food that you leave outside will go rotten.

**m̃la** *verb$_i$* **1)** yawn. **2)** noise a devil makes when talking. *Go i nrogo go ntwam nen i mer m̃la.* And he heard the devil growl again.

**mlaanr** *adjective* cold, cool. *cf:* namlaanr.

**mlaap** *adjective* **1)** final. *Ore i pi natrauswen ni nafkal mlaap ni nmalko me tuk fo inrok pak namrem.* Okay, this is the story of the final battle of darkness and we would then go into the light. **2)** last. *Etan, etan, etan, nametp̃agon wi, ga kin i pi temlaap.* Down, down, down, right at the end of the village, he is the last.

**mlag** *verb$_i$* break, like a wave in the ocean. *cf:* tfarer.

**mlakes** *adjective* blue, to be. *cf:* ksakes.

**m̃lakon** *adjective* sour, food that has gone off, like yesterday's kava.

**m̃lato** *noun* Vanuatu fruit dove (type of bird). (*Ptilinopus tannensis*).

**mlau** *noun* incubator bird, scrubduck, likes hiding under *napukmokul* tree, building its nest in a rotten tree trunk. (*Megapodius freycinet*).

**mlees** *adjective* pink, to be.

**mleo** *noun* yam, type of yam. There is a red one (*mleomiel*) and a white one (*mleotaar*).

**m̃letik** *verb$_i$* stand on tiptoes.

**mlil** *verb$_i$* roll. *Nkas i mlil su ki ntaf.* The wood rolled down the hill.

**m̃nam̃on** *adjective* yellow.

**m̃nam̃onp̃ok** *adjective* orange (colour).

**m̃ok (m̃okus)** *verb$_a$* **1)** pull something out of something else; *m̃ok npatin i skei* 'take out a tooth', *m̃ok nam̃nam̃* 'pull out weeds', *m̃ok nsankas* 'take out a splinter'. **2)** harvest *maniot* 'cassava'. Note that different terms are used for harvesting different crops. *cf:* m̃tal, namas, traf.

**m̃okur (makur)** *adjective* skinny, of a person. *cf:* mrara.

**mol** *verb$_i$* hunt (for coconut crab only).

**m̃ol** *verb$_a$* squeeze, like squeezing kava or oranges.

**m̃oltao** *verb$_a$* rinse clothes. *cf:* pnol, pnoltao, preitao.

**m̃olu** *verb* rinse, rinse yourself after a shower.

**mom** *pronoun* our (1st person plural exclusive direct possessive). *U slasol ki ntak mom.* We took it on our backs. *cf:* mam, nigmam.

**m̃on** *verb*$_i$ swim under water.

**m̃ook** *noun* sleep, the crust in your eyes in the morning.

**m̃ook** *verb* term used to describe a stupid person (slang).

**m̃ool** *verb*$_i$ **1)** live, alive (of a living being, but can also be used of a volcano, for example). *Faat nen ru soso ki faat Kalosik. Go apu nen i tua nagien. Ga i m̃ool to mees ne.* That rock is called Kalosik. And that grandfather named it. It is alive today. **2)** healthy, used of a person who is well, not sick. *Me i pitlak natam̃ool nen kin ke fo mer gaag preg naul nkas nen ke tuok p̃a mingi, go p̃af mer m̃ool.* There is a man who will get leaf medicine to give you to drink, and you will be healthy again.

**m̃ool** *noun* tree sp., orange. (*Citrus sinensis*).

**m̃or** *verb*$_i$ submerge, as in a canoe filled with water but still floating. *cf:* tut.

**m̃ori** *noun* true. *cf:* til, tilm̃ori.

**m̃orm̃rom** *verb*$_i$ stage of growth of plant just before buds. *Nawi nen i m̃orm̃rom ser ntau.* That yam buds every year.

**mos (msagi)** *verb*$_a$ **1)** transport inside something, like in a canoe, a wheelbarrow, or a car. *A tak naniu ore a msagi pak esum̃.* I husked the coconut then transported it home. **2)** transport. *Me ka fo preg loto ke fan msagi mai. Me malpei i tiik.* I will get the car to come and fetch it (the garden food). But not in the old days. *Ru ga msag serale nen.* They brought everything for her.

**m̃os** *verb* wean, time when a baby stops breastfeeding. *Ru m̃os teesa sees.* They weaned the baby.

**m̃os (m̃osi)** *verb*$_a$ massage.

**m̃osus** *verb*$_i$ withdraw, pull back, like an anemone.

**mot (moti) 1)** *verb*$_a$ bind, tie. *Ku mot nkap po slati.* You tie up the firewood then you take it. **2)** *noun* bundle of wood. *cf:* motsok.

**motsok (motsoki)** *verb*$_a$ tie tightly. *Nala, ku slati, ku mai, ku motsok, ku motsok laak kin.* The 'nala' vine, you get it, you come, you tie it, you tie the peg (in the outrigger of the canoe) with it. *cf:* mot.

**motu** *adjective* old. *Ag kui pe pi tiawi motu.* You are already an old person.

**motu** *verb* dense (of trees in a forest). *I pitlak namlas motu i skei i tu natik naum̃.* There is dense bush near the river.

**mp̃aakor (mp̃aakron)** *noun*$_i$ lid (its lid).

**mp̃ag (mp̃agon)** *noun*$_i$ **1)** buttocks. *Teesa nen m̃pagon i fag.* This child has sores on his buttocks. **2)** end, furthest point of something. *cf:* nametp̃ag, p̃ag.

**mpak** *noun* banyan, varieties of banyan are called *mpakaul, mpak m̃aau. Mpak i pi nkas p̃ur nen* *nakon ru laap.* Banyans are big trees with plenty of roots.

**mpaklep** *noun* anemone that lives in the sand. *cf:* nrmen.

**mpakot** *verb* cross quickly in front of something, as a bird flying across one's path or a dog running across quickly.

**mpakur** *noun* tree sp., tamanu. (*Calophyllum inophyllum*).

**mpakur ni euut** *noun* tree sp., 'false tamanu'. (*Garcinia pseudoguttifera*).

**m̃p̃akus** *noun* bush that is left and not cut, natural bush. It has never been a garden, unlike *namlas*. *cf:* namlas.

**mpal** *noun* tree sp., milkwood tree. Tall tree used to make canoes. Bark used to be used for making cloth. (*Antiaris toxicaria*).

**mpalag** *verb* sleep on top of something.

**mp̃alo** *noun* valley, gorge, cliff.

**mpam (mpamun)** *noun$_i$* shoulder.

**m̃p̃ar (m̃p̃aron)** *noun$_i$* **1)** side. **2)** side of face. MacDonald (late 1800s) has *bora* as the sides of the face and temple which women used to cut and tear open with sharp shells during mourning.

**mpasok (mpasoki)** *verb$_a$* **1)** engage to be married, 'block' a partner before marrying them. **2)** block a space, as in saving a place for someone who has not yet arrived. **3)** to hold a mat flat using a rock while weaving.

**mpasul** *verb* lie down among some things, e.g., *mpasul nkal* 'to lie among a heap of clothes'.

**m̃p̃atfaat** *noun* iron, metal, steel.

**mpatur** *verb* to go through a group of things, e.g., *mpatur natam̃ool* 'go through a group of people'.

**m̃pau** *noun* spirit, a *ntuam* that lives in the *namlas* bush.

**m̃p̃au** *noun* sea creature, nudibranch. Its mucus trail can make your skin itchy.

**m̃p̃et** *noun* meaning. *A tae nag ke fo nrik mam ki m̃p̃et nafsan nag i tili.* I know he will tell us the meaning of the word that he said.

**mpul** *noun* shit, piece of shit left hanging after you have been to the toilet and haven't cleaned yourself properly.

**mra** *noun* eel (general term). *cf:* taakto.

**mra** *verb$_i$* bleed. *Kano nen i to mra.* The man is bleeding.

**mra napu (mra napuen)** *noun$_i$* **1)** spinal column. **2)** small of back.

**mra ni nai** *noun* freshwater eel.

**mra ni ntas** *noun* moray eel, also *mra maat, mra tfei*.

**mra nm̃ap̃** *noun* giant moray eel. (*Gymnothorax javanicus*).

**mra tfei** *noun* banded snake eel which lives in the sand and is not eaten.

**mrag (mragi)** *verb$_a$* rule, as of a chief ruling a village. *cf:* mermer.

**mrakor** *noun* trap, animal trap, snare. *Ka fan preg mrakor reki waak.* I will go and make a pig trap.

**mralu natuen** *verb* toddle, start to walk.

**mram (mrem)** *adjective* **1)** light, shining (of light). **2)** clear, of thinking. **3)** bright. **4)** Christian times, the 'light'. *I pi mal ni tiawi, go i pi mal nen kin loto ru tiik, go i pi malnen i ta mram wi mau.* This was in the old people's time, when there were no cars, and it was a time that was not in the light (before Christianity). *cf:* malik, namram.

**mrapil** *adjective* nearly ripe (of flesh of fruit). *cf:* arum.

**mrara** *adjective* **1)** thin, e.g., of a thin person. **2)** shallow (of water). *cf:* m̃okur.

**mrat** *verb* falling apart (of clothes); worn out.

**mrer** *verb*$_i$ die down (of fire). *Malnen ku preg kapu nkap i na i mrer go ku paan, go ku po nrak.* When you make laplap the fire dies down and you can roast vegetables, then take out the stones.

**mro** *verb*$_i$ think. *Ku to mro ki nafte?* What are you thinking about? *cf:* mrosa.

**mrofaafat** *verb* believe.

**mrokasu (mrokasueki)** *verb* think heavily about something, also.

**mrolep** *verb* think about something big or important.

**mroperkat** *verb*$_i$ remember. *Go m̃aau Msaiwi ki mroperkat nafsan nig naot nig Emelp̃au.* And the warrior Msaiwi remembered the words of the chief of Emelp̃au.

**mropir (mropri)** *verb*$_a$ to doubt. *A mroprik.* I doubt you.

**mropta** *verb* think ahead and plan something. *cf:* pregpta.

**mroput** *verb*$_i$ worry, be troubled, feel burdened. *A mroput toop selwan a nrogo ku msak.* I worry when I hear you are sick.

**mrosa** *verb* **1)** think badly of, to not like. **2)** flirt. *cf:* mro.

**mrotae** *verb*$_a$ recognise by thinking about something. *cf:* letae, nrogtae.

**m̃sai** *verb* to have holes in it. *cf:* m̃saisei.

**m̃saisei** *adjective* holey, full of holes, like a tin roof with lots of holes in it. *cf:* m̃sai.

**msak** *verb*$_i$ sick, to be; *namsaki* 'sickness, disease'. *A tap tae nafte if pi nlaken kin i msak mau.* I don't know what caused his sickness.

**msal** *adjective* different, to be. *Me nam̃olien ni mees i msal toop. I tap taos nam̃olien ni malpei mau.* But life today is very different. It's not like life in the old days.

**msalsal** *adjective* special thing.

**mtaatak (mtaatakun)** *verb*$_a$ careful, be careful. *I trau mtaatak sernale.* He is careful about everything.

**mtafus** *adjective* stupid. *cf:* p̃autik.

**mtak** *verb*$_i$ fear. *Ku mtak ki naat nen i na ke watgik.* You're scared of the man who wants to hit you.

**mtakseu** *noun* carpenter. *A tae preg nasum̃ neu, tae pi mtakseu.* I can make my own house, I can be a carpenter.

**m̃tal** *verb*$_a$ harvest food from the forest, wild food, not from a garden; forage for food. Note that different terms are used for harvesting different crops. *cf:* m̃ok, namas, traf.

**mtalu (mtalua)** *verb*$_a$ choose. *Kineu a mtaluok nen p̃a fi naot.*

I choose you to become the chief. *cf:* tiptip.

**mtame** *noun* crab, small crab that looks like a small kaledoni crab (mudcrab), in the sea, edible, strong shell, about 20 cm across. Comes out at night.

**mtamurmur 1)** *verb*$_i$ smile a little. **2)** *verb* giggle. *cf:* mur.

**mtapes** *noun* orphan.

**mtar** *verb*$_i$ set (of the sun going down) (for the setting moon use *tanun*); *almtar* 'sunset'. *cf:* tanun.

**mtas** *verb*$_a$ scratch.

**mtastes** *adjective* scratched, e.g., skin scratched by something.

**mtau** *verb*$_i$ honour, respect. *Ku mtau ki maarik naot.* You show respect to the chief.

**mtel** *noun* a crack that occurs in wood.

**m̃tel** *verb* fire glowing, no longer burning brightly (*sor*). *cf:* sor.

**mten** *adjective* heavy. *Go a po to kerkrai me skel i mten, me ka fo sati ur napu ne.* I had to be strong, as the scales were heavy, but I would take them along this road. *cf:* namtenwen.

**mtet** *adjective* rotten, e.g., of wood, or of a tin roof, but not of food. *cf:* p̃o.

**mtir (mtri)** *verb*$_a$ **1)** to write. *Tiawi ni teetwei gar ru sup̃nekin mtir, tiawi ru kano mtir.* The old people from long ago didn't know how to write, they couldn't write. **2)** to paint. *cf:* namtirwen.

**mtirtir** *adjective* coloured, striped.

**mtulep** *noun* **1)** wife, also *nmatu*. *I neu paakot tiket ni plen, me komam mtulep nranru pa.* He paid for my ticket, and my wife and I both went. **2)** missus, a term of respect for a woman. **3)** spirit, respectful way of referring to a female spirit. *Trau pulp̃og nen kin ke fo pam̃ori teflan mtulep Katapel i to mai pak elau wes tekatpi elau.* This morning he went to find how Missus Katapel (a *natopu*) came from the sea with shellfish. **4)** woman, old woman deserving of respect. *cf:* maarik, natopu.

**mu** *verb*$_i$ high tide, to be high tide. *Elau i mu.* The tide is high. (*Idiom: 'The tide comes in.' The sea is full/abundant, meaning there's a lot of money.*) *cf:* namuenmokur.

**muk (mukti)** *verb*$_i$ ripen, put something aside until it is ripe. *cf:* puk.

**mul (mulsi) 1)** *verb*$_a$ peel. **2)** *verb*$_a$ strip bark, as in stripping hibiscus branches (*nap̃lel*) to make string. **3)** *verb*$_i$ slough, shed skin. *Aas i mul.* The coconut crab changes its shell.

**mulmul** *verb*$_i$ flake, peel, e.g., of skin, or paint.

**mulu (mulua)** *verb*$_a$ **1)** take out, take something out of something. **2)** peel skin from a sore.

**munwei** *noun* **1)** healer. *Munwei nen ke tae ga pam̃or nlak namsaki ga.* A healer will be able to find out the cause of his sickness for him. **2)** magician (*kleva* in Bislama). *cf:* kulmam, kulru.

**mur** *verb*$_i$ **1)** smile. **2)** laugh. *cf:* mtamurmur.

**mus** *pronoun* **1)** you (2nd person plural object). *Teesa laap a muurin nrik mus kin na nfaketanwen i pi tewi.* Children, I want to tell you that respect is a good thing. **2)** your (2nd person plural inclusive possessive). *Ko faketan ki tem mus go rait mus.* Respect your father and your mother.

**mut (muti)** *verb$_a$* keeping something for yourself. *Raf mut ntaewen go akit tu kano preg namrun.* They might protect their knowledge, and we couldn't do anything.

**mutrei** *noun* fermented breadfruit (an old word, not known today but found in writing on South Efate from the 1950s).

**muuk** *verb$_i$* wipe your bottom after going to the toilet.

**muur (muurin)** *verb$_a$* want. *A muur ka tae nafsan gamus.* I want to learn your language. *A muurin.* I want it. *cf:* na.

# N Nr

**-n** *pronoun suffix* **1)** he, she, it (3rd person singular object). *Namroan nen kin u piatlaken malpei kin u mal ki independent.* That was the thinking we had then when we didn't want independence. **2)** his, hers, its (3rd person singular direct possessive) when suffixed to inalienable body parts or used in reflexive constructions. *Ki pe pak nam̃leen pa.* She has gone back to her place. *Malen tmen i tm̃en nrea, i lee pak euut.* When his father turned around, he looked to shore.

**na** *determiner* the. *Or go na p̃og iskei i tili nag, "Ka fo pak Etog nafanu nig nam̃er taar."* Yes, and then one day he said, "I will go to the foreign place, the country of white people." *Go i mai pak Efil 1946 malnen kin nafkal i nom, 1948 a mer na Franis polis.* [I was there] until 1946 in Vila, then war finished, in 1948 I returned to the French police.

**na** *interjection* expression of hesitation. *Selwan, na, nana, lycee i nom go a pak kur normal, ru len ki teflan ru tij ki teesa.* When the lycee (high school) was finished, I went to the cours normal, they taught us how to teach children.

**na** *verb$_i$* want, to want; to intend or desire to do something. *Malnen i na ke fak, i tu sa i muur na ke fak Ermag.* When he wanted to go, he was here and he wanted to go to Erromango. *Kaaru nen a na ka trausi, a na ka traus na natrauswen gakit teni Efat.* What I want to talk about next, I want to tell our story, of those people from Efate. *cf:* muur.

**na** *COMP* in order to. *Ku p̃el ki nas na p̃a moti.* You bend your bow in order to tie it. *Ru kpasir go ru mai paa raru na ruk sef pa.* They chased them and they came by canoe in order to run away.

**na** *preverbal* begin to. *Selwan ru toto pan pan welkia nalotwen i na ke fo mai.* They stayed and stayed until Christianity began to arrive.

**na (nag)** *verb$_i$* say. *Go ru na, "E p̃a fo mer ler pak nawesien." Go a po mer ler pan tkal namba 15 atlag ne.* And they said, "You go back to work." And I went back until the fifteenth of this month.

**naal** *noun* basket. *Naal nen ku tae pai nkal wes.* A basket in which you can put clothes.

**naal** *preposition* inside, the main part of something, e.g., *naal narum* 'the palm of your hand', *naal natuen* 'sole of his/her foot'.

**naal (naalon)** *noun$_i$* crotch, part of the front of the body where the legs meet.

**naal nasum̃** *noun* household. *Go tep̃ur knen i to naal nasum̃, i wel tem me rait, ru tafnau teesa gar ki nafte kin i wi go nafte kin i sa.* And the biggest of them is in the home, where the father and mother teach their children what is good and what is bad.

**naal ni teesa** *noun* womb (lit: basket for child), also the placenta or sac the baby is in inside the womb.

**naal raru** *noun* inside a canoe.

**naala** *noun* **1)** vine. **2)** lawyer cane, used for binding, e.g., a canoe's outrigger to the cross-members. Also known as supplejack or rattan. (*Calamus vitiensis*).

**naam̃** *noun* coconut sp., green, no flesh inside, but you can drink it.

**naam̃ (naam̃on)** *noun$_i$* lung.

**naam̃er** *noun* tree sp., bead tree. The bright red hard seeds of this tree are used for necklaces. The wood is used for canoe paddles. (*Adenanthera pavonina*).

**naan** *noun* ringworm.

**naan (naanin)** *noun$_i$* shadow, photo. *Naan teem̃ool go natam̃ool.* Pictures of animals and people. *A lek naanik.* I'm looking at my own image. *cf:* tip̃ot.

**naanr** *noun* banana (general term). Also a type of banana which is very yellow and the bunch grows up on the tree rather than hanging down. *Selwan naanr i mam ku tae pami ko ku preg kapu kin.* When a banana is ripe you can eat it or you can make laplap with it.

**naap** *noun* tree sp., fish poison tree. Note: seeds are ground up with sand and water and placed into pools to kill fish. The leaf is used for roasting food. (*Barringtonia asiatica*).

**naap̃ (naap̃on)** *noun$_i$* characteristic of a person, feeling or emotion; *naap̃ wi* 'generous, good-hearted, good person', *naap̃ sa* 'bad feeling'. *Ku p̃rai naap̃on.* You broke his heart.

**naapas** *noun* fish sp., pipefish, shrimpfish.

**naapas** *noun* coconut branch, middle of the big coconut from which the leaves (*naun naniu*) grow.

**naar** *noun* **1)** tide. *Naar i su, naar i sak.* The tide is falling, the tide is rising. **2)** current, the movement of water in the sea.

**naar** *noun* tree sp., sheoak. (*Casuarina equisetifolia*).

**naar (naarun)** *noun$_i$* hand, arm. *Naarum i kerkrai toop.* Your arm is very strong. (*Idiom: 'Take one's hand.' Take care of or bring up a person who is either parentless or given for this purpose by his/her parents.*)

**naariu** *noun* lemongrass, used to make tea.

**naas** *noun* bow, for shooting arrows. *Ki pregpta ki ola, naas, plak timen nega.* He got his spear, bow and arrows ready. [Kalsarap's bow was made of mangrove (*natog*) with a string made of banyan (*mpak*). The top of the bow is called its head (*np̃au*) and the bottom is called *nakoinrok*. The bow and arrow should always be carried with the head up, ready to use.] (*Idiom: 'Walks behind a bow.' Still doing something secretly, but one will learn a lesson eventually.*) *cf:* pupuet.

**naas** *noun* day before yesterday. *cf:* aas.

**naas (naasin)** *noun$_i$* jaw, chin; *naasim ni entan* 'your lower jaw'.

**naat** *noun* **1)** person. *Naat nen i preg nawesien sa go ruk fo watgi.* That man did something bad so they would hit him. **2)** someone, a definite but non-specific person. *cf:* natam̃ool.

**naat (naaten)** *noun$_i$* **1)** soul. *Naatak i nrir.* I am scared (lit: my spirit is flying). **2)** spirit, a spirit that can't be seen and can be either good or bad. *Me Atua kin i preg naaten, naaten p̃otae, naaten nen kin i wel ag ku rog, go ke fo watgik.* God makes the *naaten*, different *naaten*, and if you do wrong he will hit you.

**naat p̃rakot** *noun* anybody, somebody. *Naat p̃rakot ke mai slati pan.* Somebody came and took it away.

**naatap** *noun* statue, idol, image, tamtam (slitgong). *P̃a fam̃ori na naatap kin rui laotu.* You will find that they stood a statue up. *cf:* natopu.

**naatfer** *noun* plant sp., small grass like pampas-grass.

**naatmat** *noun* flying insect, has an orange nose.

**naatmat** *noun* corpse. *cf:* mat, nmaten, teemat.

**naf** *noun* **1)** pumice stone. **2)** lava, liquid rock. *cf:* faatsal.

**nafakton** *noun* sugarcane sp., green (*ksakes*) and red (*miel*). *cf:* makol, nap̃rai, naus, traares, tumel.

**nafamwen** *noun* feast.

**nafanu (nfanu)** *noun* country. *Ka fo pak etog nafanu nig nam̃er taar.* I will go to the foreign country of the white people. *Go rak mer tfag na nfanu ke nrus pak elag.* And they would build the country so that it would raise up.

**nafanu sa** *noun* hell.

**nafar (nafarun)** *noun$_i$* wing. *Gar rukui mai go i na, "E, naat i lakor srakor nafarum."* And they came and he said, "Hey, someone must have hidden your wings."

**nafarifa** *noun* tree sp. (*Neisosperma sp.?*).
**nafeet** *noun* spleen.
**nafeifeien** *noun* omen. *cf:* fei.
**nafen (nafnen)** *noun*$_i$ armpit. (*Idiom: 'To look under one's armpit.' Looking everywhere for help. When a person becomes helpless or doesn't have anything or anyone to help them in an uneasy situation.*)
**nafeng (nafengan)** *noun*$_i$ flesh that is inside a shell, e.g., coconut or shellfish; also the pith around a nut, like *nafil.*
**nafenu** *noun* tree sp., with a furry leaf, used to cover fish when you cook them; it gives them a nice taste. The leaves are used as a medicine. They are also now used to clean diving glasses.
**nafer** *noun* **1)** bits. **2)** crumbs.
**naferkaal** *noun* dwarf spirit that usually moves around in groups.
**naferkaal** *noun* group of children.
**nafesaan** *noun* curse.
**nafet** *noun* group, used of plants, animals or trees. *Ale a pas nafet na korespondens nen ru neu sent ki.* I passed the bunch of courses that they had sent for me.
**nafet (naften)** *noun*$_i$ pile of fish.
**nafetfet** *noun* **1)** seat of canoe. **2)** platform between canoe and outrigger.
**nafi** *noun* taro sp. (*Alocasia macrorrhizos*). *cf:* ntal, ntal ni fiti.
**nafiaf** *noun* everything that is washed ashore and is left at the high tide mark, stones, shells, flotsam, etc. *cf:* tarisal.
**nafiefi** *noun* tree sp., like a small palm with a grooved leaf. The heart is used for roasting fish. It has bitter fruit that can be used as an emetic; eat it if you have eaten poison to vomit out the poison. (Varieties include *nafiefi ni euut* [seaside], *nafiefi ni nai* [riverside].)
**nafil** *noun* bush nut tree (navele), smaller than *napkor* or *nafil pokor,* which has a bigger pith (*nafengan*) around the nut. (*Barringtonia edulis*).
**nafilsanr** *noun* tree sp., leaves used for decoration as they smell good. Tree used for firewood. Birds eat the fruit.
**nafinaotan** *noun* chiefliness, also the chiefly line. *I pi sautog, rent, nag ru tok pregi ser ntau paakot gar pak nafinaotan.* It is rent which they gave every year, their payment to the chiefly line. *cf:* naot.
**nafinr (nafinrin)** *noun*$_i$ rib.
**nafis** *noun* Fijian asparagus (*navisa* in Bislama), small sugarcane. (*Saccharum edule*).
**nafit** *noun* slave. This could be someone who has had their land taken away as punishment and is sent away from their own village. *cf:* manmun.
**nafitiawian** *noun* old age. *cf:* tiawi.
**nafkal** *noun* **1)** battle. **2)** war. *Selwan nlaun ru paakruk ru tae preg nafkal.* When countries come together they can have big battles. *cf:* ftup̃, tup̃.

**nafkou** *noun* messenger. *P̃a fi nafkou pak Eton.* You be the messenger to Eton.

**naflak** *noun* clan. Note: You are in the same clan as your mother. You have to marry someone from another clan. Some clans no longer exist because there are no children in the line. Some of the clans and their characteristics are: *kram,* a shell which sits on the beach in good times but buries itself in the sand in bad times; *nm̃al,* a wild yam, the shoots don't follow the rope you put to train it; *namkanr,* a plant which grows quickly, takes firm hold, but dies soon after; *ntal,* taro, the skin is a little bitter but the inside is good; *nawi,* yam, these people control their feelings; *wit,* the octopus, who changes colour depending on its surroundings. There are titles associated with the clans, e.g.: *wiit* 'mama'; *namkanr* 'kaka'; *nawi* 'wiwi'; *nmal* 'nmal'; *kram* 'taata'; *naniu* 'nunu'. You call them maarik/mtulep, taata and so on. The word for father is different in some clans: naflak kram call their father *taata;* naflak namkanr call their father *gka*; and the others all call their father *apap*. *cf:* nametrau.

**naflel** *noun* dry leaves, after cooking on the hot stones and eating the laplap. *cf:* nteu.

**naflewen** *noun* fight, argument. *cf:* ple.

**nafnag** *noun* food. Mainly used to refer to vegetable food, but food in general; *nafnag ni talm̃aat* 'garden food', *nafnag ni aliat* 'dinner', *nafnag ni pulp̃og* 'breakfast'.

**nafnag ni afsak** *noun* plant sp., which grows near the sea, succulent, eat it with dry coconuts or pickle it with chilli. This is a type of *nafrofur*.

**nafofon** *noun* vine sp., strong vine which was used to make whips.

**nafolflon** *noun* behaviour.

**nafon** *noun* pubic cover, woven cloth which used to be attached by the belt and passed between men's thighs, now used of a child's nappy (napkin). *cf:* pisp̃lolo.

**naframwen** *noun* length. *cf:* pram.

**nafrofur** *noun* scrub, bush, small bushes and grass.

**nafrofursa** *noun* plant, any type of plant for which there is no use and which is regarded as a weed, e.g., Job's tears. One kind is also called kamarat from French because its seeds stick to you as you walk past it. (*Coix lacryma-jobi*).

**nafsan** *noun* **1)** story. *Me itap metp̃akor nafsan nig apap nega mau.* But he didn't forget his father's story. *Selwan Pastor Kalagis I nrog nafsan ni Sailas I nrogtesa wes.* When Pastor Kalagis heard Sailas's story he felt bad about it. **2)** language. *Na mtakseu i pi nafsan ni kastom, kapenta, mtakseu.* Mtakseu is the kastom language way of saying carpenter, mtakseu.

**nafsik** *noun* flesh (of fruit or animal).

**nafsup̃** *noun* peak. *Namlame i pakor nafsup̃ ntaf.* Dew fell on the mountaintop. *cf:* fsup̃.

**nafsup̃nar (nafsup̃narun)** *noun*$_i$ elbow.

**nafte** *interrogative* 1) what. *Ag ku pi naflak nafte?* You are what clan (naflak)? 2) pronoun what *Ale, nafte nen a to muur ka to pregi...* Okay, what I like to do... *cf:* ku.

**naftom (naftomin)** *noun*$_i$ growing part of a plant.

**naftourwen** *noun* wedding. Today also commonly *nlakwen*. *cf:* ptour, taulu.

**naftuan** *noun* **1)** gift. **2)** property (land and house) inherited by someone. *cf:* tu.

**nafum̃** *noun* flower. *cf:* fum̃.

**nafunwen** *noun* fish poisoning, putting poison in to the water to kill fish. *cf:* pun.

**nafusrekwen** *noun* conversation. *cf:* puserek.

**nafutfut** *noun* bubble.

**nafuukwen** *noun* cough. *cf:* puuk.

**nag** relativiser, used after a noun to introduce a relative clause. *Natam̃ool nag ru mat go tenag ru m̃ool ru to slatir mai psur ospitel ni Pelfi.* The people who died and those who were alive, they brought them to the hospital at Belleview.

**nagae** *noun* almond, native almond. Note: nut tree, the resin was once used for caulking canoes. (*Canarium indicum, Canarium harveyi*).

**nagel (naglen)** *noun*$_i$ gum in the mouth, that holds your teeth.

**nagi** *noun* tree sp., strong ironwood, grows on rocks by the sea, trunk can be 60 cm in diameter, succulent leaf and small flower with yellow centre. Medicinal uses. Leaves can be used to make your teeth strong. Also use it to decorate your house.

**nagi (nagien)** *noun*$_i$ name. *Me ru tua ki nagi nig etog i skei i to.* But they gave him a foreign name.

**nagis** *noun* point, cape, headland. *I piatlak nagis ni Eter ga i pi nagis pram, me m̃aat nen kin i fisktofi.* There is the point at Eter, it is a long point, and this snake split it.

**nagitpar** *noun* tree sp., leaves look like cabbage, grows near the sea, smells good. Leaves used for medicine.

**nagor (nagorin)** *noun*$_i$ **1)** nose. *Nlaken ru tao nalur i pram go i po paakor namter go nagorir go negar tete rukoi sef pan kus nkas me ru to mak leker.* Because they leave their hair long and their eyes and noses appear behind it, some of them ran away and hid in the trees and stared at them. **2)** end of a mat. **3)** tassle or special weaving.

**nagoswen** *noun* flu, cold.

**nagrof** *noun* tree sp., New Guinea rosewood. Timber used for canoes. (*Pterocarpus indicus*).

**nai** *noun* **1)** water, fresh water, spring. *I pitlak nai i skei i to Ertap.* There is a spring at Eratap. *I ser*

*ser me mtulep Katapel i to elag ntaf nrogo ki nai i ser i fiit mai tuleg ki Ewenesu.* It ran and ran, but Katapel was up on the hill and heard the water run right to Ewenesu. **2)** alcohol. *cf:* ntas.

**nai kookon** *noun* bitter drink, alcoholic drink, wine, spirits and so on. *Selwan ku min nai kookon nen, i preg np̃aum i lefek.* When you drink that alcohol it makes your head spin.

**nai latlat** *noun* beer (bubble water).

**nai miel** *noun* wine (red water).

**naiam** *noun* yam, spiky wild yam sp.

**naik** *noun* fish (general term). *Gar ru maui pitlak serale teplan ne, go i pitlak naik. Ku muurin paus ki naik ke fo tuok ki.* They all have something like this, like fish. If you want to ask for fish, he (the spirit) will give it to you.

**naik maan** *noun* **1)** lionfish. **2)** butterflyfishes. (*Pterois spp.*).

**naik nrmen** *noun* fish sp., damselfishes, anemonefishes. (*Pomacentridae*). *cf:* tametpel.

**naik taos** *noun* fish sp., remoras. (*Echeneidae*).

**naikmetpuk** *noun* fish sp., type of flying fish. (*Priacanthus macracanthus*).

**naiknrir** *noun* fish sp., type of flying fish.

**naimat** *noun* lake.

**nainom** *noun* tree sp., fruit eaten by flying foxes.

**naipir** *noun* Chinese lantern tree. (*Hernandia nymphaeifolia, Hernandia peltata*).

**nairo** *noun* yam sp., vine grows a little crooked. It has roots growing off the yam.

**nais (naisun)** *noun$_i$* breast. *cf:* mimi.

**nais (naisun)** *noun$_i$* prickle, thorn (*naisun*): *nais m̃ool* 'orange thorn'; *nais laim* 'lime thorn'; *nais mandrin* 'mandarin thorn'. *cf:* sup̃sup̃.

**naiser** *noun* river. *cf:* naum̃.

**naisig** *noun* bush with red berries. Its fruit is sweet.

**naispako** *noun* yellow spongy creature that lives on reef rocks.

**nait** *noun* fig tree, figs grow out of the trunk of the tree. (*Ficus wassa*).

**naitar** *noun* semen.

**naitarpes** *noun* yam sp., white flesh.

**nak (naken)** *noun$_i$* inside leg (an old word, not used today).

**nakerkraian** *noun* labour, giving birth. *cf.* **kerkerai.**

**nakfakof** *noun* tree sp.

**naki** *noun* pandanus, cultivated. Hanging roots are used to make tongs (*nkem*) for taking stones out of the fire. (*Pandanus tectorius?*). *cf:* nfak, nparom.

**nakiat** *noun* cross-member of a canoe, joins the canoe to the outrigger.

**nakik** *noun* poles attached to the top of a canoe, used as a handle for carrying the canoe.

**nakimtirmtir** *noun* pandanus with striped leaves.

**nakin (naknin)** *noun$_i$* finger, toe. *Me ke fo lul ki naknin ru fak nmal nanr pa.* But he would come and stick his fingers in the middle of the bananas and go.

**nakir** *noun* **1)** coral. **2)** gravel.

**nakirles** *noun* soft coral (some is edible).

**naklak** *noun* tree sp., comb tree. Its small fruit is eaten by flying foxes. (*Planchonella grayana*).

**nakm̃ou** *noun* tree sp., island teak. The bark was once used to make barkcloth. Its hardwood was used for tools and for houses. Toukolau saw a man from Eratap who also made barkcloth from *narkamet, natret, napum̃alom, nmariu*. (*Intsia bijuga*).

**naknafnag** *noun* leftover food. *cf:* kotfak.

**naknot** *noun* root, any type of root crop, e.g., *naknot ntal,* taro roots, *naknot nawi,* yam roots.

**naknrae (naknraen)** *noun$_i$* brain.

**nako (nakon)** *noun$_i$* **1)** face. *Nlaken kin nakon, nakon wan ki kin nagis ni Emut ne.* Because his face, his face, that is this point at Emut. **2)** prow of a canoe.

**nakoi** *noun* marker used to show the edge of a land area. *cf:* nmakot.

**nakoinrok** *preposition* **1)** back. *Ru preg tete kaku ni raru nen ru to nakpei ru pak nakoinrok Morinda.* They took some cargo from the front and put it at the back of the Morinda. **2)** behind. **3)** rear. *P̃a ler pak nakoinrok.* Go back behind! *Selwan ku na p̃a weswes p̃a ta le pak nakoinrok mau.* When you want to work, don't look behind you.

**nakompak** *noun* yam sp., sweet, like arrowroot.

**nakon** *noun* **1)** share. **2)** half. *A tae te nakon me a ta mrotae te nakon mau.* I know half, but I don't recognise half. *cf:* kotfak.

**nakon** *noun* verse (as in the Bible or in a song).

**nakoon** *noun* root, part of a tree.

**nakpei** *preposition* ahead, forward, front. *Ku lek nakpei selwan ku na p̃a freg namrun.* You look ahead when you want to do something.

**nakpes** *noun* tree sp., the young leaves are eaten together with *ntali* fruit. Also use the wood to make fish traps by planting sticks vertically in the water to create a fence. You can eat the new growth.

**nakrik** *noun* fig tree, small banyan. (*Ficus virgata*).

**nakrok** *noun* vine sp., strong vine.

**nakser** *noun* wild kava, creeping thick vine, the leaves are eaten, but not the root. Its leaves can stop a devil that is following you. You can hang the leaves in your house as a form of protection.

**nakte** *pronoun* my (1st person singular possessive). Unusual in being the only possessive form that precedes the object it possesses. *Ka fo puetsok nakte nkal wel a tuleg me a na ka taf.* I would hold my skirt like this, when I want to leave.

**nakul (naklun)** *noun$_i$* skin (of people only). *Ku kue ki naklum.* You are not ashamed of something you have done (idiomatic expression). Saying that your skin is bad (*naklum i sa*) means that you have goosebumps, a feeling of nervousness but you don't know why. *cf:* kuul, nasok.

**nakur** *noun* Indian mulberry, not used as a dye today, but it was used as a yellow dye for mats and hair. Layard in 1915 said it was used for sickness, and that it was mixed with lime to make a red paint. Also known for medicinal uses (as 'Tahitian noni'). (*Morinda citrifolia*).

**nakwak** *noun* coleus, used as medicine and to decorate the house. (*Coleus spp.*)

**nal (nalun)** *noun$_i$* **1)** hair. **2)** moustache. **3)** beard, body hair (his/her); *nal nfas namet*(*kit*) 'our eyebrows'.

**nalag** *noun* song. *Me mees nen i welkia, teesa ru to preg nalag mana, me rui pe to natkon sikskei to.* But today, children sing songs and so on, but they stay at their own villages.

**nalag** *noun* plant sp., from by the sea.

**nalagaan** *verb* music. *cf:* lag.

**nalaglag** *noun* scale (of a fish).

**nalap̃o** *noun* marsh, soft ground, soft mud.

**nalapul** *noun* web, spiderweb.

**nalee (naleen)** *noun$_i$* voice. *Ser teem̃ool nen ruk nomser preg naleer ke fak elag.* Each animal would send their voices on high.

**naleenaan** *noun* truth. *Teetwei if wel kuf muur p̃a sol naleenaan knen, p̃a fo mas nkas, nap̃raat ke skei me p̃a fas kin Elakmamiel.* Long ago, if you wanted to find out the truth of it, you would cut a tree, a Nap̃rat tree, and you would push it in to Elakmamiel.

**nalelewen** *noun* opinion. *Me nalelewen neu a leka teetwei i mer wi toop.* In my opinion I see the olden days as being better. *cf:* lee.

**nalepleptau** *noun* spots, white spots on skin, itchy, white and black varieties; leaf disease. Could be caught from washing in bad water, or wearing clothes of someone who has it. Use the leaf of *mismai* to treat it.

**nalewen** *noun* look, the way something looks.

**nalewen sa** *noun* ugly, something that doesn't look good.

**nalewen wi** *noun* beautiful, something that looks attractive. *Ru pregi nen ke fi nalewen wi.* They make it so that it is beautiful.

**nali** *noun* clearing, open space. *Me selwan nalotwen i mai nawesien sa laap nega ru maui tok enali.* But when Christianity comes all his bad work is out in the open.

**naliati** *noun* days, used to describe a period of time, not a specific day, which would be *aliat. Go a muurin na, naliati ke skei ka fo preg nafnag p̃ur keskei me ko fo mai.* And I want that, someday, I will have a feast and we will all come. *cf:* aliat, ser naliati.

**naliati mau ilaru** *noun* week (more commonly *wik*).

**nalik** *noun* tree sp., small tree, 3–4 metres, good for firewood.

**naliu** *noun* breadfruit sp., strong type of breadfruit that needs long cooking. *cf:* naptam.

**nalkes** *noun* medicine, leaf magic. *Ka fo tuok nalkes p̃a fo mingi.* I'll give you medicine and you will drink it.

**nalkolik** *noun* party, a celebration held between Christmas and New Year. It comes fom New Caledonia. Women hang their clothes and a man has to choose clothes (blindfolded) then take them back to the woman who owns the clothes.

**nalkolik** *noun* frame for hanging yams. *cf:* lkolik.

**nalkur** *adjective* dry banana leaves, used to burn or as a mulch to put around young seedlings.

**nalo** *noun* dust, smoke. *cf:* nam̃tam̃ot.

**nalo** *noun* tree sp., with small tasty nuts. Wood is also used for house construction and fuel. (*Finschia chloroxantha*).

**nalof (nalfen)** *noun$_i$* track. *Selwan i pan panpan na i tkal talm̃aat ki us nalof waak.* When he got to the garden he began following the pig's tracks. *Ki us nalfen panpanpan ki pe tok malik, nmalko sa ki pe tok mai.* He followed its tracks until it was dark, deep darkness was coming in. *cf:* lfalof.

**naloklokotwen** *noun* stain, something spilled that has dried.

**nalomlom** *noun* moss.

**nalotwen** *noun* prayer, Christianity. *cf:* lot.

**nalsiu** *noun* basket for carrying food from the garden.

**naltelit** *noun* spark, sparks from a fire.

**nalukor** *noun* curtain.

**nalwaniksu** *noun* sea urchin with soft bristles. It is eaten raw or cooked. *cf:* saofak, somkol.

**nam** *noun* yam sp., 'Wael yam', some are sweet, some are bitter, and there are red, yellow, and white ones. Fruit hangs down and can be eaten, it is like a potato. Kalsarap says it is not eaten today as it is too bitter. Layard in 1915 said it is the fruit of a wild yam skinned and scraped and put in a basket in which it is soaked for a day in salt water, then for another day in fresh water. It may be eaten without further preparation, or else cooked with grated coconut. (*Dioscorea bulbifera*). *cf:* nawi.

**namamao** *noun* tree sp., also known as *nkas ni Esanr* 'Santo tree', used for tree posts. (*Pipturus argenteus*). *cf:* nametal.

**namamwen** *noun* poisoning, food poisoning. Also ciguetera poisoning. *cf:* mam.

**nam̃aniu** *noun* heap of fruit, like coconuts, mangoes or *nmal* 'hog plums', heaped up on the ground; *nam̃aniu naniu* 'bunch of coconuts'.

**namas** *noun* harvest, a general term for food from the garden. Note that different terms are used for harvesting different crops. *cf:* m̃ok, m̃tal, traf, kil, kis, pupuet.

**nam̃aser** *noun* grass skirt.

**namatal** *noun* tree sp., puzzle tree. Note: the bark can be used as a rope. The leaves are medicinal. (*Kleinhovia hospita*).

**namatun (nmatun)** *noun* thing; *tenmatun* 'something'. *U tae preg tenmatun nen kin u muurin, nlaken ui pe slat independent nigmam.* We can do something that we want because we got our independence.

**name (namen)** *noun$_i$* **1)** tongue. **2)** blade, tip of something; *namen nau* is the tip of a wave.

**namee (nameen)** *noun$_i$* urine, piss. *cf:* me.

**nam̃el** *noun* namele, cycad palm. Leaves are used as a sign of peace. Fruit is not eaten today. (*Cycas seemannii*).

**nam̃el (nam̃len)** *noun$_i$* tail (of fish).

**nam̃elfer** *noun* charcoal.

**nam̃elnatu (nam̃elnatuen)** *noun$_i$* heel.

**namenkori** *noun* spleen, a part of the guts that looks like a dog's tongue (*namen* 'tongue', *kori* 'dog').

**nam̃er** *noun* people, more than one person; *nam̃er malik* 'heathen', *nam̃er nafkal* 'soldiers', *nam̃er p̃rakot* 'civilians', *nam̃er p̃afp̃of* 'adults'. *Nam̃er p̃afp̃of m̃as ki ru tae mai takinrog.* Only adults can come and listen. *cf:* natam̃ool.

**nam̃ermra** *noun* tree sp., the red bark of it (or the fruit) is scraped and rubbed in the hair to make dreadlocks. It is not good to burn the wood as its fumes are bad for asthmatics. Leaves are used as medicine (taken every five days) and to wrap things, but not for cooking.

**namesp̃al** *noun* desert, place with no vegetation.

**nameswen** *noun* game, something done for fun. *Go nameswen kaaru nen a meswes, i pi polevault.* And the next game I played was pole vault. *cf:* mes.

**namet (namten, nmet)** *noun$_i$* **1)** eye. *Naat nen, namten i malik.* The man fainted (lit: eye it is dark). **2)** door. *Polis ga ra to na, nmet, me ga, ga i pato mp̃agon.* The police were at the door, but she was at the end of the cave. **3)** window of a house (lit: the eye of the house). *cf:* faar, namet p̃ur, nametfau, namet sees.

**namet nafsan** *noun* verse.

**namet p̃ur** *noun* main door. *cf:* namet.

**namet sees** *noun* window.

**namet tkau** *noun* eye of the fishhook. *cf:* tkau.

**nametal** *noun* tree sp., used for building, but rots if put in the ground. *cf:* namamao.

**nametfaai** *noun* fish sp., emperors. (*Lethrinidae*). *cf:* nsul.

**nametfau** *noun* hole drilled in the side of a canoe used to attach cross-members. *cf:* namet.

**nametmatuan** *noun* knowledge. *Ru mro kin na gar ru metmatu tol nametmatuan nigmam tiawi.* Because they think their knowledge is better than that of us old people. *cf:* metmatu.

**nametmet** *noun* banana for cooking.

**nametmet miel** *noun* red cooking banana.

**nametmet taar** *noun* white cooking banana.

**nametnai** *noun* spring.

**nametp̃ag (nametp̃agon)** *noun$_i$* **1)** end, conclusion. *I tiik ki nametp̃agon.* There is no end to it. **2)** point of land in the sea. *Ga kin i tap̃o patu nametp̃ag nagis ne ru soso ki Katapel.* He is the one who fell over at the end of the point that they call Katapel. *cf:* mp̃ag.

**nametrau** *noun* **1)** family, close family, 'tribe'. Now many people use famle. *Nametrau neu ru to natkon kaaru.* All my family live in another village. **2)** type. *I piatlak nametrau naik i lap.* There are many types of fish. *cf:* naflak.

**namgalgal** *noun* tree sp., timber, strong wood.

**namgar** *noun* **1)** white spots in the throat and on the tongue. **2)** coconut disease.

**namgar** *noun* plant sp., small plant that grows to 20 cm, along the seashore. The leaves are roasted and then drunk as a cure for coughs.

**namiel** *noun* rust.

**nam̃ilo** *noun* dirt.

**namir** *noun* tree sp., black burao of the sea, used for spear wood, especially good because the wood is strong but floats. (*Cordia subcordata*).

**namir ni euut** *noun* tree sp., used to be used to make candles as it has a natural type of kerosene. The fruit can be used for dancing rattles.

**namkalkal** *noun* **1)** itch. **2)** scabies. *cf:* mkalkal.

**namkanr** *noun* plant sp., grows quickly, takes firm hold, but dies soon after. Grows to about 1 metre, like a weed, and is also known as wild arrowroot. It is the name of one of the clans or *naflak.* It is a food eaten after a cyclone has damaged all other food. Two kinds, red and white. The red one has no leaves and produces a bad-smelling flower.

**namlaanri** *noun* cold. *cf:* mlaanr.

**nam̃lak** *noun* dregs, small amount of drink left in a glass.

**nam̃lalop** *noun* bamboo sp. *cf:* loop.

**namlame** *noun* dew.

**namlas** *noun* an area of bush that has been used as a garden in the past, unlike *m̃p̃akus* which was not used as a garden. *Go malnen ru pak Erakor ga i pi namlas tu.* And when they went to Erakor it was bush. *cf:* m̃p̃akus, namlaskos.

**namlaskos** *noun* jungle, untouched forest. *cf:* namlas, m̃p̃akus.

**nam̃lat** *noun* tree sp., devil nettle, stinging nettle tree. (*Dendrocnide latifolia*).

**nam̃lee (nam̃leen)** *noun$_i$* **1)** place. *I p̃erik i mai lao na faat etan, go nam̃leen i to panpan tup̃ mees.* It flew and landed on the rock in the ground, and its place is there to this day. **2)** space, plenty of room.

**nam̃leenatu (nam̃leenatuen)** *noun$_i$* footprint.

**namles** *noun* plant sp., eaten in laplap, has white flowers. There are white (*taar*), red (*miel*) and green (*ksakes*) varieties. (*Graptophyllum spp.*).

**namlun (namlur)** *noun*$_i$ skin; hide (of animals).

**nam̃nam̃** *noun* grass.

**nam̃ol (nam̃olin)** *noun*$_i$ body. *Komam u weswes ki naar mam, u farfar ki nam̃ol mam, raki nawesien p̃afp̃of laap.* We worked with our hands, we moved our bodies, doing lots of hard work.

**nam̃ol nasum̃** *noun* body/outside of a house.

**nam̃olien** *noun* life. *Go taos nanre nigmam tiawi u kano piatlak mane nlaken nam̃olien ni mees i kerkerai.* And as for us old people we can't have much money because life today is hard.

**namook** *noun* tree sp., octopus tree, used for making canoes, paddles, carving (**fols tabako**). The wood is prized for its colour. The fruit is eaten raw. (*Heliotropium foertherianum*).

**namoos** *noun* ocean. *Ku lelua faat p̃ur nen ku pan lelua teflan pan pa raru gaag kai pak namoos pan.* You avoid the big rock, you avoid it when you paddle your canoe and go to the ocean. *cf:* elau, ntas.

**nam̃or** *noun* hole. *Nam̃or katnaam i to elag Ep̃or.* The mosquito hole is at Ep̃or.

**nam̃oru** *noun* deep sea. *Tete nasum̃ nlag i sati tut kin nam̃oru.* The wind took some houses and submerged them in the deep sea. *cf:* etan, paketan.

**nam̃os** *noun* tree sp., used to make the outrigger (*nsem*) and the cross-members (*nakiat*) of a canoe. The leaves can be used to stop diarrhoea. (*Macaranga megacarpa*).

**namram (namrem)** *noun* **1)** clarity. **2)** brightness, shining light. *cf:* mram.

**namrer** *noun* charcoal, coal.

**namroan** *noun* thinking. *Namroan nen kin u piatlaken malpei kin u mal ki independent, u mro ki na i sa me mees u po pam̃ori na i wi.* Before independence we thought it would be no good, but today we find it is okay.

**nam̃rom (nam̃romin)** *noun*$_i$ new leaf growth.

**namrun** *noun* something; *namrun p̃rakot* 'anything, any type of rubbish'. *P̃a fak ektem mal sees me kaonsil ko fo til tete namrun.* You go outside for a while and Council will have something to say. *P̃a tap tkali mau i pi namrun p̃rakot, p̃a lekor.* Don't touch it, it's rubbish, you look out!

**namsaki** *noun* sickness. *Nlaken nafitiawian totur namsaki nlaken neu me a po to su nmarom̃iit.* Because of old age caused by sickness, that's why I have asthma.

**namta** *noun* end of reef, where it becomes the open sea.

**namtagot** *noun* tree sp. (*Elattostachys falcata*).

**namtame** *noun* crab (general term).

**namtamiel** *noun* tree sp., the wood is used to make the frame of a thatch house.

**nam̃tam̃ot** *noun* **1)** dust, sawdust. **2)** dust on the spear of the coconut palm, *nam̃tam̃ot ni naniu* 'pollen from coconut'. **3)** rubbish. *cf:* nalo.

**namtampei** *noun* thatch, usually sewn up from sago (*rowat*) leaves, one row of thatch.

**namtau** *noun* anchor. *Selwan a na ka tkau a tut ki namtau i pu sok raru go a po tkau.* When I want to fish, I throw in the anchor to hold the canoe, then I start to fish. *cf:* torwak.

**namtenmatun** *noun* burden

**namtenwen** *noun* weight. *cf:* mten.

**namtirwen** *noun* writing. *cf:* mtir.

**namtlel (namtlen)** *noun* piece of something, section, as found in fruit, e.g., a pawpaw which has five sections, or the sections of an orange.

**namtun** *noun* tree sp. (*Cerbera odollam*).

**namuenmokur** *noun* tide, small tide. *cf:* mu.

**namuentau** *noun* tide, king tide.

**namuurien** *noun* desire, wanting something. *I preg namuurien ga i pregsa ki sernale ni em̃rom go maarik nen ki nrogtesa ki.* It [a pig] did what it wanted to and spoiled everything inside [the house] and the man felt bad about it.

**nan (nanin)** *noun$_i$* child. *cf:* tausees, teesa.

**nana** *interjection* 'thingamy', used as a filler when you can't think of the right word. *Ru pan psi nana, raru gar.* They put it in the thingamy, their canoe. *cf:* sap, sua.

**naniu** *noun* coconut, name of the tree and the fruit. (*Cocos nucifera*).

**naniu** *noun* dolphin. (*Delphinidae*).

**nanom** *adverb* yesterday. *Kia nanom na, i tli na ke fo mai kotfaan, mees.* And yesterday he said that he would come in the afternoon today.

**nanr** *noun* fish spp., needlefish, halfbeaks. (*Belonidae, Hemiramphidae*). *cf:* p̃agp̃ag.

**nanra** *noun* banana sp., where the hand of fruit stands up straight rather than hanging down.

**nanratwen** *noun* pardon.

**nanrau namet (nanrau namten)** *noun$_i$* eyelashes.

**nanre** *noun* side; *nanre ni maur* 'left side', *nanre ni matu* 'right side'. *Ru po tan kin nanre, nanre nasum̃ gar.* They would bury him by the side of their house.

**nanre nafenr (nanre nafenrin)** *noun$_i$* spouse, wife or husband

**nanre wes** *preposition* beside.

**nanrepnrep** *noun* cloth used to wrap oneself in, lavalava. *Nmatu ru piatlak nkal sees nen ru soso ki nanrepnrep ru ofa su po mer of nkal p̃ur.* Women have a small piece of material called a *nanrepnrep* which they wear under a bigger piece of clothing. *cf:* fiikot, nap̃lai, nasieg, nrepnrep, pisp̃lolo.

**nanreu** *noun* bones, fish bones, bones of small animals, like snakes.

**nanrm̃a** *noun* tree sp., its wood is used for rough house posts. It has poisonous wood, and smoke from its fire is an irritant. Used as a medicine for asthma. Used to make paddles. Has exposed buttressed roots. (*Pipturus argenteus*).

**nanrm̃anipun** *noun* tree sp., good wood for making the outrigger of a canoe (*nakiat*).

**nanrmem** *noun* ripe banana. *cf:* furaru.

**nanrmem pot** *noun* banana sp., the skin is easy to peel.

**nanrmem swit** *noun* banana sp.

**nanrognrogon** *noun* news.

**nanrogtesan** *noun* bad news, hardships. *Nkal nigmam ru map̃rap̃or, u slat nanrogtesan i toop.* Our clothes were ripped, we had too many hardships. *cf:* nrogtesa.

**nanromien** *noun* **1)** gift, present. *I wi i nrom, i nrom ser natam̃ool, me malen kin naat i skei i maet ki aslen, me i pan tua tete nanromien ga ke fo pregi.* She (the natopu) is good, she loves all people, but when a man is angry with his friend, he will give her a present and she will do something (to hurt his friend). **2)** feeling of love. *cf:* nrom.

**nanrum̃ (nanrum̃en)** *noun$_i$* chest.

**nanrup̃** *noun* plantation; *nanrup̃ naniu* 'coconut plantation'. *cf:* naroi.

**nanrur** *noun* earthquake. *Ku na p̃a tarup̃ nlaken welkia nanrur i teflan ki ag iteflan.* You feel like falling over because the earthquake is like that. *cf:* nrur.

**nanrwor** *noun* banana sp., a long banana with skin that is hard to peel, you have to twist the skin to get to the banana.

**nanrwor** *noun* yolk, egg yolk.

**nanu** *noun* pearl, bead.

**nanu (nanuen)** *noun$_i$* neck. *P̃a mai totan nanuak, me kineu ka fo pan nrookot.* Come and sit on my neck and I will go across.

**nanumtap̃es** *noun* cane sp., 'wild sugarcane'. (*Miscanthus sinensis*).

**nanwei** *noun* **1)** man. *Me nanwei ga ke fo pak etalm̃aat, i slat nafnag i p̃aunamru ke mai psi esum̃, me nmatu kin ke fo preg nafnag.* The man would go to the garden, get food, carry it and put it in the house, but the woman prepares the food. **2)** male. *Go malfane, tem teesa nanwei ga ke fo pak esum̃ ni tem teesa nmatu.* And now, the father of this boy would go to the house of the girl's father. *cf:* kano.

**nao** *noun* wave. *Ntas i mu, welkia tasuur nen ru mai pan, nafet nao p̃afp̃of ru mai pak euut pa.* The tide was high, and the tidal waves came, lots of big waves came ashore there.

**naor** *noun* place. *P̃a mai p̃atlas kineu naor p̃rakot m̃as.* You come and meet me any place.

**naor m̃al** *noun* clearing, a cleared piece of ground.

**naot** *noun* **1)** chief. *Natam̃ool ne ki pei selwan u pa paakor natkon u lek naot ni Lefenpis i tarp̃ek to esum̃ nega to.* This man led us when we found the village and saw the chief of Lefenpis had fallen in his house. **2)** boss. **3)** captain. **4)** leader. *cf:* nafinaotan.

**nap (napun)** *noun$_i$* cheek.

**nap̃aap̃ak** *noun* banana sp., not used to make laplap, you have to boil it to eat it. *cf:* niuslan.

**nap̃ak** *noun* tree sp., with hard nut seeds.

**nap̃e** *noun* slit-gong, drum made from a tree trunk.

**napeel** *noun* fish sp., sardine. (*Clupeidae*).

**napeenr** *noun* **1)** arrowroot, the plant that was collected and then used by the missionaries to raise funds for printing translations of Christian materials ('Polynesian arrowroot'). (*Tacca leontopetaloides*). **2)** manioc starch. Grate the manioc and then squeeze the water from the manioc and leave it to dry, mix it with coconut milk and put a hot stone into it. It is like a jelly.

**nap̃eiluk** *noun* puddle of water left at low tide.

**nap̃el** *noun* yam sp., metre long (or more), white yam, pink flesh.

**nap̃el (nap̃len)** *noun$_i$* belly. *Nap̃len i ptin.* His belly is sore.

**nap̃elgan** *noun* page of a book.

**napelial** *noun* fish sp., a flat type of sardine, Indo-Pacific tarpon. (*Megalops cyprinoides*).

**napelpel** *noun* fish sp., sardine, very small. They jump when chased by a *kaitao* (karong).

**napelp̃ures** *noun* fish sp., sardine, round, like a finger.

**napeltan** *noun* fish sp., sardine, very small.

**naper** *noun* side; *naper ntaaf* 'side of a hill'.

**nap̃esp̃es** *noun* foam in the mouth of someone, e.g., when they are having a fit.

**napiau** *noun* swell, surge in the sea.

**napil** *noun* lightning.

**napirket (napirketin)** *noun$_i$* stalk of coconut. Part of a coconut tree that holds the coconuts. It can be used as a rake.

**napis (napsin)** *noun$_i$* bottom, rear end of person, anus. *P̃a ta tkal napsim mau.* Don't touch your anus.

**nap̃kal** *noun* hibiscus sp. (*Hibiscus rosa-sinensis*).

**nap̃kas (nap̃kasin)** *noun$_i$* meat; *nap̃kas waak* 'pork'.

**napkor** *noun* bush nut tree, longer than *nafil.* There is also a red one (*napkor miel*). (*Barringtonia procera*).

**napkun** *noun* knot (in wood).

**nap̃laepako** *noun* sea cucumber which is long and has an anemone-like end, a long black sea cucumber. (*Holothuria leucospilota*). *cf:* litot.

**nap̃lai** *noun* belt, made of hibiscus bark or similar material, traditionally worn by both men and women, but women hung a skirt (*nasieg*) as a pubic covering from the *nap̃lai*. *cf:* fiikot, nanrepnrep, nasieg, nrepnrep, pisp̃lolo.

**nap̃laso** *noun* tree sp., puzzle-nut. (*Xylocarpus granatum*).

**nap̃lau (nap̃laun)** *noun$_i$* inside something, e.g., undergound, underwater.

**nap̃lau nkas** *noun* heartwood of tree.

**naplel** *noun* tree sp., hibiscus. (*Hibiscus tilaceus*).

**naplip** *noun* fig variety, the bud and fruit is good to eat. Its green leaf tips are eaten, and the fruit used to be eaten but not anymore and is used as pig food. The wood is used for digging sticks. It can make a medicine which makes you stronger. (*Ficus granatum*).

**nap̃o** *noun* smell, the smell of something. *cf:* p̃o.

**nap̃oi** *noun* tree sp., blackbean. Note: big seed pods. (*Castanospermum australe*).

**nap̃ooi** *noun* yam, a strong yam.

**napor** *noun* basket, made from weaving coconut leaf, for carrying crops. *cf:* fuelig, likat, nroog, tasaal.

**napos** *noun* pudding made of roast breadfruit, pounded with coconut milk. *cf:* woi.

**napot (napton)** *noun$_i$* navel, belly button.

**nap̃raat** *noun* **1)** the wood inside a hibiscus branch after you have taken the bark off it to make into string. **2)** corncob, the part of the corn left behind after the seeds are eaten.

**nap̃rai** *noun* sugarcane variety called *kramp̃og,* has stripes of purplish colour. *cf:* makol, nafakton, naus, traares, tumel.

**nap̃rairei** *noun* cane variety where wild ducks make their nests.

**nap̃rairei** *noun* tree sp., grows in the sea or by the river like a mangrove.

**nap̃raksa (nap̃raksaan)** *noun$_i$* gill of fish.

**nap̃re** *noun* dream. *Ku to lek nap̃re.* You are dreaming.

**napri** *noun* tree sp., large tree, good timber.

**naptam** *noun* breadfruit sp., burn the dry leaves to keep mosquitoes away. (*Atocarpus altilis*). *cf:* kanotaar, loof, naliu, naptamkos, naptamkuut, nateeman.

**naptamkos** *noun* breadfruit sp., strong type of breadfruit that can be cooked quickly. *cf:* naptam.

**naptamkuut** *noun* breadfruit sp., strong type of breadfruit that can be cooked quickly. *cf:* naptam.

**napu** *noun* road. *Me i ta pi napu ni natam̃ool taos napu ni loto mau.* But it wasn't a man-made road like a road for cars.

**napu (napuen)** *noun$_i$* tail (of an animal). *I pul kusu ki go, gawankin nlap̃ wiit, kilfot wan ki napu kusu to.* It slung the rat with it, and that's the octopus's ninth tentacle, that he made into the rat's tail.

**napu toraan** *noun* fork in the road.

**napuk** *noun* tree sp., canoe tree, used for making the hull of canoes. (*Gyrocarpus americanus*). *cf:* m̃eem̃.

**napukm̃opul** *noun* tree sp., a soft wood, its sticky seeds are used to trap birds. The *mlau* 'incubator bird' lays its eggs in the rotten debris under this tree. (*Pisonia umbellifera*). *cf:* pul.

**napukror** *noun* tree sp., whitewood. (*Endospermum medullosum*).

**napuktau** *noun* tree sp., type of whitewood, used to make canoes. It has a white trunk. (*Endospermum spp.*).

**napum̃** *noun* fish sp. (*Scombridae spp.*).

**napum̃** *noun ntuam,* devil that lives in the bush and has the form of a fish.

**napum̃ m̃nam̃on** *noun* fish sp., yellowtail tuna or skipjack.

**napum̃ ni faat** *noun* fish sp., fusiliers. (*Caesionidae*).

**napum̃ ni nam̃oru** *noun* green fish sp.

**napum̃ ni nskau** *noun* red fish sp., that lives on the reef.

**nap̃umaas** *noun* property, estate left behind by someone who has died, but not including their house or their land, which is called *naftuan*.

**napum̃alom** *noun* tree sp., *handel wud*, the bark was once used to make barkcloth. The fruit is not eaten by people. (Barkcloth was also made from *narkamet, natret, nmariu.*) (*Mimusops elengi*).

**napupuus** *noun* flower on the plant *nakpes*.

**nap̃ures** *noun* fish sp., milkfish. (*Chanos chanos*).

**napus** *noun* wart.

**nap̃ut (nap̃utwen)** *noun*$_i$ knee. *Nap̃utwok i kano paakor nkal neu ke mas pram pak esa.* My knee couldn't show, my clothes had to be long down to here.

**nareo** *noun* tree sp., like a *mpak* 'banyan', but smaller. The latex from the fruit is used to make cricket balls. A soft wood. (*Homolanthus nutans*).

**narfaat** *noun* **1)** rocks heaped up by people. **2)** bridge. *Me ag ku kano pak narfaat. I tap nen p̃a fa.* But you can't go to the bridge. It is taboo that you go there. *cf:* np̃arfaat.

**nariuriu** *noun* seagrass.

**narka** *noun* tree sp., 'false coffee', strong wood, firewood, also used for making a *kal* or digging stick. It has a sweet smelling flower that is either white or yellow. (*Pavetta opulina*).

**narkamet** *noun* tree sp., its bark was used to make barkcloth.

**naro** *noun* **1)** offering made to pay for something, e.g., to pay for something you have done wrong (*naro sup̃tap*). **2)** bride price, paid by a man to the family of his prospective wife in order to marry her.

**naroi** *noun* plot, allotment of land. *Ku tap̃op̃tai nmakot seserik ko naroi seserik.* You divide the small boundary to make a small plot. *cf:* nanrup̃, nmakot.

**narom** *noun* beam holding a cross-member (*nsol*) that holds the roof of a house.

**naromet (naromten)** *noun*$_i$ tears.

**naror** *noun* something that smells good.

**narup̃** *noun* chief's wives, a group of women of whom one is the head (*np̃au narup̃*), who will bear the chief's successor.

**naruut** *noun* fern, use the root to prepare a cure for dysentery.

**narwarof** *noun* tree sp., a big tree used for firewood, and for paddles.

**nasap̃** *noun* foreigner, stranger to this country. *Erakor teetwei ga i kerkerai na, nafet nasap̃, ruk taulu nam̃er ni ena, ru plak mai pak Erakor, i kerkerai.* Erakor, long ago, it (the custom) was hard, if some foreigners married women from somewhere, they (had to) came back to Erakor, it was hard.

**nasei** *noun* plant sp. (*massing* in Bislama). (*Euodia hortensis*).

**naselslam** *noun* tree sp., peanut tree (*nawaswas* in Bislama), seeds of fruit are roasted and eaten. (*Sterculia tannaensis, S. vitiensis*).

**naser (naserin)** *noun$_i$* **1)** root, taproot, sucker. **2)** bud.

**nasi (nasin)** *noun$_i$* smell, unpleasant smell. *cf:* ntae.

**nasieg** *noun* skirt, piece of bark material traditionally used by women to hang off a belt (*nap̃lai*) as a pubic covering. Men traditionally wore a *nafon*. *cf:* fiikot, nanrepnrep, nap̃lai, nrepnrep, pisp̃lolo.

**nasiin** *noun* bushfire.

**nasinrwen** *noun* shit, runny shit.

**nasitafra** *noun* rock, like pumice (lit: whale shit).

**naskeimielwen** *noun* power, to be powerful. *cf:* sup̃.

**naslag (naslagin)** *noun$_i$* banana rings, a banana bunch cut up into sections, making rings of bananas.

**nasnaki** *noun* fibre dye, dye for pandanus leaves.

**nasok (naskon)** *noun$_i$* skin (of animal or plant); *nasok nawi* 'skin of a yam'. *cf:* nakul.

**nasok nkas** *noun* bark. *Ku tae preg nkal ki nasok nkas.* You can make clothes out of tree bark.

**nasoksok (nasok)** *noun* rubbish, mess.

**nason** *noun* fish sp., silver pompano, good to eat. (*Trachinotus blochii*).

**nason** *noun* sores around the mouth, cold sores. Kids have them and are given castor oil as a cure.

**nasralesokwen** *noun* trust. *cf:* sralesok.

**nasraletuaan** *noun* confession.

**nasu** *noun* roof, and roof beam of house. *cf:* surnaot.

**nasu** *noun* tree sp., a big tree (some are at Ekasiik), now logged, it has brown bark and wood, like a natapoa.

**nasu (nasun)** *noun$_i$* juice of anything. Also a soup is called *nasun*.

**nasukefik** *noun* tree sp., the fruit is white, pink and red. (*Syzygium richii*).

**nasul** *noun* **1)** wild cane or speargrass used to build things, also used as a torch. When processed for making arrows it is called *ftok*. (*Centotheca lappacea*). **2)** light, lamp.

**nasuloop** *noun* grass, speargrass.

**nasum̃** *noun* house. *Go san kin hotel i po to i pitlak nasum̃ i skei i tu wes, family i skei ru tkos.* And where the hotel would be, there was a house that was there, a family were there. *cf:* sum̃.

**nasum̃ malik** *noun* cell.

**nasum̃ namsaki** *noun* hospital, more usually called 'ospital'.

**nasum̃ ni faat** *noun* bank.

**nasum̃ ni pi** *noun* beehive. *Nasum̃ ni pi i kaakas wi.* A beehive is sweet.

**nasum̃tap** *noun* church.
**nasusu** *noun* froth on the sea that indicates a turn of the tide.
**nasusu** *noun* liquid that comes out of a sore (not pus). *cf:* naup̃o.
**naswaf** *noun* tree sp., poisonwood, children use it to make slingshots because the branches grow in the right shape. It has sweet-smelling white flowers.
**nat** *noun* tree sp., it has a nut inside the fruit that is only eaten by flying foxes. Its wood can be used to make paddles. (*Terminalia sepicona*).
**natam̃ool** *noun* person. *Fakalomara ga i pi natam̃ool ni Samoa.* Fakalomara was a person from Samoa. *cf:* naat, nam̃er.
**natam̃ool lot** *noun* Christian.
**natam̃ool psir** *noun* liar.
**natatik** *noun* childlike adult, developmentally delayed.
**natatok** *noun* citizen, native. *Natatok ga i welkia, pati ni Erakor, nam̃er ni naor.* The 'natatok' was a (political) party from Erakor, people of that place.
**nateeman** *noun* breadfruit sp., a strong type of breadfruit that can be cooked quickly. *cf:* naptam.
**nateen** *noun* flat country.
**nati (natien)** *noun$_i$* **1)** saliva. **2)** sap of a tree. *cf:* natoo.
**natiel** *noun* vine, St Thomas bean, a plant with large disk-shaped seeds which are made into necklaces. Used for temporary binding, but the vine milk causes burning on skin. It looks like a snake. It is said that if you cut it you will die. *I piatlak natiel i skei, natiel p̃ur a leka ki namtak.* There is a vine, a big vine, I've seen it with my own eyes. (*Entada phaseoloides*).
**natik (natkin)** *noun$_i$* edge, side; *natik naum̃* 'riverbank'. *Selwan i pan panpan i siwer panpanpan i na i tkal natik erfale.* He went on until he walked to the edge of a cave. *Teesa ni mees, u tap lek esan kin Litrapog i tkos mau, me kineu a leka ki namtak, go a silwes, a pan to natkin.* Children of today, you don't see the place where Litrapong stayed, but I saw it with my own eyes, and I went in there, I stayed on the edge of it. *cf:* etik.
**natilsoksokwen (natilsoksokien)** *noun* promise, commandment. *cf:* tilsoksok.
**natir** *noun* **1)** mast of sailing canoe. **2)** tower (as in a radio communication tower).
**natkul** *noun* tree covered in vines.
**natlag** *noun* tree sp., good timber.
**natog** *noun* mangrove (general term); *natog pram* grows tall; *natog m̃it* has shorter leaves; *natog ni euut* grows on the shore away from the water. This is also the name of its seedpod that floats all over the place until it settles in one place.
**natokon (natkon)** *noun* village. *Ru pi natopu me ru tae nam̃er, ru laap tae natam̃ool ni natkon, lekor pta ki natam̃ool.* They are natopu 'spirits' but they know people, they know the people of the village, look after the people.

**naton (natonkas)** *noun* **1)** ashes. *San ku preg nkap wes sernaliati naton i laap wes.* The place where you make fire every day is full of ashes. **2)** limestone that has been burned to make into cement.

**natonifaat** *noun* cement.

**natoo** *noun* invitation to bring food or something else to an event.

**natoo (natoon)** *noun$_i$* sap (of tree), sometimes the sap can be used as a glue (*tepulsok*). Tree sap can stain your clothes. *cf:* nati.

**natoop̃** *noun* yam sp., white, bottle-shaped yam, also the name of a clan or *naflak*.

**natopu** *noun* spirit, a permanent animist presence at a place. This spirit may be an ancestor or a creature from 'before'. Usually called by the respectful terms *Maarik* (for a male *natopu*) or *Mtulep* (for a female *natopu*). Some names of such spirits include P̃umakot, Apu ni ntaf, Liportani, Katapeel. *Natopu nigmam ni esa, ga kin i to, i to i to pan, i to teetwei paakor mees.* The natopu 'spirit' from this place, he is the one who is there, who has been there from long ago until today. *cf:* maarik, mtulep, naatap.

**nator** *noun* hardwood.

**natot** *noun* tree sp. (*natoto* in Bislama), use the milk from the leaves if your skin is scraped by a stingray or stonefish, for example. (*Excoecaria agalocha*).

**natp̃olnra** *noun* plant sp., shrub with lower leaves that are green, higher leaves that are red. The leaf is fed to sows to help them get pregnant.

**natp̃opis** *noun* tree sp., sweet leaf, used for medicine, good for the blood.

**natran** *noun* twin.

**natrauswen** *noun* story. *Go i pi esuan natrauswen ki nom wes.* And that's where the story finishes.

**natret** *noun* tree sp., grows on the shoreline, good firewood and used for making hitting clubs and handles of tools. The bark was once used to make barkcloth.

**natu** *noun* tree sp., small, the wood can be used for handles of axes, it has small leaves.

**natu** *noun* poisonous vine for poisoning fish. Crush the stem and throw it in a pool to stun (*pun*) the fish. The vine can also be used for tying things.

**natu (natuen)** *noun$_i$* foot, leg. *Malen i kam leeg ki nfal ni nmakou go nmakou i puetsok natuen, i katsok natuen. Me malfane i kano puetlu natuen.* When it walked right on the lobster's hole, the lobster grabbed its legs, it held them. But now it couldn't pull its leg out.

**natuer** *noun* grass, a type of grass that is like short elephant grass.

**natuetu** *noun* tree sp., a tree that used to grow very tall in the bush but is no longer found.

**natumau** *noun* **1)** yam, strong yam. **2)** constellation of stars, no longer known which stars.

**natunr (natunron, natnron)** *noun$_i$* nape of neck.

**natuotu** *noun* choppy sea that is still able to be navigated by a canoe and so is not too rough.

**naturiai** *noun* lad, young man, unmarried man. *Ru pi naturiai, ru pe pi young children e, me, ru mat.* They were young people, they were young children, but they died. *cf:* nmatuerik.

**naturm̃os** *noun* raindrop, e.g., leak in the roof.

**naturwotu** *noun* soft wood, no good for anything.

**natus** *noun* book, text, paper; (*na*) *tus ni telumlum, nalumlumwen* 'album'. *cf:* tustap.

**natuut** *noun* appointment (lit: a time to *tuut* 'tie' together). *Ku npa ki natuut / ku preg natuut.* You make an appointment. *cf:* tuut, npa.

**nau** *noun* inside of the mouth.

**nau** *noun* **1)** pan flute. **2)** mouth organ.

**naul** *noun* **1)** credit, account, money borrowed to pay for goods. **2)** bribe, money paid to someone to get them to do something that is illegal or not entirely correct.

**naul** *noun* **1)** leaf; *naul nanr* 'banana leaf'. *Ru pau naul naniu i pi napor go ru po paai naot negar wes.* They wove coconut leaves into a basket and they put the chief into it. **2)** page, piece of paper.

**naul nmariu** *noun* crescent moon (lit: 'leaf of nmariu', which has a crescent-shaped leaf).

**naulalas** *noun* small bush, used to eat mixed with animal blood, pig's guts. (*Polyscias spp.*).

**naulum̃** *noun* pillow. *cf:* p̃aulum̃.

**naulum̃ ni afsak** *noun* starfish like a pillow (lit: turtle's pillow).

**naum** *noun* fish sp., humpnose unicornfish. (*Naso tuberosus*). *cf:* raeru, uus.

**naum̃** *noun* river. *cf:* naiser.

**naun** *noun* husk of a coconut when it is prepared to be used as a strainer for coconut milk.

**naunau** *verb*$_a$ grate the skin (of roasted yams and taro).

**naup̃ (naup̃en)** *noun*$_i$ the feeling of missing someone, weak feeling due to the absence of a friend. *Nametrau ru nrog naup̃ Endis.* The family misses Endis.

**naup̃o** *noun* pus, liquid that comes out of sores. *cf:* nasusu.

**naur** *noun* island. *Go ru pan go ru po taasai naur sees nen ru lao ki nasum̃.* And they went and would clear the small island so that they could build houses. *cf:* naurour.

**naur (nauren)** *noun*$_i$ top of tree or plant.

**naures** *noun* grater made by cleaning some coconut shell and wrapping it with wild cane. *cf:* fatma.

**naurour** *noun* islands. *cf:* naur.

**naus** *noun* wild cane, there are two varieties: freshwater and saltwater. *cf:* ftok, makol, nafakton, nap̃rai, traares.

**naustap** *noun* spear tip that has magic properties. Made from wild cane that has been sung over to make it work. Also made from the bones of special people (chiefs or those of *naflak nmal*). Even the slightest scratch from these bones will kill. *cf:* nm̃aal.

**naut puluk** *noun* a dried bullock's penis used as a cudgel.

**nawatlakien** *noun* celebration of a wedding.

**naweel** *noun* creeper with large leaves, used to feed pigs. The vine is strong and can be used to tie wood for housing. (*Gunnera macrophylla, Epipremnum pinnatum*).

**naweel ni namlas** *noun* fern sp. (*Phymatosorus grossus, Pyrrosia lanceolata*).

**nawelwel** *noun* clothes, hand-me-down clothes.

**nawen** *noun* sand. *Kusu i leka na i tae sok pak nmal nawen.* The rat saw that it could jump into the middle of the sand.

**nawes** *noun* paddle. *Selwan p̃a falus pan p̃a leka af sik naruk p̃a tao nawes me natus ruk maui pak ntas pan.* When you have paddled (out), you'll see me raise my hand, you put down your paddle then throw all the paper into the water.

**nawesien** *noun* work. *Mal sees, kineu a preg tete nawesien, ni na konstraksen.* For a little while, I did some work in construction. *cf:* weswes.

**naweskin kaaru** *noun* west.

**naweskin kaatol** *noun* north.

**naweskin kafaat** *noun* south.

**naweskin pei** *noun* east.

**nawi** *noun* yam sp., also general term for all yams. *Nawi kosu* is a strong type of yam. A bundle of yams is called a *tafra* 'whale', and when whales swim around close to shore you know yams are ready. You make a bundle of yams (*tafra nawi*) to take to a feast. Types of yams include: *afrika, martinique, toknimakil, tog, nayam, wailu, taalau, ros, ara, natop, nmal, natumau, sak, mpaisak, nap̃el, faalau, nam̃, fofile, nuwai, ntaul, tumas, nawim̃aat, ntentfa, naitarpes, rok, roktaar, rokmiel.* *cf:* nam, ntaul, ntelpou, toop̃.

**nawip̃o** *noun* rotten yam.

**nawip̃o** *noun* blotchy skin.

**nawool** *noun* bedding, also grave, 'place to lie in'. *cf:* wenr.

**nawoos** *noun* coconut, green, young (soft inside). *cf:* numotu.

**naworaan** *noun* family line, generations.

**ne** *demonstrative* this (close). *Go teesa nanwei gar ne ra soso ki Naleman.* And they called their son (this one we were just talking about) Naleman. *cf:* nen.

**neet** *verb$_i$* meet, go and meet. *Kineu a neet lek ag.* I went to see you. *Kineu ka fo neet.* I will go and meet you. *cf:* patlas, saisei, seltra.

**nega** *pronoun* **1)** he, she, it (3rd person singular subject or object). *Nega i taos naik nag ru soso ki map̃er.* He is like the fish they call map̃er. **2)** his, her, its (3rd person singular possessive). *Me i tao plak kapu nega me i po pami.* And he put them on his laplap and ate them. **3)** for him, for her, for it (3rd person singular benefactive). *A muurin na p̃a traem nega preg tete nalkes gaag, nen ag ku tae.*

I want you to try to make some medicine for him, as you know how to. *cf:* ga.

**negaag** *pronoun* **1)** your (2nd person singular possessive). *P̃a fan pa raru negaag mai sok kin eslaor Elaknatu.* You take your canoe and go to that place Elaknatu. **2)** for your benefit (2nd person singular benefactive). *cf:* gaag.

**negakit** *pronoun* **1)** our, belonging to you and us (1st person plural inclusive possessive). *A muurin nag ka gamus traus tete natrauswen nig tiawi negakit nig teetwei selwan Efat i malik.* I want to tell a story of our old people when Efate was in darkness. **2)** for us, for our benefit (1st person plural inclusive benefactive). *cf:* gakit.

**negamus** *pronoun* **1)** yours, belonging to you (2nd person plural possessive). **2)** for you, for your benefit (2nd person plural benefactive). *Raru nen ke fo to. Me matool pulp̃og me ka fo negamus sol suker mai.* The canoe will be there. And tomorrow morning then I will go and bring sugar for you. *cf:* gamus.

**negar** *pronoun* **1)** they, them (3rd person plural subject or object). *Negar ru taos mutwam, nalur i pram me if wel uf muurin u tae puetir mai nag akam ko lemsir.* They are like spirits, their hair is long but if we want we can get them so we can see them. **2)** their (3rd person plural possessive). *I lek natam̃ool kin ru to ur taon napu i toop go natam̃ool ru laap go napu negar i m̃alm̃al wi.* He saw people around town on the roads and many people, and their roads were clean. **3)** for them (3rd person plural benefactive). *Ntau 1956, komam ra mer tuer tete nanromien sees ru mer negar wesi.* The year 1956, we gave the small present again for them. *cf:* gar.

**nen** *demonstrative* that. *Go naur nra nen, me m̃aat i na i fisktofir.* And those two islands, this snake wanted to split them. *cf:* ne.

**nen** relativiser, used after a noun to introduce a relative clause. *Ser naliati nen ruk freg nsaiseiwen, mtulep Katapel i preg nafnag.* Every day that they had a meeting, Mrs Katapel made food.

**nen pa** *preposition* past, as in *ntau nen pa* 'last year'; *wik nen pa* 'last week'.

**nen tu** *preposition* next, as in *ntau nen tu* 'next year'; *wik nen tu* 'next week'.

**nep (npa)** *verb$_a$* throw, to throw a stone, to stone. *Ku nep ki naat.* You throw to the man. *A npa ki faat.* I throw a stone at it. *Malnen ku nep maan ku npalua go ru soso ki arleg.* When you throw a stone at a bird and you hit it, they say it is skilful.

**nepsok (nepsoki)** *verb$_a$* weigh down, place a weight on something to stop the wind blowing it away. *Selwan nlag i maaf ke silua ku* *nepsoki ki faat.* When the wind wants to blow everything, you put a rock on things to hold them down.

**nepsok** *verb$_i$* stay in the house of someone who recently died, to look after it and to keep a vigil.

**neu** *pronoun* **1)** I, me. *Me neu a kano kuk aliat.* But I can't cook in the daytime. **2)** my (1st person singular possessive). *Ka nrik naot kin me if wel kin af kop namuurien neu pan ruk fo wat kineu.* I would talk with the chief, but if I just followed my own way, they would hit me. **3)** for my benefit (1st person singular benefactive). *P̃a fo neu preg raru foum ke skei.* You will make a new canoe for me. *cf:* nigneu.

**nfa** *noun* plant, leaf used for wrapping laplap (*kapu*). Types include *nfamiel, nfapram, nfaliu, nfamil, nfa ni Epi. cf:* nrau.

**nfa** *noun* tree with wood that burns very well, used to carve idols (*natap*).

**nfaag** *noun* parable, story with deeper meanings. *cf:* faag.

**nfaakoton** *noun* payment, bribe, bride price. *cf:* paakot.

**nfaat** *noun* roof timbers that are under the thatch.

**nfaato** *noun* tree with fruit (*twin frut* in Bislama), two types, one round, one long. The wood is used to make canoe paddles and in making houses. The bark can be used as medicine for diabetes. (*Ochrosia elliptica*).

**nfag** *noun* sore, like a boil or similar sore on the skin. *cf:* fag, m̃tel.

**nfak** *noun* pandanus, a tall one with long leaves and big fruit. The fruit can be eaten without preparation. *cf:* naki, nparom.

**nfaketanwen** *noun* respect. *Teesa laap a muurin nrik mus kin na nfaketanwen i pi te wi.* Children, I want to tell you that respect is a good thing. *Nfaketanwen ki tiawi ko te pakelag.* Respect all old people and big men.

**nfal** *noun* hole. *Ra ta puel mau, me ra to, ra to faat, nfal i nru ra to faat, go ra m̃ool to panpan tup̃ mees.* They haven't left, they are there, they are in the rock, two holes in the rock, and they are still alive today.

**nfamwen** *noun* taste. *cf:* pam.

**nfan** *noun* tree with fragrant flowers. (*Guettarda speciosa*).

**nfar** *noun* navara, coconut, the nutty inside of sprouted coconut.

**nfas (nfaswen)** *noun$_i$* parts of something, e.g., all parts of the body, parts of a car.

**nfas namet (nfas nameten)** *noun$_i$* eyebrow.

**nfer (nferen)** *noun$_i$* handle, e.g., of spear, paddle. *Nfer ola nen i trau kerkrai wi.* This spear handle is very strong.

**ngas** *noun* when. *cf:* sefmal.

**ni** *preposition* of. *Ru preg tete kaku ni raru nen ru to nakpei ru pak nakoinrok Morinda.* They took some cargo from the front and put it at the back of the Morinda.

**nier** *noun* broom, e.g., made from the *tap̃ir* tree or from *nikniser*. *P̃a tau* *nier ka ser nasok.* Give me the broom, I'll sweep the rubbish.

**nies** *noun* bailer, canoe bailer.

**nigmam** *pronoun* **1)** our (1st person plural possessive) (inclusive and exclusive). *Apu me ati nigmam ru to nigmam trausi.* Our grandfathers and grandmothers would tell us. **2)** for us (1st person plural benefactive) (inclusive and exclusive). *cf:* mam, mom.

**nigneu** *pronoun* **1)** my, mine (1st person singular possessive). *If wel kuf lek tete nkas i ftom emat nigneu, p̃a tap m̃okus mau.* If you see a tree growing from my grave, don't pull it out. **2)** for me (1st person singular benefactive). *cf:* neu.

**niif** *noun* fan, usually made of coconut leaf. *P̃a tao niif ka fo niif nkap.* Give me the fan, I'll fan the fire.

**niif (nfe)** *verb*$_a$ fan, to fan.

**nikniser** *noun* coconut spathe, spine of a coconut leaf, commonly used to make brooms (*nier*).

**ninum̃** *verb* be barren (of a woman) (an old word not known today). An idiomatic expression used today to mean 'barren' is *nkas nmarteu* 'dry wood'.

**nipu** *noun* palm tree, the heart of palm is eaten. (*Veitchia spp.*).

**niuslan** *noun* banana sp. *cf:* nap̃aap̃ak.

**nkafik** *noun* tree sp., the fruit is white, pink and red (*nakavika* in Bislama). *Nkafik mil* is wild nakavika, smaller than *nkafik.* Make an infusion of the bark for medicine. (*Syzygium malaccense*).

**nkafik mil** *noun* tree sp., smaller than *nkafik.* (*Syzygium clusiaefolium*).

**nkafrag** *noun* scab, the crust that forms on the skin after a wound heals.

**nkal** *noun* **1)** cloth. **2)** clothes; *nkal ni namlanri* 'cardigan, jumper' (lit: clothes for the cold), *nkal ni nmatu* 'dress' (lit: woman's clothes). *cf:* kal.

**nkalwel** *verb*$_i$ change clothes, to dress as someone else (*nkalwel nanwei* 'to dress as a man').

**nkanr (nkanron)** *noun*$_i$ **1)** mouth. **2)** lips. *Kat p̃elp̃el ki nkanron.* Close one's lips (as when holding something in them).

**nkap** *noun* **1)** fire. *Ko fo mai ko fo pregi na, ko mer ler nkap, ko mai suekro.* We would go and make it, get firewood and smoke it. **2)** firewood. (*Idiom: 'You lose' [Bislama: faea i ded]. Putting out someone's fire, putting them down. S/he is a good-looking person, 'hot'.*)

**nkar (nkaren, gkaren)** *noun*$_i$ handle of basket.

**nkari** *noun* bush, red top leaves, cordyline. (*Cordyline fruticosa*).

**nkas** *noun* tree (general term), wood. *Malnen kin ku na ku msak go natam̃ool nen kin ke fo gaag preg naul nkas taos meresin.* When you feel you are getting sick, this man will make leaf medicine for you.

**nkas mel** *noun* tree sp., 'shade tree'.

**nkas ni aal** *noun* tree sp., wood used for paddles, and the sap is used as glue.

**nkas ni nap̃e** *noun* drum beater, stick used for hitting slit-gong drums.

**nkas slasol** *noun* posts holding up a house.

**nkasaap̃o (nkasaap̃on)** *noun$_i$* throat.

**nkasakien** *noun* seat, chair.

**nkaso** *noun* necklace, made of beads, seeds, or stones.

**nkasot** *noun* tree sp., blackbean. Note: it has a black strong heartwood. (*Diospyros sp.*)

**nkaspau** *noun* stake used for plants to grow up on.

**nkaspaulep** *noun* tree sp., used for firewood.

**nkaspeltakot** *noun* beam, crossbeam on the short end of a house. *cf:* raus, surnaot.

**nkasp̃o** *noun* tree sp., it has big fruit. Its wood is used as firewood. (*Dysoxylum gaudichaudianum*).

**nkau** *noun* croton, red low bush, used as cough medicine.

**nkaukofua** *noun* tree sp. (*Sterculia banksiana*).

**nkem** *noun* **1)** plant, like cane, used for making baskets and trays. (*Flagellaria indica*). **2)** tongs, made by bending a piece of wood, used for picking up cooking stones, made from the cane of the same name. **3)** constellation shaped like tongs, with Orion's belt the lower right side of the tongs.

**nkis** *interjection* hey! Term used to call out to get someone's attention.

**nkok** *noun* tree sp., Java cedar. (*Bischofia javanica*).

**nkraful** *noun* vine, nettle, which you brush by and only notice has stung you when you rub your skin or wash it. (*Dendrocnide spp.*). *cf:* gkar.

**nkur** *noun* **1)** rake, a small tree pulled up with roots which are used as a rake to level an oven before laplap is put in. **2)** constellation of stars in the shape of the rake of the same name (it is not clear which constellation they are).

**nlae (nlaen) 1)** *noun* shellfish sp., bicolor pen shell. (*Pinna bicolor*). **2)** *noun* sail, sail-like objects. **3)** *noun$_i$* fin of a fish.

**nlafkir** *noun* basket, made from pandanus leaf, a big version of *likat. cf:* nroog, polpol, sarpopot, sp̃ol, tip̃el.

**nlag** *noun* wind, air. *P̃og kin nlag nen i mai, ku lek naniu ru trau nomser pak ntan pa.* The night that the wind came, you could see coconuts all fell to the ground.

**nlag kerkrai** *noun* gale.

**nlag miel** *noun* hurricane, cyclone.

**nlag mlakes** *noun* wind that makes green leaves fall to the ground.

**nlag sumat** *noun* wind that blows when someone is dying.

**nlagwat** *noun* storm, cyclone. *Nlagwat i p̃urp̃ur nasum̃ neu.* The cyclone wrecked my house.

**nlak (nlaken)** *noun$_i$* trunk, stem (its). *Nlak mpak i piatlak ntwam i skei i to em̃rom nlak mpak.* There was a devil living in the trunk of the banyan.

**nlaken** *conjunction* because, the reason. *I preg namrun i sa nlaken i tap tae mau.* He did something bad because he didn't know. *A pan nlaken kin a na ka lek Silas.* I go because I want to see Silas.

**nlaketik** *noun* vine which grows around but you can't find its trunk. If you do find it, it is bad luck. It has green fruit. Headbands were made from it.

**nlaknait (nlaknaiten)** *noun*$_i$ ankle.

**nlakotao** *noun* vine which grows by the sea.

**nlakwen** *noun* wedding, marriage. *cf:* lak.

**nlap̃ (nlap̃en)** *noun*$_i$ tentacle, octopus arm.

**nlas** *noun* tree sp., largely avoided as a timber source due to its poisonous sap. It has spines that fly in the wind and cause itching if you pass near it. (*Semecarpus vitiensis*).

**nlas (nlason)** *noun*$_i$ genitals.

**nlas ni nmatu** *noun* vagina.

**nlasopuk natu (nlasopuk natuen)** *noun*$_i$ calf of leg.

**nlatlat** *noun* foam.

**nlaun** *noun* nation.

**nlauwen** *noun* dance. *cf:* lau.

**nlel** *noun* mud.

**nlik** *noun* **1)** snare. **2)** cord tied to a pig's foot.

**nlul** *noun* bundle of leaves.

**nma** *noun* black palm, used to tip arrows and make them poisonous. (*Blechnum gibbum, Cyathea lunulata*).

**nmaal** *noun* breadfruit sp., a type of breadfruit.

**nm̃aal** *noun* **1)** yam which grows with one leaf and has strong thorny roots. Sweet yam like a potato. **2)** one of the *naflak,* members of which are taboo and must be buried in a hidden place so that their bones cannot be found by accident. These bones are used as weapons as they have special powers for injuring the victim. *cf:* naustap.

**nmaat** *noun* low tide. *cf:* maat. (*Idiom: 'The tide is out.' 'The sea is dry.' This means that a person doesn't have any money.*)

**nmaatraar** *noun* lowest tide.

**nmae** *noun* string, twine.

**nmaeto** *noun* anger. *Selwan nmaeto i mai ku muur na p̃a wat naat.* When you get angry you want to hit someone.

**nmaf** *noun* fog.

**nmak** *noun* boil, a hot boil that has no head unless you put a special leaf on it to draw the head. *cf:* fati, nmanuk, p̃onfer.

**nmakot** *noun* **1)** border. **2)** boundary. *cf:* nakoi, naroi.

**nmal** *noun* tree, hog plum (*naus* in Bislama). Its fruit is eaten and the leaf can be used against ciguetera poisoning (*mam*). Place the leaf in the fish before cooking it. (*Spondias dulcis*).

**nmal (nmalon)** *noun*$_i$ **1)** middle. *Kusu i leka na i tae sook pak nmal nawen.* The rat saw that it could jump into the middle of the sand. **2)** waist, middle of the body.

**nmalfa** *noun* **1)** sky, space. **2)** something that doesn't touch the ground is said to be *nmalfa.*

**nmalko** *noun* **1)** dark, darkness. *Selwan kotfaan u lek ag go nmalko i toop, us i pees wo, go ntas i sa.* When it was afternoon, we saw you, and it grew dark, rain started and the sea was bad. **2)** cloud. *Go nmalko ki pe tok mai go maarik wan ki muurin nen kin ke fan sil pak erfale, me ke fo matur p̃og paakor pulp̃og ke fo mer us nalof waak p̃ur nen.* The clouds were moving in so the man wanted to go inside the cave, and then he would sleep the night until the morning when he would follow the tracks again. **3)** time before Christianity. *Ore i pi natrauswen ni nafkal mlaap ni nmalko me tuk fo i nrok pak namrem.*Okay, this is the story of the last battle of darkness and we would then go into the light. *cf:* malik.

**nmalko ni us** *noun* cloud, storm cloud.

**nmalmel** *noun* tree sp. (*namalaos* in Bislama), its wood is used for houses. Its small fruit is eaten by birds. (*Garuga floribunda*).

**nm̃alm̃ol** *noun* vine sp., a thick vine that has water that can be drunk.

**nmalnar (nmalnarun)** *noun$_i$* forearm.

**nmalnatu (nmalnatuen)** *noun$_i$* calf of leg.

**nmalnawen** *noun* beach. *Selwan ku muur p̃a nrog nlag natik ntas ku pan marmar nmalnawen.* When you want to feel the wind you can go and rest on the beach.

**nmalnkas** *noun* log of wood.

**nmalok** *noun* kava. *I to ntau laap, malpei nmalok i tiik, mal ni apap nigmam mana, nmalok ru ta ius ki nmalok teflan mau.* Before, there wasn't kava; in our parents' time, they didn't use kava like they do today. (*Piper methysticum*).

**nmanuk** *noun* boil, a small skin infection that causes a lump, usually with a head full of pus. *cf:* fati, nmak, p̃onfer.

**nmao (nmaon)** *noun$_i$* crotch, thigh.

**nmaono** *noun* sweat. *cf:* maon.

**nmaotao 1)** *preposition* between. *Kapu i to nmaotao akit.* The laplap is between us (you and me). *P̃a fo nmaotao kir.* You get between the two of them. **2)** *noun* gap in teeth.

**nm̃ap̃** *noun* tree sp., Tahitian chestnut, can be cooked on the fire, or boiled in water and is used in making laplap, and roasted and eaten. (*Inocarpus fagifer*).

**nm̃ap̃m̃ap̃** *noun* looking-glass tree, has fruit with a ridge along the top. Commonly found washed up on beaches. (*Heritiera littoralis*).

**nmar** *noun* vine sp., rosary pea, has red and black seeds. (*Abrus precatorius*).

**nmar (nmaron)** *noun$_i$* **1)** breath. *Me teetwei ga Erontp̃au naat i kano mes ki. Malen kin ag ku lek kori miel i mai pa, aal i ta ta mtar mau me nmarom ki pe nom.* And long ago, Rentapau, no one could play around with Rentapau. When you see the red dog coming by, the sun wouldn't have set but your breath would be your last (because of the taboo nature of Rentapau you would be dead). *Nmar menal ki pe to m̃it.* The barracuda's breath was getting short. **2)** puffed, out of wind.

**nmarit** *noun* rope, vine. *Ale ru kelkel ki nmarit go ru to kelkel me nao ito nrpagir.* So they held on to the rope, and they were holding it but the wave slapped them.

**nmarit (nmarten)** *noun$_i$* guts, intestines. *Tenag ru mat ru tfeir go ru pu nmarter i pan me ru pregi i kal ki nkal nega go ru pregi i ler pak nafanu nega pan.* They cut them and they pulled out their guts and they dressed them in their clothes and they took them back to their country.

**nmaritmat** *noun* vine sp., not useful, the sap can burn your eyes.

**nmaritpes** *noun* telephone (lit: talking rope).

**nmariu** *noun* tree sp., wattle tree, the smell of the leaves keeps flies away. Its bark was once used to make barkcloth. (*Acacia spirorbis*).

**nmariwenr** *noun* tree sp. (*Acacia simplex*).

**nmarom̃iit** *noun* asthma. *A ta tae naftekin i preg nmarom̃iit mau.* I don't know what caused the asthma. *cf:* mar.

**nm̃arteu** *noun* dry coconut. *Ke fan tm̃en lel nrau ke tm̃en lel nm̃arteu, nkap, mai pak esum̃ ke mer preg nafnag.* She goes herself to find laplap leaves, to look for dry coconuts, firewood, and comes back to the house to prepare the food. *cf:* numamkop.

**nmasel (nmaslen)** *noun$_i$* piece of something, piece of wood (*nmasel nkap*).

**nmaslesil** *noun* tree sp., its wood is used for spears.

**nmaten** *noun* death. *If pi nmaten, a mat kat kantri.* If it is death, I die for my country. *cf:* mat, naatmat.

**nmatu** *noun* **1)** female. *Go tekaaru nen i piatlak waak nmatu.* And the other one had a female pig. **2)** wife. *Ku neu lekor pta ki nmatu neu I sel teesa.* You will look after my wife, who is having a baby, for me. **3)** woman. *Tete nrak nanwei i nrom nmatu i leka nmatu i maos go nanwei i po welua.* Sometimes, if a man feels sorry for a woman, he will see she is tired and the man will help her.

**nmatu (nmatuen)** *noun$_i$* right side, its right side. *cf:* matu.

**nmatu lak** *noun* bride.

**nmatu ni napu** *noun* **1)** loose woman. **2)** sex worker.

**nmatuerik** *noun* young woman, virgin. *cf:* naturiai.

**nm̃au (nm̃aun)** *noun$_i$* feather.

**nm̃er** *noun* shellfish sp., strawberry conch. (*Strombus luhuanus*).

**nm̃of** *noun* fishing place, the usual place you can go to to find fish, or an octopus, for example.

**nmot** *noun* bundle of things.

**nmraksul** *noun* **1)** centipede. **2)** seaworm, a type of centipede-like seaworm.

**nognoog** *noun* senile, also someone suffering from dementia.

**nom 1)** *verb$_i$* finish. *Kui pe nom ko?* Have you finished? **2)** *auxiliary, adjective* everyone, all. *Ru nom to tm̃er plekir.* They were all arguing with each other.

**nomser** *adjective* every, all. *Ser natam̃ool ni Erakor ru nomser mtak ki natopu nen kin ru soso ki maarik.* Everyone from Erakor is scared of the natopu (spirit), which they call *'maarik'* (mister).

**noop** *noun* puddle of water.

**npa ki natuut** *verb* make an appointment. *Go rui npa ki natuut. "Mal teflan p̃a fo mai."* And they arranged to meet back again. "That is the time you will come." *cf:* tuut, natuut.

**npanep** *noun* **1)** rain sprinkled on the ground. **2)** group of fallen objects lying everywhere. *A pak talm̃aat nanom me a lek nm̃arteu ru trau npanep ur ntan pa.* I went to the garden yesterday and saw dry coconuts fallen on the ground.

**np̃arfaat (m̃p̃arfaat)** *noun* rock or boulder in the sea. *cf:* faat.

**nparom** *noun* pandanus sp., that lives near the sea, used as thatch and to make grass skirts. Varieties: *nparom wal, mil, ksakes, taar.* The fruit is eaten by flying foxes but not by people. *cf:* naki, nfak.

**npasil** *verb$_i$* **1)** knock away, using a stone or as in a ball knocking another away in petanque. *Malen kin ag p̃a fei pa, neu ka fei, kai nrok na ka npasil kik go tak fo pa.* When you go, I'll be first and then I'll knock you out of the way and we will go. **2)** stone, to throw stones.

**npat (npatin)** *noun$_i$* **1)** tooth. *Npatik i ptin.* My tooth is sore. **2)** horn, e.g., of cow. **3)** heart of pimple or boil. **4)** seed. **5)** claw. *cf:* patlep, patrik.

**np̃at** *noun* stick, hitting stick, club. *Tiawi nig teetwei ru to preg nafkal go ru to fisfis ki np̃at.* The old people used to have battles using hitting sticks.

**npatnkafik** *noun* Adam's apple.

**npatsfir** *noun* clitoris.

**npatsoru** *noun* broken teeth. *cf:* soru.

**npatwaak** *noun* tusk (pig's tooth).

**np̃au (np̃aun, mp̃aun, nap̃au)** *noun$_i$* **1)** head, the body part. *Go np̃au wiit ki mer tuul.* And the octopus's head kept swaying. **2)** the main part, the most important one. *Me san kin ru soso ki np̃au natkon ga kin Ekasufaat.* But the place they call the main village is Ekasufaat. **3)** leader, head of group, also *nap̃au;* most important, e.g., *np̃au narup̃* 'main wife', *np̃au natkon* 'main village'. **4)** top of something, e.g., a bow. *cf:* tp̃au.

**np̃au ntaaf** *noun* summit, top of hill.

**np̃auwaak** *noun* sign of leadership, to give the *np̃auwaak* 'pig's head' is like passing on the torch of leadership. *Ru ptu Ep̃ag ki np̃auwaak.* They gave Pango the 'pig's head' (meaning passing the torch to them for the next event).

**n̄pauwaak** *noun* shellfish sp., tuberose rock-shell. (*Thais bitubercularis*).

**n̄pet (n̄peten)** *noun$_i$* meaning.

**n̄pip̄** *noun* throwing wood, any small useful piece of wood, e.g., for throwing at fruit or flying foxes or other such uses. *cf:* p̄i, p̄ii.

**npoulaolag** *noun* pole, main pole of a house. Vertical pole that holds up the crossbeam (*surnaot*) at ceiling level, and the top roof beam (*nasu*). The beams (*narom*) that rest on the *npoulaolag* hold the cross-members (*nsol*) to which the roof is attached.

**nra** *noun* tree sp., false nutmeg. (*Myristica fatua*).

**nraa (nraan)** *noun$_i$* blood. *Nraa ki ser.* Blood goes around (the body). *Selwan ku tai natuom, nraa i tro.* When you cut your leg, it bleeds.

**nraap̄el** *noun* **1)** blood that is stuck inside a wound for a few days, 'rubbish blood' (of a human). **2)** clotted blood that is good to eat (of an animal's blood).

**nraasa** *noun* blood that comes out of a sore.

**nrae (nraen)** *noun$_i$* **1)** face. *Ke fo preg nanromien nen ke ur tete naor p̄tae. Me rekin kin komam ra trau tm̄om nrae ki komam, i pi namtakwen.* He will take his present around to different places (to hide the fact that he is giving it to me). But as for us giving it face to face, we were too scared. (*Idiom: Nraen go im̄aler to. Happy, be happy* (*Literally: His/her face is calm*).) **2)** forehead.

**nraenatu (nraenatuen)** *noun$_i$* shin, front of lower leg, tibia.

**nraf** *verb$_a$* weave (of weaving a fence), using, for example, wild cane (*ftok* or *naus*). *cf:* pau.

**nraf** *verb$_i$* bush bash, go through the bush where there is no track; *nrafkor* 'break through the bush holding your hands out to protect yourself'.

**nrafi** *verb$_i$* blow one's nose.

**nrafi (nrafien)** *noun$_i$* **1)** phlegm. **2)** snot.

**nrafkor** *verb$_i$* be ringed by, like a halo. *Atlag i nrafkor.* The moon is ringed (by a halo). *cf:* skakoor, tam̄as.

**nrag (nragi)** *verb$_a$* heat up.

**nrag (nragon)** *noun$_i$* claw.

**nraglaion** *noun* shellfish sp., cock's-comb oyster. (*Lopha cristagalli*).

**nragnrag** *noun* twigs.

**nraguti** *noun* plant sp., like a small tree fern, not eaten by Erakor people.

**nrak (nrakus)** *verb$_a$* take hot stones out of the fire using tongs.

**nrak** *noun* time, occasion (as in 'that time'). *Nrak i skei i piatlak apu go ati i skei ra tok.* Once there was a grandfather and grandmother. *I mer mai lek wou nrak kaaru, i mer mai nrak kaatol, go a trok.* She came and saw me a second time, and again a third time, and I agreed.

**nrak** *verb* take everything when going. *Ki pe nrak pa.* He took everything and went.

**nrakat (nrakati)** *verb*$_a$ lift up something heavy from underneath.

**nraknrak** *verb* prepare yourself to do something.

**nrakut (nrakuti)** *verb*$_a$ grab, e.g., an eagle grabbing its prey.

**nrali** *noun* plate.

**nrankas** *noun* **1)** branch. **2)** stick.

**nranru** *adjective* both. *I pu tefla nagis nranru nen kin ke pnut nai ke ta ser mau.* She pulled both points of land to try and stop the water from flowing. *cf:* nru.

**nraopet** *noun* tree sp., big shady tree with red fruit which is round and bigger than a nakatambol (*nrau*). Good timber.

**nrap** *noun* oily liquid in a germinated coconut.

**nrar** *noun* tree sp., African tulip, tree used to build the outrigger of a canoe. (*Erythrina variegata*).

**nras (nrasi)** *verb*$_a$ select, as in choosing the best among a group of things.

**nrat (nrati)** *verb*$_a$ forgive (also *nrat taap̃aar*). *I negaag nrat.* He forgives you.

**nrat (nrati)** *verb*$_a$ untie, release.

**nrau** *noun* tree sp., dragon plum, has yellow fruit, but the *nraupet* has red fruit. (*Dracontomelon vitiense*).

**nrau** *noun* leaf, used to wrap laplap for cooking underground in a stone oven. The old name was *nfa;* varieties include *nrauspun* and *nrauksakes*. (*Idiom: P̃rai nrau* 'break the *nrau* leaf' and *suer nrau* 'shit on the *nrau* leaf' both mean 'to marry too close within the family'.) (*Heliconia indica*). *cf:* nfa.

**nrau (nraun)** *noun*$_i$ edge of something, like a cliff.

**nrau (nraun)** *noun*$_i$ pubic hair.

**nre (nrea)** *verb*$_a$ turn. *I na i pak eluk sees, nen i nre faat.* He went to the small pool to turn the stone. *cf:* tare.

**nreapis** *verb*$_i$ somersault.

**nremet** *verb*$_i$ look from the side.

**nrepnrep** *verb*$_i$ wrap a piece of material around your waist, e.g., a *nanrepnrep*. *cf:* fiikot, nanrepnrep, nap̃lai, nasieg, pisp̃lolo.

**nrepnrpag (nrepnrpagi)** *verb*$_a$ pat, console, as when you put a child to sleep and pat them. *cf:* nrpag.

**nrernrer** *verb*$_i$ shine, like the sun or an angel. *cf:* paa.

**nres** *verb*$_i$ **1)** noise. *Pan ki pi teesa i nrus p̃ur, me i nrog ntas, kin i to nres elau.* Until he was a big boy, and he heard the noise of the sea. **2)** sound. *cf:* tik.

**nrfaal** *adjective* few. *Go komam u nrfaal kin u preg wi ki exam nigmam go u pas pak Onesua High School.* And there were few of us who did well in the exam and passed for Onesua High School. *cf:* warik.

**nri (nria)** *verb*$_a$ **1)** dig out the roots of a tree. *Rui mer nri mpak, me mpak i kano tarp̃ek, ale rui mer lag.* They dug it again and again, but it wouldn't fall down, so they sang again (to make it fall). **2)** dig out banana for replanting.

**nrig** *verb*$_i$ **1)** groan, moan. **2)** growl.

**nriikor** *verb* block a path with a tree that has fallen over.

**nrik** *verb*$_d$ tell. *Go Mista Adam i nrik mam kin nag, "Ko fai polet sisi negamus."* And Mister Adams told us, "We'll put bullets in our guns."

**nriksoksok** *verb*$_i$ command.

**nrilkau (nrilkaui)** *verb*$_a$ jump over.

**nripug** *verb* dig the holes for planting, after having cleared the garden.

**nrir** *verb*$_i$ fly. *Malnen ru nrir, sokfal kin i nrir ur etan.* When they flew, the owl flew down low.

**nrmen** *noun* anemone that lives on rock. *cf:* mpaklep.

**nrog (nrogo)** *verb*$_a$ **1)** feel, also used in compound forms like *pamnrog* 'taste', *minrog* 'taste by drinking'. *Go ati me apu nen ru tu elag Ep̃uf ru pam ni ntas ne, ru nrog wi ki.* And the grandmother and grandfather that stayed up at Bufa ate from the sea, they felt good for it. **2)** hear. *A ta nrog wi kin mau. P̃a pe mer ler tli?* I didn't hear well. Could you say it again?

**nrogperkat** *verb* obey.

**nrogpir (nrogpri)** *verb*$_a$ disobey.

**nrogtae** *verb* recognise by hearing something. *cf:* letae, mrotae.

**nrogtesa** *verb*$_i$ sad, be sad, feel bad, be disappointed, be sorry. *Raru i tap̃o ki tete naat go ru nrogtesa.* The canoe tipped some men out and they feel sad. *Selwan teesa i mat tmen go raiten ra nrogtesawes.* When a child dies, its father and mother are sad. *cf:* nanrogtesan.

**nrogtiawi** *verb*$_i$ well, healthy, feel good.

**nrogtor (nrogtron)** *verb*$_a$ speed, be quick.

**nroi (nroir)** *verb*$_a$ strain, as in coconut milk strained through coconut mesh, or material.

**nrokof** *verb* care for, look after someone by staying with them. *Kineu ka fo pak talm̃aat me ag p̃a nrokof teesa to.* I will go to the garden, but you look after the child.

**nrokos (nrokosi)** *verb*$_a$ follow. *Ag p̃a fei me ka fo nrokosik.* You lead and I will follow you. *cf:* taos.

**nrom (nromi)** *verb*$_a$ love. *cf:* nanromien.

**nron** *noun* **1)** sense, thinking; *nron i mat* 'to not be thinking' (lit: thinking is dead). **2)** vision, a premonition, seeing something that hasn't yet happened.

**nroog** *noun* basket for food, made of pandanus leaf with hibiscus handles. *cf:* fuelig, likat, napor, nlafkir, polpol, sarpopot, sp̃ol, tasaal, tip̃el.

**nrook** *verb*$_i$ **1)** bend. **2)** bow, bend (of a person). *Ku nrook na p̃a slat namrun.* You bend in order to get something. *A pregi ku nrook.* I make you bend over.

**nrookot** *verb*$_i$ cross. *Ale u po pa raru nrookot mai pak Efat gakit ne.* Okay, we would paddle a canoe across and come back to Efate.

**nroos (nroosi, nrsagi)** *verb*$_a$ drag something heavy, like dragging a canoe or a heavy bag.

**nrop** *verb*$_i$ **1)** be mentally unstable. **2)** intellectually disabled. **3)** be drunk.

**nros** *verb*$_i$ lose weight, be sick and lose weight. *Nam̃olin i to nros.* His body was losing weight.

**nrotik** *adjective* **1)** silly. **2)** stupid. *cf:* p̃autik.

**nrpag (nrpagi, nrepag)** *verb* slap. *A nrepagik.* I slap you. *Ale ru kelkel ki nmarit go ru to kelkel me nao i to nrpagir.* So they held onto the rope, they were holding it but the wave slapped them. *cf:* nrepnrpag.

**nrp̃asok (nrp̃asoki)** *verb*$_a$ nail, attach something using nails. *Ku nrp̃asok rowat elag nasum̃.* You nail the thatch on top of the house.

**nrp̃ei** *verb*$_a$ **1)** bark (of a dog). *Selwan ku ur esum̃ ni naat kori ga ru nrp̃ei ag.* When you go past that man's house then dogs bark at you. **2)** scold, tell someone off.

**nru** *number* two. *cf:* kaaru, nranru.

**nru** *verb*$_i$ tree losing its leaves when the flower is about to set. *Nmal i nru su to ki.* The hog plum has lost all its leaves.

**nruenru** *noun* each (two).

**nrup̃** *verb*$_i$ dive, dive for something. *Ku nrup̃ pak etan.* You dive down. *A po nrup̃ masmes.* I will dive for the knife.

**nrur** *verb*$_i$ shake. *cf:* nanrur.

**nrus** *verb*$_i$, *auxiliary* **1)** move a little. *Ale u mer nrus pak esum̃ ni natam̃ool kaaru.* Then we went to the other man's house. **2)** become, change into. *I pi natkon nen i nrus laap.* It was a village that became many villages. **3)** be a little bit like something, to have some of the characteristics of something. *I nrus miel.* It is reddish.

**nsag** *noun* forked piece of wood, used in building.

**nsaiseiwen** *noun* meeting. *Go maarik naot nig Emelp̃au ki sos nafet naot nakon me ru preg nsaiseiwen.* And the chief of Emelp̃au called all the chiefs of the place and they held a meeting. *cf:* saisei.

**nsankas** *noun* splinter, small piece of wood.

**nsat** *adjective* rotten (of a yam only).

**nsau** *noun* sky.

**nsel** *noun* spring, source of water.

**nselpot** *noun* anus.

**nsem** *noun* outrigger of canoe. *cf:* esem.

**nsem̃ (nsem̃)** *noun*$_i$ chip of wood, as from cutting a canoe, also used of waste from another product, like the sugarcane spat out after it has been chewed.

**nsem̃mantu** *noun* roll of, for example, banana or manioc in island cabbage (*simboro* in Bislama) cooked in the oven, unlike *manmon,* which is cooked in a pot. *cf:* manmon.

**nser** *noun* comb.

**nser** *noun* tree sp., used to make the cross-members of a canoe (*nakiat*) and for firewood. (*Melicope latifolia*).

**nsfen** *noun* 'something like that'. *Ru preg kram ko nsfen kia.* They made axes and things like that.

**nsik** *noun* pole for knocking a coconut off a tree.

**nsilfer (nsilfren)** *noun$_i$* blade, the edge of a knife or similar object.

**nskau** *noun* reef. *I su pak etan, ra pan me elau i mat, i lao kin nskau tefla.* He went down, they (two) went and the tide was out, he walked on the reef like that.

**nslawos** *noun* channel in the reef, small enough to step over.

**nsol** *noun* cross-member, beam to which the roof of a house is attached. It is attached on top of *narom*.

**nsul** *noun* fish sp., emperors. (*Lethrinidae*). *cf:* nametfaai.

**nsulnkanrpram** *noun* fish sp., long-nosed emperor, longface emperor. (*Lethrinus olivaceus*).

**nta** *interjection* expression of agreement, also used to conclude a conversation. *Nta ka fo tuok gaag m̃iit.* Okay, I will give you a mat.

**nta** *noun* tree (*nandau* in Bislama) that has small fruit (yellowish/reddish green). Two kinds, a red one (*nta miel*) and a green one (*nta ksakes*). (*Pometia pinnata*).

**ntaanu (ntaanuen)** *noun* spit. *cf:* taanu.

**ntaarto** *noun* **1)** cockscomb, the red crown on a cock (fowl). **2)** uvula, small piece of skin that hangs down at the back of the mouth.

**ntae** *noun* **1)** paint. **2)** plant sp., the name of a plant, of which the flower is used to make face paint or mat dye.

**ntae (ntaen)** *noun$_i$* excrement, shit. (*Idiom: You are shit, you talk nonsense.*) *cf:* nasi.

**ntaenlag** *noun* cloud.

**ntaewen** *noun* knowledge. *Me i gaag traus, ag ku pitlak ntaewen, ag p̃a fo tm̃om mtiri.* But he tells it for your benefit, you have the knowledge, you will write it yourself. *cf:* metmatu, tae.

**ntaf** *noun* **1)** hill. **2)** mountain. *Go i siwer sak ki ntaf pak elag, malen i pan pan pan pak elag ntaf go i nrog nai i ser.* And she walked up the mountain to the top; when she was high up the mountain she heard water flowing.

**ntafat (ntafatun)** *noun$_i$* midriff, hip, above the waist, and around to the small of the back. *cf:* ntap̃rai.

**ntafwen** *noun* diarrhoea.

**ntag** *noun* generation. *Ru patok naur sees kin go ru po mer pes preg natam̃ool ru laap pan pan tup̃ ntag ni mees nen.* They went to the small island and there started to be many people up until this generation.

**ntai** *noun* fish sp., soldierfish. (*Holocentridae*).

**ntak (ntakun) 1)** *noun$_i$* back, also used to describe the back of something, e.g., *ntak nanuen* 'back of his neck'. *Selwan ntakum i ptin, ru m̃osik go p̃a fo nrog tiawi.* When your back is sore they massage it and then you feel better. **2)** *noun$_i$* behind, after, later (lit: its back). **3)** *adjective* relative who should be avoided, like a son-in-law to his mother-in-law, or brothers-in-law. *Maarik ntakun* (term of respect: *maarik* mister).

**ntaknanu (ntaknanuen)** *noun$_i$* back of the neck.

**ntaknatu (ntaknatuen)** *noun$_i$* heel.

**ntal** *noun* taro. Some kinds of taro are: *ntal m̃ool,* a small plant with a red stalk; *nafia; nafimas,* has marks on the stem and leaf; *napliit,* a blue *nafi; ntal nafum̃kas,* multi-coloured leaf. (*Colocasia esculenta*). *cf:* nafi, ntal ni fiti.

**ntal ni fiti** *noun* taro sp., 'Fiji taro'. (*Caladium bicolor*). *cf:* nafi, ntal.

**ntalfan** *noun* **1)** deep ocean. **2)** horizon.

**ntali** *noun* tree sp., tropical almond. Good wood for canoes. (*Terminalia samoensis*). *cf:* ntalitas.

**ntalifam** *noun* plant sp.

**ntalig** *noun* fungus, mushroom (lit: ear) of any kind.

**ntalig (ntalgen)** *noun$_i$* ear; *ntalig nrir* 'ears sticking out', *ntaligen i p̃aar* 'his ears are blocked' (he is deaf).

**ntaligkusu** *noun* plant sp., leaf is serrated, stamen is long with violet flowers.

**ntaligp̃aar** *noun* deaf.

**ntaligpram** *noun* devil, type of devil with long ears.

**ntalimil** *noun* tree sp. (*wael natapoa* in Bislama). (*Terminalia sepicana*).

**ntalitas** *noun* tree sp., sweet fruit (*natapoa* in Bislama). (*Terminalia samoensis*). *cf:* ntali.

**ntame** *noun* reef crab, red-eyed crab, about eight cm long; crabs which keep their claws close to their shells. (*Xanthidae*).

**ntan** *noun* ground, land. *Gar ru pitlak na ntan nen naot nig Efil i tuer kin Emlap̃o, san kin Kawenu i tkos.* They had land that the chief of Ifira gave them at Emlap̃o, where Kawenu (college) is. *Go neu ka fei tu esum̃ mal sees ka traem weswes ntan, preg talm̃aat.* I went back to my house for a while, I tried working the land, making a garden.

**ntan makoren** *noun* red dirt (of the ground).

**ntan nakof** *noun* soil, white soil.

**ntankep** *noun* liver.

**ntankep** *noun* firestick.

**ntanrur** *verb* posset, small vomit like a baby does.

**ntanu (ntanuen)** *noun* spit.

**ntap̃aun** *noun* tree sp. wood used for canoes.

**ntap̃ir** *noun* tree sp. (*nil blong nasama* in Bislama). (*Murraya paniculata*).

**ntap̃rai (ntap̃rain)** *noun$_i$* hip, also used for one's bottom (more polite than *napis*). *cf:* ntafat.

**ntap̃u** *noun* heap of root crops, e.g., *nawi* 'yams' or *ntal* 'taro'.

**ntapukor (ntapukron)** *noun$_i$* shell cover, operculum. Closes the opening of the shellfish when the animal is retracted inside the shell.

**ntas** *noun* salt water, salt. *Malnen i siwer ur ntas kin i pak Ermag, go ntas i pamau nap̃utuen.* When he crossed the sea to Erromango, the sea came to his knee. (*Idiom: 'The sea is calm/clear/still.' There is peace and calm, no problems,* *things in life are okay.*) *cf:* elau, nai, namoos.

**ntatanwen** *noun* funeral.

**ntau** *noun* year; *ntau faum* or *ntau nen tu* 'next year', *ntau nen pa* 'last year'. *Selwan tu pakor nametp̃ag ntau, ra to tu teesa tete nanromien.* When we come to the end of the year they give presents to the children.

**ntau** *noun* fish sp., insular halfbeak, the top of its mouth is short, bottom is long. (*Hyporhamphus affinis*).

**ntaul** *noun* yam sp., strong yam, can stay in the ground a long time before being harvested. *cf:* nawi.

**ntaul pram** *noun* yam sp.

**ntawot (ntawotin)** *noun$_i$* bone, skeleton.

**ntawotmal** *adjective* lazy.

**ntelpou** *noun* yam sp. *cf:* nawi.

**nteu** *noun* green leaves for covering laplap. *cf:* naflel.

**ntm̃at** *noun* peace (no war), calm. *cf:* tm̃at.

**ntp̃et** *noun* heap of leaves in a garden left to dry before being burned.

**ntu** *noun* spear for spearing big fish. It has a single prong and is made from wood that floats.

**ntuk** *noun* **1)** hibiscus green branch, new growth. **2)** rope made of hibiscus; the inner bark of a green branch of hibiscus (*Hibiscus tiliaceus*) that is stripped, soaked in salt water for over a week, then made into string or rope.

**ntur** *noun* fish or crabs bound together (*ntur naik*) by sticking a string through them. One of these is a type of unit of measurement by which you can sell fish. *Ku pan kraksok nafet naik ku sati mai ku laglaga i nom, ku trus i pi ntur.* You catch fish, you bring them back and clean them, you tie them together and it is a ntur. *cf:* tur.

**ntwam** *noun* devil. *Malnen kin i nrik ntwam nen kin ntwam nen i na, "A me kineu a na ka fo pam akam kia me akam ra sef."* When he said this to the devil, the devil said, "Ah but I wanted to eat you (two), but you ran away."

**nua** *noun* **1)** fruit. **2)** balls, testicles (slang).

**nua p̃ontau** *noun* banana sp., white when ripe.

**nual** *noun* coconut, white coconut flesh, good for old people to eat.

**nuanagmos** *noun* shellfish sp., Venus comb murex. (*Murex pecten*).

**nuanpakur** *noun* coconut sp., smallest coconut. It is like the fruit of *napankura* or *tamanu* in Bislama (hence the name, fruit of *npakur*).

**nuantas** *noun* type of seaweed.

**nuasa** *noun* fish sp., short dragonfish, flatheads. (*Eurypegasus draconis, Platycephalidae*).

**nuasog** *noun* **1)** smoke. **2)** cigarette.

**nue (nuen)** *noun$_i$* vein.

**nugot** *noun* coconut sp., black leaf and black coconuts.

**nuk** *verb* have sex. *Ra to preg nuk.* They are having sex.

**nuk (nukun)** *noun$_i$* nest, a bird's nest.

**nuknimaan** *noun* bird's nest.

**numam** *noun* coconut sp., you can eat all of the nut, chew the outside husk, it is sweet all through. Your mouth goes brown.

**numamkop** *noun* coconut, flesh starting to get dry. *cf:* nm̃arteu, numotu.

**numlakes** *noun* coconut sp., a blue coconut, the coconut liquid can make you sick.

**numotu** *noun* coconut sp. with strong flesh, water is starting to get fizzy. *cf:* nawoos, numamkop.

**numtapilkap** *noun* coconut sp., its eye is red when you cut it.

**nuo** *noun* fish sp., parrotfishes; *nuo mlakes* 'redlip parrotfish', *nuo tao* 'bluebarred parrotfish', *nuo marteu* 'bridled or ember parrotfish'. (*Scaridae*). *cf:* kalap̃og.

**nuof** *noun* **1)** harbour. **2)** wharf.

**nuotpram** *noun* altar (an old word), used to be used for sacrifice. *cf:* p̃otut.

**nuotpram** *verb* tie up clothes or knot a piece of rope.

**nusoksok** *noun* coconut sp., it has small fruit and lots in one bunch.

**nutag** *noun* coconut sp., coconut tree with no flower, but no *napirkitin.* Easy to get down by throwing stones since the nuts are not held strongly.

## O OO

**of** *noun* coconut shell, dry and used.

**ofa** *verb$_i$* bury. *Selwan ra torik go temen ki mat go teesa nen i po pan ofa kin temen.* They waited and the father died, and the child went to bury his father. *cf:* taatan, tan.

**ofag** *noun* gecko, yellow belly. (*Gekkonidae spp.*).

**ofagpulsok** *noun* gecko, sticky one, hides in *nrau.* (*Gekkonidae spp.*).

**ofet** *noun* termite-like grub. *cf:* funrei.

**ola** *noun* **1)** spear. *Ki pregpta ki ola, naas, plak timen nega.* He got his spear, bow and arrows ready. **2)** penis (slang). *cf:* polpol koplog.

**olafatkau** *noun* spear, hooked spear.

**olam̃ool** *noun* spear with one tip.

**olantu** *noun* spear with three tips.

**olif** *noun* shellfish sp., olives (general term). (*Olividae*).

**ona** *verb$_i$* hesitation like 'nana', thingamy. *Me malen kin i ona tefla, me ntaf nen kin i tu euut nen kin ru soso ki esap kia Tipuet.* But when he did this thingamy, the hill that was by the sea, they called it Tipuet.

**oof** *noun* heron (type of bird), *oof taar* or *oof tau* is the white one, and *oof got* is the black one.

**oof (oofa)** *verb$_a$* **1)** bear burden, as in a chief bearing his people. *I oof namlanri ni ntas ko namlas mai sok esum̃.* He bears the cold from the sea and the bush and goes home, e.g., after fishing and hunting last night. **2)** wear clothes, but do not use this with things you wear on your head (like a hat), for which you use *su.* **3)** carry on your back, e.g., a child. *cf:* su.

**orai** *verb* wade, walk in the sea.

**oraik** *verb$_i$* fish using a spear. *cf:* tir.

**ore (or)** *interjection* yes. *Wel ga ke til, "Ore", go ke fo watgi, me wel i tli na, "I tiik", u kano.* If he says, "Yes", then he can hit him, but if he says, "No", you can't.

**orpak** *noun* fish sp., gobies. (*Gobiidae*).

# P P̃

**pa (fa) 1)** *verb$_i$* go. *Ru puetsok komam u pa, u pak namlas.* They kept us and we went to the bush. **2)** thither, away, used after a location to indicate direction of movement to that location. *Go i p̃on, ale a mer ler pak Hotel Lagon pa. It closed and I went back to the Hotel Le Lagon.* *cf:* mai, pan.

**pa** *verb$_a$* drive, also ride, e.g., in a canoe or truck. *U tap pa loto mana mau, u siwer.* We don't drive a car or anything, we walk. *Linsi Makmilen i pa lons nega mai po mos mam pak Kanal.* Lindsay McMillan drove his launch and came and took us to Kanal (Lougainville). *P̃a fa raru me p̃a falus pak elau namos.* Take the canoe and paddle out to the sea.

**p̃a=** *pronoun prefix* you (2nd person singular irrealis subject). *A tap trok na p̃a mai mau.* I don't agree that you can come.

**paa** *verb* shine brightly (of the sun). *cf:* nrernrer.

**paai (faai)** *verb$_a$* fill up, pack up (as in suitcases). *Me i kano pan paai nasok, i kano pan kuk, pan ke fei piatlak wik i nru ko i tol.* But she can't fill bags with rubbish, she can't cook, for another two or three weeks.

**paak** *verb$_i$* delouse, take lice out of hair.

**paakankan** *verb$_i$* walk with legs spread apart, to be bowlegged. *cf:* paap̃olp̃lo.

**paakor** *verb$_i$* **1)** arrive. *Malen u paakor pulp̃og, natkon i m̃alm̃aal wi.* When we arrived in the morning, the village was very clean. **2)** appear; *aal i paakor* 'sunrise'. *Go nrak i laap ru to paakor ki natam̃ool.* And many times they would appear to people. **3)** born, to be born. *Kineu a ta paakor hospital mau. A paakor esum̃.* I wasn't born at the hospital. I was born at home. **4)** happen. *I welkia ru sertep̃al wes tu pan namrun i paakor.* Well they don't listen and then something happens. *cf:* pkaal, psol.

**paakot** *verb* trap fish by encircling them.

**paakot (faakot)** *verb* **1)** pay. *Go teetwei gar ru ta paakot ki mane, go ru ta paakot ki tete namrun p̃et mau.* In those days they didn't pay for things with money, and they didn't pay with different things at all. **2)** buy. *A pato efil mai na ka* *faakot waak.* I came from Vila to buy the pig. *cf:* nfaakoton.

**paakruk** *verb* come to one place, assemble, combine. *Tuk mai paakruk naor i skei raki nsaiseiwen ko nmaten.* We come to one place together for a meeting or for a death.

**paalag** *verb* stand on something, stand up on.

**paalak** *verb*$_i$ tiptoe, creep up on. *Ku paalak reki naik.* You creep up to catch fish. *cf:* paalaklak.

**paalaklak** *verb*$_i$ creep up, sneak up on someone. *cf:* paalak.

**paalkau (paalkaui)** *verb*$_a$ step, to step over.

**paamaot** *verb*$_i$ separate.

**paam̃as** *verb* shine (of the sun). *cf:* taalag.

**paamau** *verb* fail to do something, e.g., fail to get somewhere you are trying to get to, or fail to hit something with a stone.

**paamau** *verb* end a story. *Go i pi esuan natrauswen sees nen i paamau wes.* And that is where this small story ends.

**paan (paanus)** *verb*$_a$ **1)** roast. **2)** burn, as in burning a garden. *Me reki nen u pul nkas, go nanwei kin ru to pul nkas. Ale komam u po tai nrankas i seserik, po psi ur nlak nkas nen kin ruk fo paanus.* But as for pruning trees, men prune trees. And we would cut small branches, would put them around tree trunks so they could burn them.

**paapnun** *verb* end, close (as in a meeting).

**paap̃olp̃lo** *verb*$_i$ stand with legs apart. *cf:* paakankan.

**paapuen** *verb*$_i$ walk slowly looking for things on the reef.

**paaput** *verb* walk back and forth because you are worried.

**p̃aar** *adjective* **1)** dumb, unable to speak. **2)** deaf, can't hear. *ntaligp̃aar* 'ear-closed', 'deaf'. **3)** be stuck, closed.

**paareki (paarekin, faareki)** **1)** *verb*$_a$ go for a reason, go to do something. *U pak Esanr to u pus kaku ni nafet na misnari naurur pan u ler mai pak Emlakul malnen u paareki Efat, me ki pe pi mal ni nafkal.* We went back to Santo, taking the cargo to the missionaries on different islands, then came back to Malakula then went to Efate, but war had started. **2)** *verb*$_i$ get someone.

**paariik** *noun* tree sp., cassis. (*Leucaena leucocephala*).

**paarik** *adjective* small distance, go a little way.

**paarikrik** *verb* go a little further.

**p̃aas** *noun* rhinocerus beetle, large black one that hurts if it bites you.

**p̃aas** *verb*$_i$ part hair. *Ku p̃aas nalum.* You part your hair.

**paasa** *verb*$_i$ limp, walk with a limp.

**paaskar (faaskar)** *verb* add to what has been said, extend the discussion. *Maarik naot, a muur ka faaskar nafsan.* Mister Chief, I would like to add my story. *cf:* skar.

**paat** *number* four. *U ler mai marmar naliati i paat.* We came back and rested for four days. *cf:* kaafat.

**paatan** *verb*$_i$ bury.

**paatan (pantan)** *verb*$_i$ get out of a boat or plane, disembark.

**paatlakor (paatlakro)** *verb*$_a$ be astride, stand over something.

**paatup̃tup̃** *verb* always go back to the same place.

**pafasi** *verb* step on something, as in to wash clothes or crush food.

**p̃afp̃of** *adjective* **1)** big, many. *I piatlak raru seserik go raru p̃afp̃of ru to sef ur namos ko ntas.* There are small boats and big boats that go in the ocean and the sea. **2)** adult.

**p̃afu** *verb* break open. *Ku tae neu p̃afu nua naniu ne?* Can you crack open this coconut for me?

**pag** *verb*$_i$ **1)** climb, ascend. *Mista Mi nen selwan komam u pan u laoto etan me ga i pag kin nasum̃ nega.* Mister Mi, when we stayed down there, he went up to his house. *I pag ki nkafik pak elag, me Ririal i to etan.* He climbed up the nakavika, and Ririal stayed down on the ground. **2)** copulate (of animals). *Waak i to pag ki waak nmatu.* The pig is mating with the sow.

**p̃ag** *noun* end of something. (*Idiom: You're the last one, bottom of the heap, you haven't got anything.*) *cf:* mp̃ag.

**pagos** *noun* beetle (general term). *Pagos i to tur p̃rai nkas.* The beetle drills and breaks the wood.

**pagotut** *noun* plate for liquids, like soup. *cf:* slo, trakek.

**p̃agp̃ag** *noun* fish sp., cornetfish. (*Fistularia commersonii*). *cf:* nanr.

**p̃agraap** *noun* coconut with flower, no meat inside it. *cf:* p̃orlaf.

**pagtketig** *verb*$_i$ climb with feet and hands.

**pai** *noun* bird sp., Tree martin. (*Petrochelidon nigricans*).

**paikor (paikro)** *verb*$_a$ hide to catch prey, stalk.

**pailuk (failuk)** *verb* tie a loop to hold an animal. *Ku failuk kau.* You tie up the cow.

**pak (fak) 1)** *verb*$_i$ go to, go towards (realis). *Go ru mer tp̃e ki kineu a pak Lamap Emlakul.* And they then sent me to go to Lamap in Malakula. **2)** *preposition* to. *Selwan i plak nmatu ni tekaaru i trapelpel plake pak em̃ae.* When he was with the other man's woman, he hurried with the woman and they went a long way. *Ki pe pak nam̃leen pa.* She went back to her place.

**pakelag (fakelag)** *verb*$_i$ **1)** ascend, go up. *Komam u pakelag ntaf, a plak teesa nen u pa.* We went up a hill, me with this child, we went. **2)** increase. *Go ntas i stat pakelag.* And the sea started getting higher. **3)** high, in heaven, as in Christian thought. *Leatu i pakelag.* God is on high.

**pakem̃ae** *verb*$_i$ **1)** distant, be distant, long way from. **2)** take the wrong path, stray. *Natkon i to preg nawesien wi me ku mai plak susrir nrus pakem̃ae ki natkon ko nawesien wi.* The village is doing good things and you come and lie to them and they stray from doing the good work.

**paketan (faketan) 1)** *verb$_i$* go low, below. **2)** *verb$_i$* descend. **3)** *adjective* deep. **4)** *verb$_i$* respect. *Ke fo pan lfek ur em̃ae, nlaken i paketan ki nanwei.* She will go a long way around them because she respects men. **5)** *adjective* cheap. *Nanom sernale ru paketan ru to esan sorsorwes.* Yesterday the food was cheap at the marketplace. **6)** *verb$_i$* humble, be humble. **7)** *verb$_i$* obey. **8)** *verb$_i$* honour. *cf:* etan.

**pakmaalep** *verb$_i$* mourn. *Komam uto pakmaalep.* We are mourning. *cf:* palkias.

**pako** *noun* shark.

**pakofaam** *noun* tiger shark.

**pakofai** *noun* hammerhead shark.

**pakokap̃o** *noun* ray sp., giant reef shark. (*Taeniura melanospilos*).

**p̃akor (p̃akro) 1)** *verb* cover, to cover something. *Panpan go, i p̃akoro ki puur lisaan i to.* On and on and he still covers them with a giant clam shell. **2)** *noun* cover (of pot).

**pakosgal** *noun* fish sp., puffers, e.g., guineafowl puffer, star puffer (but see also *p̃nopun*). (*Tetraodontidae*).

**pakotau** *noun* white shark.

**p̃akotkot** *verb* cut in pieces. *Me m̃aat kia i nrogtesa, go i wat ki napuen teflan panpan i pakotkot naor ne.* And the snake felt bad, and it hit its tail until it split this island into pieces.

**p̃akrau** *verb* spread the word of God. *Misnari i mai nen ke p̃akrau ki nafsan ni Atua.* The missionary came to spread the word of God.

**paktau** *verb* have sex.

**p̃al** *adjective* **1)** blank. **2)** empty. *I tiik ki namrun esum̃, esum̃ i p̃al.* There's nothing in the house, it is empty. *Ku tok p̃al to.* You do nothing. *Tep̃al m̃as.* It is easy. (It's nothing). *cf:* tep̃alp̃al.

**p̃al (p̃alun)** *noun$_i$* brother, also mother's or father's sibling's son. *Go neu taos p̃al papa neu i skei ga i pato sanpen.* As for me, my father's brother stays over there. *cf:* temp̃alp̃olun.

**palkias** *verb$_i$* mourn, *ipalkias* 'period of mourning' (five days, or could be longer). *cf:* pakmaalep.

**palkor (palkro, falkor)** *verb$_a$* observe. *Malnen naat i mat ku palkro.* When a man dies you observe five days of mourning. *Tuk falkor aliat tap nlaken i pi Sabat.* Observe Sunday because it is the sabbath.

**palsmin** *noun* plant sp., fruit is not eaten, only the flower is used for decoration. (*Elaeocarpus spp.*).

**p̃alu** *verb* throw a stone and hit something. *cf:* p̃ilu.

**palus (falus)** *verb$_i$* paddle. *Selwan ru toktan nag ruk falus go ru totooluk ki nakpei nig raru po palus.* When they sit to paddle they turn their backs to the front of the boat then paddle.

**pam (pami, fam)** *verb$_a$* **1)** eat; *natam̃ool fam toop* 'glutton'. *Ag ku fam toop.* You eat too much. **2)** consume. *I to pam mane p̃ur.* It used up lots of money. *Ntaewen i tae pam nasup̃nekien.* Knowledge can eat ignorance. *cf:* nfamwen.

**pamnrog (pamnrogo, famnrog)** *verb$_a$* taste food. *cf:* minrog.

**pam̃or (pam̃ori, fam̃or)** *verb$_a$* **1)** discover, find out about something. *Ale sup̃ nen, ale tete nigmam ru pam̃ori ru nrogtesa ru pestaf naot ki.* Okay, that way of doing things, some of us found out and felt bad about it and told the chief. **2)** find. *Go mees nametnai nen ki p̃on ku mer kano pam̃ori.* And today the spring is blocked and you can't find it.

**pan (fan) 1)** *verb, auxiliary* go. *Ale a mer ler pan, paus ki nawesien naur sees go a po weswes tkal mees.* So I went back, asked for work at the small island and I worked until today. **2)** thither, away. *cf:* pa.

**pan ki i sa** *adverb* doing something so much that it ends up being a bad thing (*gogo inogud* in Bislama), can't find a solution. *Ntwam i en mromromro pan ki i sa.* The devil thought and thought until he couldn't find a solution.

**pankot** *verb$_i$* burn (garden). *U pankot, u pankot, u taata, u suur. Go u pul nkas, u preg nawesien p̃rakot.* We burn the garden, we clear, we cut the grass. And we prune trees, we do any type of work.

**panpan** *preposition* until. *Go i pregi panpan Efat negakit nen natam̃ool ru mat panpan natam̃ool rui tiik.* And it came to be that our Efate, people died until there were no people.

**p̃anrer** *verb$_i$* coo (of a dove). *Ru to kol mapul i to kol me i to p̃anrer. Ser maan nen ru preg sup̃ nen ru to pregi.* They called – the pigeon called – but he cooed. Each bird followed its own habit.

**p̃anuk** *noun* shellfish sp., nautilus. (*Nautilidae*).

**pao** *noun* fish sp., onespot snapper or yellow-margined snapper.

**pao malagot** *noun* fish sp., snapper, with black dot on side. (*Lutjanidae*).

**paokap** *noun* fish sp., paddletail snapper.

**p̃ap̃a** *noun* shellfish. The spines of this shellfish can be used to write on slate, instead of using chalk. (*Guildfordia triumphans*).

**p̃apir** *verb$_i$* demolish, pull down.

**pare** *verb$_i$* blind, to be. *Natam̃ool nen i kano lele i pi met pare ko i pare.* A man who can't see has blind eyes, or he is blind.

**p̃aror** *noun* **1)** fool. **2)** crazy person.

**p̃arp̃aar** *verb$_i$* bland, not enough taste, as in tea with not enough sugar or meat with no salt.

**p̃arp̃or** *noun* fish sp., triggerfishes (general term), but see also *fum̃or, fuu*. (*Balistidae*). *cf:* fuu.

**p̃arp̃ormol** *noun* fish sp., strong skin. *Fuu* is the adult of *p̃arp̃ormol*. *cf:* fuu.

**p̃arsor** *noun* fish sp., surgeonfish sp., including white-freckled, lieutenant, striped bristletooth, twospot bristletooth. (*Acanthurus*).

**p̃aru** *adjective* fat, large, e.g., an extra high tide can be described as *p̃aru*.

**parut** *verb$_i$* take water (in a boat).

**pas (fas)** *verb* push, put something through something else, as in flowers in the hair. *Ku pas ki nafum̃nkas ntalgem.* You put flowers behind your ears.

**p̃as** *verb* pick (a flower).

**p̃as (p̃asi)** *verb$_a$* adopt. *Ku p̃as teesa ni naat.* You adopt a child who is someone else's. *cf:* taap̃as.

**p̃aseu** *noun* shellfish sp., horse conch (general term). (*Fasciolariidae*).

**p̃asok** *verb$_a$* hit something with something else using your hands, like a stick, stone or hammer. *cf:* nrp̃asok.

**pasprut** *noun* passionfruit, used both of the wild (*mil*) variety, which has white fruit, and the introduced variety.

**p̃asrot** *verb* destroy, knock something down. *cf:* m̃asrot, srot.

**patlas (patlasi, fatlas)** *verb$_a$* meet without planning to meet. *Me ru traef mai ko ru patlasik ru msagik.* They come driving or they meet you or they take you in the car. *cf:* neet, saisei, seltra.

**patlep** *noun* claw, the big claw (e.g., of crab); *patrik* is the little claw. *cf:* npat, patrik.

**patlep** *noun* mat, big single weave pandanus mat.

**pato (fato)** *verb$_i$* be at, distant place. *Go mam u piatlak famle ru pato Emar.* And we have family who are at Mare.

**patpat** *verb$_i$* share four ways. *cf:* inruenru, limlim, toltol.

**patrik** *noun* claw, small claw. *cf:* npat, patlep.

**patru** *noun* fish sp., wrasses. (*Labridae*). *cf:* aaf, aaf ni nariuriu, afam, laokinasusu, taktak.

**pau (pausi, fau)** *verb$_a$* weave, also used to describe the joining of boards in canoe making. *Ru pau napor.* They weave the coconut leaf (pieces tied together). *Nmatu ru na ruk fau m̃iit.* The women want to weave a mat. *A to na ka fau.* I am just about to weave. *cf:* nraf.

**pau** *verb$_i$* creep, like a vine. *Nmarit i pau ki nkas.* The vine creeps up the tree.

**p̃au kerkerai** *adjective* wilful, strong head. *cf:* np̃au.

**p̃au m̃aalm̃aal** *noun* bald head. *cf:* m̃aalm̃aal.

**p̃aufiif** *noun* drunk, a drunken person (lit: head spin).

**p̃aukaplat** *adjective* bald.

**p̃aulum̃** *verb$_i$* lie down, lay your head on something. *cf:* naulum̃.

**p̃aulum̃ ni afsak** *noun* cushion star, starfish. (*Culcita novaeguineae*).

**p̃aulum̃ ni rakum** *noun* plant sp., fairly low cover, a hiding place for crabs.

**p̃aum̃osu** *adjective* bald patch on top of the head. *Selwan ku to pi nmaloput natam̃ool np̃aum ke fo pi p̃aum̃osu.* When you become middle-aged your head becomes bald.

**p̃aumra (p̃aumran)** *verb$_a$* slaughter an animal to eat it.

**paunamru** *verb$_i$* carry two bundles of food balanced on a stick over the shoulder, one behind and one in front of you. This is typically done by men. If the stick has a load on only one end, then the type of carrying is called *sikpol. Nsag nen kin ku pau nafnag i to nametp̃agon ranru, ale ku po slati mpamum ru soso ki paunamru.* You carry a stick on your shoulders onto which you tie food at both ends, and it is called *paunamru. cf:* freg.

**paunarum** *verb* have your arms folded in front of you.

**p̃aup̃al** *noun* fish sp., grouper, the big one is *koom.* This one (lit: head-empty) is named for not having meat in its head. (*Serranidae*). *cf:* koom, **p̃autop**.

**paus (faus)** *verb$_d$* ask. *Selwan ku muur namrun p̃a freg nfauswen ke leeg.* If you want something, just ask for it.

**pausus** *verb$_i$* ask too many questions.

**p̃autik** *adjective* foolish (lit: no head). *Natam̃ool nen i tap tae namrun mau ru soso ki p̃autik.* A man who doesn't know something is foolish. *cf:* mtafus, nrotik.

**p̃autop** *noun* fish sp., groupers. *cf:* koom, **p̃aup̃al**.

**pawer** *verb$_i$* walk, hands held behind the back.

**pe** *particle* intensifier, used to increase the intensity of a verb or adjective, e.g., *maon* 'to sweat'; *maon pe maon* 'to really sweat'. *A pam̃or namrun i skei me i trau wi pe wi.* I found this thing and it is really beautiful.

**pe** *preverbal* used to show that the action has already finished. *Go Kalokis ne, mees ne ki pe lakor tkal m̃eltig ki ntau 80.* And Kalokis here, today he would have reached nearly eighty years.

**pe** *directional* there, used to indicate a distance further than that already stated, e.g., *san pe* 'over there'. *Ntwam i tarp̃ek kai mat pe.* The devil fell down and died there.

**p̃eel** *verb* to put a taboo on something, to hang a leaf of coconut or namele to show that there is a taboo on something. *I pus p̃eel talm̃aat.* He put a taboo on the garden. *cf:* p̃eelkor.

**p̃eelkor (p̃eelkro)** *verb$_a$* to block something using a taboo. *cf:* p̃eel, kamkor, laokor.

**peen** *preposition* particle used to mean 'there' (*I peen san peen-e*); *peen* precedes the location name, *-e* follows the location. *Gar ra nru mat peen Epakrar-e.* They both died at Epakrar.

**peep** *noun* moth that lays eggs in ripe bananas. (*Chromis erotus*).

**p̃eer** *noun* type of mushroom, it is white and can be eaten.

**p̃eer** *noun* dirt around the neck or armpit.

**pees (fees)** *verb$_a$* start, as in *tak fees nafuserekwen* 'you start talking', or *pees nkap,* 'start a fire' (by rubbing sticks together). *Go a po mai pees nawesien neu atlag ni Jun 1998.* And I started work in June 1998.

**pei (fei)** *verb$_i$* show. *P̃a fei ki wou ki nkal foum gaag.* Show me your new clothes. *Ka fo pei ki natam̃ool* *nen ki napu.* I will show this man the road.

**pei (fei) 1)** *verb$_i$, auxiliary* lead. **2)** *verb$_i$, auxiliary* win. **3)** *number* first. *Komam u weswes u maos u muurin na ko to wi, ko fo pei maos.* We worked and got tired, if we wanted to be well we would first have to get tired. *cf:* tepei.

**p̃el** *verb$_i$* shelter, from sun or rain, or protect from something.

**p̃el** *verb$_i$* bend, fold (bend or fold an object). *Ku p̃el ki naas na p̃a moti.* You bend your bow to tie it. *A p̃el ki natus.* I fold the paper.

**p̃elgat (p̃elgati, plag)** *verb$_a$* open, e.g., window or door; turn something; turn a page; turn on a switch. *Malen a p̃elgat botel tefla a lao kin nkanrok, a npa ki botel.* When I open a bottle, I tip it up in my mouth and I throw the bottle away. *Kineu go jastis Cook ra mer p̃elgat Aelan Kot.* Justice Cook and I opened the Island Court. *I p̃elgat faat tefla i sol kaai.* She turned the stone like that and she got cockles.

**p̃elp̃eel** *verb* sneak along.

**pelpel** *adverb* quickly. *Ag ku siwer pelpel.* You walk quickly. *cf:* fiit, trapelpel.

**p̃elp̃el** *verb$_i$* tack on, baste on, as in sewing clothes.

**p̃elpuk** *noun* soldier crab. (*Mictyris sp.*).

**p̃elpuk** *noun* full tummy.

**peltakot** *adjective* crossed. Anything crossing something else can be described as being *peltakot.*

**p̃en** *verb$_i$* whistle, not using your fingers. *cf:* safeu.

**pepelau** *noun* person who talks too much.

**pepelau** *noun* bird, a land bird.

**pepep** *noun* slipper lobster, sand lobster, 'bug'. (*Parribacus caledonicus*). *cf:* makou, unr, uur.

**p̃er** *verb$_i$* fart. *cf:* p̃erat.

**p̃erat** *verb$_t$* fart on something. *cf:* p̃er.

**p̃erik** *verb$_i$* fly magically.

**perkat** *adverb* truly, used for emphasis. *Me faat nen i sees perkati.* But that rock was really small.

**pes** *verb$_i$* talk (*nafsan* [*na-fes-an*] is language). *Gar ru pes ki nafsan gamus.* They speak your language.

**pes (pesa, psa)** *verb$_a$* produce a child.

**pes sa** *verb$_i$* **1)** curse. *Mis i pes sa kir.* The missionary cursed them. **2)** insult. *Teesa i preg tenamrun nen i kerkerai i takel me tenen kin i pi rait ko tiawi u kano preg kerkerai kir. Go u kano pes sa kir nlaken gar ruk fo develop ki mal wi nen ke fo mai.* If a child does something wrong, and the mother or the old people can't take strong action against them, we can't insult them, because they will develop, all in good time.

**pesfirfir** *verb* talk against someone, talk over someone when they are talking.

**pesfkaar** *verb$_i$* joke. *cf:* fkaar.

**pesmaomao** *verb* quieten, to calm down, to tame someone.

**pesmosmos** *verb* comfort. *cf:* pesnromnromi.

**pesmotu** *verb* talk proudly.

**pesnre** *verb*$_a$ change a story to suit your own ends, not telling it straight as it should be.

**pesnromnromi** *verb*$_i$ comfort. *I pesnromnromi selwan ru nrogtesa.* He gives comfort when they feel bad. *cf:* pesmosmos.

**pespir** *verb* disagree.

**pesp̃ot** *verb*$_i$ judge a problem. *Akam u pesp̃ot ki ntan.* You judge who is the landowner.

**pesptai** *verb* confirm, give an answer.

**pesp̃ur** *verb*$_i$ boast. *I piatlak natam̃ool nen ru tae pesp̃ur me ru kano preg namrun.* There are people who know how to boast but they don't know how to do anything; *pesp̃urp̃al* 'talk big about nothing'. *cf:* fekfek, polmatmat.

**pesrae (fesrae)** *verb* confront someone and tell them straight what you think, tell something to someone face to face.

**pestae** *verb* inform, tell someone something they didn't know.

**pestaf (pestafi, festaf)** *verb*$_a$ tell, talk to. *Tete nrak a pestafi i tap nrog wou mau.* Sometimes I talk to her, she doesn't listen to me.

**pestatakor** *verb* talk over someone. *cf:* takor.

**p̃et** *adjective* **1)** other. *I fla nrogo ki naat p̃et, i fla sati sanpe, i fla nrogo radio.* He might have heard from other people, he might have got it somewhere, he might have heard it on the radio. **2)** different. *cf:* p̃tae.

**pgai** *verb* attract someone magically.

**pi (fi)** *verb* be. *I pi tesees nen kin a tae.* It is the little that I know. *Ale ola ki nom go malfane i pi timen.* Okay, the spears were finished and now it was arrows.

**pi (fi)** *verb*$_a$ pour, as in watering a plant or drizzling coconut milk onto laplap.

**p̃i** *verb*$_a$ **1)** kick, with top of the foot. **2)** kick, as in the effect of kava or alcohol (*nmalok i p̃i,* 'the kava kicks').

**pia** *noun* banana sp., small sweet banana.

**pialoaal** *noun* crab sp., red and black small crab which lives in holes on the beach.

**piam** *noun* fish sp., damselfishes (onespot, twospot, etc.). (*Pomacentridae*).

**piatlak (pitlak, piatlaken, fitlak)** *verb*$_a$ **1)** own, have (from *pi* 'be' and *atlak* 'owner'). *Ku piatlaken ko?* Do you have it? *Ag ku piatlak sernale.* You own everything. **2)** exist, with a third person subject it also refers to general existence; *i piatlak* 'there is'. *Me i pitlak namrun i skei i to nam̃or.* But there is something in the hole.

**pier** *verb*$_i$ shout loudly, cheer. *cf:* p̃ir.

**p̃ii** *verb*$_a$ throw a small piece of wood to knock something down, e.g., to get a coconut or to hit a flying fox. *A p̃ii naniu.* I throw a stick at coconuts (to make them fall down). *cf:* np̃ip̃.

**p̃iit** *noun* fish sp., frogfishes, stonefish. They float on top of the water when they miss catching a fish to eat. (*Antennariidae*). *cf:* ftir.

**p̃il** *verb$_a$* close eyes, e.g., so that you can pray. *cf:* lee sulsul.

**pili** *noun* banana sp., a long banana. Twist it to take off its skin, which is hard to get off.

**p̃ilmet** *verb$_i$* blink.

**pilo** *verb$_i$* wake up, to be awake. *Me pulp̃og, i ta malkolik to u lefekor natkon negar, selwan ru pilo, ru lek mam, tete ru sef.* Then, in the morning, before dawn, we went around their village; when they woke up, they saw us, some ran away.

**p̃ilp̃il** *verb$_i$* close eyes. *Ku p̃ilp̃il me tuk lot.* You shut your eyes and we can pray.

**p̃ilu (p̃ilua)** *verb$_a$* **1)** kick something away. **2)** sack, make someone lose their job.

**pines** *noun* tree sp., green long fruit with black seeds, yellow when ripe, sweet and cotton-like inside that is eaten.

**pinp̃aop̃on** *noun* pin, for holding material before it is sewn together.

**pios (fios)** *verb$_i$* call out. *Ko redi me ku nrogo na menal ke fios elau, go akam ko fios euut.* You get ready and when you hear the barracuda call out from the water, you call out from the shore. *cf:* sos.

**p̃ip̃** *verb* the action of an outrigger rolling over the canoe when it capsizes. *cf:* tap̃o.

**pir (pri)** *verb$_a$* braid, tie, as in weaving; arrange your hair.

**p̃ir** *verb$_i$* scream, yell, shout, but not as loudly as *pier*. *cf:* pier.

**pirsai (pirsair)** *verb$_a$* to drill.

**pism̃alit** *noun* mantis shrimp (named for the popping noise [*m̃alit*] they make on the reef). (*Stomatopoda*).

**pisp̃lolo** *noun* loincloth, made of bark. *cf:* fiikot, nafon, nanrepnrep, nap̃lai, nasieg, nrepnrep.

**pitar** *verb$_i$* be lost.

**pitkaskei (pitoskei, fitkaskei)** *adjective* **1)** same. **2)** alike. **3)** balance. *Selwan ku pus sernale raru ku psi pitkaskei nen raru ke ta tap̃o mau.* When you put things in a canoe you must keep balance so that the canoe won't tip over. **4)** equal. *Me ntaewen go nasup̃nekien gar ra ta pitkaskei mau.* But knowledge and ignorance are not equal at all. **5)** double, be two of the same thing.

**p̃ka** *noun* breadfruit sp., strong type of breadfruit that has spines and needs long cooking.

**p̃ka** *noun* fish sp., porcupinefishes, burrfish, pufferfish with nail-like covering on skin. (*Diodontidae, Tetrodontidae*).

**pkaal** *verb$_i$* give birth (of humans). *cf:* paakor, psol.

**pkaaru** *verb* come to somewhere two times.

**p̃kafu (p̃kafua)** *verb$_a$* split, e.g., a coconut.

**pkal (pkali, fkal)** *verb$_a$* sharpen something. *Tuk fkal masmes.* We sharpen the knife. *A to pkal masmes.* I am sharpening the knife. *cf:* faatmaama, maa, maama.

**pkal** *verb$_i$* care for a person or an animal.

**p̃kapun (p̃kapni)** *verb*$_a$ kill by using something in your hands, like punching, or using a stick. *P̃a p̃kapni.* You kill him.

**p̃kasai (p̃kasair)** *verb*$_a$ poke a hole in something.

**p̃kastes** *noun* dugong. (*Dugong dugon*).

**p̃kasus 1)** *verb*$_i$ breastfeed. **2)** *adjective* woman still breast-feeding. *cf:* sus

**pko** *verb*$_i$ interested, be interested in something. *Ku pko ki nawesien gaag.* You are interested in your work.

**p̃ko** *verb*$_i$ keep secret, keep your feelings to yourself.

**pkot** *verb*$_i$ mildew, mould. Can refer to the mould on bread or on clothes, for example.

**p̃laakor (p̃laakro) 1)** *verb*$_a$ cover something. **2)** *noun* cover (of a pot).

**p̃laanr** *noun* tuna, dogtooth tuna. (*Gymnosarda unicolor*).

**plak (plake, flak) 1)** *verb*$_a$ accompany, take someone somewhere. **2)** *verb*$_a$ with, be with. *Ku plake pak sua?* Where are you going with him? *P̃a flaker pan.* Take them and go. **3)** *preposition* with. *Ki pregpta ki ola, naas, plak timen nega.* He got his spear, bow and arrows ready. *cf:* ptaan, skot.

**plak (flak)** *verb*$_i$ pregnant. *cf:* tien.

**p̃lak** *verb*$_i$ scared, to be scared, to be terrified of something.

**p̃lak** *noun* rail (type of bird). (*Gallirallus philippensis*).

**plak p̃orp̃or** *verb*$_i$ break wood in the bush, like a pig does running through the bush.

**p̃lakes** *noun* green tree lizard.

**plakori 1)** *verb*$_i$ hunt. **2)** *noun* dog used for hunting.

**plakot** *verb* escape from being tied up (of an animal).

**plaksok (plaksoki)** *verb*$_a$ teach. *Mis Kina kin i mai preg nalotwen i plaksok PW.* Miss Kina brought Christianity and taught the PW (Presbyterian Women). *cf:* faitau, tefaitau, teplaksok.

**ple** *verb*$_i$ **1)** argument, fight. **2)** dispute, not a physical fight. *Naat i nru ra ple.* Two men are fighting. *Mees ne ru ple, ru ple ki ntan.* Today they fight, they fight about ground. *cf:* fiet, naflewen, tik.

**plee** *verb* hand of bananas.

**plik (plikti)** *verb*$_a$ peel.

**plim** *verb*$_i$ change, transform, as in a magical transformation. *Munwei i plim pi kori.* The 'kleva' (wise man) changed into a dog.

**p̃log** *noun* coconut shell, empty coconut.

**plokra** *verb* frightened, be frightened, shocked by something.

**p̃lolep (p̃lolpen)** *noun*$_i$ stomach.

**plor (plori, flor)** *verb*$_a$ turn, e.g., a tap. *Ag p̃a flor nai.* Turn on the water! *Ku plor lam pak elag.* You turn the light up.

**plos** *verb* twisted, crooked, to be.

**plos (plosi, flos)** *verb*$_a$ wring clothes.

**plos (plosi)** *verb*$_a$ avoid, as in being angry with someone, you avoid them, unlike *lelu,* which means go around.

**plos (plosi)** *verb*$_a$ do something bad to someone.

**pnak (pnako) 1)** *verb*$_a$ steal; *pnak nmatu, pnak nanwei* 'adultery'. *Ku pnak nmatu nen i tapi nmatu gaag mau.* You take a woman who doesn't belong to you. **2)** *adjective* thieving; *kano pnak, natam̃ool pnak* 'thief'. *Naat nen i to slat sernale p̃et i pi natam̃ool pnak.* A person who steals things is a thief.

**pnat** *verb*$_i$ numb, be numb.

**pnol** *verb*$_a$ **1)** wash. **2)** rinse. *cf:* m̃oltao, preitao, pnoltao, sertao, p̃oktao

**pnoltao** *verb* wash things, like plates. *cf:* m̃oltao, pnol, p̃oktao, sertao.

**p̃not** *verb*$_t$ close, shut.

**pnut (fnut)** *verb*$_i$ **1)** quiet. *P̃a fnut, p̃a ta pes toop mau.* You be quiet, don't talk much. **2)** stop. *Preg nra ke fnut.* Stop the bleeding.

**po (fo)** *preverbal* future marker, used in preverbal position. Used to say that something will happen in the future. *Komam ra po plak prison nen mai pak elau Busmans Bei.* We would take the prisoner to the coast at Bushman's Bay.

**p̃o** *verb*$_i$ **1)** to smell (odour of something). **2)** rot, decay. *cf:* mtet, nap̃o.

**p̃og** *noun* night. *Komam Ben rak fo pan pueti p̃og go ra po pan.* Ben and I had to go and get him in the night, and we went.

**p̃ok** *adverb* part, something not completed. *A tu a ta weswes mau, me u skul, skul nigmam i pan p̃ok.* Well, I'm here, but I don't work, because our schooling only went halfway.

**p̃oktao** *verb* dust, to wipe, as in dusting a mat inside the house. *cf:* pnoltao.

**pol (fol )** *verb*$_i$ behave. *cf:* folfol.

**pol (plon)** *noun*$_i$ testicles. *cf:* p̃ura, teem̃iit.

**poler** *noun* pot, saucepan.

**polfai** *noun* fish spp., mullet; *p̃aurik,* small one; *naumet,* middle one; *rutiyaf,* old grey mullet. (*Mugilidae*).

**polfnak** *verb* trespass. *Ku polfnak naat.* You trespass on a man's land.

**polkirkir** *adjective* active, of a person. *Naat nen i tae preg namrun p̃elp̃el i pi natam̃ool polkirkir nen i wi.* A man who can do something quickly is an active man who is good.

**polmatmat** *verb* show off. *cf:* fekfek, pesp̃ur.

**polpilieli** *verb* look around with bad intentions. *cf:* leepilieli.

**p̃olp̃lo** *adjective* wide.

**polpol** *noun* basket, big one. *cf:* nlafkir, nroog, sarpopot, sp̃ol, tip̃el.

**polpol koplog** *noun* penis. *cf:* ola.

**polsa (folsa)** *verb* **1)** spoil. *Malpei kotkot nen a lek nanrur kerkrai teflan i ta polsa ki naur i toop mau.* Long ago I saw that the earthquake didn't spoil the island too much. **2)** behave badly. **3)** have sex with.

**p̃olul** *noun* reef crab, red shell, 15 cm. (*Etisus splendidus*).

**polwi (folwi)** *verb*$_i$ behave well, do good.

**p̃on** *verb*$_i$ **1)** shut, to be shut. **2)** end, finish. **3)** webbed feet, like a duck's feet. *Natu dakdak i p̃on.* The foot of a duck is closed (webbed).

**p̃onfer** *noun* boil that comes up in the armpit, you put a cockleshell on it to cure it. It has lots of heads. *cf:* fati, nmak, nmanuk.

**p̃onp̃on** *preposition* together.

**p̃onp̃tae** *adjective* different.

**p̃oo** *verb* crouch down to hide. *cf:* kuskor.

**p̃ook** *noun* food, typically different vegetables, cut up and prepared in a ground oven (known in Bislama as a *bougna*, a term from New Caledonia).

**pool** *verb*$_i$ fool, trick someone.

**p̃ool** *adjective* blunt. *Faatmama ne ki pe to p̃ool ki.* This sharpening stone is almost blunt.

**p̃oon** *number* thousand.

**p̃oonti** *number* million.

**poot** *noun* banana sp., plantain banana for cooking.

**p̃oot** *verb*$_i$ explain something to others.

**p̃oot** *verb* share out. *cf:* aliat p̃oot.

**p̃op̃** *noun* spirit, feeling, a person's fashion of doing things; *p̃op̃ wi* 'good way of doing things', *p̃op̃ sa* 'bad fashion of doing things'. *cf:* sup̃.

**p̃op̃ pakelag** *noun* pride.

**p̃op̃ paketan** *noun* quiet, contemplation, humility.

**p̃op̃o** *verb* **1)** brood, as in a bird sitting on its eggs. **2)** cluck, the noise a chicken makes. *Too i p̃op̃o.* The chicken is clucking. *cf:* p̃otp̃otak.

**p̃op̃or** *noun* fish sp., cardinalfish. (*Apogonidae*). *cf:* anrar.

**popot** *noun* crab sp., small white crab that lives in the sand. Good to eat.

**p̃optao** *verb* sweep with a broom.

**p̃or (p̃rai)** *verb*$_a$ **1)** chop something to break it in smaller pieces. *Me mtulep ga i to p̃or na, ntali p̃ur i skei i to em̃au ga.* But his wife was breaking the branches of the big natapoa (tropical almond tree) that was in her yard. *Tenmatun i skei namrun nen i sor, i sfe ki aian i skei i ur elag pan i pan na i p̃rai nmet klas nasum̃tap ni Efil i map̃or.* When this place burned, it threw iron high (up in the air) and it broke the glass windows at the church in Vila. **2)** break something with your hands. *cf:* map̃or, p̃rai.

**p̃orlaf** *noun* coconut, flower breaking open. *cf:* p̃agraap.

**p̃orp̃or (p̃orp̃ro)** *verb*$_a$ break everything.

**p̃orp̃rae** *verb*$_a$ break into pieces.

**p̃otp̃otak** *verb* chicken's cry as it lays an egg. *cf:* p̃op̃o.

**p̃otp̃tae** *verb* divide.

**p̃otut** *noun* **1)** standing stone, stone arrangement with religious importance. *Me faat nen ga taos ru soso ki faat Lelep a? Tenen kin ru preg p̃otut ki.* And that rock, they called it Lelep, eh? The one they made a standing stone. **2)** altar. **3)** pulpit. *cf:* nuotpram.

**p̃rai** *verb* break. *Kin nasum̃ nigmam nlag i p̃rai teflan pa me teflan kin u totan to u to.* The cyclone broke our house this way and that way and we sat and stayed. *Welkia ntas i tik p̃rair.* So the sea broke them all. *cf:* p̃or.

**p̃rakot** *adjective* **1)** ordinary. *Natam̃ool nen i trau p̃rakot m̃as.* The man just seems ordinary. **2)** any, anything. *P̃a slat tep̃rakot m̃as mai.* Take anything and come!

**pram** *adjective* **1)** long. **2)** tall. *Nap̃utuok i kano paakor, nkal neu ke mas pram pak esa.* My knee couldn't show, my dress had to be long down to here (the ankle). (*Idiom: I skei to pram.* He is unmarried.) *cf:* naframwen.

**pras** *noun* plank of wood, a piece of wood that has been shaped for use.

**preg (pregi, freg)** *verb$_a$* **1)** make, cause, also used with a following verb as a cause of the action of that verb. Note: *kaimes* is the term used for biblical creation. *Ru to sursur natam̃ool ru pregi natam̃ool ru sapot kir.* They tricked people and made people support them. **2)** do, carry out an action. *Teesa i preg tenamrun nen i kerkerai i takel me tenen kin i pi rait ko tiawi u kano preg kerkerai kir.* Children do things that are not right, but their mothers and old people can't be firm with them. *Kai pe preg nawesien su.* I have done the work. **3)** take. *Maarik naot ni Em̃eltefra i preglu nam̃er nen kin ru to preg nawesien sa.* The chief of Em̃eltefra took out the people who had been doing bad things. *cf:* kaimes.

**pregfu (pregfua, fregfu)** *verb$_a$* pierce, e.g., an abscess or a boil.

**pregi kesalsal** *verb$_i$* enlighten, show someone how to do something.

**pregnrog (pregnrogo, fregnrog)** *verb$_a$* attempt, try. *I pregnrogo nen kin ke fan, me mtulep i tap trok nen kin ke fo pan mau.* He tried to go, but this spirit woman didn't let him go. *Ku pregnrogo nen p̃a welu aslam.* You try to help your friend.

**pregpta** *verb* prepare. *Malen kin ru ga pregpta ki m̃iit, ru ga pregpta ki nkal, panpan i nom ru tatue kin raru, ru msagi raru me ru pa.* Then they prepared mats and cloth for her, and when they were done they put them in a canoe and went. *cf:* mropta.

**pregsa** *verb$_i$* spoil, damage, hurt. *Me i tfale kin maal i to pregsa ki kit, i to pam kit.* But why does the hawk hurt us, it eats us?

**pregwel (pregweli, fregwel)** *verb$_a$* imitate.

**pregwi** *verb* do good to someone. *Ru pregwi ki natam̃ool i leeg tlas nam̃olien nen kin ru tkos.* They were good to people, it was correct for their life as it was.

**prei** *verb$_i$* **1)** wash, using your hands to splash water over yourself. **2)** baptise (*paptaes* commonly used today). *cf:* tofnp̃au.

**preitao** *verb$_a$* wash (of people). *cf:* m̃oltao, pnol.

**pres (presi)** *verb$_a$* untie.

**promiel** *verb* angry, get angry (of a white person, who goes red in the face).

**p̃roro** *adjective* hard (of food, like gristle).

**p̃rot (p̃roti)** *$verb_a$* eat something hard, crunch. *Nafnag nen i p̃roro, p̃a tao kin ka p̃roti.* This food is hard, give me some and I will crunch it.

**p̃sai** *$verb_i$* clap together, like two waves hitting each other, or a single handclap. *cf:* p̃sap̃os.

**psakor (psakro)** *$verb_a$* hide, to keep secret.

**psaosus** *verb* discuss something in order to find an answer. Once you have a solution you tell people. *cf:* tilusus.

**psapir (psapri, pisapir)** *verb* disagree, oppose, stop what someone was planning.

**psaplil (fsaplil)** *$verb_i$* argue, strongly discuss. *Go faat sees i nrik faat p̃ur ki na, "Ag p̃a fei. Me kineu ka fo inrok." Go i pregi rai tm̃er psaplil kir.* And the small stone said to the big stone, "You go first. I will come behind." And they ended up arguing with each other.

**p̃sap̃os** *$verb_i$* clap hands, applaud. *cf:* p̃sai.

**psapus** *verb* farewell.

**psaput** *verb* argue, to disagree, be unsure.

**psasok (psasoki)** *$verb_a$* encourage. *Ku psasok naat nen ke kerkrai ki nawesien ga.* You encourage that man to be strong in his work.

**psawi** *$verb_i$* **1)** thanks. *Psawi ki mus natakinrogwen.* Thanks for listening. **2)** grace, the prayer said by Christians before a meal. *cf:* faftae, ta.

**psig** *$verb_i$* **1)** disobey. *Ku leka a tli na p̃a fato me ku psig.* You see, I told you to stay but you disobeyed. **2)** play, muck around. *cf:* sigpir.

**psir** *$verb_i$* lie, pretend. *I piatlak tete naat nen ru tae psir wi.* There are some people who know how to lie well. *cf:* tepsir.

**psirsir** *noun* toy, plaything for children. *cf:* tepsirsir.

**psol** *$verb_i$* give birth to (of animal). *cf:* paakor, pkaal.

**pta** *$verb_i$* make good. *Go naliati i skei i to panpan go ki nrikin kin na ke freg tenmatun ke freg pta ki em̃rom.* And one day he said she should make something, she should make the place ready (make it good).

**ptaan** *$verb_i$* accompany, go with. *cf:* plak, skot.

**p̃tae 1)** *adjective* different. *Nlaken katom p̃tae kin i to nagis kaaru, katom p̃tae kin i to nagis kaatol.* Because there were different hermit crabs at other points, there were different hermit crabs at the third point. **2)** *$verb_i$* divide. **3)** *$verb_i$* share. *cf:* kaaru, p̃et.

**ptal (ptale)** *$verb_a$* ask for something.

**ptau** *verb* be at. An old way of saying *pato*.

**p̃ti** *verb* eat a meal without meat. *Kapu p̃ti.* Laplap without anything else. *cf:* tanum̃.

**p̃ti** *verb* walk barefoot.

**ptin** *$verb_i$* sore, pain.

**ptol** *$verb_i$* hungry. *Tafra i pato elau to pul ki nam̃elen me i sook i ptur ki ntas panpan kai ptol. Go ki mro* *kin nag ke fo mer mai fam.* The whale was at the sea, it thrashed its tail in the sea until it got hungry. Then it thought it would come and eat.

**pton** *noun* coral sp., ascidian, with meat that can be eaten.

**ptour 1)** *verb* to get married (of a couple). **2)** *verb*$_a$ marry (of the pastor marrying a couple). *Gar ra ptour aliat poot wik nen pa.* They got married on Friday last week. *cf:* naftourwen, taulu, tosok.

**ptu (ftu)** *verb*$_d$ give a gift; ptu is used of ritual gifts or offerings rather than the ordinary form tu 'give'. *Gar kin ru ptu ki ntan nen kin tu tkos pan tup̃ mees ne.* They gave the land that we are on up until today. *cf:* tu.

**ptur** *verb*$_i$ squirt, spit, spurt.

**pu** See: puet

**pu sman** *verb* drive a vehicle (car, plane or boat). *Ku tae pu sman loto.* You know how to drive a car. *cf:* kel sman.

**puel** *verb*$_i$ **1)** absent, lost. *Mal nawesien me ga i puel.* Time to work, but he isn't here. **2)** disappear.

**puet (pueti, fuet, pu)** *verb*$_a$ **1)** pull. There is a form of this verb (pu) that takes a direct object. *Ru pak taon ru puetlu flaik nen kin kafman i psi i to taon.* They went to town, they pulled down the flag that the government had put up in town. *Ku pan slati elau, p̃a mai, p̃a traf nam̃or, ku pu nkap kerkrai, nkap nmarteu.* You get it from the sea, you come and dig a hole, you put in strong dry wood. **2)** suck. *I puet nasu magko.* S/he sucks the mango. **3)** bring, carry. *Ki pe puet valis ni brother neu teflan. Ki pe pueti mai me i to pai nkal wes.* That's how he brought my brother's suitcase. He brought it and he filled it with clothes.

**puetsok (puetsoki, fuetsok)** *verb*$_a$ **1)** hold. *Ka fo puetsok nakte nkal wel a tuleg me a na ka taf.* I would hold my dress when I stood up and wanted to leave. **2)** catch, capture (as in a ball or a prisoner). *Go polis ru puetsok tete go, ru sm̃olir nasum̃ malik.* And the police captured some and they pushed them into the gaol. **3)** understand, in the sense of grabbing hold of an idea. *Me tete naat ru kraksok wi ki, ru puetsok wi ki natrauswen ne.* But some people they got it well, they understood this story. *cf:* sarsok.

**pug (pugon)** *verb*$_a$ wake. *A pug ag.* I wake you.

**pui** *noun* nudibranch, sea slug (but not *litot* 'bêche-de-mer').

**puk (fuk)** *verb*$_i$ **1)** swell, to be full (of food). **2)** high tide; *ntas i puk* 'the sea is full'. *Nanrur, teni 1953, na ga i kerkrai. Ku lek ntas kin i puk.* The earthquake of 1953 was strong. You saw the sea rise. *cf:* muk.

**pukaikur** *noun* plant sp., has violet or white flowers in a ball shape.

**pukok** *noun* bud (of a flower).

**pukos (pkos)** *verb*$_a$ unfold, open a packet, as in opening a laplap, or unfolding a mat.

**pul** *verb$_i$* make a sign with the hand. *I pul ki narum na ke mai.* She waved for him to come. *cf:* napukm̃opul.

**pul** *verb$_i$* prune, cut branches off a tree, also used of clearing the land before putting in a garden. *Natam̃ool ru um, go ru pul nkas.* The people clean the garden and prune the trees.

**pul** *verb$_i$* **1)** sling. *Welkia, i preg na p̃aun pak ntas tefla me i pul ki np̃aun tefla, nen kin ntas ke fuk.* Well, he put his head in the water and he slung his head like this so that the water rose. **2)** twirl, throw a net, shake your head. **3)** thrash tail (of a fish or an animal). *cf:* fulful.

**pul** *verb$_i$* dance.

**pulmatlen** *noun* dawn. *Me selwan i mai pulmatlen i mai, kuskor mtulep Katapel.* After he came at dawn, he came and hid from Katapel. *cf:* pulp̃og.

**pulp̃og** *noun* morning. *U pan p̃og u tkal natkon gar pulp̃og rik.* We went at night and got to the village in the early morning. *cf:* pulmatlen.

**pulp̃og rik** *noun* dawn.

**pulp̃ou** *noun* hat.

**pulsok** *verb* stuck. *cf:* tepulsok.

**pultau** *noun* shell, white cowrie shell.

**pun** *verb$_a$* fish using poison. *Ru to pun naik ki natu.* They would kill fish using that vine.

**pupu** *noun* conch shell, tritons (general term). (*Cymatiidae*). *cf:* saago.

**pupu** *verb$_i$* gargle. *Ku pupu ki nai.* You gargle with water.

**pupuet (pupueti)** *verb$_a$* **1)** pull, as in pulling (taking) a breath, or pulling a bow and arrow. **2)** hold, e.g., bundle of spears. **3)** harvest water taro (*ntalm̃ol*). Note that different terms are used for harvesting different crops. *cf:* kil, kis, naas, traf.

**pur** *adjective* full, be full. *Pagotut i pur ki nai.* The dish is full of water.

**p̃ur** *adjective* big. *Faat sees i nrik faat p̃ur kin na, "E, ag p̃a fei me kineu ka fo inrok."* The small rock told the big rock, "You go first and I will follow." *Ko fo sat tep̃ur ler, me ko fo paakot ki tesees.* We would bring the biggest back, but we would spend just a little. *cf:* lep.

**p̃ura** *adjective* double, as in fruit when there are two joined together.

**p̃ura** *noun* balls, testicles. *cf:* pol, teem̃iit.

**puri (furi)** *verb$_i$* prepare fire for laplap, heating stones that will be put into the earth oven (*uum*). *P̃a fan sat maniot nen tuk fo puri.* Get the manioc and we will prepare the oven.

**p̃urkum** *noun* bat. *P̃urkum ru preg nasum̃ gar em̃rom erfale.* Bats make their home inside caves.

**purnaniu** *noun* shell of a coconut just split in two, has flesh to eat.

**pus (psi, fsi, fus)** *verb$_a$* put. *Go na naot nigmam i tli nag, "Ko fo pan psi hospitel, Kanal Santo".*

Our boss said, "We'll put him in the hospital at Luganville". *P̃a fsi ke leeg.* You put it straight. *P̃a fus nkas ke to nmaota nasum̃ go faat.* You put wood between the house and the rock.

**puser** *verb$_i$* look for something.

**puserek (fuserek, pusrek)** *verb$_i$* talk, chat. *A muurin gaag puserek, ka fo gaag puserek ki kusu go wiit.* I want to tell you, I'll tell you about the rat and the octopus. *cf:* nafuserekwen

**puspta** *verb$_i$* arrange.

**put (pti)** *verb$_a$* pluck feathers from a bird. *Ka fan put nm̃au too.* I will pluck the chicken's feathers.

**putata** *verb* shake the dirt out of something, like clothes or mats.

**putkau** *verb$_i$* against, to be against. *cf:* kitsa, ktekit.

**putmaak** *verb$_i$* withhold information, even though you know it, when someone asks you a question.

**putsak** *verb$_i$* emerge, as in from the water. *Ku nrup̃ pak etan me ku mer mai putsak nen p̃a fuet nmarom.* You dive down but you come back up to breathe your air.

**puu** *adjective* naked. *syn:* karo usrek.

**puuk** *verb$_i$* cough, to cough. *cf:* nafuukwen.

**puul** *noun* shellfish sp., cowrie shell (general term). (*Cypraeidae*).

**puun** *noun* small green bird, smaller than the red-bellied fruit dove (*sunra*). Its call is an omen of a death.

**puup** *adjective* someone who can't swim. *Ga i pi puup to.* He can't swim.

**puur 1)** *verb$_i$* empty-handed, to be. *A puur mai.* I come empty-handed. **2)** *noun* empty shell (as in eggshell, or empty coconut), so *puur kaai* is an empty cockleshell.

**puus** *adjective* dumb, unable to speak; shy.

**p̃uut** *noun* unmarried man.

**pwok** *noun* boar. *I piatlak waak nen ru soso ki pwok mil.* There is a pig which they call a wild boar. (*Sus scrota*). *cf:* klet, waak.

**pwok** *noun* slang for 'loose man or woman'.

## R

**-r** *pronoun suffix* **1)** them (3rd person plural object) when suffixed to transitive verbs. *Me tete p̃og a mes skotir.* And some nights I played with them. **2)** their (3rd person plural direct possessive) when suffixed to inalienable body part terms or used in reflexive constructions. *Selwan ru siwer pan nalur i kofkor namter.* When they walked their hair hid their eyes.

**ra=** *pronoun prefix* dual, with reference to any person (e.g., 1dl, 2dl, 3dl realis subject). We (two), you (two), they (two). *Selwan ra lak ra tap mer tm̃er tao mau.* Once they were married they did not leave each other.

**raeru** *noun* fish sp., bluespine unicornfish. (*Naso unicornis, Balistidae*). *cf:* naum, uus.

**rai=** *pronoun prefix* they (3rd person dual perfect subject). *Rai mer palus pan ra mai sak esan ru soso ki Krikai.* They (two) paddled again until they came to land at the place they call Krikai.

**rait (raiten)** *noun$_i$* mother. *Me tmer go raiter m̃as kin ra to gar preg sernale.* But it is just their father and mother who have to get everything for them. *cf:* iak.

**rak=** *pronoun prefix* dual, with reference to any person (e.g., 1dl, 2dl, 3dl irrealis subject). We (two), you (two), they (two). *Ra tok panpanpan nrak iskei ra na rak fak talm̃aat gar.* They (two) were there until one day they wanted to go to their garden.

**rakai=** *pronoun prefix* dual, with reference to any person (1st, 2nd, 3rd person dual perfect subject). We (two), you (two), they (two). *Malnen ra kel ntakun, go Kaltog i kel ntak Selwin teflan go rakai ler mai pak esum̃, Erakor.* Then they (two) held his back and Kaltong held Selwin's back like this and they came back to the house at Erakor.

**raki** See: reki

**rakum** *noun* crab (general term).

**rakum ntas** *noun* crab sp. (*krab kaledoni* in Bislama).

**ralim** *number* ten. Numbers between ten and twenty are formed with a base of ten then *atmat* and then the number, e.g., *ralim iskei atmat inru* 'twelve', *ralim iskei atmat ilim* 'fifteen'.

**ralim inru** *number* twenty.

**raolae** *noun* mat, special decorated mat for weddings. A mother wants to have a *raolae* for a good wedding.

**raru** *noun* canoe, ship, boat (often nowadays the term loto is used for a car). *I piatlak raru seserik go raru p̃afp̃of ru to sef ur namos ko ntas.* There are small boats and big boats that go in the ocean and the sea.

**raru m̃ol** *noun* canoe without a platform (*nafetfet*).

**raru ni nmalfa** *noun* aeroplane. *cf:* maan ni nmalfa.

**raru ni ntan** *noun* car, vehicle.

**raus** *noun* beam, crossbeam on top of the walls on the long side of a house. *cf:* nkaspeltakot, surnaot.

**reki (raki)** *preposition* **1)** for, to get to. *Or selwan ru tok palus reki euut...* When they paddled to shore... *Ku slati reki nafte?* What did you bring it for? *Ke fan preg naik, i mai ale i sori, ko ke sati reki esum̃ nen ruk fami.* He would go and get fish, come and sell them or take it for the house for them to eat. *Me ke fo mer kuk p̃og reki matool.* Then he would cook at night for the next day. **2)** as for. *Apu neu kin a tae tli, me reki apu ptae a kano tli.* I can talk about my own grandfather, but as for other people's grandfathers, I can't say.

**rik** *adjective* small, mainly used of islands (e.g., *Ekap̃um rik*) but also used for 'early'; *pulp̃og rik* 'early morning'. *I tok rik go ki pak emat temen pan.* He was early and he went to his father's grave.

**roktaar** *noun* fish sp., manta ray. (*Manta birostris*).

**rook** *noun* yam sp., white outside, red inside, cooks quickly.

**room̃** *noun* fish sp., striped surgeonfish, also sohal surgeonfish. (*Acanthurus lineatus, Acanthurus sohal*).

**roos** *noun* yam sp., red one and white one.

**rowat** *noun* sago palm, used for making thatch for roofs. (*Metroxylon warburgii*).

**rp̃ek** *noun* laplap wrapped and ready to cook.

**ru=** *pronoun prefix* they (3rd person plural realis subject). *Go mam u piatlak, famle ru pato Emar.* And we have family, they stay in Mare.

**ruelau** *noun* west.

**ruetu** *noun* east.

**rui=** *pronoun prefix* they (3rd person plural perfect subject). *Go i pregi panpan Efat negakit nen natam̃ool ru mat panpan natam̃ool rui tiik.* And it came to be that our Efate, our people, died until there were no people. *cf:* rukoi.

**ruk=** *pronoun prefix* they (3rd person plural irrealis subject). *U pan paus ki natam̃ool ki faat nen ruk welu nasum̃ tap.* We went and asked people for money so that they could help the church.

**rukoi=** *pronoun prefix* they (3rd person plural perfect subject). *Me malnen rukoi pe laosok silua ru tur pek.* When they finished pounding it, they sewed up the bag. *cf:* rui.

**ruum̃** *noun* shellfish sp., black wing oyster. Moves quickly through the water as if flying. (*Pteria avicular*).

## S

**sa** *verb$_i$* **1)** bad. *Mees a trau nrogo i sa.* Today I don't feel good. **2)** very, used idiomatically to intensify an adjective or verb, e.g., *i fsofus sa* 'he is very young', *i pios sa* 'he cries out loudly'.

**sa 1)** *demonstrative* here. *Ra mai tkal esa 1906. Me mama neu ki pe pi teesa nmatu p̃ur. Ra mai ra na pak sa.* They came here in 1906. But my mother was a big girl then. They came back here. **2)** *noun* place. *cf:* sago, sanpe, san, sanie.

**saago** *noun* shellfish sp., triton, big conch shell. (*Charonia tritonis*). *cf:* pupu.

**saak** *noun* yam sp., a 'strong' one, good for laplap, has prickles on the vine. Kalsarap has grown one that weighed 75 kg.

**saap̃** *verb$_i$* mistake. *Ku preg saap̃ namrun. Ku saap̃ napu.* You make a mistake. You miss the road. *cf:* sraf, sursap̃.

**saar** *verb* mix, combine. *Go, u saar a, komam nmatu go nanwei u* *saar, welkia u miks, u saar.* And we mix, us women and men, we would mix.

**safei** *verb$_i$* pull or twist a banana from a bunch.

**safeu** *verb$_i$* whistle loudly using your fingers. *cf:* p̃en.

**sago** *demonstrative* there, that one close to the addressee. *cf:* sa, san.

**sai** *verb$_i$* creep, way in which a plant grows along the ground (like *kumol* 'kumala', for example).

**sai** *verb$_i$* push. *A sai ki naaruk na ka taaloof.* I push my hand so I can shake hands. *A mai sai ki raru.* I will come by canoe (pushing the canoe).

**sai suek** *verb$_i$* poke the fire.

**saisai** *verb$_i$* slither, the way eels or snakes move.

**saisei** *verb$_i$* meet, have a meeting. *Ru saisei skot tiawi laap, tiawi laap ru trok go i pitlak hotel ito naur.* They met with many old people, many old people agreed and so there is a hotel on the island. *cf:* neet, nsaiseiwen, patlas, seltra.

**saisuek** *verb* build a fire, put the firewood together.

**sak** *verb$_i$* land, come ashore. *A mai na a sai ki raru, sak ki Ear, raru i to.* I came and pushed the canoe, came ashore at Ear.

**sak 1)** *verb$_i$* ascend, advance, go up (a hill). *I pi nlaken Vanuatu i po mer sak panpan kin go natam̃ool ru po ftom.* That is why Vanuatu has advanced and people have grown. **2)** *verb$_t$* increase.

**sak (sakes)** *verb$_a$* sit.

**sal** *verb$_i$* **1)** drift. **2)** swing. **3)** float. *Raru ni naat i sal.* The man's canoe is drifting. *Ra mai mai ra palus mai. Ra maos. Ra to sal namos.* They came, they paddled and came. They were tired. They floated on the ocean. **4)** hang, to hang someone by the neck. *I tm̃en sali.* He hanged himself. *cf:* salia, salsal.

**salia** *verb$_i$* throw into the water, to make float. *cf:* sal.

**salsal** *verb$_i$* **1)** light, to be light (not heavy). **2)** float on water. *cf:* salsal.

**sam** *verb$_i$* dunk, put something into liquid, as bread in tea, or laplap into coconut milk.

**san** *demonstrative* place, there, that place. *Ku lakor ta tae san kin a to tli mau, ko ku tae?* Maybe you don't know the place that I am talking about, or do you know it? *cf:* sa, sago.

**sanie** *demonstrative* there. *Kia olfala Kalwat ne, i po mat sanie.* This old man Kalwat, he died over there. *cf:* sa, sanpe.

**sanpe (sampe)** *demonstrative* there. *cf:* sa, sanie.

**sao** *verb$_a$* bale, scoop out water.

**saof (saofi)** *verb$_a$* visit. *I wi kin natam̃ool sikskei ru mer saof family gar.* It is good if each person visits their family. *Komam Limaas ra mer nag rak fan saofir.* Limaas and I said that we would go and visit them.

**saofak** *noun* sea urchin. *cf:* nalwaniksu, somkol.

**saolu (saolua)** *verb$_a$* remove, bail (water). *Selwan raru i p̃ur ki nai ku saolua.* When water fills up the canoe you bail it out.
**saoprei (saopreir)** *verb$_a$* splash, throw water onto something.
**sap** *noun* where, used when the speaker is unsure of the place-name. *Ale tu nrus pak elag, ru soso ki esap, me, Ntanmiel.* So we go up to a place they call, um, Ntanmiel. *cf:* nana, sua.
**sap̃el (sap̃le)** *verb$_a$* tie. *cf:* **sp̃il**
**saprek** *verb$_i$* discard, chuck out.
**sar (sari)** *verb$_a$* hug, immobilise (as in an animal or a child), restrain from moving.
**sari** *verb$_i$* wander. *Ko pan sari naor ni Linsi, i to nmaotao Hog Haba, go Pot Olry.* We wandered to Lindsay's place, between Hog Harbour and Port Olry.
**sari** *verb$_i$* filter liquid, e.g., kava or water, using cloth or coconut husk.
**sari** *verb$_i$* take the flesh from a clam shell.
**sarpopot** *noun* basket, round basket, made of coconut leaf. *cf:* nlafkir, nroog, polpol, sp̃ol, tip̃el.
**sarsok (sarsoki)** *verb$_a$* hold tight. *cf:* puetsok.
**sasaan** *verb$_i$* sick, deformed, disabled.
**saspe** *preposition* behind, there.
**sasu** *noun* fish sp., humpback grouper, pantherfish, also sweetlips. (*Cromileptes altivelis, Haemulidae*).
**sasupra** *noun* fish sp., lesson's sweetlips. (*Plectorhinchus lessonii*).
**sat** *verb$_i$* hold firmly. *cf:* slat.
**sautog** *noun* **1)** gift given with no obligation to repay it, usually at weddings. **2)** rent. *cf:* tigpiel.
**seek** *verb$_i$* paddle following the tide or wind; surf. *cf:* suar.
**seer** *noun* coconut frond.
**sees** *adjective* small, narrow. *I pi natrauswen sees m̃as, go a psawi ki mus nen ko fo nrogo.* It is just a small story and I thank you who will hear it. *cf:* seserik.
**sees** *noun* shellfish sp., general term for nerites, snail-shaped shells. (*Neritidae*).
**seeskanrp̃on** *noun* shellfish sp., costate nerite. The general term for nerites is *sees*. (*Nerita costata*).
**seesp̃al** *adjective* tiny. *cf:* seserik.
**sef** *adjective* what, which. *Ag ku paakor sef ntau?* When were you born?
**sef** *verb$_i$* **1)** escape, run away. *Go namrun nen ru sef ler pan pak Ermag pa.* And these things ran away back to Erromango. **2)** run.
**sef** *verb* avoid, get out of the way.
**sefmal** *noun* when. *Ki pe pi sefmal go? Em̃eltig ki tenklok.* What's the time? Nearly ten o'clock. *cf:* ngas.
**seltae** *verb* grasp, understand.
**seltra** *verb$_i$* go and meet someone. *cf:* neet, patlas, saisei.
**selwan** *adverb* while, at the time that. *Selwan ki ler tok etog mai ki preg nsaiseiwen p̃ur i skei go ki tili nag natam̃ool ruk fo pak efare.* When he had come back from abroad he called a big meeting and he

told them all they should go to the nakamal (meeting house). *cf:* malnen.

**semsem** *verb$_i$* happy, be happy. *A semsem toop selwan ku mai saof kineu.* I am very happy when you come to visit me.

**senai (snai)** *noun* intestines of an animal.

**seo** *verb* dig a hole for a yam to be planted in.

**ser** *adjective* every. *Ser pulp̃og Katapel i su mai pak etan, i piatlak nai sees iskei.* Each morning, Katapel would go down, there is a small waterhole. *cf:* silu.

**ser** *verb$_i$* **1)** flow. *I sel nawen nen kin ke tfag kor nai me, nai i kerkrai toop, i trau serlu nawen go i mer fiit mai to leeg ki narfaat.* She got sand and built a wall to stop the water but the water was too strong, it flowed over it and across the sand, and it flowed down to the bridge. **2)** melt.

**ser** *noun* **1)** prop used to support a leaning branch of a tree. **2)** joint, small piece of wood that holds two beams running in different planes or at right angles to each other.

**ser (sra)** *verb$_a$* hang. *Ku ser nal.* You hang the basket.

**ser (sra)** *verb$_a$* sweep; *ser nasok* 'sweep rubbish'.

**ser naliati** *adverb* every day, daily. *cf:* naliati.

**seragrag** *verb* come together in one place (an old word, not used today, see *paakruk*).

**sernale (serale)** *noun* anything, things, everything. *Ru mai plak sernale ni nafkal, ola me nana.* They came with everything for battle, spears and so on.

**sernaor** *adverb* everywhere.

**sernrak** *adverb* always. *Sernrak ru ple ko ru ftuk.* They argue or fight all the time. *Ku pes sernrak, ku pes toop sernrak.* You talk all the time, you talk too much all the time.

**serpaal** *noun* bract, part of coconut tree shaped like a boat in which the flower grows. Can be burned to use as a torch.

**sertao (sertao, sertaoer)** *verb$_a$* to sweep. *cf:* mas, pnoltao.

**sertep̃al** *verb$_i$* ignore, disobey, disbelieve. *A sertep̃al nafsan ni raitok.* I ignore my mother's words.

**seserik** *adjective* small, many small things. *Ga ke fo skel ki teesa seserik me Mis Kina ke fo preg nasum̃tap.* She would weigh the small children, but Miss Kina would give the church service. *cf:* sees, seesp̃al.

**sestau** *noun* sore, big head on the sore, cyst (an old word, not used today).

**sestau** *noun* shellfish sp., white and round, lives on stone.

**sfa** *verb* put something away secretly, like putting money in someone's pocket.

**sfir** *noun* lorikeet (green palm and rainbow) (type of bird). (*Trichoglossus haematodus*).

**sfirmer** *noun* waxbills, manakins, birds of that type. (*Estrildidae*).

**sfiu** *noun* whimbrel (type of bird). (*Numenius phaeopus*).

**si** *verb*$_{a}$ **1)** blow. *P̃a si nkap nen ke sor.* You blow to make the fire light. *Nlag i sisi kerkrai.* The wind blows strongly. **2)** shoot, with a gun. *Go komam u pan malen kin manpus ru ta to tm̃er sir.* And we went when the bush men were still shooting each other. *cf:* sisi.

**si (sir)** *verb*$_{a}$ divide a leaf using a knife, as you do to pandanus or to make a coconut broom (*nier*).

**si** *particle* completive particle, used to indicate that the action of the verb it is attached to has been completely achieved; *pamsi* 'eat all of', *slatsi* 'take all of'. It seems only to be allowed with these two and a small set of other verbs.

**si** *interjection* yes, from French and used in the same way to disagree with a question.

**sif (sfa, sfe) 1)** *verb*$_{a}$ flick with fingers; sling, using a slingshot. *Jacop i sifpun m̃aau nig Efil Kalros panpan i watpni.* Jacob hit the Ifira warrior Kalros with a stone and killed him. *Kineu a sfek ki faat sifsif neu.* I sling a stone from my slingshot. **2)** *verb* shoot. *cf:* sifsif.

**sifsif** *noun* slingshot. *cf:* sif.

**sigpir (sigpri)** *verb*$_{a}$ ignore, don't listen to. *cf:* psig.

**siig** *verb* show one's bottom, a sign of disrespect. *U pan na ko los ntas nanom trau krokur Matai kin i siig toklos mam to.* Yesterday we went swimming and were surprised to see Matai bend down and poke his backside at us.

**siik** *noun* kingfisher (type of bird). (*Alcedinidae*).

**siil** *noun* chilli.

**siil** *noun* shield. *cf:* tikor.

**siil** *noun* shellfish sp., turritellas (general term), white one that travels in the sand. (*Turritellidae*).

**siiti** *verb*$_{a}$ carry something heavy. *cf:* slat, wes.

**sik (ske)** *verb*$_{a}$ raise, lift.

**sikpol** *verb* carry something behind you hanging off a stick balanced on the shoulder, but if the stick has a load on both ends that is called *p̃aunamru. cf:* tafra.

**siksik** *verb*$_{i}$ play a game, using a large stick to hit a smaller stick out of a hole in the ground. A game that is not played much now.

**sikskaar** *adjective* messy (of hair).

**sikskei** *adjective* individual, separate, each, one or two. *Me kin tete ni mees ru ta to pregi, ru to me i sikskei, ia?* Some still do it today, they are there, but just the odd ones. *cf:* skei.

**sil** *verb*$_{i}$ **1)** enter. *Akam, teesa, teesa ni mees, u tap lek esan kin Litrapog i tkos mau, me kineu a leka ki namtak, go a sil wes, a pan to natkin.* You children of today, you don't see the place where Litrapong lives, but I have seen it with my own eyes and I went into it and was there on the edge of it (the cave in which Litrapong lives). **2)** join, come into the company of, meet.

**silfek** *verb* tuck in, push something in between something else, typically something flat such as paper money in between pages in a book, or tucking your shirt into your pants.

**silu** *adjective* every, every one. *I min silua me ki ga uut nai pan tua kin i mingi.* He drank it all, but he filled water (for the owl) and took it to give him to drink. *cf:* ser.

**sin** *$verb_i$* finish (only of rain). *Us i sin.* Rain is ending.

**sinrkat (sinrkati)** *$verb_a$* frighten someone.

**sipun (sipni)** *$verb_a$* shoot and kill.

**sireu** *verb* share things out with others.

**sirsak** *noun* wind going up.

**sirsir** *$verb_i$* **1)** drizzle. **2)** sow (seeds). **3)** germinating seed, shoot sprouting, e.g., a hibiscus stick planted in the ground that sprouts roots.

**sirsuk** *noun* wind going down.

**sisi** *noun* gun. *Go Mista Adam i nrik mam kin nag, "Ko faai polet sisi negamus."* And Mister Adams said to us, "Put bullets into your rifles." *cf:* si.

**sisi ni ntas** *noun* speargun.

**sisi p̃ur** *noun* rifle.

**sisi sees** *noun* revolver.

**siti** *verb* lift something heavy with two hands.

**siu** *verb* gather food from the reef.

**siwer** *$verb_i$* walk. *Ko natam̃ool laap ru tu me nmatu i muurin na ke siwer toolir nlaken nanwei laap ru tu.* There are lots of men there and a woman wants to walk past because of all the men there.

**ska** *verb* penetrate, as when a car smashes into another car, also used to describe having sex.

**skakoor** *noun* **1)** dark night, cloud blocking the moon. **2)** overcast, cloud cover blocking the sun.

**skakoor** *verb* put wood around a tree stump to burn it out.

**skakor (skakro)** *$verb_a$* block the road to stop someone getting through.

**skar (skari)** *$verb_a$* add, join. *Tiawi wan kin ru tli na mees i pi mal gamus. Nen ko fo skari.* The old people say that today it is up to you. That you should add to it (the good work that they have done). *cf:* paaskar.

**skarkar** *$verb_i$* scratch (of a chicken scratching the ground).

**skasook** *$verb_i$* jump around, more than once. *cf:* sook.

**skatur** *$verb_i$* pass through. *Malnen kin i ẹntan tefla nen ke enkor ntas, ntas i skatur natuen.* When she lay down to block the salt water, it went through her legs.

**skei** *adjective* **1)** one. **2)** same, as in *malskei* 'one time', 'at the same time'. *I ur nagis ne nafsan skei ne.* He went to this point, as in this same story. **3)** one, also used following a noun to indicate specificity of the noun. *Go i pi premium lis i skei.* And it is a premium lease. *cf:* sikskei.

**skeitrai** *noun* coconut grater. *cf:* fatma.

**sko (skor)** *verb$_a$* sex, to have sex with. *Ra tm̃er skor.* They have sex with each other. *cf:* ska.

**skof (skofi)** *verb$_a$* catch something as it falls. *P̃a skofir.* You catch them.

**skoot** *verb* swing, hang, like a monkey in a tree.

**skosuk** *verb$_i$* go backward. *P̃a skosuk pak nakoinrok.* You go backwards towards the rear. *Ku kaal ki skosuk ki singlet gaag.* You put your T-shirt on backwards.

**skot (skoti) 1)** *verb$_a$* with, go with. *Ku mer skotir ler.* You go back with them again. *Ag ku skot naat pak elau.* You go with the man to the sea. **2)** *verb$_a$* with, used of sexual relationship (*tm̃er skotir* 'they go with each other'). **3)** *preposition* with. *cf:* plak, ptaan.

**slaor** *noun* route, passage, as in the way through coral to get around the lagoon or to get to shore. *Kin me, ka fo to san po sol skel panpanpanpanpan pak eslaor ni Ertap.* And I would stay, bringing the scales (to weigh babies), until we went back to the passage at Eratap.

**slat (slati, sol, sat)** *verb$_a$* take, carry, bring, e.g., *sati pa,* carry something bigger than applies when using *wes*. *Me mees nmatu ke muur ke furi ke freg kapu, ga ke fan tm̃en slat nafnag.* But today if a woman wants to prepare a laplap, she must carry the food herself. *I sol teesa nafte, nmatu ko nanwei?* She is carrying what type of baby, girl or boy? *Me ag ku pan slat nanrmem sua?* But where did you bring ripe bananas from? *Me ati kaaru i na malfane ke fan slat kai.* And the other grandmother wanted to get cockles. *cf:* sat, siiti, wes.

**slati mai** *verb$_a$* bring.

**slei (slei, sleir)** *verb$_a$* action of wedging a door or window open, or wedging a table leg to make it balance. *Ku slei ki nsem̃.* You wedge it with a wood chip.

**slif** *verb* go inside, hide under.

**slo** *noun* plate used for pounding breadfruit. *cf:* pagotut, trakek.

**smaan** *noun* rudder, steering paddle, now used of a steering wheel of a car.

**sm̃ai (sm̃ai, sm̃air)** *verb$_a$* chew (kava, chewing gum).

**sman (smani, suman)** *verb* praise.

**sm̃anr (sm̃anri)** *verb$_a$* whip. *I pes kerkrai kik, tenrak i sm̃anri ki stokwip me tenrak i pes kerkrai kik m̃as.* That's it. He shouts at you, sometimes he whips you with a stockwhip, but sometimes he just shouts at you. *cf:* fis.

**smokle (smoklen)** *noun$_i$* **1)** noise made by something, like the noise of a car or of a plane. **2)** echo. *cf:* misleo.

**sm̃ol** *verb$_i$* make a noise with your mouth to call, usually a long kissing noise to call an animal or a person.

**sm̃ol (sm̃oli)** *verb$_a$* close a hole, plug, mend, caulk a hole in a canoe. *P̃a smol nkal gaag.* You mend your clothes.

**sm̃os** *noun* fish sp., rabbitfish. (*Siganidae*).

**snae** *verb* gut, take out the guts of an animal. (*Idiom: 'I will gut you.' Can mean I will severely punish you.*)

**snom** *noun* fish sp., spotted halfbeak. (*Hemiramphus far*).

**sog (sogi)** *verb*$_a$ fall, used of a house falling down.

**sog (sogi)** *verb*$_a$ kiss.

**sogkor** *verb*$_a$ block the way with a branch of wood. *cf:* laokor, tikor.

**sogsog (sogsogi)** *verb*$_a$ **1)** encircle game (animals or fish) to catch it. **2)** encircle a group of children to control them. *cf:* ti.

**sok (ska)** *verb*$_a$ throw. *Maarik ne i pei tua ki ola, ola kin ru pei, i pei ska ki ola panpan i na i nom.* The man first gave him a spear, the spear was first, he first threw the spear until it was done.

**sok** *adjective* child who is not growing.

**sok** *verb*$_2$ Emphasises the verb it is attached to. *A pei weswes a ta mrosok sef ntau mau, a weswes British kafman.* I worked, I don't remember what year, for the British government. *Malfanen Ririal i trau slatsoki me i to tagsi.* Now Ririal held him tightly and he cried for him.

**sokfal** *noun* owl (type of bird). (*Tyto alba*).

**soklep** *adjective* rich.

**soklkau (soklkaui)** *verb*$_a$ jump over.

**soksm̃anr (soksm̃anri)** *verb*$_a$ nearly hit something by slipping into it. *Loto i soksm̃anr naat.* The car nearly hit the man. *cf:* kursm̃anr.

**soksok** *verb*$_2$ used to emphasise a verb, e.g., *mrosoksoki* 'think carefully'. *Mam u po tap taesoksoki na ga i pi maarik naot mau, nlaken ru po ta tli mau.* We didn't really know that he was the chief, because they hadn't said.

**sol** See: slat

**solsol (solsla)** *verb*$_a$ **1)** rub. **2)** caress.

**somkol** *noun* sea urchin, with long black spines. (*Diadema savignyi*). *cf:* nalwaniksu, saofak.

**sook** *verb*$_a$ rise (as in the sun, the moon or a star rising). *Aal i pregnrogo nen i sook.* The sun is trying to come out.

**sook** *verb*$_a$ visit, go to see someone. *Ra pan ra sook ki asler. Rakai to puserek.* They went to see their friends. They were talking.

**sook (ska)** *verb*$_a$ leap, jump. *Ku sook nkas.* You jump from the tree. *I sook pak na nmal nawen pan, na i lek wiit pak elau.* It jumped onto the middle of the sand, and it saw the octopus in the sea. *cf:* skasook.

**sook (ska)** *verb*$_a$ collide.

**soor** *verb*$_a$ cut wood.

**soptau** *noun* shellfish sp., small shells like olive-shaped imbricaria. (*Imbricaria olivaeformis*).

**sor (sro)** *verb*$_i$ light (as of fire); be alight. If the fire is glowing or smoking then it is referred to as *fag*. *Nkap i sor.* The fire is alight. *Ka si ke sor.* I blow (the fire) to light it. *Ntas i sor.* The sea is shining (with phosphorescence). *cf:* m̃tel, taalag, paam̃as.

**sor** *verb$_a$* scrub, e.g., with coconut husk, or clean your teeth.

**sor (sori)** *verb$_a$* sell. *Ale i pan sor tete sernale hotel, nen ke sol faat sees.* Then he goes and sells something at the hotel, to get a little money.

**sorsor (sorsro)** *verb$_a$* praise.

**sorsor (sorsro)** *verb$_a$* show off by lifting something that is too heavy. *I tm̃en sorsro slat sernale mten.* She showed off carrying all the heavy things.

**soru** *adjective* gap, something missing, like a gap in the teeth, a missing tooth. *cf:* npatsoru.

**sos** *noun* grasshopper. (*Orthoptera spp.*)

**sos** *verb$_d$* **1)** to call. *Selwan i ler mai ke fo sos nam̃er nega ruk fak efare me ke fo nrikir ki tenag i leka.* When he returned he would call his people to the house and he would tell them what he had seen. **2)** to name. *Namba tortin, u pak elag, naor i skei ru soso ki Tanmililip.* But on the thirteenth we went up to this place they call Tanmililip. *cf:* pios.

**sp̃ei (sp̃eir)** *verb* cut off the head (the end that is attached to the stalk) of taro or yam (but not other root crops which don't have a 'head').

**sp̃il (sp̃ili)** *verb$_a$* tangle. *A preg nmarit ne i pi sp̃il.* I tangled this rope. *cf:* sap̃el

**sp̃ol** *noun* basket (for the garden). *cf:* nlafkir, nroog, polpol, sarpopot, tip̃el.

**sputan** *noun* dwarf, dangerous creature which lives in the bush and may eat food that is left lying around.

**sraf** *verb$_i$* **1)** miss. *Ku rog wes taosi ku rog ku sraf, a, ku sraf napu kia.* You are wrong there, you took the wrong road. **2)** mistake. *I skul wi me selwan ku sraf i taos skul masta i skei i po sm̃anri.* He was well educated, but when you made a mistake he was like a school master, he would hit you. *cf:* saap̃, sursap̃.

**srak** *noun* insect, stick insect, that can be eaten. It has a white powder inside it that can be used as paint.

**srakor (srakro)** *verb$_a$* hide something. *Me kano nen kin i kus to i srakor nafar teesa nmatu ne.* But the man who was in hiding hid the girl's wing.

**sralesok** *verb$_i$* trust. *Ku sralesok Leatu p̃a fo m̃ool.* You trust in God so you will be safe. *cf:* nasralesokwen.

**sraletu (sraletua)** *verb$_a$* **1)** confess. **2)** be sorry.

**sreniu** *noun* fish sp., squirrelfish. (*Holocentridae*). *cf:* trakap.

**srof (srofi)** *verb$_a$* **1)** suck, breathe in, drink noisily. (*Idiom: 'You breathe the ground.' After being beaten in a fight you breathe in the ground.*) **2)** grunt, the noise a pig makes. *cf:* tarp̃otik, ur.

**srosur** *noun* tool for taking coconut meat out of the shell.

**srot** *verb* destroy a house or a building. Use the word *sor* for cutting out a tree.

**sto** *noun* **1)** store (from English). **2)** Vila, also known as *sto p̃ur*.

**su (sua)** *verb$_a$* catch (as in sickness). *Nlaken nafitiawian totur namsaki nlaken neu me a po to su nmarom̃iit.* Because of old age I have got sick, because I have caught asthma. *cf:* oof.

**su** *particle* use this after a verb to say that the action has been completely done. *Ki pe mat su.* It is already dead. *Kineu a pam natam̃ool i tol su.* I have already eaten three people.

**su** *verb$_i$* descend (from a hill), get out of a canoe. *Ser pulp̃og Katapel i su mai pak etan, i piatlak nai sees iskei.* Each morning, Katapel went down, there is a small waterhole.

**sua** *interrogative* where. *Ale i paus ki na, "Ag ku to pan sel kaai sua?"* And he asked her, "Where do you get cockles from?" *cf:* nana, sap.

**suar** *verb$_i$* paddle against the tide or wind. *cf:* seek.

**suarip** *noun* common waxbill (type of bird). (*Estrilda astrild*).

**suek** *verb$_i$* put wood in fire.

**suekor (suekro)** *verb$_a$* smoke, as in drying copra, or smoking a fish.

**suer (suerai)** *verb$_a$* shit, excrete. *Kineu a suer.* I'm shitting. *P̃a fan suer!* You go and shit!

**sul** *verb$_i$* hesitate, be a little scared of, as with an in-law whom you have to avoid.

**sul** *verb$_i$* pull the head back to duck, to avoid something by pulling the head back.

**sul** *verb$_i$* fish by torchlight.

**sul (suli)** *verb$_a$* cut the eye out of a coconut.

**sulfra** *verb$_a$* to be scared, shake with fear. *A sulfra ki ntwam.* I'm scared of the devil. *A sulfrak ki m̃aat.* I scare you with a snake.

**sulkor (sulkro)** *verb$_a$* glare, blind by light.

**sulok** *noun* umbrella.

**sulprog** *noun* lizard that you find under rocks or timber.

**sulsul (sulsli)** *verb$_a$* soften something in the fire. *Ku masulsli nkap.* You soften it in the fire. *Ku sulsul tok.* You soften the wild cane (to straighten it).

**sulsul** *noun* great-grandchild (slang). *cf:* suul.

**sum̃** *noun* house. *Teflan a sees go a to naur, a tap to sum̃ ni iak neu go apaap neu m̃as mau.* When I was small and I stayed on the island, I didn't only stay at my mother and father's house. *cf:* nasum̃.

**sumat** *noun* vine sp.

**sum̃faitau** *noun* school.

**sum̃kai** *noun* yam sp., dark red inside, under the outside skin is white.

**sum̃los** *noun* bathroom.

**sum̃sees** *noun* toilet.

**sum̃sm̃o** *verb* get wet, as in being wet by the rain.

**sunra** *noun* red-bellied fruit dove, bird which cries out when someone has died. (*Ptilinopus greyii*).

**sunref** *verb$_i$* sniff.

**sup̃ (sup̃en)** *noun$_i$* **1)** character of a person or animal. *Ku tae sup̃ ni teem̃ool i tap tae nafte kin maarik nen i nrikin kin mau.* You know how animals are, it didn't understand what the man said to it. **2)** habit. *cf:* naskeimielwen, p̃op̃.

**sup̃ (sup̃ti)** *verb$_a$* stab with something sharp. Take out by stabbing, e.g., the head of a boil. *cf:* tnus.

**sup̃fu (sup̃fua)** *verb$_a$* pierce boil.

**sup̃neki (sup̃nekin)** *verb$_a$* not know, be ignorant of. Not the same as *tap tae mau* 'don't know'. *Tiawi ni teetwei gar ru sup̃nekin mtir, tiawi ru kano mtir.* The old people long ago didn't know how to write, the old people couldn't write. *Go a ta tae kastom ni Erakor i tfale mau, kineu a sup̃neki.* And I don't know how Erakor custom works, I am ignorant of it. *cf:* maak.

**sup̃otunr** *verb$_i$* bow one's head in shame.

**sup̃raan** *noun* two-faced person.

**sup̃rai (sup̃rair)** *verb$_a$* stab and break.

**sup̃sup̃** *noun* **1)** horn of an animal like a cow or a goat, or sea urchin. **2)** thorns on a plant. *cf:* nais.

**sup̃tap** *noun* punishment (which may include having to pay a fine – *naro*). *Ku preg namrun i sa, ku wat np̃au, ru tuok sup̃tap.* If you do something bad, like killing a man, they will punish you.

**sup̃ti** *verb* sting.

**sur (sura)** *verb$_a$* take out flesh of coconut, also *surlua 'take out completely'. Tiawi i fla pan sur kopra i patu komam natam̃ool kerkerai ko fo tae pan gar slati mai.* The old people would cut out the copra, and we strong ones would go and get it for them.

**surfunfnoi** *verb$_i$* erase, obliterate. *cf:* funfnoi, krakfunfnoi.

**surnaal** *verb* shave hair, pluck hair out.

**surnaot** *noun* beam, crossbeam at ceiling level of a house. *cf:* nasu, nkaspeltakot, raus, surnp̃ou.

**surnp̃ou** *noun* beam in house building, holding the roof of a house. *cf:* surnaot.

**sursap̃** *verb$_i$* miss. *Ku sursap̃ napu.* You missed the road (went the wrong way). *cf:* saap̃, sraf.

**sursur (srosro)** *verb$_a$* deceive, pretend to do something. *Ku sursur wou nanom na p̃a fo pa, me ku ta pan mau.* You tricked me yesterday saying that you would go, but you didn't go. *cf:* gien.

**surwel (surweli)** *verb$_a$* replace.

**sus** *verb$_i$* suck at the breast. *cf:* mimi, nais.

**susa** *noun* jaw harp.

**suskei** *noun* caterpillar.

**suski** *verb* plant, to put a plant in the ground.

**susmraknaniu** *noun* fish sp., goatfish (goldband, blackstriped, yellowbanded). (*Upeneus*). *cf:* konafnako.

**susu** *verb$_i$* cradle a child (rock it from side to side).

**susunatog** *noun* robin (type of bird).

**suu** *verb* **1)** to wear on the head. **2)** headbutt, head a football.

**suu (suwai)** *verb* root, as in a pig rooting in the ground. *Tenen i tok lek waak nen i to suu entan.* The man looked after the pig which was digging the ground.

**suul (suulin)** *noun*$_i$ grandchild, term used by grandparent for their grandchild. *cf:* sulsul.

**suul kaaru** *noun* great-grandchild.

**suun** *verb*$_i$ carry on the head.

**suur** *verb*$_a$ cut grass, weed the ground.

**suus** *noun* fish sp., yellowstripe goatfish, yellowfin goatfish. Note that the yellowtail barracuda is *suuspwok*. (*Mullidae*). *cf:* konafnako.

**swiit** *noun* banana sp., lady's finger.

## T

**ta** *interjection* thanks. *cf:* psawi.

**ta** *noun* aunt, the sister of your mother or father. Note: added to last syllable of some names, e.g., *ta + ana tana, ta + lilo talo.*

**ta** *preverbal* **1)** still. *Go ga kin i pi maarik kin i ta to.* And he is the *maarik* (spirit) who is still there. **2)** used to express the progressive, to be doing something.

**ta** *preverbal* not, used with *mau* as the second part of the negation. *Esan mana ru ta lom mau.* This part wasn't wet. *cf:* tap.

**ta=** *pronoun prefix* we (1st person dual inclusive realis subject). *Akit ta nru tok me selwan kineu a fla mat …* We are both here, and when, maybe, I die …

**taa** *verb*$_i$ wrap a part of the body, as in wrapping a scarf around the head. *Taa np̃aun ki gkal.* Wrap your head with a cloth.

**taag** *noun* sea slug, sea creature that is like a sea snail but without a shell. *cf:* litot.

**taag** *noun* banana sp., plantain banana for cooking. *cf:* taagmetkes, taagmol, taagsus.

**taagmetkes** *noun* banana sp., cooking banana. *cf:* taag, taagmol, taagsus.

**taagmol** *noun* banana sp. *cf:* taag, taagmetkes, taagsus.

**taagsus** *noun* banana sp. *cf:* taag, taagmetkes, taagmol.

**taai** *noun* brother.

**taak** *noun* age-mate, someone the same age as you. *Tene i pi taak neu.* He is the same age as me.

**taakau** *verb* **1)** turn a canoe quickly. **2)** hook shot in cricket, hit the ball around and behind you.

**taakot** *noun* axe, curved axe used in battles.

**taakot** *verb* cut, with an axe (*taakotkot* indicates cutting many things).

**taakto** *noun* eel. *cf:* mra.

**taakto ninai** *noun* fish sp., river eel.

**taalag** *verb*$_i$ shine (of torchlight, or of the moon, but not the sun, which is *paam̃as* 'shine'). *cf:* paam̃as, sor.

**taalaklak** *verb*$_i$ whisper.

**taalau** *noun* yam sp., wild yam, sweet, has spines along the ground around the root.

**taaloof** *verb*$_i$ shake hands.

**taalu** *verb* clean a spring of water.

**taalua** *verb* allow, permit, let something happen.

**taam̃an** *verb* scatter.

**taam̃el** *verb*$_i$ squat, crouch.

**taanre (taanrea)** *verb*$_a$ stir in a circular motion, unlike *walnre,* which involves stirring from the bottom to the top. *cf:* walnre.

**taanu (taanuei)** *verb*$_a$ spit. *cf:* ntaanu.

**taap̃aar** *noun* sin, also used of an act which could be considered 'sinful'.

**taapam** *verb*$_i$ carry under the arm.

**taapas** *verb*$_i$ wave, call someone over with a hand gesture.

**taap̃as** *verb* adopted, be adopted. *I pi teesa taap̃as neu.* He is my adopted child. *cf:* p̃as.

**taap̃es** *noun* swamphen (type of bird). *Go mees ku tae pam̃or too kin i to ur esum̃, nlaken kin i pnak kom ni taap̃es.* And today you will find that the chicken stays around the house because it stole the swamphen's comb. (*Porphyrio melanotus*).

**taap̃etu** *verb*$_i$ kneel.

**taapol** *verb*$_i$ steer, action of paddling to turn the canoe to the side.

**taap̃oos** *adjective* curved.

**taapsik** *verb*$_i$ clean the ground.

**taap̃ur** *adjective* greedy, want more than others have.

**taar** *adjective* white. *Or go na p̃og i skei i tili nag, "Ka fo pak etog nafanu nig nam̃er taar."* Yes and one night he said, "I will go to the foreign place of the white people." *cf:* tau.

**taar** *verb*$_i$ to crow, the noise a rooster makes.

**taar** *verb* broke, not to have any money (slang), 'white page'.

**taarag** *noun* net, made with coconut leaves.

**taasai** *verb*$_a$ cut the way through bush.

**taasak** *verb*$_i$ come to the shore from the sea. *Raru i sal mai taasak eslaor Elkau.* The canoe came ashore at Elkau passage.

**taasir** *verb*$_i$ scatter.

**taasok (taasoki)** *verb*$_a$ hug, hold against the chest, like a child. *cf:* wafin.

**taata** *verb* clear the ground, take out weeds.

**taata** *noun* father, the address term used by members of the *kram naflak. U pan paakor Elaknar go Taata Sailas i to esum̃ nega to.* We went to find Elaknar and Taata Sailas was at his house. *cf:* apaap, gka, tem.

**taata** *verb* peck. (*Idiom: 'The hen pecks to show her young to do likewise.' When a person does something which gets imitated [either mistakenly or deliberately] by their child.*)

**taatan** *verb* **1)** plant something. **2)** bury something. *cf:* ofa, tan.

**taatur (taaturi)** *verb* escort someone, lead the way for them; meet someone on their way to your house and come back with them.

**tae (taer) 1)** *verb*$_a$ know, also used in compounds, e.g., *nrogtae* 'recognise' (hear), *mrotae* 'understand' (know). *Go tiawi laap nen kin i taer, gar ruipe pei maui matmat.* And the many old people that he knew, they had all died before. **2)** *auxiliary* can, to be able to. *Kano taar i tae tafnau ag.* The white man can teach you. *cf:* metmatu, ntaewen.

**taf** *verb$_i$* **1)** exit, leave. *Ko fiit taf pak ektem ko ta to em̃rom nasum̃ mau.* Run and go outside, don't stay inside the house. **2)** shit, have diarrhoea. *Me ru kraksok disentri, me ru taf ki nra.* They got dysentery and they shat blood.

**tafafu** *verb$_i$* hatch, as of an egg. *Too i tafafu.* The chicken is hatching an egg. *cf:* maaf.

**tafesfes** *verb$_i$* pray.

**tafiif** *verb$_i$* **1)** boiling (of water); *nai i tafiif 'water is boiling'.* **2)** whirlpool. **3)** bad feeling (idiomatic). *Tafiif ni naflewen gar ni teetwei i ta to.* The bad feeling from their fight long ago still remains.

**tafiif ni nlag** *noun* whirly wind.

**tafin** *noun* a woman servant who helps around the house. An older meaning is 'slave'.

**tafkaaru** *verb* report, tell someone about something.

**tafnau (tafnaus)** *verb$_a$* preach, teach. *Tem me rait ru tafnau pta ki teesa gar.* The father and mother teach their children. *cf:* faitau, fnau.

**tafra** *noun* whale.

**tafra** *noun* bundle tied to a pole and carried between two people, typically root crops like taro or yams, used to take to a feast. *cf:* sikpol.

**tafrafer** *verb$_i$* scatter, go to different locations.

**tafut** *noun* fish sp., hawkfishes (that travel with big fish). Also identified as prettyfins. (*Cirrhitidae, Plesiopidae*).

**tafuu** *noun* uncivilised, used before of people from other parts of Vanuatu.

**tag (tagsi) 1)** *verb$_a$* cry. *Ale Ririal i na i satsok, i na i slati kai pe to tag.* So Ririal took him, he carried him and he cried. **2)** *noun* mourn. *I tagsi.* She cries for him.

**Tagiter** *noun* spirit, an omen of impending death. When you hear the voice of *Tagiter* calling at sea, someone has died. *Tagiter* is a spirit '*ntwam*'. *cf:* ter.

**tagralim** *noun* moth sp., black with white marks. *cf:* meer.

**tai** *verb$_a$* **1)** cut. *I tok i tai nafil panpanpanpan kai paai nafil ru pak em̃rom naal ga.* He cut the navele (nuts) and he filled up his basket with them. **2)** sting (as in a jellyfish sting).

**tai** *noun* jellyfish that stings.

**tak (tkan)** *verb$_a$* husk a coconut.

**tak (tkan)** *verb$_a$* **1)** trip over something. **2)** fall over. *A lek nafet nasum̃ nigmam ru tak tefla, tak tefla nkas ru tak.* I saw all our houses fall over, trees fell over.

**tak (tkan)** *verb$_a$* kick with your toes, stub your toes.

**tak=** *pronoun prefix* we (1st person dual inclusive irrealis subject). *Tak stat nagis ne, tak res panpan na ta fak nagis kaaru.* We (two) will start at this point, we'll race until we get to the next point.

**takai= (tkai)** *pronoun prefix* we two (1st person dual inclusive perfect subject).

**takel** *verb$_i$* crooked. *P̃a tap tai nkas nen i takel mau i sa ki nasum̃.* Don't cut crooked wood, it is not good for house building.

**takelkel** *noun* millipede which *pan* 'burns' your skin.

**takerker** *noun* grey fantail (type of bird).

**takinrog** *verb$_i$* listen.

**takinrog wi** *verb$_i$* concentrate.

**taklep** *noun* child, first born. *Neu kin a pi taklep, neu kin a pitlak rait.* I, who am the firstborn, I have rights.

**takmaloput** *noun* child, middle born.

**takor (takro)** *verb$_a$* prevent, stop someone doing something. *cf:* pestatakor.

**takotp̃au** *noun* wreath, flowers prepared for a funeral.

**takrik** *noun* child, last born. *Panpan me teesa sees, tenen i pi takrik, ga i paakot ga nalag nen ru to si, mouth organ, ga i paaktofi.* Then a small child, the last child, bought a mouth organ for them to blow, a mouth organ, he bought it.

**taktaak** *verb$_i$* **1)** sway when walking, as when drunk. **2)** roll (of a boat in the waves). *cf:* tartaar.

**taktak** *noun* duck (type of bird).

**taktak** *noun* fish sp., bird wrasse. (*Gomphosus varius*). *cf:* patru.

**taktakninai** *noun* Australian grey duck (type of bird).

**takwer** *noun* sea snake, black and white; sea krait. (*Laticauda colubrina*).

**takwerkot** *noun* plant sp., with yellow leaves that people grow as fences and boundaries in yards. A variety of *naulalas*. (*Polyscias scutellaria*).

**tal** *verb* to roll pandanus leaves that have been boiled, dried, baked in the sun and prepared to be used for weaving. *Tal* is used only of rolling pandanus. *cf:* lul, taltel.

**tal** *verb* slow, be slow. *cf:* mailum.

**talel** *verb$_i$* dodge, avoid. *cf:* lelu.

**talgolig** *noun* dizzy.

**taligftin** *noun* otitis, inflammation of the ear.

**taligme** *noun* fish sp., surgeonfishes, big one is called *p̃arsor*. (*Acanthuridae*). *cf:* map̃eriat, tiftif, weel.

**taligter** *noun* **1)** eel sp. **2)** white-eyed moray, has 'ears'. Can be eaten but doesn't have much flesh. (*Siderea grisea*).

**talm̃aat** *noun* garden. *Ku pe pak talm̃aat ko?* Have you been to the garden or not?

**talm̃aat faum** *noun* newly planted garden.

**talm̃aat fus** *noun* garden left fallow.

**talm̃aat tau** *noun* garden left fallow.

**talmat** *noun* fish sp., batfish (also *naik nasok,* when young, like a piece of rubbish floating in the water). *cf:* foik.

**talof** *verb$_i$* jump out of the way of something, duck.

**talpuk** *noun* **1)** crowd. **2)** group. *Go a leka na taos talpuk ni nanwei ru weswes kerkrai.* And I see that a group of men are working hard.

**taltel** *noun* roll of pandanus (*naki*) leaves. After they have been cured in an earth oven and dried in the sun, the edges are stripped and rolled into large (30 cm) rolls. *cf:* tal.

**tamarin** *noun* tree sp. (*Glochidion ramiflorum*).

**tam̃as** *noun* halo, ring around the moon (an old word not known today). *cf:* nrafkor.

**tametpel** *noun* fish name that includes Starck's demoiselle and blackvent damselfishes. (*Chrysiptera starcki, Dischistodus melanotus*). *cf:* naik nrmen.

**tamlaanr** *verb* go out without having had breakfast.

**tamotm̃ot** *verb* hold something tight to save yourself, like in a cyclone, or if they are trying to take you away and you cling to a tree.

**tam̃ra** *noun* starfish. (*Ophidiasteridae*).

**tam̃uk** *verb* use a cloth to hold a saucepan when it's too hot for your hands.

**tan** *verb$_i$* **1)** to bury. **2)** to plant, of plants that are buried, like root crops, otherwise, it is *lao* for plants that need to be stood up when planted. *cf:* lao, ofa, taatan.

**tanum̃ (tanm̃ei)** *verb$_i$* put meat (of any kind, including seafood) on laplap. *Ku tanum̃ nap̃kas i pak kapu.* You put meat on the laplap. *Go ati nen ser nrak nen kin ru pa, ga i sol nafnag i toop tolir siluer. Nlaken ga i to tanum̃ nap̃kas kapu.* And this grandmother, every time they went, she got more food than anyone else. Because she put meat on the laplap. *cf:* gkof, p̃ti.

**tanun** *verb* set (of the moon) (for the sun setting use *mtar*). *cf:* mtar.

**tao** *verb$_a$* **1)** leave, let go. *P̃a tao maan ki nrir pa.* You let the bird fly away. *Ku tao waak ki taf.* You let the pig escape. **2)** divorce.

**tao (taon)** *verb$_a$* bake. *Ke fo wasirlu namten me tao plak kapu nega me ke fo pami.* He would take out the (warrior's) eyes and bake them with his laplap and he would eat them. *Ku tao nafnag taos nanr, ntal, nawi.* You bake food like banana, taro, yam.

**taos** *verb* to be like; be similar to. *Ga i ta taos sisi gamus nam̃er taar mau.* It is not like your white man's guns. *cf:* nrokos.

**tap 1)** *adjective* taboo, forbidden. *Ru tu san tu, me ru kano sil. I tap. I piatlak lo knen i to.* They stand there, but they can't go inside. It is taboo. There is a law about it. **2)** *preverbal* 'no' or 'not', before the verb it is the same as ta. *cf:* ta.

**tap** *verb$_i$* lean. *A tap nkas. Kineu a tap wes.* I lean on the wood. I lean on it.

**tapiak** *verb$_i$* **1)** begin weaving a mat with a crossed pair of leaves. **2)** lean something against something, like leaning a piece of wood against the wall.

**tap̃ir** *noun* tree used to make *lak,* joints between *nsem* 'outrigger' and *nakiat* 'cross-member' on a canoe. This is a small tree, less than three metres tall, also used to make a rough broom. Its leaves can be used to numb the mouth when you have a toothache.

**tap̃o** *verb$_i$* capsize, tip over, can be of anything that tips over, a person or a canoe or car. *cf:* p̃ip̃.

**taptaan** *adjective* enough. *Mam nen kin u weswes u nrus taptaan.* We who were working had enough. *Neu i taptaan kis.* I've got enough here with me. *Natam̃ool ru taaptan kis ru patu limuuti nig nasum̃tap tau.* There are enough people at the churchyard.

**tap̃u** *noun* heap, to mound up together or group together, e.g., *tap̃u nasok* 'heap of rubbish', *tap̃u natam̃ool* 'crowd of people', or *tap̃u naik* 'school of fish'.

**tare** *verb$_i$* turn, as in an object turning, or being turned. *I tare ki glas.* He turned over the glass. *Ku tare nanre ni matu gaag.* You turn to your right side. *cf:* nre.

**tarim** *noun* armlet, coloured armlet for a chief. *cf:* leel.

**tarir** *noun* necklace worn by a chief.

**tarisal** *noun* **1)** driftwood. **2)** flotsam, anything that gets washed up by the sea. It can also be an insult to call someone *tarisal. cf:* nafiaf.

**taro** *noun* bird which eats chilli and so its meat is spicy to eat.

**tarp̃otik** *adjective* noisy; *min tarp̃otik* 'to drink noisily' (an old word not known today). *cf:* srof.

**tartaar** *verb$_i$* walk crookedly, stagger. *A nrepagik p̃a fo tartaar.* I'll hit you so you will stagger. *cf:* taktaak.

**tarup̃** *verb$_i$* fall, stumble. *Nmalko ki pe tok tarup̃ ntan.* Darkness was falling on the land.

**tas (tasi)** *verb$_a$* **1)** shave, cut hair from skin. **2)** take bark off a tree.

**tasaal** *noun* basket (pandanus or coconut). *cf:* fuelig, likat, napor, nroog.

**tasar** *noun* fish sp., deep sea fish.

**tasil** *noun* chief's bodyguard, warrior.

**taso** *noun* burned limestone used to make cement.

**tastes** *noun* plane, spokeshave, for smoothing wood.

**tasuur** *noun* tsunami wave, a wave that comes onto the land.

**tatakaal** *noun* plant with flower which opens at 11.00 am, about 30 cm high, with single leaves. The flower can be used as medicine when you spit blood. A white variant can be used as a broom.

**tataraas** *noun* plant sp., medicine can be made of the leaves.

**tatu (tatue)** *verb$_a$* load. *Malen kin ru ga preg pta ki m̃iit, ru ga preg pta ki nkal, pan pan i nom ru tatue ki raru, ru msagi raru me ru pa.* After they got mats ready for him and material ready for him, they loaded the canoe and they took the canoe and they went. *Kin po tatue skel raru.* Then put the scales in the canoe.

**tau** *verb* stay, used the same as *to. Tak fo leka, fei kin ke fo pregi nag te natam̃ool nen i tau ke slatlu gkal namlaanri nega.* We will see, who will make it so that people who stay will take off their warm clothes.

**tau** *verb$_i$* bear fruit, as in a tree bearing fruit. *Nua nkas ru tau toop.* Fruit trees bear lots of fruit.

**tau** *adjective* white. *cf:* taar.

**taulu (taulua)** *verb$_a$* marry, of a man marrying a woman. *A mro kin nag akam uf mer taulu tete go negar kin ruk fo pregwi ki nafanu negakit.* I think that you should marry some (of them) and they will then be good for our country. *cf:* lak, naftourwen, tosok, ptour.

**taum̃of** *verb$_i$* sacrifice (an old word, not used today).

**taurua** *noun* fish sp., whitespotted surgeonfish. (*Acanthurua striatus, Acanthurus olivaceus*).

**taus (tausi)** *verb$_a$* follow. *Ku tae sef teflan me i tae kop teflan kin i tae nlaken ke fo taus nalo gaag, ga i pi naik.* You can run away, but it will follow you, because it will follow your dust trail; it is a fish.

**tausees** *noun* baby. *cf:* nan, teesa.

**tauso** *verb$_i$* commit adultery.

**te-** *determiner prefix* 'the', used to make nouns out of adjectives and verbs, like *temlaap* from *mlaap* 'last' means 'the last one'. *Ru matmat pan pan tewarik m̃as kin go ru po nrookot pak naur sees.* Many died and only very few crossed across to the small island.

**teelekor** *noun* guard, person who guards something.

**teemat** *noun* corpse, dead body. *cf:* naatmat.

**teem̃iit** *noun* balls, testicles. *cf:* pol, p̃ura.

**teem̃ool** *noun* animal (general term), creature. *Me i mrokin na teem̃ool taos kori ko i tefla.* And he thought it was an animal, like a dog or something like that.

**teemtakun** *noun* respect relationship, used to describe the way that one behaves with in-laws, e.g., avoiding being near them, and using the dual form instead of the singular when talking to an in-law (e.g., *akam rakmai fam* 'you (dual) come and eat'). (Tokolau Takau recalls this from her youth but it is no longer practised.)

**teemtmen** *noun* father and his child.

**teep̃al** *noun* spirit, various kinds of bad spirits.

**teesa** *noun* child. A daughter or a girl is *teesa nmatu* and a son or a boy is *teesa nanwei. Me i piatlak teesa i skei i paakor faat elau.* But a child appeared on a rock in the sea. *cf:* nan, tausees.

**teesa nanwei** *noun* boy, son. *Ra pitlak teesa nmatu i tol me teesa nanwei i paat.* We have three girls and four boys.

**teesa napu** *noun* bastard, illegitimate child (lit: child of the road). *Nmatu nen i pan skot nanwei p̃rakot i piatlak teesa napu.* A woman who goes with any man has a bastard child.

**teesa nmatu** *noun* girl, daughter.

**teesa sees** *noun* child, baby.

**teet** *noun* sister (address term).

**teetwei** *adverb* before. *Teetwei tiawi ru tap tae maan ni nmalfa mau.*

Before, the old people did not know aeroplanes.

**tef (tfei)** *verb*$_a$ **1)** cut, to make a small cut; to cut a sore open. *Tenag ru mat ru tfeir go ru pu nmarter i pan me ru pregi i kal ki nkal nega go ru pregi i ler pak nafanu nega pan.* Those who died, they cut them and they pulled out their guts and they dressed them in their clothes and they took them back to their country. **2)** circumcise. **3)** carve (wood, or meat). *cf:* mas.

**tef** *verb*$_i$ call of the kingfisher. It brings luck if you hear it on your right side.

**tefaitau** *noun* teacher. *cf:* faitau, plaksok.

**tefkau** *noun* mat, made from coconut leaf, used for walls of houses.

**tefkot** *verb* break with the hand.

**tefla** *adverb* similar, like that. *Mees ku pam̃ori na i piatlak pasis i sees m̃as, go natrauswen ni lakun i tefla.* Today you see the passage there is only small, and the story of the lagoon goes like that.

**tefra** *verb*$_i$ line up, put things in a line.

**tego** *demonstrative* that. *E i tiik i tiik, i ta pi tego mau.* No, no, it isn't that one at all.

**tekatpi** *noun* meat, any kind. Refers to meat needed to balance a meal which is otherwise vegetables. *Tekatpi i pi teni elau ntas, pregi pregi pan me maarik naot i to leka pan me i na, "Mtulep Katapel ga i to pam̃or tekatpi elau i tfale?"* The meat was from the sea, but the chief watched and he said, "How does Katapel find meat from the sea?"

**tekor** *noun* shield, made of wood.

**teleekot** *noun* healer, traditional healer. *syn:* kulru.

**telele** *noun* **1)** television. **2)** glasses (lit: the thing to look at or with).

**telomlom** *noun* camera.

**tem (temen, tmen)** *noun*$_i$ father, father's brother. *Go malfane, tem teesa nanwei ga ke fo pak esum̃ ni tem teesa nmatu.* And now, the father of this boy would go to the house of the girl's father. *cf:* apaap, gka, taata.

**temakoren (temakorer)** *noun*$_i$ sisters, group of sisters (including women whose parents are siblings).

**temakot** *noun* property, something belonging to someone; *temakot neu* 'my property'.

**tem̃anr** *verb* carry many things in your arms (an old word, not used today).

**tem̃anrogon** *adjective* lonely, like if your child goes away and you don't think about them.

**tem̃okm̃ok** *noun* dentist.

**temotmot** *noun* bandage. *Selwan ku piatlak nfag ku tae mot nfag ki temotmot.* When you have a cut, you put a bandage on it.

**temp̃alp̃olun (temp̃alun)** *noun* brothers, a group of brothers (men whose parents are siblings). *cf:* p̃al.

**tem̃rak** *verb* stand up (of a person).

**temumu** *noun* saviour.

**tena** *demonstrative* that (same as *tene*).

**tene (tenen, tenag, tena)** *demonstrative* that. *Ga teni taap̃es, i pi nser* *ni taap̃es, tene, i pi teni taap̃es. Me tene i pi teni too.* The one belonging to the swamphen, it is the swamphen's comb; that one, it is the swamphen's. But that one is the fowl's.

**teni** *preposition* of, belonging to. *Sernale nen ru pi teni naot.* Everything here belongs to the boss; *teni fei* 'whose?, belonging to whom?'

**tenrtenr** *verb$_i$* sleepwalk, talk in your sleep.

**tep̃** *adjective* **1)** empty. **2)** dried up, as in a dry river.

**tep̃al** *noun* empty talk.

**tep̃al** *noun* balls, testicles.

**tep̃alp̃al** *adjective* for no reason. *Kori ru nrpei tep̃alp̃al m̃as.* The dogs are barking for no reason. *cf:* p̃al.

**tepei** *adjective* **1)** first. *Komam kin u pi tepei nen u sil skul.* We were the first to leave school. **2)** eldest, firstborn. **3)** most important. *Me tepei knen gawankia a tli, koperesen m̃as.* But the most important of them is the one I talked about, just cooperation. *cf:* pei.

**tep̃lag** *adjective* warped.

**teplaksok** *noun* teacher. *cf:* **plaksok.**

**tep̃las** *noun* husk of coconut.

**tep̃lasnak (tep̃lasnakin)** *noun$_i$* fingernail.

**tepsir** *noun* lie. *cf:* psir.

**tepsirsir** *noun* toy, plaything. *syn:* psirsir.

**tepulsok** *noun* glue. *cf:* pulsok.

**ter** *verb* throw, backhanded throw of something flat, like a frisbee.

**ter** *verb$_a$* iron. *Ru ter nkal.* They iron clothes.

**ter** *verb$_i$* glide (as of a bird).

**ter** *verb* warning that someone will die called out by the spirit called Tagiter. *cf:* tagiter.

**termau** *adverb* for good, forever. *Me tete nrak ra pregi nen kin ke fo mat. Ke fo mat termau.* But sometimes they made him die. He would die forever.

**tesaosao** *noun* spoon.

**tesiksik** *noun* fork.

**tetau** *noun* small baby.

**tete** *adjective* some. *Tete mal.* Sometime.

**tetrasfiu** *noun* shellfish sp. (*Astraea rhodostoma*).

**tewasir** *noun* toothpick. *cf:* wasir.

**tfa** *noun* thunder.

**tfag (tfagi)** *verb$_a$* build, pile up. *I sel nawen nen kin ke tfag kor nai me, nai i kerkrai toop, i trau ser lu nawen go i mer fiit mai to leeg ki narfaat.* She got sand and built a wall to stop the water but the water was too strong, it flowed over it and across the sand, and it flowed down to the bridge.

**tfale** *adverb* how. *I map̃or tfale?* How did it break?

**tfar (tfari)** *verb$_a$* widen a hole you have dug.

**tfarer** *verb$_i$* break (of waves breaking on the shore). *cf:* mlag.

**tfei** *verb$_a$* share out food.

**tgof (tgofi)** *verb$_a$* push away; to get up off something, pushing away from it. *Ku tgof m̃iit.* You get up from the mat.

**ti (tia)** *verb$_a$* **1)** straighten. *P̃a tia nkas ke leeg.* Turn the wood (on the fire) to make it straight (for a spear). **2)** stretch oneself. *P̃a tm̃ok tiak.* Stretch yourself. *cf:* ltia

**ti** *verb* herd, as in herding pigs or cows, also for using dogs to herd animals. *cf:* sogsog.

**tiawi** *noun* **1)** ancestors. *Ntag ni teetwei tiawi ru piatlak nam̃olien wi.* In past generations the old people had a good life. **2)** old people, elders. *Komam nen kin u pi tiawi u lek nam̃olien pei mai paakor nam̃olien ni mees.* We old people we look at the way of life before becoming life today. *cf:* nafitiawian.

**tiei** *verb$_i$* start weaving.

**tiel** *verb$_i$* laugh loudly.

**tien** *verb$_i$* pregnant (of people or of animals, same as *plak*). Idiomatic expressions for being pregnant include *oftag, ga imer to, nakon ifsofus. cf:* plak.

**tifli** *number* hundred, one hundred.

**tiftif** *noun* fish sp., butterflyfishes and some angelfishes. Note that any fish with long dorsal fins can be called *nlae* 'sail', hence *tiftif nlae* for bannerfish. (*Chaetodontidae, Pomacanthidae*). *cf:* map̃eriat, taligme.

**tiftif wel rom** *noun* surgeonfish sp.

**tigpiel** *verb$_i$* exchange. For example, at a yam dedication ceremony, yams are taken out in small groups and one from each is exchanged with another group, this is *tigpiel. If wel kin taf tigpiel kin i lakor wi.* If we exchange, it could be good. *cf:* sautog.

**tigtig** *verb$_i$* hop on one foot.

**tiik** *verb$_i$* **1)** lean on a walking stick (*tiip̃*), use a stick to walk with. **2)** push a boat along with a pole. *cf:* tiip̃.

**tiik 1)** *verb$_i$* no, nothing. *I tiik ki namrun.* There is nothing. **2)** *verb$_i$* not have. *Ru tiik ki nfaktanwen toklos tiawi.* They don't respect their elders. **3)** *interjection* no, used in conversation. *Wel ga ke til, "Ore", go ke fo watgi, me wel i tli na, "I tiik", u kano.* If he says, "Yes", then he can hit him, but if he says, "No", you can't.

**tiip̃** *noun* **1)** walking stick. **2)** pole for pushing a boat along. *cf:* tiik.

**tiisoksok** *adjective* crowded; be full (as of a basket).

**tiit** *verb$_i$* dry by sunlight.

**tik** *verb$_i$* bang, to bang into something. *Selwan i oofa nra nait mai tik ntan teflan.* When he broke the fig branch he fell and banged on the ground. *cf:* nres, ple.

**tik (tki)** *verb* **1)** punch. *Ka fo tik ag.* I will fight you. **2)** have sex with, literally to bang (slang). *I pan tki sanie.* He is going to have sex with her there. *cf:* fsok, ftik.

**tikfu (tikfua)** *verb$_a$* split (as in a nut or hard fruit), crack open.

**tikor 1)** *noun* fence, small fence to keep animals out. **2)** *noun* wall of house. **3)** *noun* ridge made next to laplap to prevent things falling into the laplap. **4)** *verb* block a road, or build in the walls of a *koof* (shed). *cf:* laokor, siil, sogkor.

**tiktao** *verb* wash rust off iron.

**tiktik** *noun* shellfish sp., like a trochus, but green.

**tiktik** *verb* make a loud noise, like music or an earthquake in the distance.

**tiktik** *verb* tap repeatedly.

**til (tli)** *verb$_a$* say, tell. *A muur ka nrik mus ki na ka til naleenan.* I want to say to you that I am telling the truth. *Ku kano lek teesa i til nafsan sa.* You can't see a child swearing (using bad language). *cf:* m̃ori, tilm̃ori.

**tilm̃aar** *verb$_i$* spin.

**tilm̃aar** *noun* shellfish sp., Hebrew cone, cone shellfish, distinguished by black squared marking. Also identified as Nielsen's cone. (*Conus ebraeus*).

**tilm̃ori** *verb, adjective* tell truth, to be honest. *Ag nen ku to meltig ki tiawi, ku fla psir ko ku fla tilm̃ori, me kuf nrog natrauswen.* You who are close to the elders, you may lie or you may tell the truth, but you would have heard the stories. *I ta pi natrauswen tilm̃ori mau.* It is not a true story. *cf:* m̃ori, til.

**tilsa** *verb$_i$* criticise.

**tilsei 1)** *verb$_i$* admit, declare, announce. *A tilsei nafte kin a pregi i sa.* I admit that what I did was no good. *Ku tilsei nasaiseiwen p̃ur ni natokon.* You announce it to a big meeting in the village. **2)** *verb$_i$* prophesy.

**tilsoksok** *verb* promise. *cf:* natilsoksokwen.

**tilusus** *verb* **1)** debate. **2)** discuss, seek a solution. **3)** talk badly of someone, run someone down. *Wel kia ru laap, ruf tae tilususik ko ruf til kik, ko.* Well, many might argue with you, or gossip about you. *cf:* psaosus.

**timen** *noun* arrow. *P̃a slat naas mai, me p̃a fo tup̃ ki timen.* You bring the bow and you will shoot the arrow.

**tipaaru** *verb$_i$* give birth, bear a child. *Selwan nmatu i piatlak teesa i to nap̃len, i maos toop, me selwan i tipaaru, p̃kal kin, go i po nrogo i wi.* When a woman is pregnant it is hard work, but when the baby is born she feels good.

**tip̃el** *noun* basket type. *cf:* nlafkir, nroog, polpol, sarpopot, sp̃ol.

**tip̃ot** *noun* picture. *Tip̃ot i pi naan natam̃ool.* The picture is a photo of a man. *cf:* naan.

**tiptip** *verb* choose. *Kineu a tiptip waak ne.* I choose this pig. *cf:* mtalu.

**tir** *verb$_i$* **1)** fish from a boat. *Ka fan tir ur elau.* I will go fishing in the sea. **2)** put something into a container. *cf:* oraik.

**tkal (tkali)** *verb$_a$* **1)** touch, reach. *Go ku tae na a tkal nagis nen kia, go ag if wel kin ku tkal nagis nen kin kineu a tkos go a na "Watetjo".* And you will know that I reached the point, and if you reach the point that I am at I will say "Watetjo". **2)** until, up until the point of something happening.

*Go a mer ler mai skul natkon pan tkal 1967.* And I went back to school until 1967. *cf:* kel.

**tkalnrog (tkalnrogo)** *verb*$_a$ feel around, feel by touching. *cf:* tonrog.

**tkanwan** *interjection* how. *Tkanwan kin ku tae pes ki Erakor?* How come you can speak Erakor language?

**tkapir (tkapri)** *verb*$_a$ comb.

**tkar** *verb*$_i$ take something that someone gives you.

**tkarkaar** *verb*$_i$ restless, can't stay still, like a baby going around and touching everything, fiddling with things.

**tkas** *noun* rooster (type of bird).

**tkau** *noun* hook, any kind, including fishhook. *cf:* fatkau, namet tkau.

**tkau** *verb*$_a$ pull, e.g., on the trigger of a rifle (*tkau sisi*).

**tkau (tkau, tkaur)** *verb*$_a$ cut, e.g., grass with a scythe.

**tlai** *verb*$_i$ warm oneself at a fire.

**tlas (tlasi)** *verb*$_a$ **1)** enough, to be. *Ru pregwi ki natam̃ool i leeg tlas nam̃olien nen kin ru tkos.* They were good to people, it was enough for their life as it was then. **2)** reach, get to the point of. *A tlas nlakwen.* I was old enough to get married.

**tlei** *verb*$_i$ steer canoe by holding paddle still in the water.

**tluk (tuluk)** *noun* a small parcel of cassava wrapped around meat and covered in leaves, cooked in an earth oven. Typically small enough to hold in the hand. *Mtulep i to i pan toto uum panpan i pam̃or tluk i nru.* The woman there felt around in the oven until she found two tuluks.

**tm̃alu** *verb*$_i$ depart. *Pulp̃og rik go kai tm̃alu Erakor pan sak Egis.* Early morning I left Erakor, and came ashore at Egis.

**tm̃an** *noun* stick, used as the drill stick for fire making. Use a hardwood, e.g., *nap̃lel. Nmatupes* is wood used by women to start a fire; *nam̃ernra* is wood used by men to start a fire. The base piece of wood that you rub against does not have a name.

**tm̃anruk** *noun* **1)** blister. *Selwan ku tai nam̃nam̃, tm̃anruk i pakor.* When you cut grass, blisters come out. **2)** shellfish sp., chiton. *I piatlak tm̃anruk nen i tok elau i to pulsok faat.* There's a chiton in the sea that sticks to rocks. (*Polyplacophora*).

**tm̃at** *adjective* **1)** calm, no wind. **2)** peaceful. *cf:* ntm̃at.

**tmawot** *noun* couple, husband and wife, two spouses together.

**tm̃en** *noun* laplap, individual pieces on a leaf.

**tm̃o (tm̃e) 1)** *preverbal* reflexive, used to indicate an action a person performs on or for themself. *Me mees nmatu ke muur ke furi ke freg kapu, ga ke fan tm̃en slat nafnag.* But today it is the woman who prepares food, makes laplap, who fetches food for herself. **2)** *preverbal* reciprocal, used to indicate an action performed by people to each other. It is formed by using *tm̃o / tm̃e* in the preverbal complex and then the direct possessive suffix. *Komam u tm̃om tumam nafnag.* We gave food to each other.

**tnol (tnoli)** *verb*$_a$ swallow.

**tnolsa** *verb*$_i$ choke.

**tnus 1)** *verb*$_i$ sting, to be stinging, like an insect bite stings when you put alcohol on it. **2)** *verb*$_a$ sting, as in what a centipede does to a person. *cf:* sup̃.

**to 1)** *verb*$_a$ stay. *I to America mai.* He is here having come from America. **2)** *auxiliary* habitual, used with an activity that occurs habitually. *Mtulep Katapel ga i to pam̃or tekatpi elau i tfale?* How does Missus Katapel find meat from the sea? **3)** progressive, used with an ongoing activity. *I gar preg nafnag panpanpan ra to fam.* She made food for them, and they ate. **4)** *directional* at (directional particle). Follows a location specified by the verb. *A mer ler mai to esum̃ to.* I came back to stay at home.

**tof (tofi)** *verb*$_a$ push. *A tof nkas.* I push the wood. *A tofi.* I push him. (*Idiom: beg*).

**tofkas** *noun* fish sp., peppered rabbitfish or coral rabbitfish. (*Siganidae*).

**tofnp̃au** *verb*$_a$ baptise. *cf:* prei.

**togtog** *noun* yam, red, white, big, small (*togtogm̃it*), etc.

**togtogm̃it** *noun* yam sp., other types are *togtogmiel, togtogtar*.

**tok** *verb*$_a$ burn.

**tokape** *noun* green-winged ground dove (type of bird). (*Chalcophaps indica*).

**tokelau** *noun* wind from the sea. *cf:* lagsu.

**tokleg** *verb*$_i$ wake up, get up.

**toklos (toklosi)** *verb*$_a$ facing, in front of, with regard to, about. *Ru tiik ki nfaktanwen toklos tiawi.* They don't show respect in front of the old people. *Teetwei perkati i piatlak nafkal toklos nanre nig ntan.* A long time ago there were fights about the issue of land.

**tokmai** *noun* bird sp., a small bird with a brightly coloured tail.

**toknak** *verb*$_i$ prepare. *Ku toknak nafnag.* You prepare the food. *cf:* aliat toknak.

**toknimakil** *noun* yam sp., shaped like a bottle, small at the top and large at the base.

**tokomai** *noun* insect, a type of insect that shines a light from its tail.

**tokor (tokro)** *verb*$_a$ block, prevent something from happening. *Nkas i tarup̃ i tokor napu.* The tree fell and blocked the road. *cf:* koor.

**tol** *number* three. *Me malfanen kineu a pam natam̃ool itol m̃as.* But I have only eaten three men. *cf:* kaatol.

**toltol** *noun* share something three ways. *cf:* inruenru, limlim, patpat.

**tom (tomi)** *verb*$_a$ suck, e.g., lolly in mouth. *Teesa i tom nasu magko.* The child sucks mango juice.

**tonrog (tonrogo)** *verb*$_a$ feel around, feel by touching something you can't see, like feeling around in a basket. *cf:* tkalnrog.

**too** *noun* fowl (type of bird).

**too mil** *noun* wild fowl (general term).

**too nmatu** *noun* hen.

**too sees** *noun* chicken.

**too waipit** *noun* chicken with ruffled feathers, or whose feathers aren't straight.

**toof** *noun* fish sp., rabbitfish. (*Siganidae*).

**took** *noun* adze, narrow adze used for cutting out the inside of a canoe. *cf:* krampel, limur.

**tool (tooli) 1)** $verb_a$ to pass, to be more than. *Kineu a kraksok naik tool ag.* I caught more fish than you. *Me u tool Janweri go komam Limaas ra mer nag rak fan saofir.* After January, Limaas and I wanted to go and visit them. *Go ati nen ser nrak nen kin ru pa, ga i to sol nafnag i toop tool siluer.* And this grandmother, every time they went, she got more food than anyone else. **2)** *preposition* pass.

**toon** $verb_i$ **1)** compare. **2)** measure, also used in the expression *pus toon* 'to speak metaphorically'. *A toon ki loop ru pitkaskei.* I am measuring the bamboo, they are the same.

**toop 1)** *adjective* big, much. *Nlaken naskulwen i tap toop malpei wan mau.* Because there wasn't much schooling in those days. *I wi toop.* It is very good. **2)** $verb_i$ swell (also *toptop*). *Ku pregi ke toop.* You make it big, enlarge it. *cf:* wi m̃esm̃es.

**toop̃** *noun* yam sp. *cf:* nawi.

**toopuk** $verb_i$ to have a full mouth.

**toor** *noun* shellfish sp., pearl oyster (general term), long oyster. (*Pteriidae*). *cf:* flefil.

**toos** $verb_i$ slip, drag.

**topi** *noun* bird sp., Vanuatu white-eye. (*Zosterops flavifrons*).

**tor (tro)** $verb_a$ fill with liquid.

**toreki** $verb_a$ wait. *Me malpei i tiik, nmatu malen tiawi i toreki nmatu i skei i slat teesa.* But not then, the old women waited for a woman to have her baby.

**tortor** *noun* **1)** heat. **2)** steam.

**torwak** $verb_i$ anchor, to throw a rock on a rope into the water to hold a canoe in place. Now a general term for using any anchor. *cf:* namtau.

**tosok (tosoki)** $verb_a$ act of marrying, either of the pastor marrying the couple, or the couple marrying each other. *Nmatu go nanwei ru to tosok kir.* The woman and man married each other. *Ru paptais, go ru tosok natam̃ool.* They baptised and they married people. *cf:* ptour, taulu.

**totan** $verb_i$ **1)** sit. *Ag ku totan sago me kineu a muurin na ka taf, o, i kerkerai toop.* If you are sitting there, but I want to leave (needing to go past you), oh that will be very hard. **2)** land, come ashore. *cf:* tutan.

**toto** $verb_i$ grope, in a place you can't see in, like in a basket, or in the dark. *Mtulep i to i pan toto uum panpan i pam̃or tluk inru.* The woman there felt around in the oven until she found two tuluks.

**totogmal** *noun* fish spp., reef needlefish, garfish, red mouth. (*Strongylura incisa*).

**totooluk** *verb$_i$* turn your back on someone. *Selwan ru toktan nag ruk falus go ru totooluk ki nakpei nig raru po palus.* When they sit to paddle they turn their backs to the front of the boat then row.

**totur** *verb$_a$* **1)** go through something. *I piatlak nai sees i skei i en faat nen ga i totur pa.* There is a small spring in that rock that goes through it. **2)** via, by means of (as in via a letter). *Ku muur na p̃a weswes me p̃a faus kin totur natus.* You want to work so you ask in (by means of) a letter (of application).

**tp̃ak** *adjective* frizzy (hair).

**tp̃au** *noun* main one, the head one of a group. *Erontp̃au i tp̃au ser naor, naor i lfek ki Efat.* Rentapau is the head place of all places around Efate. *cf:* np̃au.

**tp̃er** *noun* fence, larger than *laak,* for bigger animals, like cattle. *Telaap ru letae go teflan kin ru weswes ki tp̃er, go tete, tete ru piatlak, na tete sup̃ nen kin gar me ru mer tae pregi nen kin ru nrus ki ntan. Ru to puet ntan sees.* Many knew how to make fences, and some would make a habit of shifting (the boundaries of) the land. They got a little more land (every time they put in new fence posts). *cf:* laak.

**tp̃er** *verb$_i$* break (as of a wave on the beach).

**tp̃il (tp̃ili)** *verb$_a$* **1)** burn, light (as in a fire), blow up, kindle. *Nam̃er malik nen ru su mai, ru tp̃il nasum̃tap ni SDA, ru tp̃il, ru p̃orp̃rae pija rol, go slet, paipol, i pi nanrogtesan p̃ur.* The bush men who came down burned the SDA church; they burned, they smashed the picture roll, the slate, Bible, it was a big disaster. **2)** shoot, as in kicking something hard or shooting a goal.

**tp̃ofu (tp̃ofua)** *verb$_a$* puncture something, like a ball is punctured or pierced. *Nkas i tp̃ofu raru.* The wood pierced the canoe.

**tp̃okor (tp̃okro)** *verb$_a$* stop someone doing something. *A pak hospitel pa go dokta i tp̃okor wou sikaret.* I went to the hospital, and the doctor stopped me from having cigarettes.

**tp̃olu (tp̃olua)** *verb$_a$* send someone to take a message or to do something. *A tp̃oluok.* I send you (to take a message). *Me ka fo mas ka fo gar kuk, ko tete nrak a tp̃olu tete natam̃ool p̃tae.* I have to cook for them, though sometimes I send someone else. *cf:* tup̃ek.

**tp̃oper** *noun* fish, big redmouth, like *nsul* but bigger.

**tp̃osok** *verb* push hard against an object, like a tree or a rock. Also to pull a canoe up on the sand to stop it drifting away.

**tp̃otag** *verb* live life, struggle in own life, to go about one's own life.

*Akit tu to tp̃otag ki nam̃olien sikskei gakit ser naliati.* We just keep struggling on with our lives every day.

**tp̃otunr** *verb* nod one's head. *cf:* tunr.

**tp̃otur** *verb* pray, say prayers before going to sleep. *cf:* lot.

**tp̃otur** *verb* take a shortcut.

**traares** *noun* sugarcane sp., red one. *cf:* makol, nafakton, nap̃rai, naus.

**traf (trafi)** *verb*$_a$ **1)** *Ale teesa nen ru na ru to ru pan stat, ru na ruk wat ntwam, me ntwam i sil to mpak, ale ru traf ru traf nako mpak.* So all the children went to hit the devil, but the devil was inside the banyan, so they dug, they dug the banyan roots. **2)** harvest yams, or taro, but not water taro, which you *pupuet*. Note that different terms are used for harvesting different crops. *cf:* kil, kis, m̃ok, m̃tal, namas, pupuet.

**trai** *verb*$_a$ grate, using *kai* 'cockleshell' or *skeitrai* 'coconut grater' to grate coconuts. *cf:* maa.

**trakap** *noun* fish spp., squirrelfish (threespot squirrelfish and similar). (*Holocentridae*). *cf:* sreniu.

**trakek** *noun* plate, small flat plate. *cf:* pagotut, slo.

**trakp̃og** *verb* walk about at night. *Tefsofus ni mees ru muurin trakp̃og.* Young people today want to walk about at night.

**tralosak** *verb*$_i$ be on one's back.

**trapelpel** *verb*$_i$ hurry, to go quickly. *I ta wi na tuk trapelpel mau.* It's not good that we rush. *cf:* pelpel.

**trau** *preverbal* **1)** seems. *Ag ku trau wi ki kineu.* You seem good to me. **2)** looks, followed by an adjective: *itrau sa* 'it looks bad', *itrau miel* 'it looks red'. *Ra trau mtak.* They look scared. **3)** very. **4)** really (intensifier). *Tu pitlak grup ru trau laap.* We really have a lot of groups. **5)** just, only. *Ko ga i fla muurin na ke tao tete nanromien sees, i kano trau leeg mai tao.* And if he wanted to give me a present, he couldn't just come straight out and give it to me.

**traus (trausi)** *verb*$_a$ tell, telling a story. *A na ka traus natrauswen ni Egun.* I want to tell you a story from Nguna.

**tro** *verb* flow, bleed. *cf:* ser.

**trok** *verb*$_i$ **1)** agree. *Mtulep nen i nrikin ki na, "A tap trok nen p̃a fo plak Kaltog mau."* The old woman said to him, "I don't agree that you take Kaltong back." *Akam naat ra preg natrokwen nen rak freg namrun.* You make an agreement that you will do something. **2)** amen. *Selwan ku lot mai pak nametp̃agon nafsan ku trok.* At the end of your prayer you say amen.

**tu** *verb*$_d$ give. Note that 'give me' is *tao*. *Tuer ruk min.* Give them drink. *P̃a tua kin.* You give it to him. *Ag p̃a fo tao nai ka min.* You give me water to drink. *Kineu ka fo tuok nai p̃a min.* I give you water to drink. *cf:* naftuan, ptu.

**tu** *verb, directional* stand up, to stand. *U to panpan go, nanrur ki pak tan.*

*Ale malen ku tu leeg, ku tao nkas nen ku kel wes go u tu leeg tefla.* We were there until the earthquake died down. OK, when you stood up, you let go of the tree that you were holding onto, and you stood up like that.

**tu=** *pronoun prefix* we (1st person plural inclusive realis subject). *I tap taos raru negakit kin tu lek nakpei nig raru po palus mau.* It is not like our canoes where we look at the front of the boat then row.

**tuaal** *verb$_i$* stay for the whole day, as at a funeral.

**tuai** *verb* stain, to stain something. *cf:* mir.

**tuei** *adjective* long time, old. *Tiawi nig tuei ru piatlak natrauswen nen kin selwan ru muur tenmatun ru piatlak kastom nen ru tae pregi.* The old people have a story about when they want something, they have a custom that they can use to get it.

**tuek** *verb$_i$* make, as in making tools, or a house, or craft. But not used of cloth or mats, which would use *tur* 'to sew'.

**tui=** *pronoun prefix* we (1st person plural inclusive perfect subject). *Gawankia tui pe nrogo, na, i ta pi mal leeg nen kin tuk kraksok independent mau.* So what we heard was that it wasn't the right time for us to get independence.

**tuk (tukus)** *verb$_a$* **1)** carry on the back (as in a child, or firewood). **2)** pull or tow behind, like pulling a canoe.

**tuk=** *pronoun prefix* we (1st person plural inclusive irrealis subject). *A muurin na tuk mai pak naor keskei me tuk tai raru ke skei.* I want that we come together to cut a canoe.

**tukot** *verb* shortcut, take a shortcut.

**tuleg (tokleg)** *verb$_i$* **1)** stand. *Raiten i kano tuleg pan los, ke mas pnut to pan pan naliati i lim i nom.* The mother couldn't stand up to wash, she had to sit quietly for five days. **2)** arise. *P̃a tuleg me p̃a fa.* You get up then you go.

**tum̃ (tm̃a) 1)** *verb$_a$* point, show by pointing a finger. **2)** *verb$_a$* aim. *Ku tum̃ maan na p̃a si.* You aim at the bird in order to shoot it. **3)** *verb$_i$* erect, be erect (of a penis).

**tumel** *noun* sugarcane sp. *cf:* makol.

**tum̃otum̃** *verb$_i$* knock, e.g., on a door.

**tunkor** *verb* constipated, can't go to the toilet.

**tunr** *verb$_i$* bow, lower the head. *cf:* tp̃otunr.

**tuntun** *verb* be wobbly, have a wobbly texture such as jelly or the fat of someone's fat belly. *Mp̃agon i tuntun.* His bottom is really wobbly.

**tuntun** *adjective* delicious. *Nafnag i tuntun wi.* The food tastes good.

**tup̃ (tp̃a) 1)** *verb$_a$* hit, punch with the fist. **2)** *verb$_a$* shoot (arrow). *Tuk fan tup̃.* Let's go shoot fish. *Naat nen ke fo tp̃ak.* That man is going to hit you. **3)** *preposition* until, in the sense of 'shoot to the time'. *Ra ta puel mau, me ra to faat, nfal i nru ra to faat, go ra m̃ool to panpan* *tup̃ mees.* They didn't disappear, they are in the stone, in the two stones, and they are alive until today. **4)** *preposition* achieve, get to. *I pan lfek ki Franis i mai i mai pak esa ale i tup̃ na metotel ga.* He went around France, then came back here and became a maître d'hotel. *cf:* ftup̃, nafkal.

**tup̃** *verb* prop, support a tree branch by placing a prop of wood under it.

**tup̃roor** *noun* ant sp., red ant. *cf:* mkaal.

**tup̃tao** *verb* to wipe dry, to dust off something.

**tuput** *noun* rainbow. *Tiawi ru na if wel kin us i wo pan i na ke sin, tuput i na i pakor. P̃a ta tm̃a mai. If wel ku tm̃a go us ke fo mer ler wo.* The old people say that if it rains and stops, then the rainbow appears. Don't point at the rainbow otherwise it will start to rain again.

**tur (turus)** *verb*$_a$ **1)** drill. *Pagos i tok tur p̃rai nkas.* The beetle drills and breaks the wood. **2)** sew, sew thatch, bind fish together into a bundle (*ntur*). *Me malnen rukoi pe laosok silua ru tur pek.* When they finished pounding it, they sewed up the bag. *cf:* ntur.

**tur** *verb*$_i$ leak.

**tus ni telomlom** *noun* photo album.

**tustap** *noun* Bible. *Ku fe tustap ni Atua.* You read God's Bible. *cf:* natus.

**tusur** *verb* tease, annoy.

**tut** *verb*$_i$ drown, submerge. *Samuel i tut ki natus kai ler.* Samuel threw the paper into the water and went back. *cf:* m̃or.

**tutan** *verb*$_i$ get out on to the ground, from a boat or a car, come ashore. *cf:* totan.

**tuul** *verb*$_i$ sway, in the wind or in the water; to rock something back and forth, e.g., *tuul ki teesa* 'to rock the child'. Also used to describe the motion of your head as you nod off to sleep.

**tuumas** *noun* yam sp.

**tuup̃ur** *noun* elephantiasis, 'fat leg'.

**tuur** *noun* fish sp., flagtail. (*Kuhliidae*).

**tuut (tuuti)** *verb*$_a$ tie knot; tie a band of cloth around the chest in which to carry a baby. *cf:* natuut.

**tuutnaniu** *verb* bind coconuts together into a bundle by pulling out some of the husk and weaving it to the husk of other coconuts.

## U UU

**u=** *pronoun prefix* **1)** you (2nd person plural realis subject). *Akam u tae faat i skei i tu Ertap, teetwei, ru soso ki Trawot.* You know there's a rock at Eratap, long ago, they called it Trawot. **2)** we (1st person plural exclusive realis subject). *Komam u weswes ki naar mam, u farfar ki nam̃ol mam, raki nawesien p̃afp̃of laap.* We worked with our hands, we moved our bodies, working on many big jobs.

**ui=** *pronoun prefix* we (1st person plural exclusive perfect subject). *U tae preg tenmatun nen kin u muurin, nlaken ui pe slat independent nigmam.* We can do what we want because we got our independence.

**uli (ulin)** *noun$_i$* bladder.

**ulikookon** *noun* gallbladder.

**ulu** *verb* grow well, of a plant that is growing in the way it should and is healthy.

**ululu** *adjective* hairy.

**um̃kau** *verb* to be important, to be strong; *natam̃ool um̃kau*, used in Psalm 67 in Natus Nalag 151 (an old word, not used today).

**unr** *noun* shrimp, small crustacean. *cf:* makou, pepep, uur.

**up̃lim** *noun* The fifth day after a person dies, the day their body changes. The five days are observed by relatives eating together. *Ru pak malep panpan up̃lim.* They mourn together until the fifth day. *cf:* maalep.

**ur** *verb$_i$* grunt, noise made by a pig. *cf:* srof.

**ur** *verb$_i$* **1)** go along. *I pestaf aslen nen kin ru ur ser nagis.* He told his friends that they should go along each point. **2)** *directional* along. *U siwer preg nawesien ur ser natkon.* We walked around doing work along each village.

**ures** *noun* fish sp., wrasse, sixbar wrasse?, green with stripes.

**us** *noun* rain. *Aliat tap us i toop, u mai matur Sak Bei namba faef, go siks u matur Mafea naur.* Sunday it was raining heavily, we slept at Shark Bay on the fifth, and on the sixth we stayed at Mafea island.

**us (usi)** *verb$_a$* **1)** follow. **2)** track, follow some tracks (of a person or animal). *Selwan i panpanpan na i tkal talm̃aat ki us nalof wak.* When he got to the garden he began tracking the pig.

**us** *noun* fish sp., surgeonfish, black, with sandpaper-like skin, about 30 cm long.

**us walep** *noun* heavy rain.

**usnre** *verb* consult (an old word, not used today).

**usog** *verb$_i$* concentrate, to be determined, to focus on something. *Ka fo usog nawesien neu.* I will concentrate on my work.

**usrek (userek) 1)** *verb$_i$* go around. *Naliati nen rak fo reswes me katom i pei usrek ki ser nagis.* The day when they were to race, the hermit crab had first gone around to each point. **2)** *adjective* completely, when attached to a verb it indicates the action of the verb has been done completely. *Ku lek nafte, me naor i trau m̃al userek.* You look for something but the place is completely cleared.

**usus** *verb$_2$* follows a verb to make a new meaning, for example, *mrousus,* 'think of', *tilusus*, 'discuss', *fiitusus*, 'run after'. *I preg kineu a pan pi memba ni citizenship commission, nen u leusus fei kin ke fi citizen.*

He made me a member of the citizenship commission, which looks into who can be a citizen.

**uti** *noun* skink sp. with a blue tail.

**utikaro** *noun* skink sp., grey coloured.

**utinlag** *noun* skink sp., brown.

**uum** *noun* **1)** oven. **2)** name of a constellation, possibly the Pleiades.

**uum̃** *verb$_i$* clear a garden patch.

**uur** *noun* prawn. *cf:* makou, pepep, unr.

**uurtaiak** *noun* large crayfish or lobster.

**uus** *noun* fish sp., orangespine unicornfish, or a black fish with a yellow tail. (*Naso lituratus*). *cf:* naum, raeru.

**uus** *verb$_i$* hide. *cf:* kus.

**uut (uuti)** *verb$_a$* fetch water with a container, scoop up the water. *I min silua me ki ga uut nai pan tua kin i mingi.* He drank it all, but he poured water (for the owl) and took it to give him to drink.

# W

**waaf** *verb* swim, move yourself along the surface of the water; *waaftaal* is freestyle swimming. *Me afsak iskei, i to waaf me i sik np̃aun, i lek oof kin i tu.* And this turtle, it was swimming and it raised its head, it saw the heron there. *cf:* los.

**waak** *noun* pig. *Komam mtulep ra mai pak talm̃aat me waak p̃ur i skei i kpas komam.* We, my wife and I, we went to our garden, but a big pig chased us. (*Sus scrofa*). *cf:* klet, pwok.

**waal** *noun* nation, team, group of people, ally.

**waal** *verb* **1)** gouge a hole in something (not right through it). **2)** to scoop something out, to poke something. *A waal rakum ki masmes sees pak nap̃lau nkas.* I scoop a crab out of a hole in the tree with a knife. *A waal wiit pak nap̃lau faat skot masmes sees.* I scoop the octopus out of its hole with a knife.

**waal gakit** *noun* allies, our allies.

**waal p̃tae** *noun* enemy.

**waaloop** *noun* large white land crab, has claws and lives in a hole on the seashore.

**waalu (waalua)** *verb$_a$* take off, take out; *waalu gkal* 'take off one's clothes'. *Me malen kin i pan i pan kai waalu namlun kai oof nasok natam̃ool.* But it took off its skin and changed into wearing the skin of a man.

**wafin** *verb* embrace someone by putting arms over their shoulders or around their waist, but not hugging them.

**wailu** *noun* yam sp., said to be from New Caledonia. There is a yellow one and a white one. Has prickles on its vine.

**wair** *noun* **1)** tree sp., pangi. (*Pangium edule*). **2)** rattle made from the seed pods of the tree *wair*.

**wakm̃akur** *noun* fish sp., drummers. (*Kyphosidae*).

**wal** *verb$_i$* control a canoe, action of the person at the back of the canoe who controls the direction. Also used to refer to that person. *Ag ku wal raru.* You control the canoe.

**walnre (walnrea)** *verb$_a$* stir something from the bottom to the top, unlike *taanre,* which involves circular (horizontal) stirring. *cf:* taanre.

**walsem̃** *verb* **1)** chew. **2)** grind in your mouth.

**walu** *noun* **1)** squid. **2)** cuttlefish. The cuttlefish bone is called a *pot ni walu* 'the cuttlefish's boat'.

**wam** *verb$_i$* heal. *Nfag ki pe wam.* The sore is healed.

**wamos** *verb$_a$* tattoo.

**wanaar** *noun* fish sp., monocle breams and spinecheeks, white fish with brown stripes on its back. (*Nemipteridae*).

**wanru** *noun* least frigatebird (type of bird).

**warik** *adjective* few. *Me ki mro kin ki i warik me, namrun nen i pi tenamrun p̃ur.* And he thought there were only a few, but this thing was something big. *cf:* nrfaal.

**warof** *noun* fish spp., emperor fish. (*Lethrinus spp.*)

**was** *adjective* burned, to be burned.

**wasau** *noun* rufous-brown pheasant dove (type of bird). It hides and is hard to find. When it calls out, it is burying a wild yam. Its call is 'cuckoo'. (*Macropygia mackinlayi*).

**wasem** *verb* **1)** to like someone very much. **2)** stay close to, as in a child who stays close to its parents. *Ra tm̃er wasem wer toop.* Those two hang around with each other too much.

**waser** *verb$_i$* cough, clear one's throat.

**wasir** *verb* pick out, using a stick to pick something out, like a snail from its shell, or cleaning your teeth with a *tewasir* 'toothpick'. *Me i fiit pan tu maarik naot nig Emelp̃au ki np̃au m̃aau nig Efil wan go i po wasirlu namten.* And he ran to give the chief of Emelp̃au the head of the Vila warrior and he took out its eyes. *cf:* tewasir.

**wasket** *noun* moustache. *Me wasket ga i pram mai pak etan tepla.* But his moustache went all the way to the ground like this.

**wat (watgi)** *verb$_a$* hit. *Naat ru wat naat napu ru watgi i mat.* They attacked the man on the road and killed him. *Selwan ku maet ki naat ku watgi.* When you are cross with someone you hit them. *cf:* krakpun.

**watiam** *noun* kidney.

**watkor** *verb* woman being pregnant but her parents don't know.

**watlaak** *verb* plan something.

**watlu** *verb$_a$* influence someone, make them change their behaviour.

**watlu** *verb$_a$* hit something out of the way.

**watnru** *verb* **1)** play, play around. *I watnru ki tau sees.* He plays with the little child. **2)** senile, be senile.

**watpun (watpni)** *verb$_a$* kill. *Me nlesmp̃aum go ke fo psi ke to* *nakamal nega me ke fo to leka me mroperkat nawesien sa negar teplan ra to watpun nam̃er nig Erakor kat ntan negar.* And he would put the skull into his nakamal (meetinghouse), where he could look at it and recognise their evil, how they killed people from Erakor for their land.

**weel** *noun* fish sp., keeps company of *map̃er.* Has black and white markings. Convict surgeonfish? (*Acanthurus triostegus?*). *cf:* taligme, map̃er.

**wel** *verb$_i$* be like, thus, in this way. *Ru pausi i wel m̃iit ru motsok ki nater nasum̃.* They weave it like a mat, they tie it to the walls of the house.

**welkin** *interjection* thus. *I welkin ke fitlak nlagwat p̃ur teflan ke mai, hotel ke fo puel.* Thus if a cyclone like that came, the hotel would be wrecked. *Go i welkin kuf mer ur lakun p̃a fo pam̃ori na Ewenesu i piatlak nawen i toop.* And so if you go along the lagoon you will see at Ewenesu there is a lot of sand. *cf:* kia.

**welu (welua)** *verb$_a$* help, assist. *Selwan ru pus naat i pi np̃aukit ruk fo pus tekaru nen i welua ataf preg nawesien.* When they make a man the chief, they make another man help his assistant do his work.

**wenr** *noun* **1)** bed (wenr ni matur). **2)** copra dryer (wenr ni kopra), bêche-de-mer dryer (wenr ni litot). *cf:* nawool.

**wer** *pronoun* them (3rd person plural object). *A mer lekor wer ntau ilaru, nen a mer lekor teesa skul esa.* I looked after them for seven years, I looked after the children at the school here.

**wes (os, es)** *pronoun* it, at that place. *Eswan a sraf wes kia.* That's where I missed my chance. *Ale, Katapel i pak elag i sol kaai, i pak esan kin faat i tkos.* So Katapel goes up and gets shellfish, she goes to where there is a rock.

**wes (wesi)** *verb$_a$* carry something small in your hand. *I tok kai wes tuluk nen mai.* He stayed and took the tuluk. *Komam ra mer tuer tete nanromien sees. Ru mer negar wesi pan tuer kin.* We gave them some small presents. They then took some to give to them. *If wel kin uf taos namroan neu, go ka fo weslu apil nen a pregi to. Ka fo withdraw ki.* If we follow my way, I will retract the appeal that I have lodged (in the court). I will withdraw it. *cf:* slat.

**wes** *verb$_i$* reply.

**weswes** *verb$_a$* work. *Ru fla mai pakor pulp̃og, ru fla weswes pan, nawesien pan i pi kotfak aliat.* They might come in the morning, they might work, the work might go for half a day. *Ru tiik ki kram. Ru tiik ki sernale fserser. Me ru weswes.* They had no axes. They had none of that other stuff. But they worked. *cf:* nawesien.

**wi** *adjective* good. *I wi ko?* How's it going? (lit: good or?). *Teetwei i* *wi. Pret ku paaktofi, wan vatu.* In the old days it was good. You could buy bread for one vatu. *Selwan ru slat sernale pak naor i skei, i wi toop.* When they take everything to the one place it is very good. *Nanromien gaag i wi toop.* Your present is very good.

**wi m̃esm̃es** *adjective* excellent. *cf:* toop.

**wiit** *noun* octopus. *Ke piatlak kaai, go ke fo piatlak wiit, go ke fo piatlak naik, go ke fo piatlak tefserser i laap nen i to slati elau, ntas.* There was shellfish, and octopus, and fish, and many other things that she would get from the sea. (*Octopodidae*).

**wit ni too** *noun* brittle star, eaten by chickens at the sea. (*Ophiothrix purpurea*).

**wo** *verb$_i$* fall (as in rain). *Ga, ki pe pei leka barometer nega nag, "Wik foum go us ke fo wo." I pi nlaken tiawi ru faafat wes.* He first looked at his barometer and said, "Next week rain will fall." That is why the old people believed him.

**woi** *noun* pudding made with breadfruit and green coconut. *cf:* napos.

**wok** *verb* you, pronoun form used for 'you' as an object (2nd person singular object). *Ka fo siwer, mailum siwer nrookot wok.* I will walk, walk slowly in front of you.

**wol** *verb$_i$* flatten something, like clothes, or leaves to make them into a plate or a mat. *P̃a wol ki nrau reki kapu.* You flatten the plate for laplap.

**wolul** *verb$_i$* pull your legs back, e.g., so someone can pass.

**woor** *verb$_i$* noise of two trees rubbing together.

**woos** *noun* tooth, back tooth.

**wor** *verb$_i$* look, appear; *wor wi* 'to look nice', *worp̃onp̃et, worp̃tae* 'to look different'.

**woro** *adjective* brown. *Nkas i woro.* The wood is brown.

**wou** *pronoun* me (1st person singular object). *Malen i paakor ki wou talm̃aat, i pi malwan a pato talm̃aat to.* Then it (asthma) comes on me in the garden, it is when I am in the garden.

# English to Nafsan Finderlist

## A

**abalone** *noun kaiaraskei*
**abort** *verb kispun*
**above** *preposition elag*
**absent** *verb$_i$ puel; verb$_i$ lalu*
**accompany** *verb$_i$ ptaan; verb$_a$ plak*
**act** *verb gien*
**active** *adjective polkirkir*
**Adam's apple** *noun npatnkafik*
**add** *verb$_a$ skar*
**admire** *verb$_i$ lewi*
**admit** *verb tilsei*
**adopt** *verb$_a$ p̃as*
**adult** *adjective p̃afp̃of*
**adultery** *verb$_i$ tauso*
**adze** *noun kramp̃el; noun limur; noun took*
**aeroplane** *noun maan ni nmalfa*
**African tulip** *noun nrar* (*Erythrina variegata*)
**after** *conjunction me; noun$_i$ ntakun*
**afterbirth** *noun naal ni teesa*
**afternoon** *noun kotfaan*
**again** *auxiliary mer*
**against** *verb$_i$ putkau; verb$_i$ ktekit*
**age-mate** *noun taak*
**agree** *verb$_i$ trok*
**aim** *verb$_a$ tum̃*
**air** *noun nlag*
**albino** *noun ataat*
**alcohol** *noun nai; noun nai kookon*
**alight** *verb$_i$ tutan*
**all** *adjective userek; auxiliary, adjective nom; adjective mau*
**allies** *noun waal gakit*
**almond, tropical almond** *noun ntali* (*Terminalia samoensis*)
**along** *directional ur*
**altar** *noun p̃otut*
**always** *adverb sernrak*
**ambidextrous** *adjective arworksu*
**amen** *verb$_i$ trok*
**ancestors** *noun tiawi*
**anchor** *noun namtau; verb$_i$ torwak*
**and** *conjunction go; conjunction atmat; conjunction me*
**anemone** *noun mpaklep; noun nrmen*
**anemonefishes** *noun naik nrmen* (*Chaetodontidae, Pomacentridae*)
**angelfishes** *noun map̃eriat* (*Pomacanthidae*); *noun tiftif*
**anger** *noun nmaeto*
**angry** *verb$_i$ ftin; verb$_i$ maet*
**animal** *noun teem̃ool*
**ankle** *noun$_i$ nlaknait*
**ant**
  **black ant** *noun kaanr*
  **fire ant** *noun kaanr*
**ant sp.** *noun funrei*
**ant sp.** *noun mkaal*
**ant sp., red ant** *noun tup̃roor*
**anus** *noun nselpot; noun$_i$ napis*
**any** *adjective p̃rakot*
**anybody** *noun naat p̃rakot*
**anything** *noun sernale*
**appear** *verb$_i$ paakor*
**applaud** *verb$_i$ p̃sap̃os*
**appointment** *noun natuut*
**approximately** *adjective mana*
**argue** *verb$_i$ psaplil*
**arise** *verb$_i$ tuleg*
**arm** *noun$_i$ naar*
**armlet** *noun tarim*
**armpit** *noun$_i$ nafen*
**arrange** *verb$_i$ puspta*
**arrive** *verb$_i$ paakor*
**arrow** *noun timen*

**arrow for killing birds** *noun kuuf*
**as** *adverb malnen*
**ascend** *verb*$_i$ *sak; verb*$_i$ *pakelag*
**ashamed** *verb*$_i$ *malier*
**ashes** *noun naton*
**ask** *verb faus; verb*$_d$ *paus; verb*$_a$ *fraa; verb*$_a$ *ptal*
**assemble** *verb paakruk*
**assistant, chief's assistant** *noun ataf*
**asthma** *noun nmarom̃iit*
**astride** *verb*$_a$ *paatlakor*
**at** *to*
  **be at** *verb*$_i$ *pato; verb ptau*
**aunt** *noun iak; noun ta*
**avocado** *noun afoka* (*Persea americana*)
**avoid** *verb*$_a$ *lelu; verb*$_a$ *plos; verb sef; verb*$_a$ *maltotae; verb lelkau*
**away** *adverb em̃ae*
**awhile** *noun mal sees*
**axe** *noun taakot; noun kram*

## B

**baby, small** *noun tetau*
**back** *noun*$_i$ *ntak; preposition nakoinrok*
**bad** *verb*$_i$ *sa*
**bad behaviour** *verb polsa; verb*$_i$ *folfol sa*
**bad news, hardships** *noun nanrogtesan*
**bail (water)** *verb*$_a$ *saolu*
**bailer** *noun nies*
**bait** *noun fgan*
**bake** *verb*$_a$ *tao*
**bald** *noun p̃au m̃aalm̃aal; adjective p̃aukaplat*
  **bald patch** *adjective p̃aum̃osu*
**balls, testicles** *noun tep̃al; noun teem̃iit; noun p̃ura; noun*$_i$ *pol*
**bamboo** *noun loop* (*Bambusa*); *noun nam̃lalop*
**bamboo tube (for carrying water)** *noun kanrsip*
**banana spp.** *noun nametmet miel; noun nanra; noun taag; noun pia; noun nanrmem pot; noun taagmol; noun naanr; noun nanrwor; noun taagmetkes; noun pili; noun nap̃aap̃ak; noun niuslan; noun taagsus; noun nanrmem swit; noun furaru*
  **hand of bananas** *verb plee*
  **lady's finger banana** *noun swiit*
  **ripe banana** *noun nanrmem*
**banana sp. for cooking** *noun nametmet*
**bandage** *noun temotmot*
**bang into** *verb*$_i$ *tik*
**bank** *noun nasum̃ ni faat*
**banyan** *noun mpak*
**baptise** *verb*$_a$ *tofnp̃au; verb*$_i$ *prei*
**barb** *noun fatkau*
**bark** *noun nasok nkas; verb*$_a$ *nrp̃ei*
  **to strip bark** *verb*$_a$ *mul*
**barnacle** *noun kainintas*
**barracuda** *noun menaal* (*Sphyraenidae*)
**basket** *noun polpol; noun nroog; noun sp̃ol; noun tip̃el; noun likat; noun nlafkir; noun tasaal; noun naal; noun sarpopot; noun napor; noun fuelig*
  **carry basket** *verb*$_i$ *freg*
**bat** *noun p̃urkum*
**batfish** *noun foik*

**bathroom** *noun sum̃los*
**battle** *noun nafkal*
**be** *verb pi*
  **to be, exist** *verb$_a$ piatlak*
**beach** *noun euut; noun nmalnawen*
**beach** *noun elau*
**bead** *noun nanu*
**beam** *noun narom; noun surnaot*
**beam, crossbeam** *noun raus; noun nkaspeltakot*
**bear** *verb$_a$ oof; verb$_i$ tau; verb slasol*
**bear, give birth (of animal)** *verb$_i$ psol*
**bear, give birth to (of humans)** *verb$_i$ pkaal*
**beard, body hair** *noun$_i$ nal*
**beautiful, something beautiful** *noun nalewen wi*
**because** *conjunction nlaken*
**because of** *preposition kat*
**bêche-de-mer** *noun litot (Holothuriidae)*
**become** *auxiliary mai*
**bed** *noun nawool; noun wenr*
**bedroom** *noun ep̃ag*
**beehive** *noun nasum̃ ni pi*
**beer** *noun nai latlat*
**beetle** *noun frap̃o; noun pagos*
  **rhinocerus beetle** *noun p̃aas*
**before** *adverb teetwei; adverb malpei*
**beg** *verb$_a$ fraa*
**behave** *verb$_i$ folfol*
**behave well** *verb$_i$ polwi*
**behaviour** *noun nafolflon*
  **bad behaviour** *verb polsa; verb$_i$ folfol sa*
**behind** *preposition saspe; adverb inrok; preposition nakoinrok*
**believe** *verb mrofaafat*
**belly button** *noun$_i$ napot*
**below** *verb$_i$ paketan*
**belt** *noun nap̃lai*
**bend** *verb$_i$ nrook; verb$_i$ p̃el; verb$_i$ map̃el*
**berry, wild** *noun krusperi (Passiflora foetida)*
**beside** *preposition nanre wes*
**between** *preposition nmaotao*
**big** *adjective p̃ur; adjective p̃afp̃of; adjective lep; verb$_i$ adjective toop*
**big toe** *noun kinm̃aat*
**bind** *verb$_a$ mot*
**bind coconuts** *verb tuutnaniu*
**bird** *noun maan*
**bird sp./spp.** *noun pepelau; noun taro; noun manim̃aat*
  **brahminy kite** *noun malpwas (Haliaștur indus)*
  **brown booby** *noun mantas (Sula leucogaster plotus)*
  **dove sp.** *noun maan nap̃lo (Macropygia mackinlayi)*
  **eagle hawk (strong one)** *noun mankerkrai*
  **fantail, grey fantail** *noun takerker*
  **fowl** *noun too*
  **goshawk** *noun malp̃erik. (Accipiter fasciatusaustrale)*
  **green-winged ground dove** *noun tokape (Chalcophaps indica)*
  **hawk (strong one)** *noun mankerkrai*
  **heron** *noun oof*
  **honeyeater** *noun alak (Lichmera incana)*
  **incubator bird** *noun mlau (Megapodius freycinet)*
  **kingfisher** *verb$_i$ tef; noun siik (Alcedinidae)*
  **lorikeet** *noun sfir (Trichoglossus haematodus)*
  **manakin** *noun sfirmer (Estrildidae)*

**myna bird** *noun kipwi* (*Acridotheres tristis*)
**owl** *noun sokfal* (*Tyto alba*)
**Pacific swallow** *noun mantilsei* (*Hirundo tahitica*)
**pigeon, Baker's imperial pigeon** *noun mapul ni ntaf* (*Ducula bakeri*); **Pacific imperial pigeon** *noun mapul* (*Ducula pacifica*)
**rail** *noun p̃lak* (*Gallirallus philippensis*)
**red-bellied fruit dove** *noun sunra* (*Ptilinopus greyii*)
**robin** *noun susunatog*
**rooster** *noun tkas*
**scrubduck** *noun mlau* (*Megapodius freycinet*)
**swamp harrier** *noun maal* (*Circus approximans*)
**swamphen** *noun taap̃es* (*Porphyrio melanotus*)
**swiftlet** *noun kapkaap*
**tree martin** *noun pai* (*Petrochelidon nigricans*)
**Vanuatu fruit dove** *noun m̃lato* (*Ptilinopus tannensis*)
**Vanuatu white-eye** *noun topi* (*Zosterops flavifrons*)
**wagtail** *noun farfar*
**waxbill** *noun sfirmer* (*Estrildidae*)
**whimbrel** *noun sfiu* (*Numenius phaeopus*)
**wild fowl** *noun too mil*

**birth, give birth** *verb$_i$ tipaaru*
**bite** *verb fket; verb$_a$ kat*
**bits** *noun nafer*
**bitter** *adjective kookon*
**black** *adjective got*
**black ant** *noun kaanr*
**black burao** *noun namir* (*Cordia subcordata*)
**black palm** *noun nma* (*Blechnum gibbum, Cyathea lunulata*)
**blackbean** *noun nkasot* (*Diospyros sp.*); *noun nap̃oi* (*Castanospermum australe*)
**blackspot snapper** *noun pao alagot* (*Lutjanus fulviflamma*)
**bladder** *noun$_i$ uli*
**blade** *noun$_i$ name; noun$_i$ nsilfer*
**bland** *verb$_i$ p̃arp̃aar*
**blank** *adjective p̃al*
**bleed** *verb$_i$ mra*
**blind** *verb$_i$ pare*
**blink** *verb$_i$ p̃ilmet*
**blister** *noun tm̃anruk*
**block** *verb$_a$ laokor; verb$_a$ kor; verb$_a$ sogkor; verb$_a$ tokor*
**block road** *verb$_a$ kamkor; verb$_a$ skakor*
**blood** *noun$_i$ nraa*
**blow** *verb$_a$ si*
**blow hard** *verb$_i$ fuu*
**blow one's nose** *verb$_i$ nrafi*
**blue** *adjective mlakes*
**blunt** *adjective p̃ool*
**blurring** *verb$_i$ funfnoi*
**boar** *noun pwok* (*Sus scrota*)
**boast** *verb$_i$ pesp̃ur*
**body** *noun$_i$ nam̃ol*
**boil** *noun nmanuk*
**heart of boil** *noun$_i$ npat*
**boil on skin** *noun nmak*
**boiling** *verb$_i$ tafiif*
**bone** *noun naustap; noun$_i$ ntawot*
**bonefish, Indo-Pacific** *noun marikwi* (*Albula glossodonta*)
**booby, brown** *noun mantas* (*Sula leucogaster plotus*)
**border** *noun nmakot*

**boss** *noun naot*
**bottom** *noun$_i$ napis*
**bottom stones of an oven** *noun faatftak*
**bougainvillea** *noun anisakel*
**bougna** *noun p̃ook*
**boundary** *noun nmakot*
**bow** *verb$_i$ nrook; noun naas; verb$_i$ tunr*
**bow one's head in shame** *verb$_i$ sup̃otunr*
**bowlegged** *verb$_i$ paakankan*
**boxfishes** *noun mateu* (*Ostraciidae, Tetraodontidae*)
**box crab** *noun arm̃afaf* (*Calappidae*)
**box jellyfish** *noun litas* (*Chironex fleckeri*)
**bracelet, rolled pandanus leaves** *noun leel*
**bract** *noun serpaal*
**braid your hair** *verb$_a$ pir*
**brain** *noun$_i$ naknrae*
**brake** *verb$_a$ kamsok*
**branch** *noun nrankas*
**breadfruit sp.** *noun nmaal; noun naliu; noun p̃ka; noun kanotaar; noun m̃nam̃on; noun nateeman; noun naptamkuut; noun naptamkos; noun loof; noun naptam* (*Atocarpus altilis*)
**break** *verb enkot; verb krakp̃orp̃or; verb$_a$ p̃or; verb$_a$ laokot; verb$_i$ mlag; verb p̃afu; verb$_i$ tp̃er; verb$_a$ kraktof; verb$_a$ laop̃or; verb$_i$ tfarer; verb$_a$ kamp̃or*
**break everything** *verb$_a$ p̃orp̃or*
**breast** *noun$_i$ nais; noun mimi*
**breastfeed** *verb$_i$ sus; verb$_i$ p̃kasus*
**breath** *noun$_i$ nmar*
**breathe** *verb$_i$ mar*
**breathe out** *verb lainmar*
**bribe** *noun naul*
**bride** *noun nmatu lak*
**bridegroom** *noun kano lak*
**bridge** *noun narfaat*
**bright** *adjective mram*
**brightness** *noun namram*
**bring** *verb$_a$ slati mai*
**brittle star** *noun wit ni too* (*Ophiothrix purpurea*)
**broke, penniless** *verb taar*
**broken** *verb$_i$ map̃or; verb$_i$ mafmaf; verb$_i$ map̃rap̃or; verb$_i$ makot*
**broken teeth** *noun npatsoru*
**brood** *verb p̃op̃o; verb$_i$ mermer*
**broom** *noun nier*
**brother** *noun taai*
  **group of brothers** *noun temp̃alp̃olun*
**brother-in-law** *noun maariktakun*
**brown** *adjective woro*
**brown booby** *noun mantas* (*Sula leucogaster plotus*)
**bubble** *noun nafutfut*
**bud** *noun pukok; noun$_i$ naser; verb$_i$ fum̃*
**bug** (lobster) *noun pepep* (*Parribacus caledonicus*)
**build** *verb$_a$ tfag*
**bullock's penis cudgel** *noun naut puluk*
**bundle** *noun mot; noun nmot; noun furfur; noun nlul*
**bundle carried on a pole** *noun tafra*
**burn** *verb$_a$ tok; verb$_a$ paan; verb$_i$ pankot; verb$_a$ tp̃il*
  **burned** *adjective was*
**burst** *verb$_i$ maaf; verb$_i$ maaf*
**bury** *verb$_i$ ofa; verb$_i$ tan*
**bury something** *verb taatan*
**bush** *noun m̃p̃akus; noun namlas*

**bush sp.** *noun nkari* (*Cordyline fruticosa*)
  **small bush** *noun naulalas* (*Polipcias spp.*)
**bush bash** *verb*$_{i}$ *nraf*
**bush nut tree** *noun napkor* (*Barringtonia procera*); *noun nafil* (*Barringtonia edulis*)
**bush with red berries** *noun naisig*
**bushfire** *noun nasiin*
**busy, be** *verb m̃aniek*
**but** *conjunction me*
**butterfly** *noun lipeep*
**butterflyfishes** *noun naik maan* (*Pterois spp.*)
**buttocks** *noun*$_{i}$ *mp̃ag*
**buy** *verb paakot*

# C

**cabbage** *noun altuk*
**calf** *noun*$_{i}$ *nmalnatu*
**calf of leg** *noun*$_{i}$ *nlasopuk natu*
**call** *verb*$_{i}$ *tef;* *verb*$_{d}$ *sos*
  **call out** *verb*$_{i}$ *pios*
**calm** *adjective tm̃at; adjective m̃aler*
**camera** *noun telomlom*
**can, to be able to** *auxiliary tae*
**cane** *noun nap̃rairei; noun ftok*
  **wild cane** *noun naus*
**canoe** *noun raru; noun raru m̃ol*
**can't swim** *noun puup*
**capsize** *verb*$_{i}$ *tap̃o*
**captain** *noun naot*
**car** *noun raru ni ntan*
**cardinalfish** *noun anrar; noun p̃op̃or* (*Apogonidae*)
**care for** *verb nrokof;* *verb*$_{i}$ *pkal*
  **watch over** *verb*$_{a}$ *maturkor*
**careful** *verb*$_{a}$ *mtaatak*
**caress** *verb*$_{a}$ *solsol*
**carpenter** *noun mtakseu*
**carry** *verb*$_{a}$ *lei;* *verb*$_{a}$ *wes;* *verb*$_{a}$ *slat;* *verb*$_{i}$ *tkar;* *verb*$_{a}$ *tuk;* *verb sikpol;* *verb*$_{a}$ *oof;* *verb*$_{i}$ *paunamru;* *verb*$_{a}$ *siiti*
**carry basket** *verb*$_{i}$ *freg*
**carry on head** *verb*$_{i}$ *suun*
**carry under the arm** *verb*$_{i}$ *taapam*
**carve** *verb*$_{a}$ *tef*
**cassava** *noun maniot* (*Manihot esculenta*)
**cassia wilt** *noun metmatur* (*Mimosa pudica*)
**cassis** *noun paariik* (*Leucaena leucocephala*)
**cast a spell** *verb*$_{i}$ *laglaga*
**catch** *verb*$_{i}$ *kraksok;* *verb*$_{a}$ *puetsok;* *verb*$_{a}$ *skof*
**catch (as in sickness)** *verb*$_{a}$ *su*
**caterpillar** *noun suskei*
**caulk** *verb*$_{a}$ *sm̃ol*
**cause** *verb*$_{a}$ *preg*
**cave** *noun erfale*
**cavity in a canoe** *noun luuk*
**cell** *noun nasum̃ malik*
**cement** *noun natonifaat*
**cemetery** *noun emat*
**centipede** *noun nmraksul*
**change** *verb*$_{i}$ *plim*
**change clothes** *verb*$_{i}$ *nkalwel*
**channel** *noun nslawos*
**character** *noun*$_{i}$ *sup̃*
**charcoal** *noun nam̃elfer*
**chase** *verb*$_{t}$ *kop;* *verb*$_{a}$ *kpas*
  **chase fish** *verb*$_{i}$ *fkop*
**chat** *verb*$_{i}$ *pusrek*

**cheap** *adjective paketan*

**check** *verb*$_a$ *leefra*

**cheep** *verb*$_i$ *fesfes*

**chest** *noun*$_i$ *nanrum̃*

**chew** *verb walsem̃*

**chew (kava)** *verb*$_a$ *sm̃ai*

**chicken** *noun too sees*

**chief** *noun naot*

**chiefliness, chiefly line** *noun nafinaotan*

**chief's bodyguard** *noun tasil*

**chief's wives** *noun narup̃*

**child** *noun*$_i$ *nan; noun teesa sees; noun teesa*

**firstborn** *noun taklep*

**last born** *noun takrik*

**middle born** *noun takmaloput*

**child not growing much** *adjective sok*

**chilli** *noun siil*

**chin** *noun*$_i$ *naas*

**Chinese lantern tree** *noun naipir* (*Hernandia nymphaeifolia, Hernandia peltata*)

**chip of wood** *noun*$_i$ *nsem̃*

**chiton** *noun tm̃anruk* (*Polyplacophora*)

**choose** *verb tiptip; verb*$_a$ *mtalu*

**chop** *verb*$_a$ *krakfufu; verb*$_a$ *p̃or; verb*$_a$ *kraktof; verb*$_a$ *p̃or*

**Christian** *noun natam̃ool lot*

**Christianity** *adjective mram*

**church** *noun nasum̃tap*

**cicada** *noun kasfaas*

**cigarette** *noun nuasog*

**circumcise** *verb*$_a$ *tef; verb*$_a$ *mas*

**citizen** *noun natatok*

**clam** *noun lisaan* (*Hippopus hippopus*); *noun kram* (*Tridacnidae, Mitridae*); *noun kramp̃el*

**giant clam** *noun kramkon*

**clan** *noun naflak*

**clap** *verb*$_i$ *p̃sai*

**clarity** *noun namram*

**claw** *noun*$_i$ *npat; noun*$_i$ *nrag; noun patlep*

**small claw** *noun patrik*

**clean** *verb*$_i$ *taapsik; verb*$_a$ *mas*

**clear** *adjective mram; adjective m̃aalm̃aal; verb taata; verb*$_i$ *uum̃*

**clearing** *noun limuti; noun em̃au; noun nali; noun naor m̃al; noun malpa*

**climb** *verb*$_i$ *pag*

**climb with feet and hands** *verb*$_i$ *pagketig*

**cling** *verb*$_i$ *kelsok*

**clitoris** *noun npatsfir*

**close (near)** *preposition m̃eltig*

**close (as in a meeting)** *verb paapnun*

**close (shut)** *verb*$_t$ *p̃not*

**close eyes** *verb*$_i$ *p̃ilp̃il; verb*$_a$ *p̃il*

**close one's mouth, refuse to drink** *verb kat soksok npatin*

**closed** *adjective p̃aar*

**cloth** *noun nkal*

**clothes** *noun nkal; noun nawelwel*

**cloud** *noun nmalko; noun ntaenlag*

**storm cloud** *noun nmalko ni us*

**cloudy, overcast** *noun malkolik*

**club** *noun np̃at; noun maltali*

**cluck** *verb p̃op̃o*

**cockle** *noun kaai* (*Arcidae*)

**cockroach** *noun feek*

**cockscomb** *noun ntaarto*

**coconut** *noun numam; noun numtapilkap; noun naniu* (*Cocos nucifera*); *noun nugot; noun numotu; noun nusoksok; noun nuanpakur; noun numlakes; noun nutag; noun p̃agraap* (coconut with flower); *noun p̃orlaf* (coconut with flower breaking open)

**dry coconut** *noun nm̃arteu*
**germinated coconut** *noun klat*
**green coconut** *noun naam̃; noun naniu motu; noun nawoos*
**coconut branch** *noun naapas*
**coconut crab** *noun aas* (*Birgus latro*)
**coconut cream, thick** *noun loorktal*
**coconut frond** *noun seer*
**coconut mesh** *noun kaak*
**coconut shell** *noun of; noun purnaniu*
**coconut spathe** *noun nikniser*
**coconut sprout** *noun nfar*
**coconut stalk** *noun*$_i$ *napirket*
**coconut weaving** *noun fuelig araskei*
**cold** *adjective mlaanr; noun namlaanri*
**coleus** *noun nakwak* (*Coleus spp.*)
**collect** *verb*$_i$ *kruuk*
**coloured** *adjective mtirtir*
**comb** *verb*$_a$ *tkapir; noun nser*
**comb tree** *noun naklak* (*Planchonella grayana*)
**combine** *verb paakruk*
**come** *verb*$_i$ *mai*
**come ashore** *verb*$_i$ *taasak*
**comfort** *verb*$_i$ *pesnromnromi; verb pesmosmos; verb*$_i$ *fokfkaal*
**command** *verb*$_i$ *nriksoksok*
**commandment** *noun natilsoksokwen*
**compare** *verb*$_i$ *toon*
**competition** *noun fusurtol*
**concentrate** *verb*$_i$ *takinrog wi*
**conch shell (tritons)** *noun pupu* (*Cymatiidae*)
**confess** *verb*$_a$ *sraletu*
**confession** *noun nasraletuaan*
**conjunctivitus** *noun metmaat*
**conquer** *verb krakp̃og*
**constellation (of stars)** *noun natumau; noun nkur; noun uum; noun nkem*
**contemplation** *noun p̃op̃ paketan*
**conversation** *noun nafusrekwen*
**coo** *verb*$_i$ *p̃anrer*
**cooked** *verb*$_i$ *maas*
**copulate** *verb*$_i$ *folfol sa*
**copy** *verb*$_a$ *leperkat*
**coral** *noun pton; noun nakir*
**soft coral** *noun nakirles*
**cord (tied to a pig's foot)** *noun nlik*
**corncob** *noun nap̃raat*
**cornetfish sp.** *noun p̃agp̃ag* (*Fistularia commersonii*)
**corpse** *noun naatmat; noun teemat*
**correct** *adjective matu*
**be correct** *verb*$_i$ *leeg*
**cough** *verb*$_i$ *puuk; noun nafuukwen*
**clear one's throat** *verb*$_i$ *waser*
**country** *noun nafanu*
**couple** *noun tmawot*
**courageous** *adjective m̃aarak*
**cousin** *noun*$_i$ *p̃al*
**cover** *verb*$_a$ *kuul; verb*$_a$ *kuulkor; verb p̃akor; verb*$_a$ *p̃laakor; verb*$_i$ *kuulkul; noun p̃laakor; noun p̃akor*
**covet** *adjective metm̃akur*
**coward** *noun malp̃al*
**crab** *noun namtame; noun kaftan; noun rakum; noun kafrali; noun pialoaal; noun kaaf; noun kafeer*
**box crab** *noun arm̃afaf* (*Calappidae*)
**coconut crab** *noun aas* (*Birgus latro*)
**ghost crab** *noun kaap̃* (*Ocypode cerathopthalma*)
**hermit crab** *noun katom* (*Coenobitidae*); *noun katp̃aar* (*Diogenidae*)
**reef crab** *noun ntame* (*Xanthidae*); *noun p̃olul* (*Etisus splendidus*)
**small crab** *noun mtame*

**small white crab** *noun popot*

**soldier crab** *noun p̃elpuk* (*Mictyris sp.*)

**crack** *verb m̃altelit; noun mtel*

**cramp** *verb*$_i$ *metmer*

**crawl** *verb*$_i$ *krak; verb kraf*

**crayfish** *noun uurtaiak*

**crazy person** *noun p̃aror*

**cream** *noun loor*

**create** *verb*$_i$ *kaimes*

**credit** *noun naul*

**creep** *verb*$_i$ *sai; verb*$_i$ *pau*

**creep up on** *verb*$_i$ *paalak*

**crescent moon** *noun naul nmariu*

**crippled** *adjective kool*

**criticise** *verb*$_i$ *tilsa*

**crooked** *verb*$_i$ *takel*

**cross (move across)** *verb mpakot; verb*$_i$ *nrookot*

**cross one's arms** *verb*$_i$ *krum*

**crossed** *adjective peltakot*

**cross-member** *noun nsol; noun nakiat*

**crotch** *noun*$_i$ *naal*

**croton** *noun nkau*

**crouch** *verb p̃oo*

**crow** *verb*$_i$ *taar*

**crowd** *noun talpuk*

**crowded** *adjective tiisoksok*

**crumbs** *noun nafer*

**crush in one's hand** *verb*$_a$ *kut p̃orp̃rai*

**cry** *verb*$_i$ *kai*

**cry for** *verb*$_t$ *kait*

**cup** *noun laas*

**current** *noun naar*

**curse** *verb*$_i$ *pes sa; noun nafesaan*

**curtain** *noun nalukor*

**curved** *adjective taap̃oos*

**cushion star** *noun p̃aulum̃ ni afsak* (*Culcita novaeguineae*)

**cut** *verb*$_a$ *tef; verb*$_a$ *taasai; verb*$_a$ *tai; verb*$_a$ *tkau; verb taakot; verb*$_a$ *lat*

**cut grass** *verb*$_a$ *suur*

**cut in half** *verb*$_a$ *masp̃rai*

**cut laplap** *verb*$_i$ *kot*

**cut the eye out of a coconut** *verb*$_a$ *sul*

**cuttlefish** *noun walu*

**cycad palm** *noun nam̃el* (*Cycas seemannii*)

**cyclone** *noun nlag miel; noun nlagwat*

# D

**daily** *adverb ser naliati*

**damselfishes** *noun naik nrmen* (*Pomacentridae*); **onespot, twospot, king, etc.** *noun piam* (*Pomacentridae*)

**dance** *verb*$_i$ *lau; noun nlauwen; verb*$_i$ *pul*

**dark** *noun malik; noun nmalko*

**dawn** *noun pulmatlen; noun pulp̃og rik*

**day** *noun m̃au naliati; noun aliat*

**day after tomorrow** *noun aas*

**day before yesterday** *noun naas*

**days** *noun naliati*

**deaf** *noun ntaligp̃aar; verb p̃aar*

**death** *noun ntanwen*

**debate** *verb tilusus*

**deceive** *verb*$_a$ *sursur*

**declare** *verb*$_i$ *tilsei*

**decorate** *verb*$_a$ *fakis*

**deep** *adjective paketan*

**deep ocean** *noun ntalfan; nam̃oru*

**deformed** *verb*$_i$ *sasaan*

**delicious** *adjective tuntun*

**delouse** *verb*$_i$ *paak*

**demolish** *verb*$_i$ *p̃apir*

**dense** *verb motu; adjective kos*

**dentist** *noun tem̃okm̃ok*

**depart** *verb*$_i$ *tm̃alu*

**depend** *verb*$_i$ *lereki*

**derib** *verb*$_a$ *m̃asel*

**descend** *verb*$_i$ *su; adjective paketan*

**desert** *noun namesp̃al*

**desire** *noun namuurien*

**destroy** *verb p̃asrot*

**determined** *verb*$_i$ *usog*

**devil** *noun ntaligpram; noun ntwam*

**devil nettle tree** *noun gkar; noun nam̃lat* (*Dendrocnide latifolia*)

**devil ray** *noun faai mantu*

**dew** *noun namlame*

**diarrhoea** *noun ntafwen; verb*$_i$ *taf*

**die** *verb*$_i$ *mat*

**die down** *verb*$_i$ *mrer*

**different** *verb*$_i$ *p̃tae; adjective msal; adjective p̃onp̃tae; verb*$_i$ *fserser; adjective p̃et*

**dig** *verb*$_a$ *traf; verb*$_a$ *kil*

**dig hole for yam** *verb seo*

**dig out tree** *verb*$_a$ *nri*

**dirt** *noun nam̃ilo*

**dirt, red** *noun ntan makoren*

**dirty** *adjective m̃ilo*

**disabled** *verb*$_i$ *sasaan*

  **intellectually disabled** *verb*$_i$ *nrop*

**disagree** *verb psapir*

**disappear** *verb*$_i$ *puel; verb*$_i$ *funfnoi*

**discard** *verb*$_i$ *saprek*

**disclose** *verb mgal*

**discover** *verb*$_a$ *pam̃or*

**discuss** *verb tilusus*

**disease** *noun namgar*

**disembark** *verb*$_i$ *paatan*

**disobey** *verb*$_a$ *nrogpir; verb*$_i$ *psig*

**display** *verb*$_i$ *fekfek*

**dispute** *verb*$_i$ *ple*

**dissolve** *verb*$_i$ *fanei*

**distant** *verb*$_i$ *pakem̃ae*

**dive** *verb*$_i$ *nrup̃*

**divide** *verb p̃otp̃tae; verb*$_a$ *si; verb*$_i$ *p̃tae*

**divorce** *verb*$_a$ *tao*

**dizzy** *noun talgolig; verb manin*

**do** *verb*$_a$ *preg*

**do by accident** *verb*$_i$ *krakpel*

**do good** *verb pregwi*

**do something bad to** *verb*$_a$ *plos*

**dodge** *verb*$_i$ *talel*

**dog** *noun kori*

**dolphin** *noun naniu* (*Delphinidae*)

**don't know** *verb maak*

**don't recognise** *verb*$_t$ *lesap̃*

**door** *noun namet p̃ur*

**double** *adjective p̃ura*

**doubt** *verb*$_a$ *mropir*

**dove sp.** *noun maan nap̃lo* (*Macropygia mackinlayi*)

  **green-winged ground dove** *noun tokape* (*Chalcophaps indica*)

  **red-bellied fruit dove** *noun sunra* (*Ptilinopus greyii*)

  **Vanuatu fruit dove** *noun m̃lato* (*Ptilinopus tannensis*)

**down** *preposition etan*

**downhill** *noun etan ntaf*

**drag** *verb*$_a$ *nroos; verb*$_i$ *toos*

**dragon plum** tree *noun nrau* (*Dracontomelon vitiense*)

**dragonfly** *noun kaltag*

**draw curtain** *verb*$_a$ *lukor*

**dream** *noun nap̃re*

**dregs** *noun nam̃lak*

**dress** *verb*$_i$ *kal*

**dried up, as in a dry river** *adjective tep̃*

**drift** *verb*$_i$ *sal*

**driftwood** *noun tarisal*
**drill** *verb*$_a$ *pirsai; verb*$_a$ *tur*
**drink** *verb*$_a$ *min*
**drip** *verb lao*
**drive** *verb*$_a$ *pa; verb*$_i$ *kel sman; verb pu sman*
**drizzle** *verb*$_i$ *sirsir*
**drop** *verb*$_a$ *kraksmanr*
**drown** *verb*$_i$ *tut*
**drum beater** *noun nkas ni nap̃e*
**drummers** *noun wakm̃akur* (*Kyphosidae*)
**drunk** *verb*$_i$ *nrop; noun p̃aufiif*
**dry** *adjective gar*
**dry by sunlight** *verb*$_i$ *tiit*
**dry leaves** *noun naflel*
**dry taste** *adjective kfet*
**dryer for copra or bêche-de-mer** *noun wenr*
**duck** *noun taktak; noun taktakninai* (*Anas superciliosa*)
**duck** *verb*$_i$ *talof*
**dugong** *noun p̃kastes* (*Dugong dugon*)
**dumb** *verb p̃aar; adjective puus*
**dunk** *verb*$_i$ *sam*
**dust** *noun nam̃tam̃ot; noun nalo; verb p̃oktao*
**dwarf** *noun sputan; noun naferkaal*
**dye** *verb*$_i$ *mir; noun nasnaki*

# E

**each** *adjective sikskei; noun nruenru; adjective inruenru*
**eager** *adjective m̃aarak*
**ear** *noun*$_i$ *ntalig*
**earth** *noun emeromen*
**earthquake** *noun nanrur*
**east** *noun naweskin pei; noun ruetu*
**easy** *adjective mailum*
**eat** *verb*$_a$ *pam; verb*$_a$ *fam*
  **eat something hard** *verb*$_a$ *p̃rot*
**edge** *noun*$_i$ *natik*
**eel** *noun mra*
  **banded snake eel** *noun mra tfei*
  **freshwater eel** *noun mra ni nai*
  **giant moray eel** *noun mra nm̃ap̃* (*Gymnothorax javanicus*)
  **moray eel sp.** *noun mra ni ntas*
  **river eel** *noun taakto ninai*
**eel** *noun taakto*
**eel sp.** *noun taligter*
**egg** *noun atol*
**eight** *number latol*
**eighth** *adjective klatol*
**elbow** *noun*$_i$ *nafsup̃nar*
**elders** *noun tiawi*
**elephantiasis** *noun tuup̃ur*
**embrace** *verb wafin*
**emerge** *verb*$_i$ *putsak*
**emperor (fish spp.)** *noun warof* (*Lethrinus spp.*) *noun nsul; noun nametfaai* (*Lethrinidae*);
  **long-nosed emperor, longface emperor** *noun nsulnkanrpram* (*Lethrinus olivaceus*)
**emphasis** *verb*$_2$ *sok*
**empty** *adjective tep̃; verb m̃asm̃as; adjective p̃al*
**empty-handed, to be** *verb*$_i$ *puur*
**encircle, encircle fish** *verb*$_a$ *sogsog*
**encourage** *verb*$_a$ *psasok*
**end** *noun*$_i$ *nametp̃ag; verb paamau; noun*$_i$ *mp̃ag; noun maumaau; verb*$_i$ *p̃on*
**end (as in a meeting)** *verb paapnun*

**end of a mat** *noun*$_i$ *nagor*
**enemy** *noun waal p̃tae*
**engage** *verb*$_a$ *mpasok*
**enlighten** *verb*$_i$ *pregi kesalsal*
**enough** *verb*$_a$ *tlas*
**enter** *verb*$_i$ *sil*
**envy** *verb*$_i$ *kitsa*
**epilepsy** *noun leet*
**equal** *verb fitkaskei*
**erase** *verb*$_i$ *krakfunfnoi*
  **obliterate** *verb*$_i$ *surfunfnoi*
**erect, of a penis** *verb*$_i$ *tum̃*
**erection** *noun m̃ak*
**erupt** *verb*$_i$ *m̃alit*
**escape** *verb*$_i$ *sef*
**escort** *verb taatur*
**establish** *verb*$_i$ *lao*
**evening** *noun kotfaan*
**evening star** *noun m̃asei lep ni kotfaan*
**ever, forever** *adverb termau*
**every** *adjective nomser; adjective silu; auxiliary, adjective nom; adjective ser*
**everywhere** *adverb sernaor*
**excellent** *adjective wi m̃esm̃es*
**exchange** *verb*$_i$ *tigpiel*
**exclamation** *interjection iuui; interjection kau; verb koloini; interjection kala*
**exit** *verb*$_i$ *taf*
**explain** *verb*$_i$ *p̃oot*
**explode** *verb*$_i$ *m̃alit*
**eye** *noun*$_i$ *namet*
**eye of the fishhook** *noun namet tkau*
**eyebrow** *noun*$_i$ *nfas namet*
**eyelashes** *noun*$_i$ *nanrau namet*

# F

**face** *noun*$_i$ *nako; noun*$_i$ *nrae*
**facing** *verb*$_a$ *toklos*
**fail** *verb paamau*
**faint** *verb*$_i$ *matmaal*
**fall** *verb*$_a$ *sog; verb*$_i$ *wo; verb*$_i$ *m̃el; verb*$_i$ *tarup̃*
**fall, of water over a waterfall** *verb laolao*
**fallow** *noun talm̃aat fus*
**false nutmeg** *noun nra* (*Myristica fatua*)
**family** *noun nametrau*
**fan** *verb*$_a$ *niif; noun niif*
**fancy** *adjective lagi*
**fantail, grey fantail** *noun takerker*
**far** *adverb em̃ae*
**farewell** *verb psapus*
**fart** *verb*$_i$ *p̃er*
**fart on something** *verb*$_t$ *p̃erat*
**fasten mat (on body)** *verb*$_a$ *fiikot*
**father** *noun taata; noun gka; noun apaap; noun*$_i$ *tem*
  **father and his child** *noun teemtmen*
**fear** *verb*$_i$ *mtak*
**feast** *noun nafamwen*
**feather** *noun*$_i$ *nm̃au*
**feel** *verb*$_a$ *tkalnrog; verb*$_a$ *nrog; verb*$_a$ *tonrog*
**feel bad** *verb*$_i$ *nrogtesa*
**feel with the foot** *verb*$_a$ *kamnrog*
**female** *noun nmatu*
**female name marker** *noun li*
**fence** *noun laak; noun tp̃er; noun koor; noun tikor; noun elkao*
**fermented breadfruit** *noun mutrei*
**fern** *noun naruut; noun naweel ni namlas* (*Pyrrosia lanceolata, Phymatosorus grossus*)

**fetch water** *verb$_a$ uut*
**few** *adjective warik; adjective nrfaal*
**fierce** *verb fiet*
**fifth** *adjective kalim*
**fifth day** *noun up̃lim*
**fig tree** *noun naplip* (*Ficus granatum*); *noun nakrik* (*Ficus virgata*); *noun nait* (*Ficus wassa*)
**fight** *verb$_i$ ftup̃; verb$_i$ ple; verb kuf; noun naflewen*
**filefishes** *noun knopun* (*Monacanthidae, Tetrodontidae*)
**fill** *verb$_a$ tor*
**fin** *noun$_i$ nlae*
**final** *adjective mlaap*
**find** *verb$_a$ pam̃or*
**fine** *noun naro*
**finger** *noun$_i$ nakin*
  **index finger** *noun kinm̃aat*
  **little finger** *noun kinrik*
  **middle finger** *noun kinliu*
  **ring finger** *noun kintapul*
  **thumb** *noun kinlep*
**finish** *verb$_i$ nom*
**fire** *noun nkap*
  **start a fire** *verb$_a$ pees*
**fire ant** *noun kaanr*
**firestick** *noun ntankep*
**firewood** *noun nkap*
**firm** *adjective masoksok*
**first** *adjective tepei; number pei; number fei*
**fish** *noun naik*
**fish from a boat, to** *verb$_i$ tir*
**fish using poison, to** *verb$_a$ pun*
**fish using a spear, to** *verb$_i$ oraik*
**fish by torchlight, to** *verb$_i$ sul*
**fish sp./spp.**
  *noun kig; noun us; noun tasar; noun weel* (*Acanthurus triostegus*); *noun napum̃* (*Scombridae spp.*); *noun meramok; noun fumatol; noun map̃er; noun kaitao* (*Carangidae*)
**anemonefishes** *noun naik nrmen* (*Pomacentridae*)
**angelfishes** *noun map̃eriat* (*Chaetodontidae, Pomacanthidae*); *noun tiftif*
**anthiases** *noun aaf* (*Serranidae*)
**barracuda** *noun menaal* (*Sphyraenidae*)
**batfish** *noun foik*
**bonefish, Indo-Pacific** *noun marikwi* (*Albula glossodonta*)
**boxfishes** *noun mateu* (*Ostraciidae, Tetraodontidae*)
**butterflyfishes** *noun tiftif* (*Chaetodontidae, Pomacanthidae*); *noun naik maan* (*Pterois spp.*)
**cardinalfish** *noun anrar; noun p̃op̃or* (*Apogonidae*)
**cornetfish** sp. *noun p̃agp̃ag* (*Fistularia commersonii*)
**damselfishes** *noun naik nrmen* (*Pomacentridae*); **onespot, twospot, king, etc.** *noun piam* (*Pomacentridae*)
**drummers** *noun wakm̃akur* (*Kyphosidae*)
**emperors** *noun nsul; noun nametfaai* (*Lethrinidae*); **long-nosed emperor, longface emperor** *noun nsulnkanrpram* (*Lethrinus olivaceus*)
**filefishes** *noun knopun* (*Monacanthidae, Tetrodontidae*)
**flagtail** *noun tuur* (*Kuhliidae*); **fiveband flagtail** *noun lailaipako*

**flounder** *noun kapuenrar* (*Bothidae*)
**flying fish** sp. *noun naikmetpuk* (*Priacanthus macracanthus*); *noun naiknrir*
**frogfishes** *noun p̃iit* (*Antennariidae*)
**fusiliers** *noun napum̃ ni faat* (*Caesionidae*); **common mojarra** *noun maar*
**garfish, red mouth** *noun totogmal*
**goatfish** *noun konafnako* (*Mullidae*); **goldband, blackstriped, yellowbanded** *noun susmraknaniu* (*Upeneus*); **yellowstripe goatfish, yellowfin goatfish** *noun suus* (*Mullidae*)
**gobies** *noun orpak* (*Gobiidae*)
**green fish sp.** *noun napum̃ ni nam̃oru*
**grouper** *noun koom; noun p̃aup̃al* (*Serranidae*); *noun p̃autop*; **humpback grouper** *noun sasu* (*Cromileptes altivelis, Haemulidae*)
**grunter, crescent-banded** *noun koser*
**halfbeak, insular** *noun ntau* (*Hyporhamphus affinis*)
**halfbeak, spotted** *noun snom* (*Hemiramphus far*)
**hawkfishes** *noun tafut* (*Cirrhitidae Plesiopidae*)
**Indo-Pacific tarpon** *noun napelial* (*Megalops cyprinoides*)
**lesson's sweetlips** *noun sasupra* (*Plectorhinchus lessonii*)
**lionfish** *noun naik maan*
**mackerel, striped** *noun aslel* (*Rastrelliger kanagurta*)
**milkfish** *noun nap̃ures* (*Chanos chanos*)
**monocle breams** *noun wanaar* (*Nemipteridae*)
**needlefish, reef** *noun totogmal* (*Strongylura incisa*)
**parrotfish** *noun kalafiai*
**parrotfish, bumphead** *noun kalap̃og* (*Bolbometopon muricatum*)
**parrotfishes** *noun nuo* (*Scaridae*)
**picasso fish, strong skin, or brush-sided filefish** *noun fumasei*
**pipefish** *noun naapas*
**pompano, silver** *noun nason* (*Trachinotus blochii*)
**porcupinefishes** *noun p̃ka* (*Diodontidae Tetrodontidae*)
**puffers** *noun knopun* (*Monacanthidae, Tetrodontidae*)
**rabbitfish** *noun toof* (*Siganidae*); *noun sm̃os;* **peppered rabbitfish or coral rabbitfish** *noun tofkas* (*Siganidae*); **vermiculate rabbitfish or forktail rabbitfish** *noun fser* (*Siganidae*)
**rays, bluespotted ribbontail ray** *noun faai kuul* (*Taeniura lymma*)
**remoras** *noun naik taos* (*Echeneidae*)
**sand bass** *noun fup̃eel* (*Centropomidae*)
**sandperch** *noun lao* (*Pinguipedidae*)
**sardine** *noun napeel* (*Clupeidae*); **flat kind** *noun napelial* (*Megalops cyprinoides*); **round, like a finger** *noun napelp̃ures;* **very small** *noun napeltan*

**scorpionfishes** *noun fti* (*Scorpaenidae*); **smallscale scorpionfish** *noun ftir* (*Scorpaenidae*)
**seahorse** *noun maikel* (*Hippocampus*)
**shrimpfish** *noun naapas*
**slipmouth** *noun m̃aor* (*Leiognathidae*)
**snapper, blackspot snapper** *noun malagot;* **sp. with black dot on side** *noun pao malagot* (*Lutjanidae*); **onespot or yellow-margined** *noun pao;* **paddletail snapper** *noun paokap;* **twinspot snapper** *noun fuknra*
**soldierfish** *noun ntai* (*Holocentridae*)
**Spengler's mactra** *noun kaluspam* (*Scissodesma spengleri*)
**spinecheeks** *noun wanaar* (*Nemipteridae*)
**squirrelfish** *noun sreniu* (*Holocentridae*); **threespot squirrelfish and similar** *noun trakap* (*Holocentridae*)
**stonefish** *noun p̃iit* (*Antennariidae*); **small stonefish** *noun ftir* (*Scorpaenidae*)
**strongskin, dark coloured** *noun fum̃os*
**surgeonfish sp.** *noun tiftif wel rom;* **including white-freckled, lieutenant, striped bristletooth, twospot bristletooth** *noun p̃arsor* (*Acanthurus*)
**tuna, dogtooth tuna** *noun p̃laanr* (*Gymnosarda unicolor*); **yellow tail or skipjack tuna** *noun napum̃ m̃nam̃on*
**unicornfish, bluespine unicornfish** noun *raeru* (*Naso unicornis, Balistidae*); **humpnose unicornfish** *noun naum* (*Naso tuberosus*); **orangespine unicornfish** *noun uus*
**white fish, small** *noun laorpek*
**wrasses** *noun patru* (*Labridae*); **bird wrasse** *noun taktak* (*Gomphosus varius*); **cigar wrasse** *noun aaf ni nariuriu* (*Cheilio inermis*); **humphead wrasse** *noun afam* (*Cheilinus undulatus*); **nebulous wrasse** *noun laokinasusu* (*Halichoeres nebulosus*); **sixbar wrasse?, green with stripes** *noun ures*

**fish bones** *noun nanreu*
**five** *number lim*
**flagtail** *noun tuur* (*Kuhliidae*);
**fiveband flagtail** *noun lailaipako*
**flake** *verb$_i$ mulmul*
**flat** *adjective matit*
**flat country** *noun nateen*
**flatten** *verb$_i$ wol*
**flesh** *noun nafsik; noun$_i$ nafeng*
**float** *verb$_i$ m̃el; verb$_i$ salsal*
**flood** *verb slasol; verb$_i$ me*
**flotsam** *noun tarisal*
**flounder** *noun kapuenrar* (*Bothidae*)
**flow** *verb$_i$ ser*
**flower** *noun nafum̃*
**flower on nakpes** *noun napupuus*
**flu, get a flu** *verb$_i$ gos*
**flu** *noun nagoswen*
**fly** *noun laag*
**fly** *verb$_i$ nrir*

**fly magically** *verb$_i$ p̃erik*
**flying fish sp.** *noun naikmetpuk* (*Priacanthus macracanthus*); *noun naiknrir*
**flying fox** *noun mantu*
  **red flying fox and white flying fox** *noun kotfeel*
**foam** *noun nap̃esp̃es; noun nlatlat*
**fog** *noun nmaf*
**follow** *verb$_a$ taus; verb$_a$ us; verb$_t$ kop; verb$_a$ nrokos; verb$_2$ usus*
**fols tabaco** *noun namook* (*Heliotropium foertherianum*)
**food** *noun nafnag*
  **hard food** *adjective p̃roro*
**fool** *noun p̃aror; verb$_i$ pool*
**foolish** *adjective p̃autik*
**foot, leg** *noun$_i$ natu*
  **sole of foot** *noun$_i$ naal natu*
**footprint** *noun$_i$ nam̃leenatu*
**forage** *verb$_a$ m̃tal*
**forearm** *noun$_i$ nmalnar*
**forehead** *noun$_i$ nrae*
**foreign place** *noun etog*
**foreigner** *noun nasap̃*
**forget** *verb$_a$ metp̃akor*
**forgive** *verb$_a$ nrat*
**fork in the road** *noun napu toraan*
**four** *number paat*
**fourth** *adjective kaafat*
**fowl** *noun too*
  **wild fowl** *noun too mil*
**frame, for hanging yams** *noun nalkolik*
**Friday** *noun aliat p̃oot*
**friend** *noun$_i$ asel*
**frighten** *verb$_a$ sinrkat*
**frightened** *verb plokra*
**frizzy (hair)** *adjective tp̃ak*
**frogfishes** *noun p̃iit* (*Antennariidae*)
**front** *preposition nakpei*
**froth** *verb$_i$ latlat; noun nasusu*
**fruit** *noun nua*
**fruit of napuk** *noun m̃eem̃*
**fuck** *verb tik; verb polsa*
**full** *adjective tiisoksok; adjective pur*
  **to have a full mouth** *verb$_i$ toopuk*
**full tummy** *noun p̃elpuk*
**fully** *suffix -lu*
**funeral** *noun ntatanwen*
**fungus** *noun ntalig*
**fusiliers** *noun napum̃ ni faat* (*Caesionidae*); **common mojarra** *noun maar*
**future** *noun matool*

## G

**gale** *noun nlag kerkrai*
**gall bladder** *noun ulikookon*
**game** *noun nameswen*
**gap** *noun nmaotao*
**garden** *noun talm̃aat*
**garfish, red mouth** *noun totogmal*
**gargle** *verb$_i$ pupu*
**gather** *verb$_2$ kruuk; verb karo*
**gecko** *noun ofagpulsok*; *noun ofag* (*Gekkonidae spp.*)
**generation** *noun ntag*
**genitals** *noun$_i$ nlas*
**germinate (seed)** *verb$_i$ sirsir*
**get out of a car or boat** *verb$_i$ tutan*
**ghost crab** *noun kaap̃* (*Ocypode cerathopthalma*)

**giant** *noun m̃aau*
**giant clam** *noun kramkon*
**giant reef ray** *noun pakokap̃o* (*Taeniura melanospilos*)
**gift** *noun naftuan*
**giggle** *verb mtamurmur*
**gill** *noun*$_i$ *nap̃raksa*
**give** *verb*$_d$ *tu; verb*$_d$ *ftu*
**glare** *verb*$_a$ *sulkor*
**glasses** *noun telele*
**glide** *verb*$_i$ *ter*
**glue** *noun tepulsok*
**go** *verb fa; verb fan*
**go along** *verb*$_i$ *ur*
**go around** *verb*$_i$ *lfek; verb*$_i$ *usrek*
**go backward** *verb*$_i$ *skosuk*
**go for** *verb*$_a$ *paareki*
**go quickly** *verb, adverb fuu*
**go through** *verb mpatur; verb*$_a$ *totur*
**go to** *verb*$_i$ *pak*
**goatfish** *noun konafnako* (*Mullidae*); **goldband, blackstriped, yellowbanded** *noun susmraknaniu* (*Upeneus*); **yellowfin goatfish** *noun suus* (*Mullidae*); **yellowstripe goatfish**
**gobies** *noun orpak* (*Gobiidae*)
**good** *adjective wi*
**goshawk** *noun malp̃erik*
**gossip** *verb*$_i$ *ftil*
**gouge** *verb*$_a$ *sur; verb waal*
**grab** *verb*$_a$ *nrakut*
**grace** *verb*$_i$ *psawi*
**grandchild** *noun*$_i$ *suul*
**granddaughter with the same name as their grandmother** *noun ati sees*
**grandfather** *noun apu*
**grandmother** *noun ati*
**grandson with the same name as their grandfather** *noun apu sees*
**grasp** *verb seltae*
**grass** *noun nam̃nam̃*
**grass skirt** *noun m̃alm̃al; noun nam̃aser*
**grass sp.** *noun natuer; nanumtap̃es* (*Miscanthus sinensis*)
**grasshopper** *noun sos* (*Orthoptera spp.*)
**grate** *verb*$_a$ *trai; verb*$_a$ *maa; verb*$_a$ *kar*
**grate, to grate roasted yam and taro skin** *verb*$_a$ *naunau*
**grater** *noun skeitrai; noun naures; noun fatma*
**grave** *noun*$_i$ *emat*
**gravel** *noun nakir*
**great-grandchild** *noun suul kaaru; noun sulsul*
**great-grandfather** *noun apu motu*
**great-grandmother** *noun ati motu*
**greedy** *verb taap̃ur; verb katp̃o*
**green** *adjective ksakes*
**grey** *adjective karo*
**grind** *verb walsem̃*
**grind one's teeth, also a sign of anger** *verb kat soksok npatin; verb kat p̃orp̃ros npatin*
**groan** *verb*$_i$ *nrig*
**grope** *verb*$_i$ *toto*
**ground** *noun ntan*
**group** *noun npanep; noun talpuk; adjective mana; noun nafet*
**group of kids** *noun naferkaal*
**grouper (fish)** *noun koom; noun p̃aup̃al* (*Serranidae*); *noun p̃autop*; **humpback grouper, pantherfish, also sweetlips** *noun sasu* (*Cromileptes altivelis, Haemulidae*)
**grow** *verb*$_i$ *ftom*
**growl** *verb*$_i$ *m̃la; verb*$_i$ *nrig; verb*$_i$ *fusuer*

**grunt** *verb*$_i$ *ur*
**grunter, crescent-banded** *noun koser*
**guard** *noun teelekor; verb*$_a$ *mut*
**guava** *noun koiaf* (*Psidium guajava*)
**gum** *noun*$_i$ *nagel*
**gun** *noun sisi*
**guts** *noun*$_i$ *nmarit*

# H

**habit** *noun*$_i$ *sup̃*
**hair** *noun*$_i$ *nal*
  **pubic hair** *noun*$_i$ *nrau*
**hairy** *adjective ululu*
**half** *noun kotfak; noun nakon*
**half dry** *adjective maus*
**half ripe** *adjective mamp̃ok*
**halfbeak, spotted** *noun snom* (*Hemiramphus far*)
**halo** *noun tam̃as*
**hammerhead shark** *noun pakofai*
**handle** *noun*$_i$ *nfer; noun*$_i$ *nkar, gkar*
**hang** *verb*$_a$ *ser; verb*$_i$ *sal; verb kof; verb*$_i$ *liksaal*
**hang, like a monkey in a tree** *verb skoot*
**hang yams** *verb lkolik*
**happy** *verb*$_i$ *semsem*
**harbour** *noun nuof*
**hard** *adjective kerkerai*
**hard food** *adjective p̃roro*
**hardwood** *noun nator*
**harvest** *noun namas; verb*$_a$ *kis; verb*$_a$ *m̃tal*
**hat** *noun pulp̃ou*
**hatch** *verb*$_i$ *maaf; verb*$_i$ *tafafu*
**have** *verb*$_a$ *piatlak*
  **not have** *verb*$_i$ *tiik*
**hawkfishes** *noun tafut* (*Cirrhitidae Plesiopidae*)
**he/she** *pronoun ga*
**he/she/it (irrealis)** *pronoun prefix ke=*
**he/she/it (perfect)** *pronoun prefix ki=*
**he/she/it (realis)** *pronoun prefix i=; pronoun nega*
**head** *noun*$_i$ *np̃au; verb entaf*
**heal** *verb*$_i$ *wam*
**healer** *noun teleekot; noun munwei; noun kulru*
**healthy** *verb*$_i$ *m̃ool*
**heap** *noun tap̃u*
**heap of fruit** *noun nam̃aniu*
**hear** *verb*$_a$ *nrog*
**heart** *noun*$_i$ *am̃kano*
**heartwood** *noun nap̃lau nkas*
**heat** *noun tortor; verb*$_a$ *nrag*
**heaven** *noun elagsau*
**heavy** *adjective mten*
**heavy rain** *noun us walep*
**Hebrew cone (shellfish)** *noun tilm̃aar* (*Conus ebraeus, Conus nielsenae*)
**heel** *noun*$_i$ *ntaknatu; noun*$_i$ *nam̃elnatu*
**hell** *noun nafanu sa*
**help** *verb*$_a$ *welu*
**helper, chief's assistant** *noun ataf*
**hen** *noun too nmatu*
**herbs** *noun nalkes*
**her, for her** *pronoun ga*
**her/his/its** *pronoun nega*
**hers/his** *pronoun ga*
**here** *demonstrative sa, esan*
**hermit crab** *noun katom* (*Coenobitidae*); *noun katp̃aar* (*Diogenidae*)
**heron** *noun oof*
**hesitate** *verb*$_i$ *sul*

**hey!** *interjection nkis*
**hibiscus sp.** *noun naplel* (*Hibiscus tilaceus*); *nap̃kal* (*Hibiscus rosa-sinensis*)
**hiccup** *verb*$_i$ *m̃aser*
**hide** *verb*$_i$ *uus; verb*$_i$ *kus; verb*$_a$ *kuskor*
**hide, keep secret** *verb*$_a$ *psakor*
**hide by covering** *verb kuulkus*
**hide something** *verb*$_a$ *srakor*
**hide to catch prey** *verb*$_a$ *paikor*
**high** *preposition elag*
**hill** *noun ntaf*
**hip** *noun*$_i$ *ntap̃rai*
**him, for him/her** *pronoun ga*
**his/her/its** *pronoun nega*
**his/hers** *pronoun ga*
**hit** *verb*$_a$ *wat; verb*$_a$ *tup̃*
**hog plum tree** *noun nmal* (*Spondias dulcis, S. cythera, S. edulis*)
**hold** *verb fuetsok; verb*$_i$ *kel; verb*$_a$ *puetsok; verb*$_a$ *kut; verb*$_a$ *pupuet; verb*$_i$ *katsok*
**hold a mat flat** *verb*$_a$ *mpasok*
**hold firmly** *verb*$_i$ *sat*
**hold tight** *verb*$_a$ *sarsok*
**hole** *noun nam̃or; noun nfal*
**hole drilled in the side of canoe** *noun nametfau*
**holey (full of holes)** *adjective m̃saisei; verb m̃sai*
**honeyeater** *noun alak* (*Lichmera incana*)
**honour** *adjective paketan*
**hook** *noun tkau*
**hook shot** *verb taakau*
**hooked** *adjective fatkau*
**hooked stick** *noun fatkau*
**hop** *verb*$_i$ *tigtig*
**horizon** *noun ntalfan*
**horn** *noun sup̃sup̃*
  **cow horn** *noun*$_i$ *npat*
**hornet** *noun liit ni ntan*
**hospital** *noun nasum̃ namsaki*
**hot** *verb*$_i$ *ftin*
**hour** *verb mal*
**house** *noun sum̃; noun nasum̃*
**household** *noun naal nasum̃*
**how** *interjection tkanwan; adverb tfale*
**how much** *adjective kefi*
**hug** *verb*$_a$ *taasok*
**humble, be humble** *adjective paketan*
**humility** *noun p̃op̃ paketan*
**humpback grouper** *noun sasu* (*Cromileptes altivelis, Haemulidae*)
**hundred** *number tifli*
**hungry** *verb*$_i$ *ptol*
**hunt** *verb*$_i$ *plakori; verb*$_i$ *mol*
**hurry** *verb*$_i$ *trapelpel*
**husband** *noun maarik*
**husk** *noun naun; noun tep̃las; verb*$_a$ *tak; verb*$_a$ *kat naniu*
**hut** *noun koof*

# I

**I** *pronoun prefix kineu; pronoun prefix a=; pronoun prefix kai=*
**I/me** *pronoun neu*
**identify** *verb*$_a$ *letae*
**idol** *noun naatap*
**ignore** *verb*$_i$ *sertep̃al; verb*$_a$ *sigpir; verb*$_a$ *maltotae*
**imitate** *verb*$_a$ *pregwel*
**important** *adjective lesok*
**increase** *verb*$_t$ *sak; verb*$_i$ *pakelag*

**incubator bird** *noun mlau* (*Megapodius freycinet*)
**index finger** *noun kinm̃aat*
**Indian mulberry** *noun nakur* (*Morinda citrifolia*)
**individual** *adjective sikskei*
**Indo-Pacific tarpon** *noun napelial*
**inheritance** *noun naftuan*
**insects & bugs**
  **ant sp.** *noun funrei; noun mkaal*
  **ant sp., red ant** *noun tup̃roor*
  **beetle** *noun frap̃o; noun pagos*
  **black ant** *noun kaanr*
  **butterfly** *noun lipeep*
  **centipede** *noun nmraksul*
  **cicada** *noun kasfaas*
  **cockroach** *noun feek*
  **dragonfly** *noun kaltag*
  **fire ant** *noun kaanr*
  **fly** *noun lag*
  **grasshopper** *noun sos* (*Orthoptera spp.*)
  **hornet** *noun liit ni ntan*
  **insect** *noun matuktukurik*
  **louse** *noun$_i$ kut* (*Pediculidae*)
  **millipede** *noun takelkel*
  **mosquito** *noun katnaam*
  **moth** *noun meer; noun tagralim*
  **rhinocerus beetle** *noun p̃aas*
  **spider** *noun kalum̃*
  **stick insect** *noun srak*
  **termite-like grub** *noun ofet*
  **wasp** *noun liit*
  **wriggler (mosquito larva)** *noun funrei*
**inside** *noun$_i$ nap̃lau; preposition em̃rom; preposition naal*
**inside leg** *noun$_i$ nak*
**inside of the mouth** *noun nau*
**insult** *verb$_i$ pes sa*
**intellectually disabled** *verb$_i$ nrop*
**interested** *verb$_i$ pko*
**investigate** *verb$_a$ leusus*
**invitation** *noun natoo*
**iron** *verb$_a$ ter; noun m̃p̃atfaat*
**ironwood** *noun nagi*
**island** *noun naur*
**island cabbage** *noun altuk*
**island teak tree** *noun nakm̃ou* (*Intsia bijuga*)
**it** *pronoun wes*
**it/he/she (irrealis)** *pronoun prefix ke=*
**it/he/she (perfect)** *pronoun prefix ki=*
**it/he/she (realis)** *pronoun prefix i=; pronoun nega*
**itch** *verb$_i$ kar; noun namkalkal*
  **be itchy** *verb$_i$ mkalkal*

## J

**Java cedar** *noun nkok* (*Bischofia javanica*)
**jaw harp** *noun susa*
**jealous** *verb$_i$ fetkasu*
**jellyfish** *noun karkor*
  **box jellyfish** *noun litas* (*Chironex fleckeri*)
**jellyfish that stings** *noun tai*
**join** *verb$_i$ sil*
**joint** *noun ser*
**joke** *verb$_i$ fkaar; verb$_i$ pesfkaar*
**judge** *verb$_i$ pesp̃ot*
**juice** *noun$_i$ nasu*
**jump** *verb$_a$ sook*

**jump around** *verb$_i$ skasook*
**jump over** *verb$_a$ nrilkau; verb$_a$ soklkau*
**jungle** *noun namlaskos*
**just** *preverbal trau*

## K

**kastom gift** *noun sautog*
**kava** *noun nmalok* (*Piper methysticum*)
**keep on** *auxiliary en*
**keep something out of sight** *verb$_i$ liaki*
**keep vigil** *verb$_i$ nepsok*
**kick** *verb$_a$ p̃i*
**kick away** *verb$_a$ p̃ilu*
**kidney** *noun watiam*
**kill** *verb$_a$ krakpun; verb$_a$ watpun*
**kingfisher** *verb$_i$ tef; noun siik* (*Alcedinidae*)
**kiss** *verb$_a$ sog; verb koo*
**knee** *noun$_i$ nap̃ut*
**kneecap** *noun kaifar*
**kneel** *verb$_i$ taap̃etu*
**knife** *noun masmes*
**knock** *verb$_i$ tum̃otum̃*
**knock away** *verb$_i$ npasil*
**knot in bamboo** *noun klop*
**knot in wood** *noun napkun*
**know** *verb$_a$ tae*
  **not know** *verb$_a$ sup̃neki*
**knowledge** *noun ntaewen; noun nametmatuan*
**krait, sea krait** *noun takwer* (*Laticauda colubrina*)
**kumala, sweet potato** *noun kumol* (*Ipomoea batatas*)

## L

**labour** *noun nakerkraian*
**lad** *noun naturiai*
**land** *noun ntan*
**land** *verb$_i$ totan; verb$_i$ sak; verb$_a$ lao*
**language** *noun nafsan*
**lantana** *noun latana*
**laplap** *noun kapu; noun tm̃en; noun rp̃ek*
**last** *adjective mlaap*
**late** *verb$_i$ frak*
**later** *noun$_i$ ntakun*
**laugh** *verb$_i$ mur; verb$_i$ tiel*
**lava** *noun naf*
**lavalava** *noun nanrepnrep*
**lawyer vine** *noun naala* (*Calamus vitiensis*)
**lay** *verb$_i$ en*
**lay down** *verb$_i$ entan*
**lay on** *verb$_a$ ensok*
**lazy** *adjective ntawotmal*
**lead** *verb$_i$, auxiliary pei*
**leader** *noun$_i$ np̃au; noun naot*
**leadership** *noun np̃auwaak*
**leaf** *noun$_i$ nam̃rom; noun naul*
  **laplap leaf** *noun nrau* (*Heliconia indica*)
**leaf fall from a tree** *verb$_i$ nru*
**leak** *verb$_i$ tur*
**lean** *verb$_i$ tap; verb malof*
**leap** *verb$_a$ sook*
**learn** *verb$_i$ faitau*
**leave** *verb$_a$ tao*
**leaves heaped** *noun ntp̃et*
**left** *adjective maur*
**left-handed** *verb armaur*
**leftover food** *noun kotfak*

**leg, foot** *noun*$_i$ *natu*
**leg, inside leg** *noun*$_i$ *nak*
**lemongrass** *noun naariu*
**length** *noun naframwen*
**lesson's sweetlips** *noun sasupra* (*Plectorhinchus lessonii*)
**liar** *noun natam̃ool psir*
**lick** *verb*$_a$ *limnai*
**lid** *noun*$_i$ *mp̃aakor*
**lie** *verb*$_i$ *psir; noun tepsir*
**lie, lay down** *verb*$_i$ *entan*
**lie down** *verb mpasul;* *verb*$_i$ *p̃aulum̃*
**life** *noun nam̃olien*
**lift** *verb siti*
**lift up** *verb*$_a$ *kaflag;* *verb*$_a$ *nrakat*
**light** *noun faar; adjective mram;* *verb*$_i$ *salsal*
**light, as of fire** *verb*$_i$ *sor*
**light, lamp** *noun nasul*
**lightning** *noun napil*
**light-skin** *noun kulmer*
**like, be like** *verb taos;* *verb*$_i$ *wel*
**limp** *verb*$_i$ *paasa*
**line up** *verb*$_i$ *tefra*
**lionfish** *noun naik maan*
**lips** *noun*$_i$ *nkanr*
**listen** *verb*$_i$ *takinrog*
**little finger** *noun kinrik*
**little toe** *noun kinrik*
**live** *verb*$_i$ *m̃ool*
**liver** *noun ntankep*
**lizard** *noun uti; noun sulprog; noun utinlag; noun p̃lakes; noun utikaro*
**load** *verb*$_a$ *tatu*
**lobster** *noun makou*
  **sand lobster** *noun pepep* (*Parribacus caledonicus*)
**location** *particle e-*
**log** *noun nmalnkas*
**loincloth** *noun pisp̃lolo*
**lonely** *adjective tem̃anrogon*
**long** *adjective pram*
**long time** *adjective tuei*
**look** *verb*$_i$ *lee;* *verb*$_t$ *lek;* *verb*$_i$ *wor*
**look after** *verb*$_i$ *mermer;* *verb*$_a$ *leperkat*
**look at** *verb*$_a$ *lemis*
**look for** *verb*$_a$ *leel*
**look for something** *verb*$_i$ *puser*
**look forward** *verb*$_i$ *lereki*
**look from the side** *verb*$_i$ *nremet*
**look out** *verb*$_a$ *leperkat*
**look up** *verb*$_i$ *m̃alosak*
**looking-glass tree** *noun nm̃ap̃m̃ap̃* (*Heritiera littoralis*)
**looks** *preverbal trau*
**loose** *adjective m̃elm̃el*
**loose woman** *noun nmatu ni napu*
**lorikeet** *noun sfir* (*Trichoglossus haematodus*)
**lose weight** *verb*$_i$ *nros*
**lost, be lost** *verb*$_i$ *pitar*
**loungeroom** *noun etkuum*
**louse** *noun*$_i$ *kut* (*Pediculidae*)
**love** *verb*$_a$ *nrom*
**low** *verb*$_i$ *paketan*
**low tide** *noun nmaatraar*
**low tide, to be** *verb*$_i$ *maat*
**lower back** *noun*$_i$ *ntafat*
**lucky** *verb mar*
**lung** *noun*$_i$ *naam̃*

# M

**mackerel, striped** *noun aslel* (*Rastrelliger kanagurta*)
**magician** *noun munwei*
**maiden** *noun nmatuerik*
**main** *noun tp̃au*
  **main part of something** *noun$_i$ np̃au*
**make** *verb$_a$ preg; verb$_i$ tuek*
**make good** *verb$_i$ pta*
**male** *noun nanwei*
**male name marker** *noun kalo*
**man** *noun kano; noun nanwei*
**manakin (type of bird)** *noun sfirmer* (*Estrildidae*)
**mangrove** *noun natog; noun maurkat*
**manioc** *noun maniot* (*Manihot esculenta*)
**manioc starch** *noun napeenr*
**manta ray** *noun roktaar* (*Manta birostris*)
**mantis shrimp** *noun pism̃alit* (*Stomatopoda*)
**many** *adjective laap*
**mark rhythm** *verb$_i$ ferfer*
**marked** *adjective fuet*
**marker** *noun nakoi*
**marriage** *noun nlakwen*
**marry** *verb$_a$ tosok; verb$_a$ ptour; verb$_a$ taulu; verb$_i$ lak*
**marsh, soft ground, soft mud** *noun nalap̃o*
**mash** *verb maama*
**massage** *verb$_a$ m̃os*
**mast** *noun natir*
**masturbate** *verb$_i$ fisfis*
**mat** *noun tefkau; noun m̃iit; noun raolae; noun patlep*
**material, piece of material** *noun gaaf*
**mature** *verb$_i$ maf*
**may, might** *preverbal fla*
**maybe** *auxiliary lakor*
**me** *pronoun suffix -m; pronoun kineu; pronoun wou*
  **for me** *pronoun nigneu; pronoun neu*
**meaning** *noun$_i$ np̃et; noun m̃p̃et*
**measure** *verb$_i$ toon*
**meat** *noun tekatpi; noun$_i$ nap̃kas*
**mediate** *verb$_i$ maomao*
**meet** *verb$_i$ neet; verb$_i$ seltra; verb taatur; verb$_i$ saisei; verb$_a$ patlas*
**meeting** *noun nsaiseiwen*
**melt** *verb$_i$ ser*
**men's house** *noun efare*
**mentally unstable** *verb$_i$ nrop*
**messenger** *noun nafkou*
**messy (of hair)** *adjective sikskaar*
**metre** *noun gaaf*
**midday** *noun aliat motu*
**middle** *noun$_i$ nmal; preposition maloput*
**middle finger** *noun kinliu*
**middle toe** *noun kinliu*
**midrif** *noun$_i$ ntafat*
**might, may** *preverbal fla*
**mildew** *verb$_i$ pkot*
**milkfish** *noun nap̃ures* (*Chanos chanos*)
**milkwood tree** *noun mpal* (*Antiaris toxicaria*)
**million** *number mantap̃arp̃ar; number p̃oonti*
**miss** *verb$_i$ sraf; verb$_i$ sursap̃*
**mistake** *verb$_i$ saap̃*
**mister** *noun maarik*
**mix** *verb saar*

**Monday** *noun aliat pei*
**monocle breams** *noun wanaar* (*Nemipteridae*)
**month** *noun atlag*
**moon** *noun atlag*
  **crescent moon** *noun naul nmariu*
  **new moon** *noun atlag foum*
  **no moon** *noun atlag malik*
**moon shell** *noun fneslu* (*Naticidae*)
**mooning (showing bottom)** *verb siig*
**moonlight** *noun atlag mrem*
**moray eel sp.** *noun mra nm̃ap̃* (*Gymnothorax javanicus*)
  **white-eyed moray** *noun taligter* (*Siderea grisea*)
**morning** *noun pulp̃og*
**morning star** *noun m̃asei lep ni pulp̃og*
**mosquito** *noun katnaam*
**moss** *noun nalomlom*
**moth** *noun meer*
**mother** *noun iak*
**mould** *verb*$_i$ *pkot*
**mountain** *noun ntaf*
**mourn** *verb*$_i$ *palkias;* *verb*$_i$ *pakmaalep*
  **observe five days after death** *verb*$_i$ *maalep*
**mouse** *noun kusu*
**moustache** *noun*$_i$ *nal; noun wasket*
**mouth** *noun*$_i$ *nkanr*
  **inside of the mouth** *noun nau*
**mouth organ** *noun nau*
**move** *verb*$_i$*, auxiliary nrus*
**much** *verb*$_i$*, adjective toop*
**mud** *noun nlel*
**mullet** *noun polfai* (*Mugilidae*)
**music** *verb nalagaan*
**my** *pronoun suffix -k; pronoun nigneu; pronoun nakte; pronoun neu*
**myna bird** *noun kipwi* (*Acridotheres tristis*)

# N

**nail** *verb*$_a$ *nrp̃asok; noun*$_i$ *tep̃lasnạk*
**nakavika** *noun nkafik* (*Syzygium malaccense*)
**naked** *adjective puu; verb*$_i$ *karo usrek*
**namalaos** *noun nmalmel* (*Garuga floribunda*)
**name** *noun*$_i$ *nagi; verb*$_d$ *sos*
**namele** *noun nam̃el* (*Cycas seemannii*)
**nandau** *noun nta* (*Pometia pinnata*)
**nation** *noun nlaun; noun waal*
**native almond** *noun nagae* (*Canarium indicum, Canarium harveyi*)
**nautilus** *noun p̃anuk* (*Nautilidae*)
**navel** *noun*$_i$ *napot*
**navele** *noun nafil* (*Barringtonia edulis*)
**neck** *noun*$_i$ *nanu*
**neck, back of the neck** *noun*$_i$ *ntaknanu*
**necklace** *noun tarir; noun nkaso*
**needlefish, reef** *noun totogmal* (*Strongylura incisa*)
**nephew** *noun ftook*
**nest** *noun nuknimaan; noun*$_i$ *nuk*
**net** *noun taarag*
**new** *adjective foum; adjective met*
**New Guinea rosewood** *noun nagrof* (*Pterocarpus indicus*)
**news** *noun nanrognrogon*
**next** *adjective kaaru; preposition nen tu*
**niece** *noun ftook*
**night** *noun p̃og*

**nine** *number ilfot*
**ninth** *adjective kilfot*
**no** *interjection tiik; verb$_i$ tiik*
**no reason, for no reason** *adjective tep̃alp̃al*
**nod** *verb tp̃otunr*
**noise** *noun misleo; verb$_i$ nres*
  **make noise** *verb$_i$ krakpes*
  **make a noise with your mouth to call** *verb$_i$ sm̃ol*
**noise of two trees rubbing together** *verb$_i$ woor*
**noisy** *adjective tarp̃otik*
**north** *noun naweskin kaatol; noun ep̃au*
**nose** *noun$_i$ nagor*
**not** *preverbal ta*
**not have** *verb$_i$ tiik*
**not know** *verb$_a$ sup̃neki*
**not want** *verb$_i$ mal; auxiliary mal*
**now** *preposition kis; adverb malfane*
**nudibranch** *noun m̃p̃au*
**numb** *verb$_i$ pnat; verb$_i$ mer*

# O

**obey** *adjective paketan*
**observe** *verb$_a$ palkor*
**observe five days after death** *verb$_i$ maalep*
**obstruct** *verb$_a$ laokor*
**ocean** *noun namoos*
**octopus** *noun wiit (Octopodidae)*
**octopus tree** *noun namook (Heliotropium foertherianum)*
**of** *preposition teni; preposition ni*
**of it** *adjective knen*
**off, bad food** *adjective m̃lakon*
**oily liquid in a germinated coconut** *noun nrap*
**okay** *interjection nta*
**old** *adjective motu*
**old age** *noun nafitiawian*
**old people** *noun tiawi*
**old person** *noun kapuer*
**omen** *noun nafeifeien*
**on one's back, be** *verb$_i$ tralosak*
**one** *adjective skei*
**only** *adverb m̃as*
**open** *verb$_i$ maag; verb$_a$ p̃elgat*
**opinion** *noun nalelewen*
**or** *conjunction ko*
**orange** *adjective m̃nam̃onp̃ok*
**orange tree** *noun m̃ool (Citrus sinensis)*
**ordinary** *adjective p̃rakot*
**orphan** *noun mtapes*
**other** *adjective p̃et; adjective kaaru*
**otherwise** *idiom ifmertiik*
**otitis** *noun taligftin*
**'ouch' (exclamation)** *interjection awe*
**our (exclusive)** *pronoun mom*
**our (inclusive)** *pronoun gakit; kit*
**our (inclusive)** *pronoun negakit*
**our (inclusive and exclusive)** *pronoun nigmam*
**out of sight, keep something out of sight** *verb$_i$ liaki*
**outside of a house** *noun nam̃ol nasum̃*
**outrigger of canoe** *noun nsem*
**outrigger rolling over** *verb p̃ip̃*
**outside** *preposition ektem*
**oven** *noun uum*
**oven stone** *noun lelep*
**overcast noun** *malkolik*
**owl** *noun sokfal (Tyto alba)*

**own** *adjective fser*
**owner** *noun lakle; noun atlak*
**oyster, black wing oyster** *noun ruum̃* (*Pteria avicular*)

## P

**Pacific swallow** *noun mantilsei* (*Hirundo tahitica*)
**pack** *verb$_a$ paai*
**paddle** *verb$_i$ seek; verb$_i$ suar; verb$_i$ palus; noun nawes*
**page, piece of paper** *noun naul*
**page of a book** *noun nap̃elgan*
**pain** *verb krakfai*
**paint, to paint** *verb$_a$ mtir; noun ntae*
**palm**
  **black palm** *noun nma* (*Blechnum gibbum, Cyathea lunulata*)
  **cycad palm** *noun nam̃el* (*Cycas seemannii*)
  **sago palm** *noun rowat* (*Metroxylon warburgii*)
  **palm tree** *noun nipu* (*Veitchia spp.*)
**pan flute** *noun nau*
**pandanus** *noun nparom; noun nfak* (*Pandanus dubius?*)*; noun naki* (*Pandanus tectorius?*)*; noun nakimtirmtir*
**paper** *noun natus*
**parable** *noun nfaag*
**parrotfish** *noun kalafiai*
**parrotfish, bumphead** *noun kalap̃og* (*Bolbometopon muricatum*)
**parrotfishes** *noun nuo* (*Scaridae*)
**parry** *verb$_a$ kor*
**part** *adverb p̃ok; verb$_i$ p̃aas*
**parts** *noun$_i$ nfas*
**party** *noun nalkolik*
**pass** *preposition tool; verb$_a$ tool*
**pass through** *verb$_i$ skatur*
**passage** *noun slaor*
**passionfruit** *noun pasprut*
**past** *preposition nen pa*
**pat** *verb$_a$ nrepnrpag*
**pawpaw tree** *noun lees* (*Carica papaya*)
**pay** *verb paakot*
**payment** *noun nfaakoton*
**peace** *noun ntm̃at*
**peaceful** *adjective tm̃at*
**peanut tree** *noun naselslam* (*Sterculia tannaensis, S. vitiensis*)
**pearl** *noun nanu*
**peek** *verb$_i$ m̃aak*
**peel** *verb$_a$ plik; verb$_a$ mul; verb$_a$ kar*
**peel skin** *verb$_a$ mulu*
**peg** *noun laak*
**penetrate** *verb ska*
**penis** *noun polpol koplog; noun ola*
**people** *noun nam̃er*
**perfect, to be** *adjective m̃anopnop*
**person** *noun natam̃ool; noun naat*
**phlegm** *noun$_i$ nrafi*
**photo album** *noun tus ni telomlom*
**photograph, take a photo** *verb$_a$ lom*
**picasso fish, strong skin, or brush-sided filefish** *noun fumasei*
**pick** *verb p̃as*
**pick (as in flowers)** *verb p̃as*
**pick fruit** *verb$_a$ lei*
**picture** *noun tip̃ot*
**piece** *noun$_i$ nmasel; noun kotieu; noun namtel*
**pierce** *verb$_i$ lul; verb$_a$ tp̃ofu*
**pierce (as in an abscess)** *verb$_a$ pregfu*

**pierce boil** *verb*$_a$ *sup̃fu*

**pig** *noun waak* (*Sus scrota*); *noun inror*

**female pig which has no piglets** *noun konrkai*

**pigeon, Baker's imperial pigeon** *noun mapul ni ntaf* (*Ducula bakeri*)

**pigeon, Pacific imperial pigeon** *noun mapul* (*Ducula pacifica*)

**piled** *verb*$_i$ *liu*

**pillow** *noun naulum̃*

**pimple, heart of pimple** *noun*$_i$ *npat*

**pin** *noun pinp̃aop̃on*

**pinch** *verb*$_a$ *kin*

**pineapple** *noun laufal*

**pink** *adjective mlees*

**pipefish** *noun naapas*

**piss** *verb*$_i$ *mem; verb*$_t$ *me; noun*$_i$ *namee*

**place** *noun naor; demonstrative san; noun*$_i$ *nam̃lee; noun sa*

**plan** *verb watlaak*

**plane** *noun tastes*

**plank** *noun pras*

**plant** *verb suski; verb*$_a$ *lao*

**plant just before buds** *verb*$_i$ *m̃orm̃rom*

**plant something, to** *verb*$_a$ *laosok*

**plant sp.** *noun naatfer; noun nafnag ni afsak; noun nalag; noun namgar; noun namkanr; noun natp̃olnra; noun nfa; noun nraguti; noun ntalifam; noun tataraas; noun tatakaal; noun kopnan* (*Plectranthus scutellarioides*); *noun nafis* (*Saccharum edule*); *noun nafrofursa* (*Coix lacryma-jobi*); *namles* (*Graptophyllum spp.*); *noun nasei* (*Euodia hortensis*); *noun palsmin* (*Elaeocarpus spp.*); *noun takwerkot* (*Polyscias scutellaria*)

**bamboo** *noun loop* (*Bambusa*); *noun nam̃lalop*

**banana spp.** *noun nametmet miel; noun nanra; noun taag; noun pia; noun nanrmem pot; noun taagmol; noun naanr; noun nanrwor; noun taagmetkes; noun pili; noun nap̃aap̃ak; noun taagsus; noun nanrmem swit; noun furaru*

**bougainvillea** *noun anisakel*

**bush sp.** *noun nkari* (*Cordyline fruticosa*)

**bush with red berries** *noun naisig* (*Malopia scondens*)

**cane** *noun nap̃rairei; noun ftok*

**cassava** *noun maniot* (*Manihot esculenta*)

**cassia wilt** *noun metmatur* (*Mimosa pudica*)

**coleus** *noun nakwak* (*Coleus spp.*)

**fern** *noun naruut; noun naweel ni namlas* (*Pyrrosia lanceolata, Phymatosorus grossus*)

**grass** *noun nam̃nam̃*

**island cabbage** *noun altuk*

**kumala, sweet potato** *noun kumol* (*Ipomoea batatas*)

**lantana** *noun latana*

**lawyer vine** *noun naala* (*Calamus vitiensis*)

**lemongrass** *noun naariu*

**manioc** *noun maniot* (*Manihot esculenta*)

**moss** *noun nalomlom*

**pawpaw** *noun lees* (*Carica papaya*)

**pineapple** *noun laufal*

**Polynesian arrowroot** *noun napeenr* (*Tacca leotopetaloides*)

**rattan** *noun naala* (*Calamus vitiensis*)
**small bush** *noun naulalas* (*Polyscias spp.*)
**staghorn** *noun lp̃eslilip*
**sugarcane** *noun nap̃rai*
**tuber** *noun naknot*
**vine** *noun nafofon; noun nkraful; noun natu; noun natiel* (*Entada phaseoloides*)*; noun laktau; noun nlakotao; noun sumat; noun naala; noun nlaketik; noun nakrok; noun nm̃alm̃ol; noun nmaritmat*
**wild kava** *noun nakser*
**wild cane** *noun nasul* (*Centotheca lappacea*)
**yam, a strong yam** *noun nap̃ooi*
**yam sp.** *noun nap̃el; noun ara*
**wild peanut** *noun mismai*

**plantation** *noun nanrup̃*
**plate** *noun trakek; noun nrali; noun pagotut; noun slo*
**platform between canoe and outrigger** *noun nafetfet*
**play** *verb*$_i$ *mes; verb*$_i$ *siksik*
**Pleiades** *noun uum*
**plot** *noun naroi*
**point (headland)** *noun nagis; noun*$_i$ *nametp̃ag*
**point, with finger** *verb*$_a$ *tum̃*
**pointed** *verb*$_i$ *fsup̃*
**poisoned** *verb*$_i$ *mam*
**poisoning, food poisoning** *noun namamwen*
**poke** *verb*$_a$ *p̃kasai; verb waal*
**poke the fire** *verb*$_i$ *sai suek*
**poke tongue** *verb limen*
**pole** *noun nsik; noun npoulaolag*
**poles (attached to canoe)** *noun nakik*
**Polynesian arrowroot** *noun napeenr* (*Tacca leotopetaloides*)
**pompano, silver** *noun nason* (*Trachinotus blochii*)
**poor** *adjective faria*
**porcupinefishes** *noun p̃ka* (*Diodontidae Tetrodontidae*)
**possessed, be possessed** *verb kof*
**posts holding up a house** *noun nkas slasol*
**pot** *noun poler*
**pound** *verb*$_a$ *laosok*
**pour** *verb*$_a$ *lig; verb*$_a$ *lup̃*
**praise** *verb*$_a$ *sorsor*
**prawn** *noun uur*
**pray** *verb*$_i$ *tafesfes; verb tp̃otur*
**prayer** *noun nalotwen*
**preach, teach** *verb*$_a$ *fnau; verb*$_a$ *tafnau*
**prefer** *verb*$_i$ *meet*
**pregnant** *verb*$_i$ *plak; verb*$_i$ *tien*
**prepare** *verb*$_i$ *toknak; verb pregpta; verb nraknrak*
**present** *noun nanromien*
**press** *verb*$_a$ *kis*
**prevent, stop someone doing something** *verb*$_a$ *takor*
**prickle** *noun*$_i$ *nais*
**pride** *noun p̃op̃ pakelag*
**prisoner** *noun manmun*
**private place** *noun ep̃rom*
**promise** *verb tilsoksok; noun natilsoksokwen*
**prop** *verb tup̃*
**property** *noun nap̃umaas; noun temakot*
**proud** *adjective lagi*
**prow of a canoe** *noun*$_i$ *nako*
**prune** *verb*$_i$ *pul*
**pubic cover** *noun nafon*
**pudding** *noun napos; noun woi*

**puddle** *noun nap̃eiluk*
**puddle of water** *noun noop*
**puffers** *noun knopun* (*Monacanthidae, Tetrodontidae*)
**pull** *verb*$_a$ *tkau;* *verb*$_a$ *puet;* *verb*$_a$ *pupuet*
**pull a banana** *verb*$_i$ *safei*
**pull behind** *verb*$_a$ *tuk*
**pull out** *verb*$_a$ *m̃ok*
**pull your legs back** *verb*$_i$ *wolul*
**pulpit** *noun p̃otut*
**pumice** *noun naf*
**punch** *verb tik*
**puncture** *verb*$_a$ *tp̃ofu*
**punishment** *noun sup̃tap*
**pus** *noun naup̃o*
**push** *verb*$_i$ *sai;* *verb*$_a$ *tof;* *verb tp̃osok; verb pas*
**push away** *verb*$_a$ *tgof*
**put meat on laplap** *verb*$_i$ *tanum̃*
**put something away secretly, like putting money in someone's pocket** *verb sfa*
**put wood in fire** *verb*$_i$ *suek*
**puzzle tree** *noun namatal* (*Kleinhovia hospita*)
**puzzle-nut tree** *noun nap̃laso* (*Xylocarpus granatum*)

## Q

**quickly** *adverb pelpel*
**quiet** *verb*$_i$ *pnut; noun p̃op̃ paketan*
**quieten** *verb pesmaomao*

## R

**rabbitfish** *noun sm̃os; noun toof* (*Siganidae*); **peppered rabbitfish or coral rabbitfish** *noun tofkas* (*Siganidae*); **vermiculate rabbitfish or forktail rabbitfish** *noun fser* (*Siganidae*)
**rail (bird)** *noun p̃lak* (*Gallirallus philippensis*)
**rain** *noun us*
**rainbow** *noun tuput*
**raindrop** *noun naturm̃os*
**raise** *verb*$_a$ *sik*
**rake** *noun nkur*
**rash** *noun frofur*
**rat** *noun kusu*
**rattan** *noun naala* (*Calamus vitiensis*)
**rattle** *noun wair*
**raw** *adjective met*
**ray sp.**
- **bluespotted stingray** *noun faai pumat* (*Dasyatis kuhlii*)
- **devil ray** *noun faai mantu*
- **eagle ray** *noun faai suar*
- **giant reef ray** *noun pakokap̃o* (*Taeniura melanospilos*)
- **manta ray** *noun roktaar* (*Manta birostris*)
- **spotted eagle ray** *noun faai p̃og* (*Aetobatus narinari*)
- **stingray** *noun faai*

**reach** *preposition tup̃;* *verb*$_a$ *tkal;* *verb*$_a$ *tlas*
**read** *verb*$_a$ *fe;* *verb*$_i$ *fef*
**real** *adjective matu*
**realise** *verb*$_a$ *letae*
**really** *preverbal trau*
**rear** *preposition nakoinrok*

**reason** *noun nlaken*
  **for no reason** *adjective tep̃alp̃al*
**recognise** *verb*$_a$ *letae; verb*$_a$ *mrotae; verb nrogtae*
**red** *adjective miel*
**red bean tree** *noun naam̃er* (*Adenanthera pavonina*)
**red dirt** *noun ntan makoren*
**red fish sp. that lives on the reef** *noun napum̃ ni nskau*
**red-bellied fruit dove** *noun sunra* (*Ptilinopus greyii*)
**red-eyed crab** *noun ntame* (*Xanthidae*)
**reef** *noun nskau*
  **end of reef** *noun namta*
**reef crab** *noun ntame* (*Xanthidae*)*; noun p̃olul* (*Etisus splendidus*)
**regarding** *verb*$_a$ *toklos*
**remember** *verb*$_i$ *mroperkat*
**remoras** *noun naik taos* (*Echeneidae*)
**replace** *verb*$_a$ *surwel*
**reply** *verb*$_i$ *wes*
**respect** *noun nfaketanwen; noun teemtakun; adjective paketan*
**rest** *verb*$_i$ *marmar*
**restless** *verb*$_i$ *tkarkaar*
**restrain** *verb*$_a$ *sar*
**return** *verb*$_i$*, auxiliary ler*
**revolver** *noun sisi sees*
**rib** *noun*$_i$ *nafinr*
**rice** *noun atol kanr* (*Oryza sativa*)
**rich** *adjective soklep*
**riddle** *verb*$_i$ *faag*
**rifle** *noun sisi p̃ur*
**right** *adjective matu*
**right-handed** *adjective armatu*
**right side** *noun*$_i$ *nmatu*
**ring** *verb*$_i$ *kii; verb*$_i$ *nrafkor*
**ring finger** *noun kintapul*
**ringed, be ringed** *verb*$_i$ *nrafkor*
**ringworm** *noun naan*
**rinse** *verb*$_a$ *pnol; verb*$_a$ *m̃oltao*
**ripe, over-ripe** *verb*$_i$ *mam; adjective mamtop; adjective matu*
  **nearly ripe** *adjective mamis; verb*$_i$ *arum; adjective mrapil*
**ripen, put something aside until it is ripe** *verb*$_i$ *muk*
**rippled** *adjective kanin*
**rise (star)** *verb*$_a$ *sook*
**river** *noun naum̃; noun naiser*
**riverbank** *noun naum̃*
**road** *noun napu*
**roast** *verb*$_a$ *paan; verb*$_a$ *gkof*
**robin (type of bird)** *noun susunatog*
**rock** *noun faatfar; noun nasitafra; noun np̃arfaat*
**rocks heaped up along the seashore** *noun narfaat*
**roll** *verb*$_i$ *mlil; noun taltel; verb*$_i$ *lul*
**roll fibre** *verb*$_i$ *lul*
**roll pandanus** *verb tal*
**roll up** *verb*$_i$ *fiif*
**roof** *noun nasu*
**roofing** *noun nfaat*
**rooster** *noun tkas*
**root** *noun nakoon*
  **taproot** *noun*$_i$ *naser*
**rope** *noun nmarit; noun ntuk*
**rot** *verb*$_i$ *p̃o*
**rotten** *verb*$_i$ *mla*
**rotten wood** *adjective mtet*
**rotten yam** *noun nsat*
**round** *adjective m̃anopnop*
**row** *verb*$_i$ *kau*
**rub** *verb*$_a$ *solsol; verb*$_i$ *folfolm̃ak; verb*$_a$ *lof; verb*$_i$ *loflof*
**rubbish** *noun nasoksok; noun etak; noun nam̃tam̃ot*

**rudder** *noun smaan*
**rule** *$verb_i$ mermer; $verb_a$ mrag*
**run** *$verb_i$ sef; $verb_i$ fiit*
**rust** *noun namiel*

## S

**sack** *$verb_a$ p̃ilu*
**sail** *noun nlae*
**saliva** *$noun_i$ nati*
**salt water** *noun ntas*
**sand** *noun nawen*
**sand bass** *noun fup̃eel* (*Centropomidae*)
**sand lobster** *noun pepep* (*Parribacus caledonicus*)
**sandperch** *noun lao* (*Pinguipedidae*)
**sandalwood** *noun makos* (*Santalum austrocaledonicum*)
**sap** *$noun_i$ natoo; $noun_i$ nati*
**sardine** *noun napeel* (*Clupeidae*)
**sardine, flat kind** *noun napelial* (*Megalops cyprinoides*)
**sardine, round, like a finger** *noun napelp̃ures*
**sardine, very small** *noun napeltan*
**Saturday** *noun aliat toknak*
**saviour** *noun temumu*
**saw** *$verb_a$ mas*
**sawdust** *noun nam̃tam̃ot*
**say** *$verb_i$ na; $verb_a$ til*
**scab** *noun nkafrag*
**scabby** *verb fag*
**scabies** *noun namkalkal*
**scale** *$verb_a$ laglag; noun nalaglag*
**scar** *noun kapil*
**scared, to be** *verb sulfra; $verb_i$ p̃lak*
**scatter** *$verb_i$ taasir; $verb_i$ frafer; $verb_i$ tafrafer*
**school** *noun sum̃faitau*
**scold** *$verb_a$ nrp̃ei*
**scoop** *$verb_a$ sao; verb waal*
**scorpionfishes** *noun fti* (*Scorpaenidae*); **smallscale scorpionfish** *noun ftir* (*Scorpaenidae*)
**scratch** *$verb_a$ mtas; $verb_i$ skarkar; $verb_a$ kar*
**scratched** *adjective mtastes*
**scream** *$verb_i$ p̃ir*
**scrub** *$verb_a$ sor; noun nafrofur*
**scrubduck** *noun mlau* (*Megapodius freycinet*)
**sea** *noun elau*
**sea cucumber** *noun nap̃laepako* (*Holothuria leucospilota*)
**sea krait, sea snake** *noun takwer* (*Laticauda colubrina*)
**sea slug** *noun m̃p̃au; noun taag*
**sea urchin** *noun kool; noun nalwaniksu; noun somkol* (*Diadema savignyi*); *noun saofak*
**seagrass** *noun nariuriu*
**seahorse** *noun maikel* (*Hippocampus*)
**search** *$verb_i$ kafkaf; verb kaftaal*
**seat** *noun nkasakien*
**seat of canoe** *noun nafetfet*
**seaweed** *noun nuantas*
**seaworm, centipede-like** *noun nmraksul*
**second** *adjective kaaru*
**second toe** *noun kintapul*
**section** *noun malmal*
**section, as found in a pawpaw** *noun namtel*
**seed** *$noun_i$ npat; noun kuut*
**seems** *preverbal trau*

**select** *verb$_a$ nras*
**selfish** *verb katp̃o*
**sell** *verb$_a$ sor*
**semen** *noun naitar*
**send** *verb$_a$ tup̃ek*
**send message** *verb$_a$ tp̃olu*
**senile** *noun nognoog; verb watnru*
**sensitive grass** *noun metmatur* (*Mimosa pudica*)
**separate** *verb$_i$ paamaot*
**servant, woman servant** *noun tafin*
**set, sunset** *verb$_i$ mtar*
**set something aside,** *verb$_i$ liaki*
**setting moon** *verb tanun*
**seven** *number laru*
**seventh** *adjective klaru*
**sew** *verb$_a$ tur*
**sex worker** *noun nmatu ni napu*
**sexual intercourse** *verb$_i$ ftik; verb$_a$ sko*; *verb paktau*
**shade** *noun meel*
**shadow** *noun meel; noun$_i$ naan*
**shake** *verb$_i$ farfar; verb$_i$ nrur; verb$_i$ ligligp̃au*
**shake a rattle** *verb farfarsa*
**shake hands** *verb$_i$ taaloof*
**shake out** *verb$_i$ folfolm̃ak*
**share** *verb$_i$ limlim; verb$_i$ patpat; noun toltol; noun nakon; verb$_i$ p̃tae*
**share out** *verb p̃oot*
**shark** *noun pako*
  **hammerhead shark** *noun pakofai*
  **tiger shark** *noun pakofaam*
  **white shark** *noun pakotau*
**sharp** *adjective mkal*
**sharpen** *verb$_a$ maa; verb maama; verb$_a$ pkal*
**shave** *verb$_a$ tas*
**she/he** *pronoun ga*
**she/he/it** *pronoun prefix i=; pronoun nega*
**she/he/it (irrealis subject)** *pronoun prefix ke=*
**she/he/it (perfect subject)** *pronoun prefix ki=*
**shell** *noun mgal*
  **cowrie shell** *noun pultau*
**shell cover** *noun$_i$ ntapukor*
**shellfish sp./spp.** *noun konr* (*Strombus*)*; noun kufa; noun kramtig; noun p̃ap̃a* (*Guildfordia triumphans*)*; noun tetrasfiu;* (*Astraea rhodostoma*); *noun siil* (*Turritellidae*)*; noun sestau*
  **bicolor pen shell** *noun nlae* (*Pinna bicolor*)
  **cockles** *noun kalus* (*Cardiidae*)
  **conches** *noun memelim* (*Conidae*);
    **horse conch** *noun p̃aseu* (*Fasciolariidae*)*;* **Mauritian conch** *noun memelim* (*Strombus decorus decorus*)*;* **strawberry conch** *noun nm̃er* (*Strombus luhuanus*)
  **cone (no poison)** *noun fakfak* (*Conidae*)
  **cone shellfish, e.g., Hebrew cone** *noun tilm̃aar* (*Conus ebraeus, Conus nielsenae*)
  **cowrie shells** *noun puul* (*Cypraeidae*)
  **mactra, ornate** *noun kaisur* (*Mactra ornata*)
  **murex, Venus comb** *noun nuanagmos* (*Murex pecten*)
  **nerites, snail shaped shells** *noun sees* (*Neritidae*)*;* **costate nerite** *noun seeskanrp̃on* (*Nerita costata*)

**olives** *noun olif* (*Olividae*)
**oyster, black wing oyster** *noun ruum̃* (*Pteria avicular*)
**oyster, long oyster, pearl oysters** *noun toor* (*Pteriidae*); **pearl oyster sp.** *noun flefil* (*Pinctada margaritifera*); **black wing oyster** *noun ruum̃* (*Pteria avicular*); **cock's-comb oyster** *noun nraglaion* (*Lopha cristagalli*)
**rock-shell, tuberose** *noun np̃auwaak* (*Thais bitubercularis*)
**small shells like olive-shaped imbricaria** *noun soptau* (*Imbricaria olivaeformis*)
**tellin, virgate** *noun kaiwi* (*Tellina virgata*)
**triton** *noun saago* (*Charonia tritonis*)
**trochus-like, but green** *noun tiktik*
**Venus clams** *noun kaip̃aar* (*Veneridae*)

**shelter** *verb*$_i$ *p̃el*
**sheoak** *noun naar* (*Casuarina equisetifolia*)
**shield** *noun tekor; noun siil*
**shin** *noun*$_i$ *nraenatu*
**shine** *verb*$_i$ *nrernrer; verb*$_i$ *taalag; verb paa; verb paam̃as*
**shining** *noun namram*
**shit** *verb*$_a$ *suer; noun mpul; verb*$_i$ *taf*
**shoot** *verb*$_a$ *tup̃; verb*$_a$ *si*
**shoot a goal (football)** *verb*$_a$ *tp̃il*
**short** *adjective m̃it*
**shortcut** *verb tp̃otur*
**shoulder** *noun*$_i$ *mpam*
**shoulderblade** *noun*$_i$ *etan mpam*
**shout** *verb*$_i$ *pier; verb*$_i$ *kol*
**show** *verb*$_i$ *pei*
**show off** *verb*$_i$ *fekfek; polmatmat*
**show off by lifting something heavy** *noun sorsor*
**shrimp** *noun unr*
**shrimpfish** *noun naapas*
**shrink, to get smaller** *verb*$_i$ *kuk*
**shut** *verb*$_i$ *p̃on*
**sick** *verb*$_i$ *msak; verb*$_i$ *sasaan*
**sickness** *noun namsaki*
**side** *noun naper; preposition etik; noun*$_i$ *m̃p̃ar; noun nanre*
**side of a canoe** *noun ekate; noun esem*
**side of face** *noun*$_i$ *m̃p̃ar*
**sign, make a sign with the hand** *verb*$_i$ *pul*
**silly** *adjective nrotik*
**similar** *adverb tefla*
**sin** *noun taap̃aar*
**sing** *verb*$_a$ *lag*
**sink** *verb*$_i$ *m̃or*
**sister** *noun teet; noun*$_i$ *kor*
**group of sisters** *noun*$_i$ *temakoren*
**sit** *verb*$_a$ *sak; verb*$_i$ *totan*
**six** *number lates*
**sixth** *adjective klates*
**skilful** *adjective arleeg*
**skilled at singing** *adjective aure*
**skin of an animal** *noun*$_i$ *namlun*
**skin of a person** *noun*$_i$ *nakul*
**skin sickness** *noun kulsa*
**skinny, of a person** *adjective m̃okur*
**skirt** *noun nasieg*
**skull** *noun*$_i$ *lesmp̃au*
**sky** *noun nmalfa; noun nsau*
**slap** *verb nrpag*
**slaughter** *verb*$_a$ *p̃aumra*
**slave** *noun nafit*
**sleep** *verb*$_i$ *matur*
**sleep badly** *verb*$_i$ *enflos*

**sleep on** *verb mpalag*
**sleep on the side** *verb*$_i$ *entaak*
**sleepy** *adjective metmatur*
**sling** *verb*$_i$ *pul*
**slingshot** *noun sifsif*
**slip** *verb*$_i$ *kursm̃anr*
**slip** *verb*$_i$ *toos*
**slipmouth** *noun m̃aor* (*Leiognathidae*)
**slipper lobster** *noun pepep* (*Parribacus caledonicus*)
**slippery** *adjective m̃asenrsenr*
**slitgong** *noun nap̃e*
**slither** *verb*$_i$ *saisai*
**slough** *verb*$_a$ *mul*
**slow** *adjective mailum*
**small** *adjective sees; adjective rik; adjective seserik*
**smell** *verb*$_i$ *mar; noun nap̃o*
**smell, to smell (something)** *verb*$_i$ *p̃o*
**smile** *verb*$_i$ *mur*
**smile a little** *verb*$_i$ *mtamurmur*
**smoke** *noun nuasog; verb*$_a$ *suekor*
**smooth** *adjective matit; adjective m̃aal*
**smooth, to smooth (pandanus leaves)** *verb*$_i$ *faar*
**smoulder** *verb*$_i$ *fag*
**snake** *noun m̃aat*
    **sea snake, black and white** *noun takwer* (*Laticauda colubrina*)
**snapper, blackspot snapper** *noun pao malagot;* **sp. with black dot on side** (*Lutjanidae*); **paddletail snapper** *noun paokap;* **onespot or yellow-margined** *noun p̃ao;* **twinspot snapper** *noun fuknra* (*Lutjanidae*)
**snare** *noun nlik*
**sneak** *verb*$_i$ *paalak; verb p̃elp̃eel*
**sneeze** *verb*$_i$ *m̃etu*
**sniff** *verb*$_i$ *sunref*
**snore** *verb*$_i$ *gor*
**snot** *noun*$_i$ *nrafi*
**soft** *adjective mailum*
**soft wood** *noun naturwotu*
**soil** *noun ntan nakof*
**soldier crab** *noun p̃elpuk* (*Mictyris sp.*)
**soldierfish** *noun ntai* (*Holocentridae*)
**sole of foot** *noun*$_i$ *naal natu*
**someone** *noun naat*
**somersault** *verb*$_i$ *nreapis*
**something** *noun namrun*
**something beautiful** *noun nalewen wi*
**'something like that'** *noun nsfen*
**something that doesn't touch the ground** *noun nmalfa*
**song** *noun nalag*
**sore** *noun sestau; verb*$_i$ *ptin; verb krakfai; noun nfag*
**sores** *noun loot; noun lakle; noun nason*
**sorry** *verb*$_a$ *sraletu*
**soul** *noun*$_i$ *naat*
**sound** *verb*$_i$ *nres*
**soup** *noun*$_i$ *nasu*
**soursop** *noun katnraap*
**south** *noun ep̃ag; noun naweskin kafaat*
**sow** *verb*$_i$ *sirsir; noun klet*
**spark** *noun naltelit*
**spear** *noun ola; verb*$_a$ *lao; noun olam̃ool; noun olantu; noun olafatkau; noun ntu*
    **women's spear** *noun kalsiu*
**speargrass** *noun nasuloop*
**speargun** *noun sisi ni ntas*
**speed** *verb*$_a$ *nrogtor*
**Spengler's mactra** *noun kaluspam* (*Scissodesma spengleri*)
**spicy, to be** *adjective fket*

**spider** *noun kalum̃*
**spiderweb** *noun nalapul*
**spilled** *verb*$_i$ *malig*
**spin** *verb*$_i$ *lfek; verb*$_i$ *tilm̃aar; verb*$_i$ *fiif*
**spinal column** *noun*$_i$ *mra napu*
**spinecheeks** *noun wanaar* (*Nemipteridae*)
**spirit** *noun maarik; noun lilip̃; noun p̃op̃; noun Tagiter; noun*$_i$ *naat; noun natopu; noun mtulep*
**spit** *verb*$_a$ *taanu*
**spit out** *verb*$_a$ *lai*
**splash, throw water onto something** *verb*$_a$ *saoprei*
**spleen** *noun namenkori*
**splinter** *noun nsankas*
**split** *verb*$_a$ *p̃kafu; verb*$_a$ *tikfu*
**spoil** *verb*$_i$ *pregsa; verb polsa*
**spots on the tongue** *noun namgar*
**spring** *noun nsel; noun nametnai*
**squat** *verb*$_i$ *taam̃el*
**squeeze** *verb*$_a$ *m̃ol*
**squid** *noun walu*
**squint** *verb*$_i$ *lee sulsul*
**squirrelfish** *noun sreniu* (*Holocentridae*); **threespot squirrelfish and similar** *noun trakap* (*Holocentridae*)
**squirt** *verb*$_i$ *ptur*
**stab and break** *verb*$_a$ *sup̃rai*
**stab with something sharp** *verb*$_a$ *sup̃*
**staghorn** *noun lp̃eslilip*
**stake** *noun nkaspau*
**stand** *verb*$_i$ *tuleg; verb*$_a$ *lao; verb tu; verb paalag*
**stand on and break** *verb*$_a$ *kamkot*
**stand up** *verb laotu*
**stand with legs apart** *verb*$_i$ *paap̃olp̃lo*
**standing stone** *noun p̃otut*
**star** *noun m̃asei*
**stare** *verb*$_i$ *maag*
**starfish** *noun naulum̃ ni afsak; noun tam̃ra* (*Ophidiasteridae*)
**stars, constellation shaped like tongs** *noun nkem*
**start** *verb*$_a$ *pees; verb*$_i$ *maaf*
**start fire** *verb*$_a$ *pees*
**startled** *verb*$_i$ *krokur*
**statue** *noun naatap*
**stay** *verb*$_a$ *to; verb tau*
**stay for the whole day** *verb*$_i$ *tuaal*
**steal** *verb*$_a$ *pnak*
**steam** *noun tortor*
**steer** *verb*$_i$ *tlei; verb*$_i$ *taapol*
**steering paddle** *noun smaan*
**steering wheel of a car** *noun smaan*
**stem** *noun*$_i$ *nlak*
**step over** *verb*$_a$ *paalkau*
**stick** *noun nrankas; noun kalsaar; noun tm̃an*
  **digging stick** *noun kaal*
**still** *preverbal ta*
**sting** *verb*$_i$ *verb*$_a$ *tnus*
**stinging nettle tree** *noun gkar; noun nam̃lat* (*Dendrocnide latifolia*)
**stingray** *noun faai*
**stir** *verb*$_a$ *taanre; verb*$_a$ *walnre*
**stone** *noun faat; noun faatsal*
**stone arrangement** *noun p̃otut*
**stone on the top an oven** *noun lm̃es*
**stonefish** *noun p̃iit* (*Antennariidae*); **small stonefish** *noun ftir* (*Scorpaenidae*)
**stop** *verb*$_i$ *pnut*
**stop someone doing something** *verb*$_a$ *tp̃okor*
**store** *noun sto*
**storm** *noun nlagwat*
**story** *noun natrauswen; noun nafsan*
**straight, be straight** *verb*$_i$ *leeg*

**strain** *verb*$_a$ *nroi*
**stranger to this country** *noun nasap̃*
**stray** *verb*$_i$ *pakem̃ae*
**stretch** *verb*$_a$ *ti*
**string** *noun nmae*
**strip bark** *verb*$_a$ *mul*
**striped** *adjective mtirtir*
**strong, be strong** *verb*$_i$*, auxiliary kerkerai*
**strong man** *noun m̃atoktok*
**strongskin, dark coloured** *noun fum̃os*
**stub your toe** *verb*$_a$ *tak*
**stuck** *verb pulsok; verb*$_i$ *kon*
**stuck, to be stuck** *verb*$_i$ *p̃aar*
**study** *verb*$_i$ *faitau*
**stupid** *adjective mtafus; adjective nrotik*
**submerge** *verb*$_i$ *tut*
**suck** *verb*$_a$ *tom; verb*$_a$ *kom; verb*$_a$ *srof*
**suck at the breast** *verb*$_i$ *sus*
**sucker** *noun*$_i$ *naser*
**suckle** *verb*$_i$ *mimi, sus*
**sugarcane sp.** *noun kram; noun nafakton; noun kramteu; noun nap̃rai; noun tumel; noun kramp̃og; noun makol; noun traares*
**summit** *noun np̃au ntaaf*
**sun** *noun aal*
**Sunday** *noun aliat tap*
**sunset** *noun aalmtar*
  **setting sun** *verb*$_i$ *mtar*
**surgeonfish sp.** *noun tiftif wel rom;* **including white-freckled, lieutenant, striped bristletooth, twospot bristletooth** *noun p̃arsor* (*Acanthurus*)
**swallow** *verb*$_a$ *tnol*
**swamp harrier** *noun maal* (*Circus approximans*)
**swamphen** *noun taap̃es* (*Porphyrio melanotus*)
**sway** *verb*$_i$ *tuul; verb*$_i$ *taktaak*
**sweat** *noun nmaono; verb*$_i$ *maon*
**sweep** *verb*$_a$ *sertao; verb*$_a$ *ser; verb*$_i$ *mas*
**sweet** *verb*$_i$ *kaakas*
**swell** *verb*$_i$ *puk; verb*$_i$ *adjective toop; noun napiau*
**swiftlet (type of bird)** *noun kapkaap*
**swim** *verb waaf; verb*$_i$ *los*
**swim under water** *verb*$_i$ *m̃on*
**swing** *verb*$_i$ *sal*
**swing, like a monkey in a tree** *verb skoot*
**sword** *noun loof*

# T

**taboo** *adjective tap*
**taboo, to put a taboo on** *verb p̃eel*
**tack on** *verb*$_i$ *p̃elp̃el*
**Tahitian chestnut tree** *noun nm̃ap̃* (*Inocarpus fagifer*)
**tail** *noun*$_i$ *nam̃el; noun*$_i$ *napu*
**take** *verb*$_a$ *preg*
**take a photo** *verb*$_a$ *lom*
**take everything** *verb nrak*
**take off** *verb*$_a$ *waalu*
**'take on', as in taking on a new task or responsibility** *verb slasol*
**take out** *verb*$_a$ *mulu*
**take stones out of a fire** *verb*$_a$ *kamti*
**take this** *interjection gki*
**take water (boat)** *verb*$_i$ *parut*
**talk** *verb*$_i$ *pes*
**talk badly** *verb tilusus*

**talk over someone** *verb pestatakor*
**talk to** *verb$_a$ pestaf; verb festaf*
**talkative** *noun pepelau*
**tall** *adjective pram*
**tame** *verb$_i$ maomao*
**tangle** *verb$_a$ sp̃il*
**taro** *noun ntal* (*Colocasia esculenta*); *noun nafi* (*Alocasia macrorrhizos*)
**tassle or special weaving** *noun$_i$ nagor*
**taste** *verb$_a$ katnrog; noun nfamwen; verb kaat*
**taste a drink** *verb$_a$ minrog*
**taste food** *verb$_a$ pamnrog*
**tattoo** *verb$_a$ wamos*
**teach** *verb$_a$ plaksok*
**teacher** *noun tefaitau; noun teplaksok*
**tears** *noun$_i$ naromet*
**tease** *verb tusur*
**telephone** *noun nmaritpes*
**television** *noun telele*
**tell** *verb$_d$ nrik*
**tell story** *verb$_a$ traus*
**tell truth** *verb, adjective tilm̃ori*
**ten** *number ralim*
**tentacle** *noun$_i$ nlap̃*
**termite-like grub** *noun ofet*
**testicles** *noun p̃ura; noun tep̃al; noun$_i$ pol; noun teem̃iit*
**thanks** *interjection ta; interjection faftae; verb$_i$ psawi*
**that** *demonstrative tego; demonstrative tena; demonstrative nen; demonstrative tene*
**that's it** *interjection gawa*
**thatch** *noun namtampei*
**their** *pronoun negar*
**theirs** *pronoun gar*
**them** *pronoun negar; pronoun wer*
  **for them** *pronoun gar; pronoun negar*
**then** *pronoun prefix kai=; adverb malnen; interjection ale*
**there** *preposition peen; demonstrative sago; directional pe; demonstrative sanie*
**they** *pronoun gar*
**they (plural irrealis subject)** *pronoun prefix ruk=*
**they (plural perfect subject)** *pronoun prefix rukoi=; pronoun prefix rui=*
**they (plural realis subject)** *pronoun prefix ru=*
**they (two irrealis subject)** *pronoun prefix ra=; pronoun prefix rak=*
**they (two perfect subject)** *pronoun prefix rai=; pronoun prefix rakai=*
**thick** *adjective matol*
**thick coconut cream** *noun loorktal*
**thigh** *noun$_i$ nmao*
**thin** *adjective mrara*
**thing** *noun namatun*
**thingamy** *interjection nana*
**think** *verb$_i$ mro*
**think ahead** *verb mropta*
**think heavily** *verb mrokasu*
**thinking** *noun namroan*
**third** *adjective kaatol*
**thirsty** *verb$_i$ manreu*
**this** *demonstrative ne*
**thousand** *number p̃oon*
**thrash** *verb$_i$ pul*
**three** *number tol*
**throat** *noun$_i$ nkasaap̃o*
**throw** *verb p̃alu; verb ter; verb$_a$ sok; verb$_a$ nep; verb m̃aal*
**throw a small piece of wood** *verb$_a$ p̃ii*
**throwing wood** *noun np̃ip̃*
**thumb** *noun kinlep*
**thunder** *noun tfa*
**Thursday** *noun aliat faitaumlap*

**thus** *interjection welkin*
**tickle** *verb$_a$ kirkis*
**tickle quickly** *verb$_a$ kistup̃*
**tidal wave** *noun tasuur*
**tide** *noun naar*
  **high tide** *verb$_i$ mu*
  **low tide** *verb$_i$ maat*
**tie** *verb$_a$ sap̃el; verb$_a$ motsok; verb$_a$ mot*
**tie a loop** *verb pailuk*
**tie cloth** *verb$_a$ fiikot*
**tie knot** *verb$_a$ tuut*
**tie your hair** *verb$_a$ pir*
**tiger shark** *noun pakofaam*
**time** *noun nrak; noun mal*
**tiny** *adjective seesp̃al*
**tiptoes, stand on** *verb$_i$ m̃letik*
**tired** *verb$_i$ maos*
**to** *preposition pak*
**today** *adverb mees*
**toe** *noun$_i$ nakin*
  **big toe** *noun kinm̃aat*
  **little toe** *noun kinriky*
  **middle toe** *noun kinliu*
  **second toe** *noun kintapul*
**together** *preposition p̃onp̃on*
**toilet** *noun sum̃sees; noun etak*
**tomorrow** *noun matool*
**tongs** *noun nkem*
**tongue** *noun$_i$ name*
**tool** *noun srosur*
**tooth** *noun$_i$ npat*
  **back tooth** *noun woos*
**toothless** *adjective golgol*
**top** *noun$_i$ np̃au*
**top stones of an oven** *noun faat ni uum*
**topless** *verb$_i$ karo*
**touch** *verb$_a$ tkal*
**tower** *noun natir*
**toy** *noun psirsir; noun tepsirsir*
**track** *verb$_a$ us; noun$_i$ nalof*
**transport** *verb$_a$ mos; verb$_a$ mos*
**trap** *noun mrakor*
**trap fish by encircling them** *verb paakot*
**tree (general term)** *noun nkas*
**tree sp./spp.** *noun nafilsanr; noun naswaf; noun pines; noun nfan* (*Guettarda speciosa*); *noun nametal; noun nlas* (*Semecarpus vitiensis*); *noun nanrm̃anipun; noun napum̃alom* (*Mimusops elengi*); *noun nkaukofua* (*Sterculia banksiana*); *noun nap̃rairei; noun narka* (*Pavetta opulina*); *noun nafenu; noun namgalgal; noun nfaato* (*Ochrosia elliptica*); *noun natret; noun nagitpar; noun nat* (*Terminalia sepicona*); *noun faresor; noun nmaslesil; noun nkasp̃o* (*Dysoxylum gaudichaudianum*); *noun nainom; noun nasukefik* (*Syzygium richii*); *noun namtun* (*Cerbera odollam*); *noun nareo* (*Homolanthus nutans*); *noun ntap̃ir* (*Murraya paniculata*); *noun nkaspaulep; noun nraopet; noun namtamiel; noun nakpes; noun namir ni euut; noun nam̃ermra; noun nakfakof; noun napri; noun nkafikmil* (*Syzygium clusiaefolium*); *noun nalo* (*Finschia chloroxantha*); *noun tamarin* (*Glochidion ramiflorum*); *noun fanikoro; noun nafarifa* (*Neisosperma sp.?*); *noun nkas ni aal; noun leskes; noun ntap̃aun; noun tap̃ir; noun nakm̃ou* (*Intsia bijuga*); *noun nfa; noun nmariwenr* (*Acacia simplex*); *noun narwarof;*

*noun nalik; noun napukm̃opul* (*Pisonia umbellifera*); *noun naap* (*Barringtonia asiatica*); *noun namtagot* (*Elattostachys falcata*); *noun natot* (*Excoecaria agalocha*); *noun nser* (*Melicope latifolia*); *noun nanrm̃a* (*Pipturus argenteus*); *noun napuktau* (*Endospermum spp.*); *noun napuk* (*Gyrocarpus americanus*); *noun narkamet; noun mpakur ni elau* (*Calophyllum inophyllum*); *noun natp̃opis; noun nkas mel; noun nmalmel* (*Garuga floribunda*); *noun kaori* (*Agathis macrophylla*); *noun nafiefi; noun natu*

**African tulip** *noun nrar* (*Erythrina variegata*)

**avocado** *noun afoka* (*Persea americana*)

**banyan** *noun mpak*

**bead tree** *noun naam̃er* (*Adenanthera pavonina*)

**black burao** *noun namir* (*Cordia subcordata*)

**black palm** *noun nma* (*Blechnum gibbum, Cyathea lunulata*)

**blackbean** *noun nkasot* (*Diospyros sp.*); *noun nap̃oi* (*Castanospermum australe*)

**bougainvillea** *noun anisakel*

**breadfruit sp.** *noun nmaal; noun naliu; noun p̃ka; noun kanotaar; noun m̃nam̃on; noun nateeman; noun naptamkuut; noun naptamkos; noun loof; noun naptam* (*Atocarpus altilis*)

**bush nut** *noun napkor* (*Barringtonia procera*); *noun nafil* (*Barringtonia edulis*)

**cassis** *noun paariik* (*Leucaena leucocephala*)

**Chinese lantern tree** *noun naipir* (*Hernandia nymphaeifolia, Hernandia peltata*)

**coconut** *noun nutag*

**comb tree** *noun naklak* (*Planchonella grayana*)

**cycad palm** *noun nam̃el* (*Cycas seemannii*)

**devil nettle** *noun gkar; noun nam̃lat* (*Dendrocnide latifolia*)

**dragon plum** *noun nrau* (*Dracontomelon vitiense*)

**false nutmeg** *noun nra* (*Myristica fatua*)

**'false tamanu'** *noun mpakur ni euut* (*Garcinia pseudoguttifera*)

**fig tree** *noun nait* (*Ficus wassa*); *noun naplip* (*Ficus granatum*); *noun nakrik* (*Ficus virgata*)

**fols tabaco** *noun namook* (*Heliotropium foertherianum*)

**guava** *noun koiaf* (*Psidium guajava*)

**hibiscus** *noun nap̃kal* (*Hibiscus rosa-sinensis*); *noun naplel* (*Hibiscus tilaceus*)

**hog plum tree** *noun nmal* (*Spondias dulcis, S. cythera, S. edulis*)

**Indian mulberry** *noun nakur* (*Morinda citrifolia*)

**ironwood** *noun nagi*

**island teak** *noun nakm̃ou* (*Intsia bijuga*)

**Java cedar** *noun nkok* (*Bischofia javanica*)

**looking-glass tree** *noun nm̃ap̃m̃ap̃* (*Heritiera littoralis*)

**mango** *noun maagko*
**mangrove** *noun maurkat*
**milkwood tree** *noun mpal* (*Antiaris toxicaria*)
**nakavika** *noun nkafik* (*Syzygium malaccense*)
**namele** *noun nam̃el* (*Cycas seemannii*)
**nandau** *noun nta* (*Pometia pinnata*)
**natapoa** *noun ntalitas* (*Terminalia samoensis*)
**native almond** *noun nagae* (*Canarium indicum, Canarium harveyi*)
**navele** *noun nafil* (*Barringtonia edulis*)
**New Guinea rosewood** *noun nagrof* (*Pterocarpus indicus*)
**octopus tree** *noun namook* (*Heliotropium foertherianum*)
**orange tree** *noun m̃ool* (*Citrus sinensis*)
**palm tree** *noun nipu* (*Veitchia spp.*)
**pandanus** *noun naki* (*Pandanus tectorius?*); *noun nakimtirmtir; noun nparom; noun nfak* (*Pandanus dubius?*); *noun nakimtirmtir*
**peanut tree** *noun naselslam* (*Sterculia tannaensis, S. vitiensis*)
**puzzle tree** *noun namatal* (*Kleinhovia hospita*)
**puzzle-nut tree** *noun nap̃laso* (*Xylocarpus granatum*)
**red bean tree** *noun naam̃er* (*Adenanthera pavonina*)
**sandalwood** *noun makos* (*Santalum austrocaledonicum*)
**sago palm** *noun rowat* (*Metroxylon warburgii*)
**sheoak** *noun naar* (*Casuarina equisetifolia*)
**soursop** *noun katnraap*
**stinging nettle tree** *noun gkar; noun nam̃lat* (*Dendrocnide latifolia*)
**Tahitian chestnut** *noun nm̃ap̃* (*Inocarpus fagifer*)
**tamanu** *noun mpakur* (*Calophyllum inophyllum*)
**tree sp. with hard nut seeds** *noun nap̃ak*
**tropical almond** *noun ntali* (*Terminalia samoensis*)
**wael navenu** *noun nam̃os* (*Macaranga megacarpa*)
**wattle tree** *noun nmariu* (*Acacia spirorbis*)
**whitewood** *noun napukror* (*Endospermum medullosum*)
**wild natapoa** *noun ntalimil* (*Terminalia sepicana*)
**wud blong Santo** *noun namamao* (*Pipturus argenteus*)

**triggerfish** *noun p̃arp̃or* (*Balistidae*)
**trip over** *verb*$_{a}$ *tak*
**triton** *noun pupu* (*Cymatiidae*)
**triton sp.** *noun saago* (*Charonia tritonis*)
**trochus** *noun arkao*
**true** *noun m̃ori*
**truly** *adverb perkat*
**trunk** *noun*$_{i}$ *nlak*
**trust** *verb*$_{i}$ *sralesok; verb*$_{i}$ *faafat; noun nasralesokwen*
**truth** *noun naleenaan*
**try on, clothes** *verb*$_{a}$ *kalnrog*
**tube of bamboo (for carrying water)** *noun kanrsip*
**tuber** *noun naknot*

**tuck** *verb silfek*
**Tuesday** *noun aliat kaaru*
**tuluk** *noun tluk*
**tuna, dogtooth tuna** *noun p̃laanr* (*Gymnosarda unicolor*); **yellow tail or skipjack tuna** *noun napum̃ m̃nam̃on*
**Turbo shell** *noun fnagot*
**turn** *verb*$_i$ *tare; verb*$_a$ *nre; verb*$_a$ *plor*
**turn a canoe quickly** *verb taakau*
**turn back** *verb*$_i$ *totooluk*
**turn inside-out** *verb*$_a$ *lum̃nre*
**turn off** *verb*$_a$ *krakpun*
**turn on (lamp)** *verb*$_a$ *kis*
**turn something** *verb*$_a$ *p̃elgat*
**turtle** *noun afsak*
**turtle shell** *noun lel*
**tusk** *noun npatwaak*
**twenty** *number ralim inru*
**twigs** *noun nragnrag*
**twin** *noun natran*
**twine** *noun nmae*
**twirl** *verb*$_i$ *fulful*
**twist** *verb*$_i$ *fiif*
**twisted** *verb plos*
**two** *number nru; adjective nra*
**type** *noun nametrau*

## U

**umbrella** *noun sulok*
**unable** *auxiliary, verb kano*
**unafraid** *verb*$_i$ *fiar*
**uncivilised** *noun tafuu*
**uncle, father's brother** *noun apaap; noun*$_i$ *alu*
**uncle, mother's brother** *noun awo*
**unconscious, be unconscious** *verb*$_i$ *matmaal*
**uncountable** *number maan*
**undercooked** *verb*$_i$ *maasp̃ok*
**understand** *verb*$_i$ *kraksok*
**unicornfish, bluespine unicornfish** noun *raeru* (*Naso unicornis, Balistidae*); **humpnose unicornfish** *noun naum* (*Naso tuberosus*); **orangespine unicornfish** *noun uus*
**unripe** *adjective met*
**unroll** *verb*$_a$ *lupir*
**untie** *verb*$_a$ *nrat; verb*$_a$ *pres*
**until** *verb*$_a$ *tkal; preposition tup̃; preposition panpan*
**up** *verb*$_i$ *pakelag*
**urinate** *verb*$_t$ *me*
**urine** *noun*$_i$ *namee*
**us (inclusive)** *pronoun kit*
  **for us** *pronoun nigmam;* **for us (inclusive)** *pronoun negakit; pronoun gakit*
**uvula** *noun ntaarto*

## V

**vagina** *noun kaai; noun nlas ni nmatu; noun lisaan*
**valley** *noun mp̃alo*
**Vanuatu white-eye** *noun topi* (*Zosterops flavifrons*)
**vatu** *noun faat*
**vehicle** *noun raru ni ntan*
**vein** *noun*$_i$ *nue*
**verdict** *noun metp̃ag*
**verse** *noun namet nafsan*

**very** *verb*$_i$ *sa; preverbal trau*
**vigil, keep vigil** *verb*$_i$ *nepsok*
**Vila (town)** *noun sto*
**vine sp./spp.** *noun nkraful*; *noun natu; noun natiel* (*Entada phaseoloides*); *noun laktau; noun nlakotao; noun sumat; noun naala; noun nlaketik; noun nakrok; noun nm̃alm̃ol; noun nmaritmat*
**lawyer vine** *noun naala* (*Calamus vitiensis*)
**vision** *noun nron*
**visit** *verb*$_a$ *lemis; verb*$_a$ *saof*
**voice** *noun*$_i$ *nalee*
**vomit** *verb*$_i$ *lu*

## W

**wael navenu** *noun nam̃os* (*Macaranga megacarpa*)
**wagtail** *noun farfar*
**waist** *noun*$_i$ *nmal*
**wait** *verb*$_a$ *toreki*
**wake** *verb*$_i$ *pilo; verb*$_a$ *pug*
**wake up** *verb*$_i$ *tokleg*
**walk** *verb*$_i$ *siwer*
**walk crooked, stagger** *verb*$_i$ *tartaar*
**walk in the bush** *verb*$_i$ *lfalof*
**walk on** *verb*$_a$ *kam*
**walk slowly** *verb*$_i$ *paapuen*
**walk with hands held behind the back** *verb*$_i$ *pawer*
**walking stick** *noun tiip̃*
**wall** *noun tikor*
**wander** *verb*$_i$ *sari*
**want** *verb*$_i$ *na; verb*$_a$ *muur*
**not want** *verb*$_i$ *mal; auxiliary mal*
**war** *noun nafkal*
**warm oneself at a fire** *verb*$_i$ *tlai*
**warning** *verb ter*
**warped** *adjective tep̃lag*
**wart** *noun napus*
**wash** verb$_i$ *los; verb*$_a$ *pnol; verb*$_i$ *prei; verb pnoltao; verb*$_a$ *preitao*
**wash the face** *verb*$_i$ *fanfan*
**washstrake** *noun kortas*
**wasp** *noun liit*
**watch** *verb*$_i$ *lekor*
**watch over** *verb*$_a$ *leperkat*
**water** *noun nsel nai; noun nai*
**wattle tree** *noun nmariu* (*Acacia spirorbis*)
**wave** *verb*$_i$ *taapas; noun nao*
**waxbill (type of bird)** *noun sfirmer* (*Estrildidae*)
**we (exclusive)** *pronoun komam; pronoun mam; pronoun prefix ko=*
**we (inclusive)** *pronoun akit; pronoun kit*
**we (plural exclusive perfect)** *pronoun prefix ui=*
**we (plural inclusive irrealis subject)** *pronoun prefix tuk=*
**we (plural inclusive perfect subject)** *pronoun prefix tui=*
**we (plural inclusive realis subject)** *pronoun prefix tu=*
**we (plural perfect subject)** *pronoun prefix koi=*
**we (two inclusive irrealis subject)** *pronoun prefix tak=*
**we (two inclusive perfect subject)** *pronoun prefix takai=*
**we (two inclusive realis subject)** *pronoun prefix ta=*

**we (two irrealis subject)** *pronoun prefix rak=*

**we (two perfect subject)** *pronoun prefix rakai=*

**weak** *adjective mailum*

**wean** *verb m̃os*

**wear** *verb*$_a$ *oof*

**weather** *noun mal*

**weave** *verb lgaskei; verb*$_i$ *tiei; verb*$_a$ *pau; verb*$_i$ *lgaru; verb*$_a$ *nraf*

**web** *noun nalapul*

**webbed feet** *verb*$_i$ *p̃on*

**wedding** *noun nlakwen*

**wedge** *verb*$_a$ *slei*

**Wednesday** *noun aliat fnau*

**weigh down** *verb*$_a$ *nepsok*

**weight** *noun namtenwen*

**well, be well** *verb*$_i$ *nrogtiawi*

**west** *noun naweskin kaaru; noun ruelau*

**wet** *verb sum̃sm̃o; adjective lom*

**whale** *noun tafra*

**wharf** *noun nuof*

**what** *pronoun nafte; adjective sef*

**when** *noun ngas; noun sefmal*

**where** *interrogative sap; interrogative sua*

**while** *adverb selwan*

**whimbrel (type of bird)** *noun sfiu* (*Numenius phaeopus*)

**whip** *noun krip; verb fisktof; verb*$_a$ *fis; verb*$_a$ *sm̃anr*

**whirly wind** *noun tafiif ni nlag*

**whisper** *verb*$_i$ *taalaklak*

**whistle** *verb*$_i$ *p̃en; verb*$_i$ *safeu*

**white** *adjective taar; adjective tau*

**white shark** *noun pakotau*

**whitewood** *noun napukror* (*Endospermum medullosum*)

**who** *interrogative fei*

**why** *verb ku*

**wide** *adjective p̃olp̃lo*

**widow** *noun malep*

**wife** *noun mtulep; noun nmatu*

**wild** *adjective mil*

**wild berry** *noun krusperi* (*Passiflora foetida*)

**wild cane** *noun nasul* (*Centotheca lappacea*)

**wild kava** *noun nakser*

**wild natapoa** *noun ntalimil* (*Terminalia sepicana*)

**wild peanut** *noun mismai*

**wilful, strong head** *adjective p̃au kerkerai*

**wilt** *verb*$_i$ *matuktuk*

**win** *verb*$_i$*, auxiliary pei*

**wind** *noun tokelau; noun lagsu*

**wind** *noun nlag*

  **whirly wind** *noun tafiif ni nlag*

**wind going down** *noun sirsuk*

**wind going up** *noun sirsak*

**wind that blows when someone is dying** *noun nlag sumat*

**wind that makes green leaves fall to the ground** *noun nlag mlakes*

**window** *noun namet sees; noun*$_i$ *namet*

**wine** *noun nai miel*

**wing** *noun*$_i$ *nafar*

**wise** *verb*$_i$ *metmatu*

**with** *preposition skot; verb*$_a$ *skot*

  **be with** *verb*$_a$ *plak*

**withdraw, pull back** *verb*$_i$ *m̃osus*

**wither** *verb*$_i$ *matuktuk*

**withhold information** *verb*$_i$ *putmaak*

**wobble** *verb farfarsa; adjective p̃aru*

**wobbly, be** *verb tuntun*

**woman** *noun nmatu; noun mtulep*

**woman still breast-feeding** *adjective p̃kasus*

**womb** *noun naal ni teesa*
**wood** *noun nkas*
  **chip of wood** *noun*$_i$ *nsem̃*
  **forked piece of wood** *noun nsag*
  **soft wood** *noun naturwotu*
**work** *noun nawesien; verb*$_a$ *weswes*
**world** *noun emeromen*
**worm** *noun aslot*
**worn out** *verb mrat*
**worry** *verb*$_i$ *mroput*
**worship** *verb*$_i$ *lot*
**would have** *auxiliary mer*
**wounded** *adjective mankotik*
**wrap** *verb*$_i$ *nrepnrep*
**wrasses** *noun patru* (*Labridae*); **bird wrasse** *noun taktak* (*Gomphosus varius*); **cigar wrasse** *noun aaf ni nariuriu* (*Cheilio inermis*); **humphead wrasse** *noun afam* (*Cheilinus undulatus*); **sixbar wrasse?, green with stripes** *noun ures;* **nebulous wrasse** *noun laokinasusu* (*Halichoeres nebulosus*)
**wreath** *noun takotp̃au*
**wrestle** *verb fsar*
**wriggler** *noun funrei*
**wring clothes** *verb*$_a$ *plos*
**write, to write** *verb*$_a$ *mtir*
**wud blong Santo** *noun namamao* (*Pipturus argenteus*)

# Y

**yam sp./spp.** *noun togtog; noun nap̃ooi; noun sum̃kai; noun roos; noun natoop̃; noun saak; noun toknimakil; noun mleo; noun taalau; noun nap̃el; noun nam* (*Dioscorea bulbifera*); *noun togtogm̃it; noun nakompak; noun wailu; noun nm̃aal; noun nawi; noun tuumas; noun ntelpou; noun naitarpes; noun nairo; noun ara; noun toop̃; noun nm̃aal*
  **spiky wild yam** *noun naiam*
**yard** *noun elol*
**yawn** *verb*$_i$ *m̃la*
**year** *noun ntau*
**yellow** *adjective m̃nam̃on*
**yes** *interjection ore*
**yesterday** *adverb nanom*
**yolk, egg yolk** *noun nanrwor*
**you (one person)** *pronoun ag*
**you (plural perfect subject)** *pronoun prefix koi=*
**you (plural realis subject)** *pronoun prefix u=*
**you (plural)** *pronoun mus; pronoun akam; pronoun gamus*
**you (singular irrealis subject)** *pronoun prefix p̃a=*
**you (singular perfect subject)** *pronoun prefix kui=*
**you (singular realis subject)** *pronoun prefix ku=*
**you (two irrealis subject)** *pronoun prefix ra=; pronoun prefix rak=*
**you (two perfect subject)** *pronoun prefix rakai=*
**you, for you** *pronoun negaag;* **(plural)** *pronoun negamus*
**young** *adjective fsofus*
**your** *pronoun gaag*
**your (plural)** *pronoun negamus; pronoun mus*
**your (singular)** *pronoun negaag*

OCEANIC LINGUISTICS SPECIAL PUBLICATIONS

Alexander D. Smith
*Series Editor*

Oceanic Linguistics Special Publications are occasional publications issued under the sponsorship of the Department of Linguistics of the University of Hawai‘i. The series consists of independently subsidized studies bearing on the languages of the Oceanic area. The "Oceanic area" is defined for this purpose as the combined Austronesian, Papuan, and Australian language areas. The Special Publications are published and distributed for the Department by the University of Hawai‘i Press.

Manuscripts may be submitted to
smithad@hawaii.edu